Good Arabs

The publisher gratefully acknowledges the generous support of the Humanities Endowment Fund of the University of California Press Foundation

Good Arabs

THE ISRAELI SECURITY AGENCIES
AND THE ISRAELI ARABS, 1948-1967

Hillel Cohen

Translated by Haim Watzman

UNIVERSITY OF CALIFORNIA PRESS

BERKELEY   LOS ANGELES   LONDON

University of California Press, one of the most
distinguished university presses in the United States,
enriches lives around the world by advancing scholarship
in the humanities, social sciences, and natural sciences.
Its activities are supported by the UC Press Foundation
and by philanthropic contributions from individuals and
institutions. For more information, visit www.ucpress.edu.

University of California Press
Berkeley and Los Angeles, California

University of California Press, Ltd.
London, England

Library of Congress Cataloging-in-Publication Data

Cohen, Hillel.
['Aravim tovim. English]
    The Israeli security agencies and the Israeli Arabs,
1948–1967 / Hillel Cohen ; translated by Haim Watzman.
        p.   cm.
    Includes bibliographical references and index.
    ISBN 978-0-520-25767-2 (cloth : alk. paper)
    1. Palestinian Arabs—Israel—Political activity.
2. Israel.Sherut ha-bitahon ha-kelali.   3. Intelligence
service—Israel.   4. National security—Israel.   5. Israel—
Ethnic relations.   6. Minorities—Israel.   I. Title.
II. 'Arvim tovim.

DS113.7.C61513   2009

323.1192'74009045—dc22   2009010473

Manufactured in the United States of America

18   17   16   15   14   13   12   11   10
10   9   8   7   6   5   4   3   2   1

This book is printed on Natures Book, which contains
30% postconsumer waste and meets the minimum
requirements of ANSI/NISO Z39.48–1992 (R 1997)
(Permanence of Paper).

*To my beloved family (the Cohen-Bars)
in our beloved city, Jerusalem.*

CONTENTS

ILLUSTRATIONS / ix

PREFACE / xi

ACKNOWLEDGMENTS / xiii

Introduction / 1

1 Beginning a Beautiful Friendship:
The Rise of the Collaborator Class / 11

2 Communists vs. the Military Government,
Collaborators vs. Communists / 39

3 Boundary Breakers: Infiltrators, Smugglers, Spies / 65

4 The Land / 95

5 The Battle of the Narrative: Symbols,
Pronouncements, Teachers / 123

6 Minorities within a Minority: Dilemmas of Identity / 159

7 Circles of Control, Circles of Resistance / 195

Conclusion / 231

NOTES / 239

BIBLIOGRAPHY / 265

INDEX / 269

ILLUSTRATIONS

1. The Israeli army enters the Triangle and imposes military rule, Kafr Qasim, 1949. / 14

2. The Arab inhabitants of the Triangle celebrate the first anniversary of their annexation to Israel, 1950. / 19

3. Sayf al-Din Zuʿbi during his campaign for the municipal elections of Nazareth, 1966. / 24

4. A Communist activist distributes leaflets, before the first elections to the Israeli Knesset, 1949. / 43

5. Israeli president Haim Weizmann with Bishop Hakim, Israel's Independence Day, 1951. / 48

6. The Catholic Scouts march in Nazareth on Israel's Independence Day, 1954. / 49

7. David Hacohen, of Mapai, with Arab MKs from lists affiliated with his party: E. Nakhle, D. ʿUbeid, and A. K. al-Daher, 1961. / 63

8. Many Bedouins helped the IDF prevent infiltration. / 74

9. March in Ramla, 1949. / 76

10. An Israeli bus attacked by Palestinian infiltrators in Meron, Upper Galilee, 1953. / 90

11. An Israeli soldier, a foreign reporter, and the mukhtar share supper in the village of Iqrit, before the uprooting of its inhabitants, 1948. / 107

12. An Arab girls choir welcomes the minister of education, Nazareth, 1949. / 124

13. Bishop Hakim and Druze religious leader Sheikh Amin Tarif in Tel Aviv, watching the IDF parade on Israel's Independence Day, 1959. / 136

14. In addition to preventing the Arabs from commemorating the massacre of Kafr Qasim, Israel manipulated the inhabitants to participate in a formal *"sulha"* (forgiveness ceremony) with state officials, 1957. / 144

15. A resident of Tira brings a radio to his house after electrification reached the village in 1957. / 153

16. Arab figures from the Nazareth area at a party organized by the military governor, 1950. / 157

17. Druze leader Jaber Dahash Mu'adi congratulates a Druze soldier who volunteered to serve in the IDF during the 1948 war. / 165

18. A Circassian language course, sponsored by the state, in the cultural center of the Circassian village of Kufr Kama, 1966. / 176

19. Sheikh 'Oda Abu-M'ammar grants the "desert sword" to Prime Minister Yitzhak Shamir, 1988. / 182

20. Eleanor Roosevelt with Sheikh al-Huzayyel and the Negev MG, 1952. / 184

21. Arab prisoners who were captured and returned to Shatta prison after their failed attempt to escape, 1958. / 191

22. Ibrahim Qasem, the head of the local council of Tira, near the local mosque with Sheikh Sultani from the village, 1966. / 197

23. The mayor of Tamra, al-Diab, visits his brother, who was accepted into the much-desired tractor course, 1957. / 213

24. Arab fishermen in Acre, 1960. / 215

PREFACE

In recent years, thousands of police files stored in the Israel State Archives have been opened to the public. These include files from the Israel Police's central headquarters and its divisions, from district headquarters, and from police stations all over the country. They are gold mines for students of Israeli society and history. The material is, in many cases, embarrassing to those it names. Among these files are hundreds dealing with Arab citizens—files of police stations in Arab villages, files of the force's Special Branches (which were responsible for Arab affairs), intelligence files, interrogation files, and files of the Regional Committees on Arab Affairs. Here one does not find debates over policy, political strategy, or ideology. Rather, coming from the grass roots, the materials in these files include reports by collaborators about events in their villages; summaries of meetings with General Security Service (GSS) agents, police officers, and military government officials about issues falling under their responsibility; and reports on political activity in Arab communities and the attempts to stymie such activity. Also included are personality profiles of mukhtars and Arab public figures, and reports about infiltrators and murders and other crimes. These documents are the principal raw material of this book.

Intelligence documents must, of course, be read critically and cautiously. The evaluations they contain are often biased, and the officials' and officers' pseudopsychological analyses of Arab individuals should be taken with many grains of salt. Nevertheless, they contain valuable information about life in

Arab communities under a military government and about the tensions prevailing in them. They also portray the methods and tactics used by the security authorities to control the Arab population and the thought patterns of field agents of the security agencies.

One ethical note: In many cases I have omitted the names of the people involved in the events I describe, even though I cannot know whether they are ashamed or proud of their actions, whether they prefer that their deeds be brought to light or remain in the dark. I have applied this rule to both collaborators and nationalist figures. The exceptions are public officials, regarding whom I have acted in accordance with the rule that their public standing permits full disclosure of their deeds. The same applies to activists whose actions were reported in the press during the period under study.

And one note regarding terminology: I alternatively use the terms "the Arabs in Israel," "the Arab citizens of Israel," "Israel's Arab citizens," "the Palestinians in Israel," "Israeli Arabs," and "the Palestinian Arabs in Israel" in order to represent the variety of views and analyses about the contemporary and the desired identities of these communities, as demonstrated in this book.

ACKNOWLEDGMENTS

I wish to thank the Harry S. Truman Institute for the Advancement of Peace at the Hebrew University of Jerusalem, the Department of Middle East Studies at Ben Gurion University in the Negev, and the Budgeting and Planning Committee *("Vatat")* of the Israeli Council for Higher Education for their financial support. I am grateful to the University of California Press for the generous grant that made possible the translation of this book into English.

Introduction

IN 1949, WHEN ISRAEL SIGNED ARMISTICE AGREEMENTS with its Arab neighbors at the end of the war in which it was born, the Jewish state found itself with an unwelcome 156,000 Arabs, approximately 15 percent of the new country's population. At the same time, these Arabs found that they were citizens of a state whose creation they had largely opposed and against which the Arab world had launched a war just two years earlier. The Israeli authorities, lacking any experience of governance and with contradictory traditions about relations with non-Jews, faced a presumptively hostile national minority within their new polity. The Palestinian citizens, on their part, had to find ways to live under the new masters.

The Arabs in Israel faced circumstances entirely different from those they had previously known. Instead of being a majority, as they had been in Mandatory Palestine, they became a minority as a result of the uprooting of some seven hundred thousand who became refugees. The country's landscape had also metamorphosed before their eyes. Many of the Arab villages they were accustomed to seeing on their travels through the country were in ruins, and Jewish towns were built in their place to house the hundreds of thousands of Jews who flowed into the country from Europe and the Islamic world. Cities that had served as political, economic, and social centers were emptied almost entirely of their Arab inhabitants. Hebrew became the language of the institutions of government. The Arabs' sense of being a marginal minority was reinforced by the restrictions imposed on them. Most Arab villages, towns, and cities were placed under military rule, and their fates— personal and collective—were determined by Israeli security authorities, whose principal concern was the security of the Jewish state.

The establishment of the state of Israel against the will of the Palestinian Arabs, and their and the neighboring Arab countries' defeat in a war they had instigated against the new state, created an atmosphere of enmity and mistrust between the state and its Arab citizens. The Israeli authorities viewed the Arab population as hostile and potentially seditious. Israeli decision makers' anxiety was exacerbated when leaders of the Arab states declared time and again that they intended to destroy the Jewish state. Sometimes, Israeli leaders exaggerated the Arab threat for political reasons. Israel's leaders were inclined to portray Israel's Arab citizens as a potential fifth column. In retrospect, it is possible to state that Israel's Arab population presented no real danger to Israel's security. At that time, there was no way to be certain. To prevent hostile activity and to establish their firm political control over the country's Arab populace, Israeli security forces quickly created networks of informers and collaborators in the Arab community. It was an extremely effective policy that operated on three levels: tactical, political, and in relation to consciousness and identity.

On the tactical level, security officials worked with Arab collaborators to prevent Arab citizens of Israel from joining the intelligence and military efforts of the Arab countries. Collaborators carried out a variety of missions to this end; among other things, they tracked belligerent underground cells, reported on Arabs who maintained contact with Arab intelligence organizations, and supplied information on infiltrators and smugglers who crossed the border. Some collaborators were sent out to the frontiers to recruit informers among their acquaintances in refugee camps in the West Bank (then part of the Kingdom of Jordan), in Lebanon, and in the Gaza Strip (which was under Egyptian rule).

The activities of the collaborators also related to a second level of policy operation: an attempt to ensure maximal control over the political and social behavior of Israel's Arab population. To this end, collaborators were pressed to provide information about the political leanings of prominent people in their villages and about the interrelationships among them and their families. They were also planted in political groups to collect information about activities and plans. Israeli security agencies were also involved in the appointment of mukhtars (village representatives who dealt with the authorities), who served as mediators between the inhabitants and the regime during the period before elected village councils and mayors were instituted. Even after this change, the security agencies continued to intervene in Arab local politics; for instance, they were involved in postelection coalition negotiations to ensure that "their" Arabs received positions of power. On the national level, the security forces encouraged Arabs to vote for Arab slates that eschewed nationalist ideology and were subservient to Mapai, the ruling party.[1] The Israeli authorities filled leadership positions in the Arab community with "moderates"—the official term for Arabs who refrained from taking nationalist positions and who accorded legitimacy not only to Israel's existence but also to its actions, such as the imposition of military rule over the Arab population and the expropriation of Arab lands.

On the third level, that of consciousness and identity, the aspiration was to reshape Arab consciousness and identity in accordance with the hegemonic Israeli worldview by controlling the society's political discourse. Israel's leadership understood that consciousness guides the behavior of individuals. The state's goal was to detach the Palestinian Arabs in Israel from the Palestinian Arab identity that was central for many of them and to create something new—the Israeli Arab. The consolidation of such an identity may well have been inevitable in light of the peculiar circumstances that prevailed after the 1948 war—principally, these Arabs' new status as a minority in a Jewish state—but the regime wanted to sever their ties to the Arab national movement. Through its loyalists, the state sought to indoctrinate Arab schoolchildren with the Zionist narrative, to widen the fissures between and within religious communities (Muslims, Christians, and Druze), to promote obedience to the authorities, and to challenge non-Israeli national identities (Palestinian or pan-Arab). No less important, by reporting on the day-to-day speech of Arabs and by summoning and interrogating those Arabs who spoke against the state, the security authorities "taught" the minority what was fit to be said and what was unacceptable, thus shaping the contours of Arab political discourse in Israel.

The state's actions, almost without exception, won the support of some figures in the Arab public. Informers who served in their communities as the authorities' eyes and ears, mukhtars, and members of Israel's parliament, the Knesset, voiced unreserved support for government policy. They helped transfer Arab land to the state, and others internalized the Zionist narrative of the 1948 war and thus ceased to speak of themselves and their communities as part of the Palestinian nation (which was in any case undergoing a crisis of identity under Jordanian rule and in its diaspora). Over the course of this book, I will discuss the reasons that Arab citizens of Israel supported the Israeli state and its policies. These reasons included individual opportunism; the weakness of the Palestinian national movement; the Jewish state's strength; their perception that Israel was Western and modern; the severity of the state system of control and oversight; fatalism; and the risks of resistance as compared to the benefits of cooperation.

But this is only one side of the picture. In fact, throughout the 1950s and 1960s, nationalist Arab groups and figures stood against the authorities and acted to reinforce Arab national identity as they challenged government policies. They set in motion mass protest actions, created radical frameworks for debate and action, and offered an alternative to the Zionist narrative and to the model of submissive collaboration. The Communist Party (known in Hebrew by its acronym, Maki, and later as Rakah), was the principal framework in which this took place. While the authorities kept it under surveillance and worked to limit its actions and influence, it was never outlawed. A number of reasons account for this: the party's recognition, in principle, of the Jewish state; the authorities' view of it as a pressure valve through which the Arab public could let off steam in the form of political protest without descending into violence; and fear of harming Israel's relationship with the Soviet Union. Another, smaller, Arab national movement was al-Ard, a group active for only a short period. It was not allowed to participate in elections to the Knesset and was subsequently outlawed because it did not recognize Israel's right to exist. Local groups were active in some cities and villages in promoting Palestinian Arab identity, to the authorities' displeasure. Intelligence material and reports from police files and from the office of the prime minister show that lively nationalist activity took place in many Palestinian population centers in Israel.

This is a fascinating phenomenon. Just a few months after the Nakba, the catastrophe of the 1948 war, in which hundreds of thousands of Palestinians, including their political and religious leadership, left or were driven out of their country to become refugees, and immediately after the imposition of Israeli military rule, the Arabs who remained and became Israeli citizens organized large-scale, adamant protest activity that lasted for two decades. This occurred despite close surveillance by Israeli intelligence and despite the military regime's intensive use of emergency regulations that enabled it to place uncooperative Arabs in administrative detention and to exile political activists from their homes to distant parts of the country. In other words, the first generation of Israel's Palestinian citizens, besides being beaten and subservient, were also engaged in far more protest activity than were subsequent generations, including the current generation, which the sociologists Dan Rabinowitz and Khawla Abu-Baker have called "the stand-tall generation."[2]

In this book I examine the social and political history of Israel's Arab citizens, from 1948 until 1967, with regard to the triangle of relationships that shaped it—among the Israeli regime and its agencies, the Arab nationalists (the "extremists," to their opponents), and those Arabs who favored cooperation with the state's agencies (the "collaborators," to their critics). But I do not make do with general analysis, nor is it my intention to offer a bird's-eye view of events. I seek, rather, to portray, at the local and individual level, the tensions between the Israeli state and its Arab citizens and among the different currents within that population. As I wrote this book, I realized how little we know about the history of the Arabs in Israel and how shallow our knowledge is of the actions of Israel's security agencies within the Arab community during the early years of the state. Who, other than old Communists, remembers the burning of the party's local headquarters in the village of 'Eilabun, in the Lower Galilee, in which a local activist was killed? Who remembers the accusation that the military government sent the arsonist on his mission? Who remembers the beatings that army enlistment personnel received when they handed out conscription orders in Druze villages in the Galilee, or the police foray into Daliat al-Karmel, another Druze village, aimed at compelling the village's young men to enlist? Who has heard that a gallon of paint was dumped on Tawfiq Toubi, an Arab Communist member of the Knesset, when he came to visit the village of Taybe, and of the Arab who did the deed, winning a gun license from the military government afterward? Who knows about the agents, Arab citizens of Israel, whom Israel sent to refugee camps in Lebanon, the Gaza Strip, and the West Bank in order to obtain information about teams of Palestinian infiltrators? Who has read the proclamation drafted by none other than Israel's General Security Service (GSS, the secret intelligence and surveillance agency also known by its Hebrew acronyms, Shabak and Shin Bet) that attacked "the criminal policy of the Israeli government" and that GSS agents sought to persuade Arab public figures to sign? Who recalls the five young Arab men killed near the border with the Gaza Strip in October 1961 and the turbulent demonstrations that broke out in Sakhnin as a result, during which the jeep of the regional GSS commander was pelted with rocks and shoes? Who remembers the Arabs who hid infiltrators in their homes and those who turned infiltrators over to the authorities? Where can one find written accounts of the struggle against the establishment of the new Jewish city of Karmiel on land expropriated from the surrounding Arab villages, and learn about the collaborators from one of these Galilean villages, Dir al-Asad, who reported to the police and the GSS on Arab and Jewish protestors against the expropriation?

These local events and many others that make up the core of this book are of great value in their own right; connecting them enhances their significance, since together they create a mosaic of Arab life in Israel during the military regime that most Israeli Arabs lived under during the years 1948–66 and for the brief period between the dismantling of that regime and the war of 1967. The picture includes collaborators and military governors, Communists and Arab farmers, robbers and mukhtars, GSS agents and infiltrators, parliamentarians and intelligence officers, teachers and merchants, children and parents, bourgeois Arabs from Nazareth and Bedouin sheikhs from the Negev, traditional leaders from the Triangle in central Israel and workers from the Galilee in Israel's north. These people interacted in innumerable ways, reacting to one another, sometimes in reciprocal relations, as I will show.

The picture that arises from this study calls into question, or tempers, some common conceptions in scholarship on Israel's Arab population. First, the extent of active opposition by Arab citizens to the state's actions was much greater than is generally thought. Second, this opposition, expressed in a variety of ways, was successful in no small measure. In other words, we are not speaking of a situation in which one side possessed all the power and the other was entirely helpless. One success for the Arabs (not addressed in this book) was the unauthorized construction of homes and sometimes entire neighborhoods, a phenomenon the state was never able to prevent. Another important achievement, discussed at length below, was the abetment of infiltrators. More than twenty thousand Arab refugee-infiltrators managed to cross into Israel during its first five years of existence. They hid in Arab settlements, and in the end the state had no choice but to grant them Israeli citizenship. This augmented the country's Arab population by about 15 percent. True, pressure from the United States government was an important factor in the decision to allow them to stay, but without the aid they received from the Arabs already in Israel they could not have been absorbed into the country.

Yet another success of Israeli Arabs came in the area of historical narrative and collective memory. The Israeli educational system, in coordination with the security agencies, tried to thwart the development of an Arab national memory. The effort was almost a complete failure. All these successes show that Israel's Arab citizens were not merely passive and subservient. They were active agents with significant influence over their fate. This conclusion was also reached by Ahmad Sa'di, whose interest is cultural forms of resistance.[3] As I demonstrate, these successes also show that Israel's security agencies were not omnipotent, as they are sometimes perceived to be. In fact, they were often bested by the routine needs of Arab citizens. I examine why in this book. It certainly has something to do with the paradoxical situation of Israel's Arab citizens, who lived under a military administration that made them simultaneously "citizens of a liberal nation-state and subjects of colonial administration," in Shira Robinson's words.[4]

A third conception about Israel's Arab population that emerges clearly from the material here involves the inaccuracy of the claim that the Israeli state did not demand of its Arab citizens severe tests of loyalty. This position has been taken by senior Israeli scholars such as Elie Rekhess and Sammy Smooha, as well as Yohanan Peres and Nira Davis.[5] To the best of my understanding, the demand to turn in infiltrators (as mandated by the Infiltration Prevention Law of 1954), the demand to inform on work colleagues who spoke out against the state, and the demand not to mark commemorative days in the Arabs' own national history were fundamentally loyalty demands of the most blatant type. Surveillance of school lessons and daily conversation in Arab communities, discussed below, also requires a modification of the common claim that Israel did not seek to change its Arab citizens' political consciousness.

Another point: Being a "collaborator" was a more complex experience than the stereotype would have it. First, not all collaborators were obedient tools of the state's control systems. Some of them knew how to demand their rights and to maneuver around the security forces. More critical, some used their influence not only for their own benefit but also for their communities' benefit. Attitudes toward them in the Arab community were thus not identical in each case. Some were despised, but others were looked at in a mixture of contempt, fear, and esteem, not only because of the power that they derived from their contacts with the establishment, but also because of what they did for their people.

The collaborators' motives and their relationships with their home communities lie at the center of this book's first chapter. The emergence of a class of collaborators immediately after the war, the privileges this class won for itself, and the mutual dependence that developed between the collaborators and the state are discussed at length. In some cases, they simply continued connections they had maintained with intelligence agents during the prestate period, connections discussed in my previous book, *Army of Shadows*.[6] Others chose to aid the security forces in order to "atone" for their involvement in combat against the Jews in 1948. And of course there were other motives as well.

The bodies that coordinated the activities of the security forces in Arab settlements were the Regional Committees on Arab Affairs, which were subordinate to a Central Committee composed of senior representatives of the GSS, the police, the army (the Israel Defense Forces—IDF), and the prime minister's adviser on Arab affairs. The three regional committees—the Galilee (northern), the Triangle (central), and the Negev (southern)—were composed of field personnel from these same agencies. Their intimate acquaintance with the population they oversaw and the powers placed in their hands gave them the ability to implement the carrot-and-stick policy they adopted. They fostered the collaborator class and did harm to those involved in anti-establishment political initiatives. Their fundamental views, work practices, and actions to channel votes for the Knesset and for local governments and to prevent the spread of anti-establishment ideas lie at the center of the book's seventh and final chapter.

These two chapters, the first and the seventh, serve as the book's frame. In its center are five chapters in which I address five key issues in the lives of Israel's Arab citizens. The different attitudes of this population toward these issues are presented on an axis stretching between resistance and collaboration. I analyze the methods that state representatives used to maneuver the Arab public into acting in ways most convenient to the state.

A central issue in Arab politics in Israel from 1948 to 1967 was organization. Opposing the collaborator class promoted by the state in its first years was the Communist Party. An examination of the rivalry between them reveals that they represented two opposing views of what the appropriate attitude toward the state should be (with neither side denying Israel's right to exist). The national current led by the Communists claimed that it was the right and duty of Israel's Arab (and Jewish) citizens to protest against what they perceived to be the regime's injustices. They believed that it was proper and imperative to fight against the state's nondemocratic conduct. The opposing current, the accommodationists, claimed that the state and its institutions should not be confronted head-on and that Israel's Arabs could make gains only if they adopted the code of behavior that the state expected of them. State agencies and officials did much to aid the Communists' opponents. The support received by people such as Muhammad Nimer al-Hawwari and Bishop George Hakim, bitter opponents of the Communist Party, and the struggle between these forces in the field are described and analyzed in chapter 2.

Another subject that had great emotional weight in the 1950s and 1960s was the treatment of infiltrators. Tens of thousands of Arab refugees attempted to enter the country and were defined by Israel as infiltrators. Thousands were killed by the Israeli army. Many others succeeded in crossing the border. The state demanded that its Arab citizens turn in these newcomers. Facing this dilemma, some Arabs living in Israel acceded to this demand; others, motivated by national feelings, helped hide the infiltrators. In the middle were many others—those who aided infiltrators from their own families, those who exploited the refugees' plight to profit from them, and others who had close ties with the authorities and used their connections to help infiltrators close to them. Chapter 3 is devoted to these complex considerations and shows that nationalist sentiments, or lack thereof, were not always the major determinant of these people's actions.

Chapter 4 addresses land. Throughout the period of the military government, the state worked to acquire ever more land owned by Arabs—owned by those who had abided on their land and by those who had been displaced from their homes but who remained within Israel and became its citizens. This land also included tracts that had belonged to Arabs who were now refugees outside Israel's borders. Although the Arab nationalist discourse since the late Ottoman period had forbidden the transfer of land to the Zionists, Arabs nevertheless sold land to Zionist institutions before and after the establishment of Israel. As a response, from the 1950s on, an entire culture developed that exalted devotion to the land. Songs condemning land sellers were sung at village weddings, secret threats were sent to Arabs who functioned as land agents, and the collaborators themselves responded to these intimidations.

Devotion to the land was a cornerstone of the Palestinian ethos. But the extent to which Arabs in Israel adopted this ethos (both that of the Mandate period and that of the Palestinian national movement that reawakened in the 1960s) was also affected by contention between the Arab nationalists and the state. Naturally, a large proportion of Israel's Arab citizens conceived of the recent and more distant past (including the 1948 war) in ways that were entirely different from how the Israeli state viewed those years. Beginning in the mid-1950s, Israel's Arab citizens were inspired by the pan-Arab ideology of Egypt's president, Gamal 'Abd al-Nasser. At the same time, the Israeli state sought—with the help of its own Arab loyalists—to indoctrinate its Arab citizens with its own national narrative and symbols and with the justice of the Zionist cause. The result was that Palestinians in Israel faced two opposing value systems, two narratives, and two sets of symbols competing for their hearts. Close oversight of the Arab school system was one of the means used by the state to fight pan-Arab identity. In parallel, the state employed Arab informers to report on the expression of nationalist sentiment—both in public and in private—in their villages. The security agencies' methods of shaping the political discourse and narratives of the Arabs in Israel are at the center of chapter 5.

Another aspect of identity was the position within the Arab community of minorities within the minority—Christians, Druze, Circassians, and Bedouin (the first two are religious minorities; the third, an ethnic Muslim minority; and the last, a minority among Muslim Arabs because of their different lifestyle and location in Israel's geographical periphery). These sub-minorities became another battleground between the state, which sought alliances with these minorities against the Muslim Arab majority-within-the-minority, and the Arab nationalists, who sought to include these groups in an inclusive Arab national community. The state indeed found allies among these groups. The most salient manifestation of this alliance was military service and conscription, the central issue addressed in chapter 6. The self-perceptions of these groups—which also had internal divisions—and the state's attempt to influence their identities are another focus of that chapter. Then, as noted above, the book concludes with a chapter that analyzes the daily work of the Regional Committees on Arab Affairs.

Beginning a Beautiful Friendship

The Rise of the Collaborator Class

NEW ENCOUNTERS IN A NEW REALITY

An unexpected welcome awaited officers of the Israel Defense Forces, the Israel Police, and the military government when they entered Taybe in May 1949. Taybe, like the other Palestinian Arab villages in the area constituting "the Triangle" in the central part of the country, had been annexed to Israel under the terms of the Rhodes Agreements between Israel and Jordan. One of the village's most notorious inhabitants (at least in Israeli eyes) reported to the military government's headquarters and offered his services as a consultant. 'Abd al-Ra'ouf 'Abd al-Razeq had been a prominent figure in the Arab revolt of 1936–39, directed against the British and the Zionists, and in the early 1940s had visited Berlin as a guest of the Third Reich. 'Abd al-Razeq's offer was accepted by the military governor on the recommendation of Yehoshua Palmon, who just a year previously had surfaced from his underground service as an agent of the Shai, the Haganah's intelligence service, to become an official in the new country's foreign ministry. The erstwhile Arab nationalist rebel was given an office in the military government building in town.

It was an unexpected development in the tortuous life of 'Abd al-Razeq, who was about forty years old at the time. Behind him was a long, peripatetic history of rebellions and incarcerations. His family was one of the village's most powerful clans, with large tracts of land to its name. When 'Abd al-Razeq reached high school age, his parents enrolled him at Mikveh Yisra'el, a Hebrew-language agricultural school. (Almost every class in the school, one of the icons of Zionism's back-to-the-land ethos, included a few young Arabs, mostly the sons of large landowners.) Upon graduation, he was employed by the British Mandatory government as an agricultural instructor. When the Arab uprising broke out in 1936, he joined the rebels and took part in important battles in Samaria. Captured by the British and then imprisoned for several months, at the height of the uprising in 1938 he returned to the battlefield, serving alongside his brother, 'Aref 'Abd al-Razeq, one of the rebellion's senior commanders. A year later, when the insurgency was gasping its last breaths, with the British executing many of its leaders, the two brothers fled to Syria. There they were arrested by the French authorities, who intended to turn them over to the British Mandatory police. By subterfuge they managed to slip away into Iraq; while they were there they joined the anti-British (and pro-Nazi) forces led by Rashid 'Ali al-Kilani in Baghdad in 1940–41. When the al-Kilani rebellion aborted, they returned to Syria to fight alongside pro-German French forces against Charles de Gaulle's Free French army, which was supported by the British. After the Allies defeated their rivals in Syria later that year, the brothers fled to Turkey. They were arrested there as well but were released through the intervention of the German consul, who was acquainted with their pro-Nazi work in Syria and Iraq. Their next stop was Sofia, the capital of Bulgaria.[1]

'Abd al-Ra'ouf married a local woman and lived peacefully in Sofia for two years, interrupted only by a visit to Berlin, where he met Himmler and Goebbels. (The latter suggested that he enlist young Arabs in the SS.) His brother 'Aref came down with a fatal illness and died in a German hospital in 1943. At the end of the war, when Bulgaria was occupied by the Red Army, 'Abd al-Ra'ouf was imprisoned for fifteen months because of his pro-German activity. When he was released, he asked the British consulate in the city to allow him to return to Palestine. He received a permit in 1946, in the framework of an amnesty granted to Arab leaders that was meant to counterbalance the release of the senior Jewish Agency and Haganah leaders who had been arrested on Black Saturday.[2] Hundreds of ecstatic admirers came to greet him at the Rosh HaNikra border crossing and took him in an automobile convoy to Taybe. 'Abd al-Razeq spent only a short time in his village before moving to Jaffa, where he became a produce wholesaler. It was in this large coastal city that he first met and entered into a close relationship with Palmon. The bond was based on a common enemy, Hajj Amin al-Husseini, the mufti of

Jerusalem and the leader of the Palestinian national movement. ʿAbd al-Razeq was convinced that the mufti, fearing ʿAref's burgeoning popularity, had instigated the brothers' arrest by the Turks. At the time, Palmon oversaw an intelligence network, and one of its missions was to track the mufti and his activities.

In early 1948, after the war between Palestine's Jews and Arabs was well under way, the two men continued to meet from time to time. Consistently reaffirming his hatred of the mufti, ʿAbd al-Razeq provided the Jewish intelligence operative with his analysis of events in the inter-Arab and local theaters.[3] After the armies of the surrounding Arab countries invaded Palestine in May of that year, his ties with the Shai disintegrated. He served as an officer in al-Qawuqji's Arab Liberation Army (ALA), which was initiated by the Arab League and was based on volunteers from the Arab states—a position he later claimed to have accepted at Palmon's behest. He was stationed in his home village of Taybe, where an Iraqi expeditionary force was headquartered. During the armistice negotiations between Israel and the Arab governments, in Rhodes at the beginning of 1949, Jordan represented Iraq. In its agreement with Israel, Jordan agreed to hand over the villages of the Triangle, Taybe included. ʿAbd al-Razeq reestablished his ties with Israeli intelligence personnel, who proposed that he move to Tulkarem, in the Jordanian-controlled West Bank, and pass on information from there. He refused, remaining in Taybe and, after the annexation, became an Israeli citizen. When a military government was set up in the Triangle, he "placed himself at the disposal of the government as an adviser on Arab affairs." To provide him with a steady livelihood, the Israeli authorities appointed him agricultural supervisor of the southern Triangle.[4] From that time onward he aided Israeli security officials in various capacities, some of which will be detailed below.

While ʿAbd al-Razeq's reversal was dramatic, and somewhat exceptional, he was hardly the only Arab to offer the new state his services after the Little Triangle was annexed to Israel. Many of the thirty thousand inhabitants of the region, which stretched from Kafr Qasim in the south to Umm al-Fahm and its surrounding villages in the north, welcomed IDF and Israel Police personnel joyfully. So, at least, reported the officers who were placed in command of the area. When they took control of the Triangle, military government and police officers conducted brief ceremonies in central villages to mark the beginning of Israeli rule. They reported that "the group was welcomed enthusiastically in all villages, which declared their loyalty to the government of Israel."[5] Many inhabitants told them they would be glad to

Figure 1. Without battle. The Israeli army enters the Triangle and imposes military rule, Kafr Qasim, 1949. Photograph courtesy Israeli Government Press Office.

cooperate. The officers also reestablished direct ties with people who had aided Zionist institutions during the Mandate period and the Jewish forces in the 1948 war. They met such people in Kufr Qara', Baqa al-Gharbiyyeh, Kafr Qasim, Taybe, Tira, Jaljulia, and elsewhere.[6]

The Israeli forces' first concrete mission was to round up the arms left in the villages after the long months of fighting. After the ceremonies, mukhtars (generally appointed by the British) and other influential people were summoned to police stations and military government headquarters and ordered to see to it that all weapons in their villages were turned over. At the same time, the Israeli forces, aided by mukhtars and collaborators, drew up lists of inhabitants who remained in the villages and those who left and became refugees. The land belonging to the latter was transferred to the state. Police officers and security services personnel immediately began putting together networks of informants. They correctly estimated that this was the best, and perhaps only, way to gain maximal control of the populace.

Just as collaboration with the Jews was not foreign to some inhabitants of the Arab villages, neither was the art of managing collaborators unfamiliar to Israeli security officials. Some had overseen Arab informers during the Mandate and the war, mostly in the framework of the Shai, but in some cases in the framework of the British police. They were well-acquainted with the principles laid down by Ezra Danin, founder of the Shai's Arab Department: establish intimate acquaintance with the villagers, get to know their weaknesses and feuds, and use these as a tool for enlisting informers. The method had worked well during the Mandate, when the Jewish operatives functioned in the framework of an underground national movement. Now they represented a sovereign victorious state, and the Arab population they were assigned to cover was beaten and hurting. It is hardly surprising, then, that the ranks of the veteran informers they knew were enlarged by many new informers who volunteered for the job. Before long the police, the security services, and IDF intelligence had informers in every village and every neighborhood. They would often compete with one another for the authorities' favor and at times also informed on one another.

Police officer Shlomo Ben-Elkana headed the police force that entered the villages of Wadi 'Ara (the area called the northern Triangle). On 22 May, he arrived in the village of 'Ara at the head of a detachment of ten policemen. First came a ceremony installing army rule, held in the presence of the military governor, Captain Efrayim Ben-Natan. After the ceremony, Ben-Elkana summoned Mahmoud 'Abd al-Qader Yunis, who had led the village's forces during the war. The policeman demanded that Yunis hand over all the village's arms. He turned in dozens of rifles, among them two machine guns and three Stens. The mukhtars of 'Ar'ara, Kufr Qara', and Barta'a also helped the police collect the weapons in their villages. There was no lack of volunteers ready to provide information. Locals came to the police stations and offered to help verify the lists of owners of weapons, prepared by the mukhtars and the commanders of the local Arab forces. Others offered the names and accounts of the actions of local fighters in the 1948 war, who had participated in the attack on Kibbutz Ma'anit and who had been in the detachment that shot to death a Jewish employee of the electric company during the war.[7]

A few days later, Ben-Elkana took his men and Governor Ben-Natan to show the Israeli flag, for the first time, in Umm al-Fahm. Their purposes were to acquaint themselves with the village's social fabric, to establish relations with influential figures, to round up weapons, and to lay the foundation of a network of informants. To achieve these goals, Ben-Elkana took advantage of the inhabitants' fear of Jewish retribution. "Everyone is frightened that we will take revenge for their past deeds, so I took advantage of that. It was sufficient to send a little note to some Arab and tell him that [we knew] he had a pistol, and within two hours he'd produce it," he reported to his superiors. His impression was that the mukhtars had begun to carry out the military government's orders reliably. Several of the people with whom he had struck up an acquaintance, he wrote, would "be useful to the police in providing information." He had already received information about a grudge between two of the village's influential men, and he explained, "By treating both of them politely it will always be possible to know what is going on in the village." Ben-Elkana had also been provided with preliminary information on a blood feud from the recent past. His working assumption was that additional villagers would cooperate with him in the hope of getting back their lands to the west of the village, which had been placed under the control of the custodian of absentee property before the annexation of the Triangle to Israel. The village's network of informants took form.[8]

The Arab population as a whole was crushed and smarting from its defeat, and it was also confused and lacked clear political direction. Only two years previously, in December 1947, the Palestinian Arab leadership had declared a war to the death against the impending Jewish state, yet now the Arabs who remained within the boundaries of the young polity had become Israeli citizens. Moreover, the Arab armies that had declared it to be their duty to prevent the establishment of Israel had signed armistice agreements with the new country. King 'Abdallah of Jordan had even gone so far as to hand over to Israel a large chunk of the Triangle, containing many Arab villages with tens of thousands of inhabitants. On the ideological level, many Arabs considered this treason, but because of the harsh conditions they had suffered under the Iraqi army (whose soldiers had reportedly committed acts of rape and robbery against Palestinian communities), many welcomed the change, which confused the picture even more.[9] Under the circumstances, it is hardly surprising that many were willing to cooperate with the authorities. The same atmosphere prevailed in the Galilee and the Negev, which had been conquered by the IDF a few months earlier.

Nazareth had been occupied in mid-July 1948. IDF infantry and armored forces surrounded the city, the most important urban center in the Lower Galilee and headquarters of al-Qawuqji's Liberation Army, after first taking the large village of Saffuri and others in the area. Nazareth's inhabitants decided to open the city's gates to the IDF without a battle. In any case there was no one in town who could fight—the Arab Liberation Army's volunteers had retreated from the city two days before its surrender, when their commanders realized that the balance of forces was not in their favor. The city's men who had fought with them also left. A delegation headed by Mayor Yusef al-Fahoum presented itself to the Jewish forces and announced the city's surrender. The IDF undertook not to harm the city's people, entered the city, and imposed a curfew. Arms held by inhabitants (about a thousand hunting rifles, military rifles, pistols, two machine guns, and two mortars) were collected by the soldiers. A military governor, Elisha Soltz, was appointed to see to the urgent needs of the city's inhabitants.

It took only a few days for the local police to return to work, but now they were under Israeli command, and Jewish policemen and officers were integrated into the force. The city's magistrate's court also reopened its doors. The inhabitants began to make contact with police officers and officials of the military government and security services. Delegations of locals appeared before the governor, and, as conquered populations do almost everywhere, they declared their loyalty to the new state and their willingness to cooperate with it. Some of the visitors referred to their historical rights, claiming that they had aided the Jews even before the war. A few Arabs from Nazareth and the surrounding area had indeed cooperated with Zionist institutions during the Mandate period and the recent war. After the conquest, locals were even more inclined to cooperate.[10]

Like Nazareth, many Galilean Arab settlements surrendered without a fight (among them were the Zu'biyya villages in the eastern Lower Galilee; the town of Shefa'amr; and the villages of Kabul, Tamra, Dir Hanna, 'Arrabe, Sakhnin, Daburiyya, Iksal, al-Reine, Mash-had, and Kafr Kanna).[11] In general, most of the Galilean villages left standing were those that did not offer armed resistance to the Jewish forces or that actually surrendered to the Jews. The veteran collaborators who lived in these villages—those who had been in contact with Zionist intelligence operatives or officials of the Jewish National Fund (Keren Kayemet LeYisra'el—KKL), the Zionist land-acquisition organization—initiated and promoted the surrender agreements. They were joined by people who had the foresight to discern the decisive military advantage of the IDF. When Jewish forces approached, whether during the Dekel operation of July or the Hiram operation a hundred days later, these Arabs persuaded their fellow villagers to refrain from fighting and made contact with IDF officers or KKL officials whom they knew in order to arrange a surrender.[12] Afterward, they encouraged a culture of cooperation with the new military government. In the postwar atmosphere of uncertainty, following the uprooting of hundreds of thousands of refugees, among them senior members and supporters of the Arab national leadership, such a decision was certainly comprehensible.

Some of the Bedouin tribes in the Negev, conquered soon afterward, acted in a similar fashion. Some allied themselves with the Jewish forces during the fighting, while others sought Israel's protection and promised to help the state when hostilities ended.[13] Those that fought against the Jews generally left the country. A letter sent by Sheikh 'Oda Abu-M'ammar, leader of the Mas'oudin tribe (a tribe in the 'Azazmeh federation), to the commander of the Beersheva District in December 1948 demonstrates the approach of those Bedouin who chose to remain within Israel and succeeded in doing so:

> We request to be annexed to Israel and request of the Israeli government that it supply us with food and clothing as needed and weapons to defend ourselves from the other members of our tribe and their Egyptian cohorts. We obligate ourselves before Allah the supreme to be loyal to the Israeli government, its leaders, and its governors, and to obey their orders without any question or doubt, and we will not use our arms for illegal purposes. We will use them to assist [the country] if we are asked to do so.[14]

The warm reception of Israeli forces in the Negev and elsewhere and the Arabs' willingness to cooperate with them led many Israeli field personnel to conclude that the Arabs were pleased to be under Israeli rule. They assumed that this would allow them to recruit significant numbers of collaborators and assessed that it would not be difficult to establish a system of self-supervision, in which the collaborators would serve as the long hand of the state.[15] In July 1949, the Nazareth police reported, "Cooperation between the police and the mukhtars proves its effectiveness in the war against infiltrators. Each day infiltrators are captured and handed over to the army for deportation from the country."[16] Two months later, the Haifa District Headquarters reported that forty young men from Baqa al-Gharbiyyeh, former soldiers in the Jordanian army, the Arab Legion, requested to enlist in the IDF and that most of the population was "beginning to recognize the state." At the beginning of October 1949, the Haifa police pointed out that the Arabs of Wadi 'Ara were pleased with the government, "which treats them justly."[17]

But this honeymoon did not last long, and the atmosphere quickly changed. In mid-November, the police station in Karkur (which was in charge of the northern Triangle) reported to its district headquarters, "Hatred for the authorities is growing steadily," and toward the end of this month a report written by the Haifa District Headquarters stated, "The mood regarding the authorities has definitely changed. [People] in all the villages are saying that the government is not looking after them."[18] Given that atmosphere, coop-

Figure 2. Honeymoon? The Arab inhabitants of the Triangle celebrate the first anniversary of their annexation to Israel, 1950. Photograph by Fritz Cohen; courtesy Israeli Government Press Office.

eration with the authorities became more and more problematic. "People who are seen in the village as being loyal to the government feel themselves isolated."[19] Very soon, the police began hearing of nationalist activists who were collecting information on collaborators and passing it on to intelligence operatives in nearby Arab countries. The state and its Arab citizens, who had almost become allies, were now arranged on either side of a divide.

The police and army tried to fathom the drastic change. Police reports quoted Arabs who accused the military government of running affairs "as its mood pleases," in a manner "reminiscent of the time of the gangs in 1936–39, and the days of the Iraqis."[20] The IDF general staff's operations branch, for its part, accused the police of failing to prevent "robbery and the movement of armed bands, [which] have caused considerable fear among the Arab population, and especially among collaborators with the Israeli authorities."[21]

These factors indeed affected the Arabs' attitude toward the state, but another important factor was economic crisis. The Arabs of the Galilee and the Triangle had lost much of their land. In the latter region, Israel had conquered large tracts during the war, while the villages were under Arab (Iraqi-Transjordanian) military rule. When these villages were handed over to Israel under the Rhodes Agreements of April 1949, Israel persisted in seeing these lands as the property of the state, assigned to the custodian of absentee property. Many villages thus lost their principal source of livelihood, and some reached the point of famine. The imposition of military government on the Arabs in Israel and the restrictions on movement imposed by this regime made it difficult for them to work outside their villages, and the resulting hardship made them hostile to the state. Resentment grew because the relevant state institutions knew very well that the country's Arab citizens were in great distress, but not one endeavored to help them (especially after the Ministry of Minorities was dismantled in July 1949).

While police officers informed their superiors about the harsh living conditions and hunger in some of the villages, the common wisdom was that the response should not be an effort to ameliorate the Arabs' economic circumstances. Instead, the minority population should be treated more harshly. "The Arabs' impudence is growing because they don't feel the hard fist that was routine during Arab army rule," maintained the officer who was responsible for the southern Triangle, Aryeh Kleper.[22]

Nationalist sentiments also played a role in the growing antipathy to Israel. A year after the Triangle's annexation, Ben-Elkana prepared a detailed report with the title "The Southern Triangle's Activity in the Past and Present," in which he stressed the nationalist (that is, Palestinian Arab anti-Zionist) orientation of the region's inhabitants. The purpose of the report, written in a cynical tone and from the perspective of the Israeli establishment, was to play down the state's responsibility for the reversal in Arab attitudes. He noted correctly, however, that economic factors were not the only ones that had brought about resistance to Israeli rule. Nationalist ideology also played a role. After surveying the involvement of the Triangle's inhabitants in the Arab rebellion of 1936–39 and in the war of 1948, the report stated:

> From the above, we can see that the villages of the southern Triangle were faithful to Arab tradition and did not miss any opportunity to prove their capacity and determination in aggressive and hostile acts against the Yishuv [the Jewish community in Palestine]. Today, too, after annexation of these villages under Israeli rule, these villages have not come to terms with that fact, and they eagerly await the time when they will return to Arab rule and, by their own account, to the "blessed" day when their lives will resume their "course" and their "path."[23]

The rapid change in attitude toward Israel, whatever its causes, did not produce any significant acts of rebellion. Despite their aspiration to live under Arab rule, many Arabs reasoned that there was not much chance of that happening. They realized that Israel would not disappear anytime soon and that it would not consent to return to the constricted borders decided on by the United Nations in its partition resolution. They observed Israel's moves to expand Jewish settlement throughout the country and perceived the real balance of power between Israel and its neighbors. The military government they lived under also contributed to their sense of weakness. Clearly, they saw, Israel rule over a large number of Arab communities was an established fact. Under the circumstances, every individual had to formulate his own position and his attitude toward the state. Many decided to lay aside the big national questions and to focus on everyday life, in particular on making a living for their families. Whatever their ideologies and nationalist sentiments, they chose political passivity. Others began to organize themselves into groups that demanded equal rights for all Israeli citizens—to the displeasure of the authorities. And there were also some who focused on the profit that could be had from establishing relationships with government officials and helping them dominate the country's Arab population. Some of these belonged to a class of people accustomed to serving in high positions. But this was hardly the case with all of them. Their motives were varied, as was their activity and their level of awareness. Some took the initiative and offered their services. Others waited until officials came to them. They acted and were run on three levels: as small-time informers and collaborators, local leaders, and national leaders. The boundaries between these levels were not always clear. Some members of the national Arab leadership began as local leaders (and sometimes returned to that category), and leaders at either level also conveyed information to Israeli authorities. They quickly became a central cog in the machine of control established by the state.

Some of those who showed up in the offices of the military government or in police stations to offer their assistance or who invited security service agents into their homes were veteran collaborators who had worked with Zionist institutions before the war and during its progress. They had arranged the surrender of their cities and villages without a fight, conveyed information to Jewish forces during the war, facilitated land sales to the KKL, opposed Hajj Amin al-Husseini during the rebellion of 1936–39 and afterward, and worked in tandem with the Haganah or the Jewish Agency. Before the establishment of Israel, when Hajj Amin headed the national movement, his opponents had been persecuted outcasts. Now they were on the strong side. Foreign Minister Moshe Sharett and Bechor Shalom Shitrit, who was minister of minorities and police, agreed in 1949 that these people should be given special treatment: "In any arrangement of internal administration for the Arab inhabitants of the conquered territories, we should depend principally on those groups and people who cooperated with us before, including those who established strong relations with the Political Department of the Jewish Agency and with the Keren Kayemet LeYisra'el."[24] In addition, many Arabs who had been active in the national movement and who feared that Israel would retaliate against them swiftly put themselves at the state's disposal. These newly "repentant" collaborators quickly became part of the state's control system. I have already recounted the story of 'Abd al-Ra'ouf 'Abd al-Razeq. Here are two more examples of how veteran collaborators, one from the Negev and one from the Galilee, became part of Israel's system of rule.

Sheikh 'Oda Abu-M'ammar of the Mas'oudin tribe had, as we have seen, requested the IDF's protection toward the end of the war. He declared his loyalty to the government and his willingness to cooperate. This was not his first contact with Zionist officials. Beginning in 1943, he served as a guard in Jewish settlements, and in the years that followed he took part in acquiring stolen British weapons and handing them over to the Haganah. His uncle Salameh, chief of the 'Azazmeh tribes, had been involved during the 1940s in land deals with the KKL. When the 1948 war began, nationalist activists called for his assassination, because it was rumored that he planned to form a Bedouin unit that would fight alongside the Jews. To clear his name, Sheikh Salameh sent his men to attack Jewish settlements in the Negev. Sheikh 'Oda, in contrast, kept up his ties to Haganah intelligence and served as an informant during the war. When Jewish forces conquered the Negev, Salameh and his men, fearing retribution, moved across the border. 'Oda and his supporters remained. It was only natural that, after the conquest, Israel appointed Sheikh 'Oda chief of the 'Azazmeh federation.[25]

Sayf al-Din Zu'bi lived in the Galilee, but his life in many ways paralleled that of Sheikh 'Oda Abu-M'ammar. Sayf al-Din was born in 1914 to the head of the Zu'biyya family, Muhammad Sa'id, of the village of Nin, who was close to Emir (later King) 'Abdallah of Transjordan. During the rebellion of 1936–39, most of the Zu'biyya family numbered among the opposition to Hajj Amin al-Husseini. (Sayf al-Din's father, Muhammad Sa'id, was briefly placed under arrest by the British and was released after the emir intervened.) In the 1940s, Sayf al-Din served in various capacities in the Mandatory administration's agriculture office and in the Nazareth municipality. Along with other members of his family—in particular, his father and uncle—he furthered the sale of land belonging to the Zu'biyya clan in the area east of Mt. Tabor to the KKL. (The family lived in the villages of Nin, Na'ura, Tamra-Zu'biyya, Taybe-Zu'biyya, and the surrounding area.) As a result, he became acquainted with Aharon Danin, a KKL land buyer, as well as with Zionist intelligence agents. In 1947, Sayf al-Din survived two attempts on his life, apparently made in revenge for his sale of land to the Jews and his opposition to Hajj Amin al-Husseini.[26] In his memoirs, he wrote that he had realized on the eve of the war that Hajj Amin's policies would lead to catastrophe and that the Jews could not be defeated. Accepting the partition proposal of 1947 was, he believed, in the Arab interest.[27]

During the war, the Zu'biyya villages entered into a peace treaty with the adjacent Jewish settlements. Sayf al-Din himself served, according to the Arab Liberation Army's intelligence, as an agent of the Jewish forces. The Arab command sent out orders that he was to be captured and brought in for interrogation. He was very nearly caught by his enemies once when he crossed the lines between the area under IDF control and that controlled by the ALA, but he managed to evade his pursuers. (One of Sayf al-Din's men was killed.)[28] After the IDF captured Nazareth and its surrounding territory, he moved naturally into the role of liaison between the Arab population and the military government. He accompanied the military governor on his visits to villages and suggested to the villagers that they demonstrate their loyalty to the state, "so that it will take care of all their needs."[29] At the same time, he worked to make life easier for the inhabitants of the Nazareth area.

The Israeli regime considered Sheikh 'Oda Abu-M'ammar, 'Abd al-Razeq, and Sayf al-Din Zu'bi to be "good Arabs," who helped establish Israeli rule over the Arab population within its borders. Others like them were active in every Arab town and village in the country. One of their tasks was to block "negative" influences—that is, nationalist and Communist ones. In addition to utilizing these men, the Israeli security agencies recruited informers to collect intelligence on Arab settlements in Israel (and sometimes over the border). To encourage these various kinds of collaborators, the state developed a sophisticated system of rewards.

Figure 3. Life of service. Sayf al-Din Zu'bi (left) was a member of the Knesset, then the mayor of Nazareth, and believed that he served his community. Here, during his campaign for the municipal elections of Nazareth, 1966. Photograph by Moshe Pridan; courtesy Israeli Government Press Office.

As with the appointment of Sheikh 'Oda to the position of chief of the 'Azazmeh tribes and the advancement of Sayf al-Din, the state acted at the village and neighborhood levels to appoint to positions of influence figures who were inclined to cooperate. Its goal was twofold: to enhance its control, and to reward its collaborators. Appointments to the position of mukhtar served, in many places, to achieve both goals. During Israel's early years, there were three distinct types of mukhtars. First, there were those who had collaborated with the Zionists during the British period and continued to do so. These, of course, retained their positions. Second were those who had been involved in militant Palestinian circles but began to collaborate with Israel after the IDF's entry into their areas. These, too, remained in place. The third category consisted of those who did not cooperate. Israeli security forces sought to remove them from their jobs or to persuade them to cooperate. All mukhtars were monitored constantly by the security forces, who produced frequent reports on them. These included brief descriptions of their characters (in the eyes of these officials, who generally evaluated positively those who cooperated and negatively those who did not), assessments of their attitudes toward the state, and recommendations regarding their future. So, for example, the mukhtar of one village was portrayed as "an honest man of good character who aids the authorities," and the recommendation was to retain him in his job. In contrast, a colleague of his was described as "an Israel-hater, who outwardly presents himself as a friend, [but] does not help and does not cooperate. The police recommended that he be dismissed." In other cases, the Israelis recalled earlier acts of favor: "During the War of Independence, he provided the Yishuv with food supplies."[30] But what determined a man's security in his sinecure, more than anything else, was his current cooperation with security forces.

In some villages and neighborhoods there was competition for the post of mukhtar, and winning the job was itself adequate compensation for assistance offered. But other mukhtars and collaborators frequently expected more concrete returns, and security officials grappled with the subject of how to compensate collaborators from the time the state was founded. They were especially concerned that collaborators might get frustrated, a phenomenon that they began to see as early as the end of 1949. Police officer Hayyim Geffen of the Hadera District brought up the subject at a meeting of security officials in the Triangle and stated his concerns: "This thing [unmet expectations] is liable to rebound on us in the future, and people will be afraid to be our intelligence agents." That, however, was not the opinion of everyone. Intelligence officer Rehavia Vardi couldn't understand what was bothering Geffen. "Nowhere in the world do they reward secret service men after they finish their jobs. On the contrary. There is no place for that with us," he said. A military government officer, Captain Go'el Levitzki, took a similar position: "We are in charge today, and the Arabs who work with us do so because it's worth it for them to do so. We have no obligations to them."[31]

The position that the collaborators deserved no compensation did not last for long. Security officials soon realized that they could not put together an intelligence network without offering fit compensation. It was not hard for them to do so. The difficult conditions under the military government offered them a variety of options. For example, compensation could come in the form of helping a collaborator find a job. One case in point is that of a refugee from Sa'sa', in the Upper Galilee, a village that was evacuated during the war. He already had a history of extensive collaboration; at the end of the 1930s, he had worked alongside the British against the rebels while also working as an agent for the KKL in the purchase of land in the Galilee. During the 1948 war he tried to establish contact with Jewish forces but did not succeed. When his village was occupied, he preferred not to go to Lebanon, as most of his fellow villagers did, and instead settled in another Arab village in the Galilee, where he became a police informant. He faced economic difficulties; his extensive holdings at Sa'sa' were declared absentee properties and transferred to the state. His connections proved useless in getting his land back. Instead, the police helped him find work.[32] A collaborator from the Triangle who had been in contact with Israeli intelligence prior to the arrival of the IDF also benefited from similar employment assistance. He, too, had suffered economic hardship after the imposition of military rule. In an effort to put him on his feet, as well as to continue enjoying his services, security officials recommended that he be employed as a guard at one of the local Jewish-owned quarries. Another collaborator from the same area was made a foreman in a nearby quarry. Others were given permits to travel freely throughout Israel—permits most villagers found it hard to obtain—so that they would have more employment opportunities. They took advantage of this in a number of ways. Some found jobs, while others opened small businesses—like the man from Tira who "received compensation in the form of help in getting an exit [permit] from the territory [of the Triangle] so that he could buy and sell old and used clothing."[33]

A more significant economic perquisite was the right to lease abandoned farmland. After independence, large areas of the Galilee were declared to be absentee lands (that is, land whose owners were no longer present in Israel), and other areas were classified as state land of one sort or another. Much land in the Triangle was also declared to be absentee property. Most of these tracts were used for the establishment of Jewish settlements, and this was the major reason for the economic crisis in the Arab areas. A small portion was assigned to the Arab inhabitants, principally to provide subsistence to the internal refugees and to collaborators. In the summer of 1951, the office of the prime minister's adviser on Arab affairs contacted the land-leasing division of the custodian of absentee property and asked that it lease land to informers who had previously worked with military intelligence.[34] This was on top of the policy of leasing local collaborators more than the standard allocation of land. For example, a mayor from the Triangle who had faithfully done the bidding of the security forces received an additional 150 percent over the standard allocation; collaborators were also given the privilege of first choice of plots.[35]

The professionals in the Ministry of Agriculture sometimes objected to these special favors. But when the director of the ministry's Lands Department, Re'uven Aloni, tried to put an end to the practice, he was opposed by a representative of the military government, Major Pinhas Amir. The latter argued that the collaborators' demands should be met. He was seconded by the KKL's representative on the Land Leasing Committee, Ya'akov Liftzin: "There is no reason to balk at cases in which Arabs who have served the state receive leases on additional lands," he said.[36] Their goal was to demonstrate to all that the state stood by its collaborators. "If we don't help him, the villagers will laugh at him," one official said at a discussion about a collaborator from al-Rameh, in the Galilee. "Right now that is really the case. He is under constant threat from the villagers. I want to show the village that we help those who help us."[37]

As a result of such displays of gratitude and with the goal of reinforcing Israeli rule, the authorities brought about the creation of a small class of wealthy collaborators at the beginning of the 1950s. The state gave them leases for relatively large tracts of land, on which they employed refugees and landless Arabs. In this way they proved that cooperating with the authorities was worthwhile, at least economically. The class included mukhtars and mayors who supported the government, regional and national leaders, and veteran collaborators who continued to work with the Israeli authorities.

Another way to reward collaborators economically was to allow them to engage in what the authorities defined as "the legal smuggling business," especially regarding meat. In the country's early years, a time of mass immigration and rationing of basic foodstuffs, one way Israel obtained meat was to bring herds of sheep and cattle in from neighboring countries with which Israel was officially at war. The smugglers were small-time informers who were paid for their work, but more senior collaborators were also involved. They used their connections on both sides of the new border to locate owners of livestock who were interested in selling their animals. The senior figures sent out shepherds to drive the herds to particular points along the border, and received a commission from the state for doing so. (Apparently they also received commissions from the sellers in the Arab countries.) Smugglers often also performed routine intelligence missions in the neighboring countries. Hajj Muhammad 'Omar Qays, a notable of the Circassian village Reihaniyya and an old friend of Moshe Dayan's (under Dayan's command, Qays guided a Palmach unit that went on an operation in Syria during the rule of the pro-Nazi regime), received the "franchise" for smuggling over the Lebanese border. It was an important source of income for him, until he was murdered in 1953. In the Triangle, the smuggling business was assigned to Fares Hamdan of Baqa al-Gharbiyyeh, a landowner who was involved in local and national politics. At the end of the Mandate period, he had zigzagged between maintaining good relations with the Jewish settlements in the region and supporting Hajj Amin al-Husseini. After the establishment of Israel, he tightened his ties to IDF intelligence and served as a link between it and several cattle dealers in Tulkarem. At the time, he was considered to be the strong man in Baqa; in 1951 he was elected to the Knesset on the Agriculture and Development slate, a satellite of Mapai, the ruling party. This, however, hardly meant an end to his extraparliamentary cross-border activity.[38]*

Approval of their requests to grant an entrance permit into Israel or a residence permit for someone who had entered illegally was a further privilege

---

* Hamdan's main smuggling partner was C., a Tulkarem notable who had been a member of the Husseini Party until 1948. In addition to trading cattle, he maintained contact with IDF intelligence agents. Despite this, when he entered Israel (via one of the paths used by infiltrators) in order to split his smuggling profits with Hamdan, the chief of the Tulkarem police and the commander of the regional Jordanian National Guard accompanied him to the border—even though their job was to prevent the border from being crossed. In this they testified to their nonrecognition of the border and beyond that to the fact that many did not recognize the official state of hostilities between Israel and Jordan. On the other hand, Arab nationalists exacted retribution from Hamdan for his collaboration by infiltrating from Jordanian territory and stealing cows from his herds. Another indication of how complex the situation was and how changeable loyalties were is that one of the Arab employees of the military governor's office in Baqa al-Gharbiyyeh, ostensibly a collaborator with Israel, routinely provided a Jordanian officer with reports on Hamdan's activities.

given to collaborators. Sometimes such permits were provided as a reward for past assistance, generally in the hope of further collaboration in the future. During the years immediately following the war, when many refugees were still living in tents and scrap-metal shanties on the edges of villages and cities in the West Bank, the Gaza Strip, and Lebanon and when the splitting of families and the pain of their separation were still fresh, such a gesture was of immense significance. Furthermore, the power that accrued to those who were able to obtain such permits for their families would be difficult to exaggerate.[39] Here was another dimension of the permits policy: when the state wanted to strengthen a political collaborator, it would approve the "list of recommendations for identity cards" that he had submitted to the authorities, which would enhance his influence and broaden the circle of his dependents—as well as the circle of collaborators. Bishop (in Arabic: "the mutran") George Hakim, head of the Greek Catholic Church in Israel, was a prominent example. In order to strengthen his hand in his battle with the Communists, the government allowed refugees who were members of his community to return to Israel. As a result, he became his community's savior and a political figure of the first order. At the same time, he was expected to sign a letter of gratitude in which he declared, "From this point forward I, other spiritual leaders, and all members of the community will aid government institutions in preventing the entry of undesirable elements into the villages in which members of our community reside." He was also asked to give up the right of his Haifa coreligionists to return to their homes, which had been handed over to the custodian of absentee property.[40] We will take a further look at the mutran (as Bishop Hakim was commonly referred to) in the next chapter.

Another way of remunerating collaborators and enhancing their power was arming them. A rifle or pistol not only served a man as self-protection (and self-confidence) but also gave him prestige. The expression "Msadso hal-qad" (His pistol is this big), accompanied by an open-armed gesture, served in some villages as an idiom to express not only how large a given man's pistol was but also how important the pistol's bearer was (at least, in the eyes of the authorities). One man who possessed an impressive arsenal was Sheikh Saleh Khneifes, a Druze leader in Shefaʿamr who had been of considerable assistance to the IDF in its conquest of the area in 1948. Two years after the war, Khneifes received a Bren light machine gun and seven rifles "for the protection of his property and home." This privilege reflected Israel's attitude toward the Druze community as a whole, which was given the right to bear arms. When it was decided in the spring of 1949 to collect some of the weapons held by the Druze, it was done in coordination with a committee of Druze representatives and with the mutual understanding that the Druze would retain more weapons than would the members of other communities.[41] This was on the national level; similarly, on the village and community levels, security officials granted gun permits to people they sought to reward.

The distribution (as well as the confiscation) of weapons was not based solely on security considerations. Ultimately, the decisions were made by a coordinating committee of security forces: "The distribution of weapons to an element or exclusively to members of a particular community that can benefit us will create desirable tension between different sectors of the population and enable us to control the situation."[42] The claim that Israel distributed arms to certain elements in the Arab population in order to intensify tensions within the Arab community was sometimes dismissed by Israelis as a conspiracy theory. But in fact the documents show it to be a policy set in place by an official committee.

These methods of rewards, the product of the realities of life under military rule, were of course supplemented by more traditional rewards in the form of money. Informers who provided information about armed infiltrators received one-off prizes. In addition, intelligence officers employed informers who were paid regular fees. The Karkur police, for example, paid a monthly retainer of eight Israeli pounds to informers who worked with them on an ongoing basis.[43] Another form of payment used by intelligence agencies around the world and adopted in some measure by Israel was erasing criminal charges. The IDF unit that maintained agents in countries bordering on Israel, Modi'in 10 (later called Unit 154, and still later Unit 504), occasionally made requests of this sort of the police, as did other intelligence agencies.[44]

Officer Ovadiah Novoselsky, a Karkur police inspector who utilized collaborators in the northern Triangle, referred to another motive. He wrote of one of his informers: "He has a character of a type that enjoys being in touch with the police or the army and other elements." About another he noted: "He gets satisfaction from having ties with the police on intelligence affairs."[45] This was the case with many collaborators. Some even refrained from accepting any concrete compensation. The feeling of power that their work with Israeli intelligence gave them sufficed.

They could also enjoy this sense of power when the activity was covert, when the informer could affect the lives of his fellow villagers without their knowledge. But some collaborators advertised their activities and were thus sought after not only by the security forces but also by members of their own communities who needed something from state institutions. As mediators, the collaborators enjoyed special standing. Arab nationalists in Israel censured them, but this was not always a deterrent. The collaborators were able to place themselves in key positions in their villages and neighborhoods.

The variety of forms of compensation reinforces the image of the collaborators as people whose primary motive was personal interest. This is largely true but not absolutely so. Some collaborators internalized the Zionist discourse to one extent or another. For example, they accepted the fundamental claim that the Zionist movement aspired to live in peace with its neighbors and to endow Israel's Arab citizens with equal rights once the state of emergency ended. Some among them thought that it was in the best interests of the Arabs in Israel to accommodate themselves to the Jewish state and that direct conflict with the state and its agencies would rebound on them. But even these "believers" often needed an incentive to collaborate actively. Sayf al-Din Zu'bi was (at least by one report) a classic example of this type. By the final stretch of the British Mandate he had come to believe that it was in the interest of the Arabs of Palestine to cooperate with the Jews, and he thus maintained contact with the Jewish forces during and after the war. He battled with the Communists for years, for political, ideological, and personal reasons. But in 1957, when the Development Authority (responsible for abandoned refugee property) refused to lease him an additional tract of land he was interested in, Sayf al-Din shouted at the responsible official, "I don't give a damn about you and your Mapai. I swear that this time I'll vote Communist."[46] It would be hard to believe that Sayf al-Din really voted for the Communists, but certainly his general view of Jewish-Arab relations was supplemented by a very firm view of what the state's obligations to him were.

This is a sensitive subject. Despite the well-developed system of compensation, more than a few collaborators felt, justly or unjustly, that the state used them for its own purposes and then left them to suffer. Rabbah 'Awad of the village of Ghabsiyya in the Galilee (known in the western Galilee as Sheikh Rabbah) provided significant assistance to the Haganah's intelligence during the 1948 war. He smuggled arms to the Jews and worked to arrange the surrender of his and other villages during the war.[47] After the state was established, he assumed that this activity would entitle him, if not to extensive privileges, then at least to protection from the arbitrariness of the state and from the inhabitants of the nearby Jewish villages. Instead, 'Awad and his men were expelled from their village, and the state expropriated most of their land. The villagers petitioned Israel's Supreme Court, which ordered the state to allow them to return to their village. But when they returned, they encountered a military police detachment that refused to let them enter their homes. The IDF demolished the village's houses, except for the mosque.[48] In the months that followed, the inhabitants of the nearby Jewish kibbutzim and moshavim vandalized 'Awad's orchards and fields. 'Awad wrote to the prime minister:

> When the War of Independence broke out, I cooperated closely with the Israel Defense Forces. I knew how much damage and risk this involved, but I threw down my life and acceded to all the demands made of me. . . . I see no need to detail all these actions here.
>
> I did all this not in expectation of reward, but out of a hope founded on mutual trust that, after the winds of war had subsided, I would be able to live in this land as a citizen with equal rights in practice and living a proper life as befits every citizen.
>
> To my great regret, I must state unequivocally and without trepidation that all my hopes have been proven false and that I am filled with a disappointment that increases day by day. I stand today shamed and disgraced before all my acquaintances because of the spiteful lawsuits and tribulations that rain down on me. . . .
>
> My above-mentioned neighbors [from the nearby Jewish settlements] have made me a target of persecution and have at every opportunity impeded me. Their actions intensify by the day, in order to harass me in every way. . . .
>
> This being the case, I am sick of my life, and I cannot understand why I am being paid in evil currency for good deeds. If it is bad for the authorities that I live in this country, I should be told that explicitly and a way found to remove me. But the deeds being done today do not befit men of culture and a progressive regime.
>
> I therefore petition his Excellency that word be given me that his Excellency will not suffer such actions against an innocent man, whose only sin is to be an Arab, and that he order all the necessary people to investigate this matter sincerely and truthfully, so that the forces of evil not prevail over the values of justice and honesty.[49]

'Awad's operational and intelligence services to the Jewish community did not protect him. The inhabitants of Ghabsiyya, and he first among them, never returned to their village. (They continue today to fight for their right to return.) It turns out that the desire to compensate collaborators could be trumped by a much more fundamental Zionist aspiration, that of transferring as much land as possible to Jewish hands.

Just as the state's sense of responsibility for its Palestinian collaborators was limited, so was the collaborators' sense of obligation toward the state. Ideology was not the collaborators' principal motivation, so it is hardly surprising that Israeli interests were not always foremost in their minds. Even when they carried out intelligence or security missions, they did not necessarily feel any identification with the state of Israel. Their connection, and perhaps also their identification, was with the specific intelligence apparatus they worked for. This feeling was reinforced in part because the various state agencies— the General Security Service (Israel's secret internal security organization), military intelligence, the police, and the military government—operated in overt or veiled competition with one another. Their interests were not necessarily identical. As a result, some of the collaborators saw themselves as working with a particular organization rather than with the state. Some even viewed themselves as collaborators with a specific intelligence officer. So, for example, a member of the Baqa al-Gharbiyyeh village council who served as a police informer stressed that he did so as a personal favor to a local officer and not in order to help Israel.[50]

Competition among different intelligence services also had implications for the other relations among them and for their relations with the collaborators. As early as the summer of 1949, police officer Ze'ev Steinberg discerned the negative consequences of this competition and recommended consolidating intelligence work into one professional agency—meaning the police. He claimed,

The military government and all sorts of intelligence services view themselves as having unlimited control. . . . Each one has his own "Ahmad," Intelligence Service 1 and Intelligence Service 3, the Front Intelligence Division and the Middle East [Department in the Foreign Ministry], and so on. And each such "Ahmad" is permitted to move freely in the region as well as near the border. And in a case when one of them has crossed the border, he should be treated leniently, because he is doing it for the country. And while I have often argued with all sorts of intelligence services that their work is military security and no more, and that the methods they use are old-fashioned and not appropriate for peacetime, and that smuggling and cattle slaughtering and beatings are not their work, I have not succeeded in convincing them. Every kid in the village knows the "secret officer," whoever he is. I proved once to Intelligence Service 3 that there's a type of person who comes up to him in the middle of the village and asks how he's doing or what time it is or the like, and after that the same Arab goes back to his café and tells everyone that this secret officer is his friend, and anyone who dares to give the police officer information about him will be arrested by the secret officer. By having all sorts of intelligence we organize groups of Arabs who take advantage of their work for the sake of their personal interests.[51]

Steinberg's recommendation was not accepted, of course, and intelligence organizations continued to compete in the field. One thing they competed for was the hearts of the collaborators. This created a tangled web of connections among the organizations themselves, between each organization and its collaborators, and between each organization and the collaborators of its competitors. In the Lod area, this competition reached a climax in 1954, when a local police officer, Ezra Goldberg, complained to his superior officers that the GSS was interfering with police work. First, he claimed, the GSS was pressuring police informers to stop working with the police and to transfer their allegiance to the GSS's agents. In addition, GSS personnel in the city were, he believed, leaking information about his informers and thus putting their lives in danger. The sequence of events, from the police's point of view (all GSS documents are still classified) was as follows: GSS agents in Lod identified a leading family in the city and, through it, planned to achieve political control of Lod's Arab population. To buttress the family's standing, the GSS helped find its members work, provided them with covert political support, and offered other benefits. Police officer Goldberg argued that the family was misleading the GSS and was in fact running a network of infiltrators and smugglers. The background to this debate was the police force's view that priority should be given to the war against crime and infiltration, while the GSS put most of its energy into political policing.

Goldberg saw this case as especially serious. The family, according to information he had received, was linked to the infiltrator and murderer Mustafa Samwili, number one on the police's most-wanted list at the time. He had been involved in the murder of Jews at Motza, 'Agur, Even-Sapir, Mishmar Ayalon, and Jerusalem. Wiping him out was the first mission given to the elite Unit 101, under the command of Ariel Sharon, when it was founded in 1953.[52] Goldberg took an exceptional step. He sent an infiltrator he knew, who was tied to Samwili, to visit the family, in order to see if they reported the visit to the GSS. As he expected, the family did not notify any intelligence agency that the infiltrator had come to their home. Goldberg told the relevant GSS personnel about this, but they did not, he claimed, cut off their ties with the family. Instead, the GSS told the family that their friend the infiltrator was connected to the police, and they passed on this information to Samwili's men in Ramallah.[53] The police claimed that the GSS had knowingly put their informer's life in danger, out of spite. Perhaps there is historical justice in the fact that, two years later, Samwili was killed, not by Unit 101, or on the basis of GSS intelligence, but by a police ambush made up of men who did not know who Samwili was.[54]

The charges made by the police against the GSS in this case were harsh. In other cases and other locales, complaints were more muted. The most common of them seems to have been connected to attempts by GSS agents to recruit police collaborators or to tales the GSS spread about them. An officer in the police force's investigations division, Aharon Shlush, had no choice but to remind the GSS, "It is inappropriate to recruit informers by slandering mukhtars or other persons with ties to the police."[55]

The police were also sharply critical of the conduct of the military government in the Triangle. Re'uven Dorenzaft, who coordinated police intelligence in the southern Triangle, did not trust the military government and its collaborators. In his best judgment, the collaborators had turned tables on the military government's officials and become the real rulers of the area.

> I think that the military government in the Triangle villages I have visited is being conducted precisely according to the old Mandatory routine. What stands out is the lack of any change in the Arab village's social structure; the same mukhtars from the eminent families and wielders of local influence act in accordance with the old Oriental approach, ingratiating themselves with the new conqueror while lording over their fellow villagers and treating them as wards. Some of them have become permanent residents of the government's centers and local buildings and without a doubt gained themselves perquisites, directly or indirectly. They know how to tilt the management of affairs according to their whim and as they wish.[56]

The picture painted here is one of collaborators adept at taking advantage of their connections with multiple intelligence organizations to strengthen themselves politically and for their personal benefit. Some exploited the divisions and rivalries among different institutions. If any further proof were needed that many collaborators did not put the state's interest at the top of their priorities, one only need point to the phenomenon of mutual betrayal among collaborators who were sent into Jordanian territory. In December

1949, a group of GSS collaborators from the Triangle who had been sent to Tulkarem to track infiltrators were reported to have turned in to Jordanian intelligence another detachment of Arab collaborators from Israel who had been sent on a similar mission by IDF intelligence. Such incidents occurred again and again.[57] The reason, apparently, was personal rivalries and competition, but presumably the pressure placed on the participants in such missions and the resulting tension were also factors. In any case, the last thing that could be said about these collaborators was that they were mere pawns in the hands of the Israeli authorities. It was often the collaborators who knew how to maneuver and exploit intelligence rivalries in order to maximize their own advantage.

To limit disputes among security organizations that dealt with Israel's Arabs, coordinating committees were established as early as 1949. These bodies addressed problems that arose regarding certain persons and established consistent policies regarding a number of pressing issues. In 1952, the cabinet moved to establish the Supreme Committee on Arab Affairs at the level of ministry directors-general, and two years later a central committee for coordination among security agencies was established, to which three regional committees—in the Galilee, the Triangle, and the Negev—were subordinated.[58] The regional military governor chaired each of these, and its members included representatives of the police, the GSS, and the office of the prime minister's adviser on Arab affairs. Support for "positive" figures and the fight against "negative" ones were a major issue addressed by these committees, as will be seen below.

These committees—the most important bodies that operated among Israel's Arab population—were also the most important apparatus that worked to establish the collaborators as a distinct class with rights of its own. The committees were the professional authority that made decisions regarding every aspect, large and small, of the lives of each and every one of Israel's Arab citizens: who would receive a building permit and whose house would be demolished, who would be sent to administrative detention and who to vocational training, who would be appointed mukhtar or sheikh of each tribe and who would be laid off from his job, who would receive land for farming and grazing and who would have to live from hand to mouth, who would be arrested if caught smuggling and who would win the authorities' consent to engage in just such activities. So, while most of the Arab population lived under close supervision, with restrictions on their movements and only limited opportunities to make a living, senior collaborators enjoyed many perquisites, and their position as intermediaries between the population and the regime—along with that position's associated benefits—also became well-founded. So grew the collaborator class.

Collaborators are generally perceived as people who help the regime oppress the collaborators' own kind and who benefit from doing so. But among the Arab collaborators with Israel, as elsewhere, we see some who tried to minimize the harm done to their fellow Arabs and who offered the state only limited and conditional assistance. Many of them maneuvered constantly between the need to please the regime and the need to preserve their standing within the society in which they lived. They believed that they were serving both sides well. Those who were local leaders not only represented the authorities to their communities but also used their connections with the authorities to provide for their people's basic needs. The result was a delicate balance between them and the authorities; their ability to control their communities was dependent on their prestige, which was dependent on the extent to which the authorities acceded to their requests. Thus, in order to keep the system functioning, the government was required to listen to these men and accept at least some of their demands. Hence, the popular expression "the regime's tails" did not always apply to them. Sometimes they wagged state institutions.

Arab society's attitude toward collaborators corresponded to its attitudes toward Israel and its institutions. That attitude was in turn determined for the most part by three factors. The first was nationalist sentiments. These dictated opposition to the state of Israel, because it was founded on the ruins of the Palestinian society and because it defined itself as a Jewish country and discriminated against Arabs. In the area under discussion here, this factor acted as a restraint on Arabs' willingness to collaborate and led them to view collaborators negatively.

The second factor was life under Israeli rule, for better and for worse. On the worse side were the limitations on personal and public rights (for example, no freedom of movement, land confiscation), and on the better side was improvement in the standard of living (for example, enlargement of the education system, the physical infrastructure). The state's ambivalent or contradictory treatment of its Arab inhabitants—and, indeed, contradiction is one of the central characteristics of Israel's treatment of its Arab citizens—affected different people in different ways. Some resented the state because of the negative aspects of its conduct and virulently opposed the collaborators in all their manifestations; others were grateful for the positive aspects of Israeli rule and so did not always see collaboration as bad. In most cases, many Israeli Arabs had mixed feelings about Israel, and this was reflected in mixed feelings regarding the collaborators.

The third factor affecting the Israeli Arabs' attitude toward collaborators was their evaluation of the power equation between Israel and the Arab world. To the extent that they perceived the Arab world as united and strong (as in the high days of Nasserism), they viewed Israel as vulnerable or even a temporary phenomenon. And this in turn made them unwilling to cooperate with Israeli institutions and led them to view collaborators in a negative light. The opposite was also true.

The collaborators—and in fact every individual in Arab society in Israel—were affected by these three factors in deciding their attitudes toward the state and in making a choice among resistance, passivity, integration, and collaboration. But another factor also affected their choice—the state's treatment of collaborators. When former collaborators were abandoned and did not receive support from the state, potential collaborators were deterred; when the reverse happened, they were encouraged.

But keep in mind that frequently the decision to collaborate with one security body or another was not conscious, unambiguous, or irreversible. Beyond matters of principle and the adoption of a general position ("I help the state," "I am a Communist," "I am an Arab nationalist," "I don't have anything to do with either side"), a concrete decision about how to relate to a specific request from, say, a police intelligence officer or a GSS agent was influenced by other factors. These included the Arab's personal relationship with the specific Israeli making the request, the Arab's feelings about the person on whom he was asked to inform, his sentiments regarding the state at that given moment, and the profit-and-loss equation inherent in any such decision. Such individual factors were thus intrinsic to any decision made by collaborators or by those who refused to collaborate on the personal, national, social, or economic level.

These were the complex and conflicting considerations faced by every potential collaborator. As far as the state was concerned, things were much simpler. In every area in which state agencies operated among Israel's Arab citizens—the war against infiltration, the struggle against the Communist Party and other Arab nationalist organizations, land issues, counterintelligence, propaganda, and political and civilian policing—Israel sought aid from them. The counterforces were Arab groups, led firstly by the Communist Party, which sought to limit cooperation with the establishment. They opposed the military government, sought to reconstruct Palestinian Arab identity, and battled for equal rights for Arab citizens in Israel.

TWO

Communists vs.
the Military Government,
Collaborators vs. Communists

THE FOLLOWING LETTER ARRIVED at the Nazareth police station in August 1955:

Dear Inspector of the Nazareth Police Station
We, some of the elders of the village of 'Eilabun, make the following presentation to your excellency:

1. Mu'in Salim Zureiq owns a grocery store in the village of 'Eilabun.

2. This said man sells alcoholic and soft drinks without a license.

3. The said drinks are situated under a bench in his living room across from the store.

4. The young men of 'Eilabun come to play *cards* secretly in his store.

5. The store is located across the street from the Communist Party in the village, and Communists come and teach the young men about communism.

6. You can look into the matter on Saturdays in particular.

7. And this will ruin our children's education and turn them into communists.

We request that your excellencies put an end to these deeds at once![1]

Such letters informing on compatriots were not unusual in Israel's Arab villages in the 1950s and 1960s. Some reported on people who provided safe houses for infiltrators, and others turned in Arabs who owned weapons. Some fingered inhabitants of their village who had engaged in combat against Israel in the 1948 war or who worked in the black market. On occasion, such letters were sent by known collaborators who sought to prove their efficacy or by Arabs who wanted to ingratiate themselves with the authorities. In other cases, the motive was personal revenge. The security or political charges the letters contained were, in such cases, intended to prompt police action. The elders of 'Eilabun, whoever they were, assumed that implicating Zureiq in Communist activity would induce the police to act. They knew that the authorities viewed the Communist Party as their major rival for the support of the Arab public and as the only organization that offered, as early as the beginning of the 1950s, a solid alternative to the collaborator class.

Sa'id M. of the village of Makr, who corresponded with the minister of police and other establishment figures, was more aggressive in his war on communism than 'Eilabun's elders were. He had no qualms about signing his name to letters, even when they reported his own semi-illegal activity. Here is a section from an account he offered of a Communist meeting in his village in April 1952:

> During the assembly, Yusef 'Abdu stood up and began to slander the government to the point that he referred to it as a dog. When I learned of this I went and disrupted the assembly. The mukhtar [Na'if Salim] opposed me and said: "We don't want to follow the government party [Mapai], which robs us of our land and demolishes our homes, and the Communists are those who speak the truth and they are those who have prevented the government party from taking such actions." As a result, an argument broke out between me and him. Afterward I sent people who threw stones at them [the assemblers] until the assembly dispersed.
>
> I am astonished that the government has not dismissed him from the position of mukhtar after he has displayed such behavior, and I do not know why the government remains silent with regard to him. I have written about him previously to the offices of the military governor in Nazareth and to the department of the adviser on Arab affairs in the office of the prime minister.[2]

Sa'id M. was more intent on the fight against communism than was the military government itself. It is not clear if his motivation was simply to maintain the good graces of his overseers or to promote a personal grudge.

Whatever the case, the Communists' conduct leaves no reason to ask why they incensed the authorities and their collaborators. Their overt opposition to the military government and its laws, their fundamental position that Israel should withdraw to the 1947 partition borders, and the systematic way they recruited supporters all made them the major rival of Mapai (and the security agencies, which were in the hands of Mapai) in the Arab public. The Communists organized mass demonstrations, urged internal refugees to return to their villages without permits, and conducted other protest activities—some under the banner of Jewish-Arab partnership. The Israeli establishment thus viewed them as a clear and present danger to the Jewish state. The Communists also attacked collaborators vociferously and constantly tried to shame them publicly, coining terms like "the government's tails," which quickly became very popular. Indeed, if in the confusing circumstances that followed the 1948 war many Arabs chose to collaborate, the Communists offered a nationalist alternative, although a complex one that recognized Jewish national aspirations, and the right of Israel to exist within restricted borders.*

The authorities used a variety of political and security mechanisms to challenge the Communists' cachet in the Arab public. They promoted anti-Communist Arabs and placed them in key positions, maintained a group of local informers, tracked party activists, and pursued a carrot-and-stick policy (the carrot for Mapai's supporters; the stick for the Communists). The strategy was successful in part. In the elections of 1949, the Communists won 20 percent of Arab votes, making them the second-largest political party in the Arab sector. (Mapai, along with its Arab satellite parties, received 61 percent of the Arab vote.) In the three national elections that followed, Communist support declined significantly. They returned to their 1949 strength only in the elections to the fifth (1961) and sixth (1965) Knesset.[3] Nevertheless, their intensive, diverse, and sometimes mass activity throughout these years remained a unique instance of popular resistance under military rule.

In fact, the new state's relationship with the Communist Party began in an almost idyllic way, for two principal reasons. First, at the beginning of the 1948 war, Jewish Communists helped the Haganah conclude a critical arms deal with Czechoslovakia, which granted the Jewish forces an advan-

---

* Some Arab activists charged the Communists with being insufficiently nationalist, because of their recognition of Israel. The party's ability to operate within Israeli law served as proof of this. Yet it was unquestionably the Communist Party that led the fight of Israel's Arab population against military rule in the 1950s.

tage in armaments and enabled them to switch from defense to offense in the spring of that year.[4]* This activity affected Jewish attitudes toward Arab Communists as well, who united with their Jewish comrades in a single party in November 1948. Second, the Soviet Union's support for the UN partition resolution in November 1947 induced at least some Arab Communists to adopt a discourse that accepted the right of a Jewish state to exist in part of Palestine and to oppose the Arab invasion of the prospective state. It is hardly surprising, then, that in August 1948 they had advocates in the establishment. An IDF document that analyzed the activities of members of the National Liberation League (the Arab Communist organization in Mandatory Palestine) stated, "The League's activities should not be seen as a military threat to the state of Israel. Our enemies are their [the Communists'] enemies. In all their activities and appearances, they demonstrate a loyal attitude to the state. . . . It [the league] should be seen as a political force of stature and a potential ally for the state of Israel."[5] This view, and the Communists' ties with Jewish officials, earned them the privilege of running the employment office in Nazareth immediately after the city was conquered by the IDF. This allowed the Communists to reward their supporters and expand their influence.[6]

But by the end of 1948 the Communists were already at the forefront of the struggle against military rule and land confiscation and the struggle for civil rights. They were aggressive, well-organized, and imbued with a profound inner sense of natural justice. In December of that year, David Ben-Gurion already perceived their subversive potential, and he told the commander of the military government "to prevent a Communist takeover of the Arabs."[7] The commander passed on these instructions to the military governors. He suggested several ways of carrying out the mission, such as prohibiting the distribution of Communist placards and organizing locals to work against the party, and these proposals were put into action.[8] From that point forward, the history of the Arabs under Israeli military rule was riddled with frontal

* The deal with the Czechoslovakian government was already signed at the time of that country's Communist coup of 1948. To make sure the deal went through, the Haganah needed the mediation of the members of the Yishuv's Jewish Communists, who were quick to help. The first shipments began to arrive in April 1948; by the end of May, more than twenty thousand rifles, three thousand submachine guns, and ammunition "in quantities not yet known in the country" had arrived. In the months that followed the quantities of small and medium arms doubled, and, no less important, seventy-five combat aircraft were delivered. At the same time, the Czechs stopped selling arms to the Arabs. See Meir Pa'il, "The Fighting Forces," in Yehoshua Ben Arye, ed., *Ha-Historia shel Eretz Yisrael: Milhemet ha-Atzma'ut* [The history of the land of Israel: War of independence] (Jerusalem, 1983), vol. 10, pp. 112, 147–48.

Figure 4. A new, just world. A Communist activist distributes leaflets, before the first elections to the Israeli Knesset, 1949. Photograph courtesy Israeli Government Press Office.

clashes between the two sides, to the point that fighting the Communists became one of the justifications cited for leaving the military government in place.[9]

One of the bluntest weapons the military government used was preventing Communist Party rallies. This began during the first year after the conquest of the Galilee. In May 1949, the Communist Party of Israel (known also by its Hebrew acronym, Maki) organized a rally in Acre, in which the writer Emil Habibi was supposed to take part. To prevent the rally from taking place, the military governor issued orders confining two central party activists, Ramzi Khuri and Nadim Musa, to their villages. But the Communists did not give in and held the rally anyway. The party's Knesset representatives attacked the military government for using its powers for political purposes, and one of its Jewish parliamentarians, Meir Vilner, noted that Khuri and Musa had headed an anti-Qawuqji underground in the Galilee during the war. Prime Minister Ben-Gurion was not impressed and said from the Knesset podium that the Communists had used violent tactics to force storekeepers to close and that they had assaulted an Arab "working for the government."[10]

This theme of protecting "pro-government" Arabs worked well in the battle against the Communists.

In the months that followed, the conflict intensified. In February 1950, a number of Communist demonstrators in Nazareth were wounded when police fired on them. This also came before the Knesset. "The police force's gunfire assault on peaceful demonstrators demanding food and work is an act that the working class in this country has not yet experienced," declared the Communist Tawfiq Toubi, a member of the Knesset (MK). The gunfire had been unprovoked, he claimed. Minister of Police Bechor Shalom Shitrit called Toubi's statement "impudent and insolent." Mapai MK Pinhas Lavon, a leader of the Israeli trade union congress, Histadrut (or the General Federation of Laborers in Israel), and soon to be appointed minister of defense, declared, "We are dealing . . . with a party interested in fomenting riots, overturning the order of our lives, slandering the state, and giving it a bad name."[11] The Communist Party's image in the eyes of the establishment was now fixed.

Clashes between Communist activists and the police and military government became routine. Security forces made intensive use of British emergency regulations—which remained part of Israeli law—for punitive purposes. These acts included exiling party activists to other cities or placing them under house arrest. The regulations were also invoked to prevent party meetings and to prohibit the distribution of written materials. The governor of Nazareth told a group of Communist women who came to request a permit for a rally that "he would not allow demonstrations, and that the Communists can voice their protests in the press or in the Knesset."[12] But the party was not willing to give up its right to direct action, and it repeatedly organized demonstrations without permits. Some of them ended in violence, such as one in Nazareth at the end of 1954. Nearly three hundred people attended the event. A police car drove up and down the street where the demonstration was being held, its loudspeaker announcing that the gathering was illegal. The crowd ignored the warning. Habibi, the keynote speaker, now a member of the Knesset, was greeted with applause. He climbed up on a truck to give his speech: "Dear workers, down with the repressive regime. Down with the military government. Speak out against the discrimination of the regime of permits and restrictions." A policeman was sent to start the truck and so prevent Habibi's speech. The truck would not start. The police began dragging away the people standing on the improvised stage. According to Habibi, he was dragged by his feet the entire way to the police station, even though he informed the police officer at the site that he was a parliamentarian and therefore immune from arrest. The policemen claimed afterward that they had not known who he was. Whatever the case, they succeeded in dispersing the rally.[13]

During this period, the Communist Party worked to position itself as the only organization that looked after the interests of the Arabs in Israel—both as individuals and as a collective. It also sought to portray its rivals as people who were selling out these interests for honor and jobs. The Communists skillfully integrated parliamentary activity, extraparliamentary activity, and writing. Its daily newspaper in Arabic, *Al-Ittihad*, reported on the work of each and every village party branch, on the injustices perpetrated by the regime, and on the state of employment. Writers, intellectuals, and central party activists organized meetings and made speeches around the country—with or without permits—and recruited supporters. The newspaper reported this as well. In parallel, problems that Arab citizens presented to party representatives were submitted as parliamentary questions in the Knesset. The Communists attacked their rivals—in particular the Zionist parties' Arab parliamentarians—again and again, calling them lackeys of the regime.

There were, in fact, Arabs who opposed the Communists in order to gain support from the authorities, but there were also others who did so because of their different analysis of the political situation. The latter maintained that the way to improve conditions for Arabs was through cooperation with the government, not through confrontation. Sometimes class, personal, and family motives were also involved, as was rivalry over leadership positions on the local or national level. State agencies identified opponents of the Communists and joined in common cause with them, helping them organize anti-Communist fronts in their localities. As always, common interests enabled cooperation. The 'Eilabun affair of the mid-1950s, of which the elders' letter was part, can serve as a typical example. Some historical background is in order.

At the end of 1954, the Special Branch of the Israeli Police (the police unit assigned to national security matters) in the Safed Police District prepared a report on 'Eilabun, as part of the unit's set of reports on Arab villages. The nature of the report reveals what interested the security forces and what determined their treatment of different villages and families within each. After providing basic information about the community's location, its clan structure and size, and so on, the report surveyed 'Eilabun's history in "the various [anti-Jewish] riots" during the Mandate period. It is noteworthy that, half a century after the riots of 1929—in which Jewish communities throughout the country were attacked by Arabs—the police thought it important to note, regarding each village, whether any of its inhabitants had participated in the attacks. The report on 'Eilabun noted that its inhabitants had been passive in 1929. However, during the Arab rebellion of 1936–39, this village, in particular the Zureiq clan, had provided shelter to Arab rebels (*gangs,* in the report's terminology). The report stated that, although 'Eilabun's Arabs had displayed hostility to the gangs, they had "collaborated" with them out of fear. Neither were they active in 1948, but they "collaborated" with a unit of al-Qawuqji's Arab Liberation Army that had deployed in and around the village. The locals dug trenches, organized a village guard, and provided food to the fighters. It is interesting that the term *collaborate* appears frequently in official Israeli documents from this period in the context of "collaborating" or "cooperating" with Arab forces. (The Hebrew word for both English terms is identical.) The tacit assumption (justifiable in some cases) was that most of the Arabs of Palestine, and later of Israel, had been passive, had taken no political position, and had lacked any ability to act on their own.

One important incident occurred in the village in 1948: Arab combatants beheaded the bodies of two IDF soldiers who were killed in a battle with the Arab Liberation Army not far from the Golani Junction (called Maskana Junction in Arabic). The Arab fighters paraded the heads through the streets of 'Eilabun on poles. "Some say the inhabitants applauded and cheered when they saw this. Villagers acknowledge that the heads were paraded through the village but adamantly deny that the villagers rejoiced; on the contrary, most of them, upon seeing this, hid in their homes in order not to view the sight, and many of the inhabitants, especially women, protested it."[14]

This event almost sealed the village's fate. When the IDF succeeded in conquering 'Eilabun at the end of October 1948, the report related, "thirteen of the inhabitants were killed and the [other] inhabitants fled in the direction of Mughar Marun and scattered among the villages on the other side of the northern border. Only the priests and their families remained in the village, along with a number of elderly people."[15] In other words, as happened with many other villages, 'Eilabun was almost entirely emptied of its inhabitants, most of whom became refugees in Lebanon. But why did they leave, and why were they allowed to return? It turns out that matters were more complex than the report makes out. According to a letter sent by the village's mukhtar, Freij Srour, and several local priests to Minister of Minorities Bechor Shitrit about four months after the village was occupied, the thirteen dead villagers were not killed in an engagement with the IDF. Rather, they were executed by an Israeli officer as revenge for the murder and beheading of the two Jewish soldiers (even though the perpetrator of that crime had been an Arab Liberation Army soldier, not a villager). Furthermore, the remaining residents had not fled; rather, they were expelled from the village. The signatories to the letter requested that the 'Eilabun refugees be allowed to return to their homes. The Vatican soon lent its support to the request, as did political figures in Israel. The pressure was effective. In the summer of 1949, the state reached an agreement with Bishop George Hakim, the Greek Catholic primate, according to which the villagers would return and receive Israeli citizenship, and the church would cooperate with the Israeli state.[16]

It was no coincidence that the mutran Hakim had conducted the negotiations with the government. Hakim was not just the leader of the largest religious community in 'Eilabun. He was also an active politician. Born in Egypt in 1908, he had been educated and taught in church institutions. In 1943, he was promoted to the rank of bishop and appointed to head the Greek Catholic Church in northern Palestine. At that time he became associated with nationalist circles and was identified with the mufti Hajj Amin al-Husseini. Nevertheless, he had also been involved in the sale of land in the area of Mt. Tabor to the KKL.* In 1946 he appeared before the Anglo-American Committee of Inquiry that came to study the question of Palestine and the problem of the displaced Jews in Europe. Along with the secretary of the Higher Arab Committee, Jamal al-Husseini, he called for preventing the Jews from immigrating to Palestine. Alongside the mufti in January 1948, Hakim took part in a meeting of the Arab League in Cairo, and he founded an armed force to protect the Christians of the Galilee. In June of that year he left the country with the refugees, after helping evacuate Arab children from Haifa to Lebanon. He returned in February 1949, with the permission of the Israeli Foreign Ministry. At that time he resumed publishing his monthly journal, *Al-Rabita,* which covered the Arab minority in Israel, and took his first steps toward assuming a leadership role in Israel's Arab public. The common presumption was that Hakim had been brought back to Israel to lead the fight against the Communists.[17] Indeed, upon submitting a request to open a printing press, he wrote to Ben-Gurion that he sought "to clear the air that has been inundated with Communist poison, to disseminate the truth and correct principles to Arab circles."[18] On many

---

* KKL agent Aharon Danin related that, subsequent to the land sale, Palestinian national institutions (i.e., the Nation's Fund) had pressured Hakim to renege on the sale. He went back to Danin and asked to cancel the transaction, adding, "You won't be sorry." His request was granted. Danin believed that this was one of the reasons behind his later support for the state. Aharon Danin testimony, 31 December 1970, OHD-HU 57/9.

Figure 5. Anti-Communists. Israeli president Haim Weizmann (left, sitting) with Bishop Hakim, Israel's Independence Day, 1951. Photograph by Fritz Cohen; courtesy Israeli Government Press Office.

issues, his positions were opposed to the nationalist-Communist position. For example, he supported a government initiative (which was unsuccessful) to evacuate the Arab inhabitants of the village of Tarshiha, on the Lebanese border, to villages in the country's interior.[19]

Rivalry between Hakim and the Communists began soon after he returned and was not restricted to politics. Their fight for dominance led to a series of clashes. The following are two examples.

In 1949 in the framework of one of Hakim's many tours of the Arab villages in Israel, he came to 'Iblin, where Christians and Muslims lived side by side. During his visit he made a speech in which he thanked the government

Figure 6. The church and the state. The Catholic Scouts march in Nazareth on Israel's Independence Day, 1954, demonstrating their support of the state. Photograph courtesy Israeli Government Press Office.

of Israel, the IDF, and the police for the help they had extended to him. A Communist activist approached him and offered him a copy of *Al-Ittihad*, perhaps to show him a different point of view. Hakim's men hustled the Communist away, and a scuffle broke out. The mutran had in the meantime gotten into his car in order to leave the village. "Some members of the Communist Party began stoning the car, but no one was hurt," reported the police officer who rushed to the site, where he arrested twenty-three people.[20]

In Nazareth, Hakim's own supporters committed the provocation. A group of Catholic Scouts—a youth movement that operated under Hakim's inspiration and was funded by the church—was on its way from Mt. Tabor to the village of Shefaʿamr. Israeli flags flew on the bus they were traveling on, along with a Vatican flag and a Scout flag. When the bus stopped in Nazareth, the youngsters gave a loud rendition of a favorite song: "We are the Scouts of Hakim, we'll finish off Stalin." Communist youth standing nearby threw stones, and the Scouts got off the bus and threw stones back.[21]

The ideological competition between the church and communism was supplemented by a dispute over how to relate to the state and its organs. It was no coincidence that the Catholic Scouts flew Israeli flags in Nazareth, while the Communists called for Israel to withdraw to the partition borders (according to which Nazareth would have been part of a Palestinian state). It was also no coincidence that Hakim met with the Arabs who had been expelled from the village of Iqrit and insisted that they change their minds and abandon their demand to return there, while the Communists supported these and other internal refugees.[22]

Back in 'Eilabun, the Catholic Scouts served as one of the bishop's most important organizational tools. A young man, H. M., active in the movement in 'Eilabun, was involved in a tragedy that rocked the Galilee—especially Arab politics in the region—in the 1950s. The case, an exceptionally serious one, reflected the atmosphere in the village at the time and the dynamics among Hakim's supporters, the Communists, and the Israeli regime. The following is H. M.'s version of the incident:

When I lived in 'Eilabun I was a member of the Catholic Scout movement, and in 1951 the Communist Party had enormous influence in 'Eilabun, so they called it Red 'Eilabun then. I and a tiny number of villagers took it upon ourselves to found the Catholic Scout movement in the village, and then I began persuading members of the Communist Party to leave their party and join the Catholic Scouts. I was so successful that soon no members were left to the Communist Party except the members of the Zureiq family. [I became] the enemy of the Communist Party and the Zureiq family. As soon as the Communist Party's influence declined in 'Eilabun, the Zureiqs began organizing parties in the village, with the help of party members from Nazareth, with the purpose of drawing the villagers to the parties and persuading them to return to the Communist Party, and at the parties they made venomous speeches against the state and its founders, and then we'd go and kick all the outsiders out of the village by force, which means there was always a conflict in 'Eilabun among the Catholic Scouts and the Zureiq family and members of the Communist Party, and I was always accused of causing the conflict, and the members of the Communist Party were always looking to get back at me but didn't succeed. Until one day the village's Communist Party headquarters was burned down, and as a result Suheil Zureiq died, who was the brother of Lutf Zureiq, Communist Party secretary in 'Eilabun. Then the Communists accused me of burning down the headquarters and causing the death of Suheil Zureiq. In Nazareth and in the court, all the members of the Zureiq family testified that they saw me burning the Communist Party headquarters with their own eyes. The district court in Haifa sentenced me to ten years in prison. I appealed to the Supreme Court, and they sentenced me to life in prison. A few years later, after many petitions from my family to his Excellency the president, my punishment was reduced to ten years in prison.

At the beginning of my imprisonment I was in the Tiberias police station, where Zureiqs were being held for burning down houses belonging to us and to Niqola . . . whose son was also accused with me. And there in the Tiberias police station the Zureiqs told me, "We won't testify against you if you join our party and sign a petition stating that the military government and Bishop Hakim sent you and members of the Catholic Scouts to burn down the Communist Party headquarters, and we will also pay you what you've lost, and we'll rebuild your house." But I wouldn't consent.[23]

H. M. chose to place himself at the vanguard of the battle against the Communists and paid a heavy personal price (although no heavier than his adversaries paid). When he was released from prison, he still believed in the old alliance among the Communist Party's opponents and sought to enlist the military governor in his favor. He wrote to the governor that Communists were willing to make peace with him according to their old conditions— that he declare that the military government and Bishop Hakim had been behind the arson. But he had refused. He asked the governor to pressure the Communists to conduct a *sulha,* a reconciliation ceremony, without any political conditions attached. He noted the interests that he and the military government shared:

> Honored sir, after explaining these things to you, I request that you try, as quickly as possible, to intervene in this matter and save me from certain death and my family from long suffering. I fought the Communists because I knew that they are the agents of foreign countries that are trying to destroy our country, and I heard the Communists making virulent speeches against the state and against the heads of the state regime. The Communists have always and will always try to persuade the members of the Arab nation in Israel to serve these foreign countries, and that is why we see that every Arab spy is a Communist or Communist sympathizer.

H. M. added one more reason he was worthy of assistance:

> After my release I had the opportunity to talk with some of the young people in 'Eilabun, and I asked them why they had joined the Communist Party, and they answered me: we saw how you fought the Communists and fell, no one helped you or asked after your parents, so we entered the Communist Party because they help every party member and do not leave them and their families to suffer, and instead help them in all ways. In this

and other ways, the members of the Arab minority are drawn into the ranks of the Communist Party.[24]

The police and military government had no practical way of helping H. M. The police investigated whether his life was being threatened but found no evidence of that. It concluded that the demand being made of him was a purely political one and that the Communists did not intend to avenge the blood of Suheil Zureiq. Under the circumstances, the police had no way to intervene. One sign of this was the Zureiq family's position that the contacts regarding a *sulha* were not to be conducted on the family level but rather through Communist Party channels. This being the case, the investigations officer of the Northern District wrote to his associates in the military government and the GSS that the only avenue open to him was to try, diplomatically, to convince Bishop Hakim to help H. M. as a released prisoner in distress, rather than as a political activist.

These events contributed to the Communist Party's growing strength in 'Eilabun and in the Galilee as a whole. Suheil Zureiq's death became a symbol of the establishment's unbending struggle against the Communists and thus a symbol of the party's position as the most significant force in opposition to the policies of the Israeli government. Not everyone in 'Eilabun—not even all members of the Zureiq clan—became Communist supporters (some even publicly disassociated themselves from the party), but one important reason for this seems to have been fear of the state's reprisals against the Communists.[25] The letter from the elders of 'Eilabun about the sale of alcoholic drinks and Communist activities in Mu'in Zureiq's store should be seen in this context.

In the years that followed, Hakim maneuvered among the Israeli authorities, the Arab states, and the Arab community in Israel. His good relations with the Israelis enabled him to regain church lands and reap other benefits; he saw the Arab states as a potential arena for his own advancement in the church hierarchy; and the Christian Arabs in Israel were his principal reservoir of political support. After failing to put together his own slate for the Knesset, he called on Israel's Arabs to vote directly for Mapai rather than for its satellite Arab slates in the elections of 1955. Such a voting strategy was aimed at sustaining his relations with the political establishment while weakening his rivals for leadership in the Arab community. Here and there he made attempts to mediate between Arab countries and Israel, principally regarding the refugee issue. In general, he voiced opinions that differed from those of Arab nationalists. In 1963 he declared that 99 percent of the refugees would not want to return to their homes in Israel and that the way to achieve peace was "goodwill and money." He called on Israel to pay reparations to the Palestinian refugees residing in Arab countries. In response, a refugee wrote in *Al-Ittihad:* "As a refugee, I assert to him and others like him that he has no right to speak in the name of our displaced people who have lived in wooden shacks for the last fifteen years. Bishop Hakim should stay at home and chant religious hymns."[26] But Hakim was not the type to stay at home. He continued to make waves among the Arab public in Israel until he left the country when he was named patriarch of Damascus in 1967.

HAWWARI RETURNS TO ISRAEL!

Mutran Hakim was not the only Arab personage who enjoyed the support of the Israeli establishment in his contention with the Communists. Another storied figure, Muhammad Nimer al-Hawwari, an attorney, fought the same battles in parallel, and sometimes in coordination, with Hakim. Hawwari also received a special permit to return to Israel at the beginning of 1950, in order to lead an anti-Communist crusade. His return, after long months of drifting and of national and personal metamorphoses, set off a storm in the Jewish and Arab publics. Hardly a year had passed since the end of the war, in which Hawwari had commanded the Najjadah, a paramilitary organization that had taken an active part in fighting against the Jews. The Jewish public in Israel was divided on the question of the wisdom and morality of allowing him to return. The Arab Communists were among those who claimed he should be put on trial rather than received with open arms. His ties to Zionist elements during and after the war were not then known to all.

Hawwari was born in Nazareth in 1907. He worked as a teacher in Hebron and as a lawyer in Jaffa, and he was a leader of the Arab Scout movement. He founded the Najjadah after World War II to serve as a counterweight to the Jewish underground military organizations. The first initiative of its type in the Arab public of Mandatory Palestine, the Najjadah was centered in Jaffa and had branches throughout the country. Hawwari declared it to be unaffiliated with any political group, but the Arab Party, affiliated with the mufti's Husseini faction, soon organized a rival organization called the Futuwwa, and a power struggle between the two militias ensued. Following pressure from the mufti and his associates, Hawwari agreed to merge the organizations under the leadership of the Higher Arab Committee and the mufti, but he did not moderate his criticism of the political conduct of the Palestinian leadership. Neither did hostility to him decline; in the months that followed, agents of the mufti tried to murder him more than once.[27]

At the end of 1947, when hostilities commenced, Hawwari realized that the Jews had the military advantage in the Tel Aviv–Jaffa region, so he tried to prevent the spread of the battle. To this end, he established contacts with figures in the Haganah. In Arab nationalist circles, this was looked on as treason, and he had to flee Palestine for Transjordan. When a peace conference was convened in Lausanne by the United Nations Conciliation Commission in an attempt to reach a mutually acceptable solution to the question of Palestine (April–September 1949), Hawwari participated as head of one of the organizations that represented Palestinian refugees. During the conference he renewed his contacts with Israeli representatives, to the displeasure of delegates from the Arab states. They attacked him in particular for supporting direct negotiations between the refugees and Israel and for advocating that the refugees return to their homes under Israeli sovereignty. Before long, he commenced contacts to carry out this principle himself and to return to what was now Israel.[28]

In mid-December 1949, Hawwari made his way across the Lebanese border, with the consent of Israeli officials, for a meeting with the prime minister's adviser on Arab affairs, Yehoshua Palmon. He brought his family—his wife and ten children—as well as three of his supporters. (Since he lacked an official permit, his party was detained by the police for a week.)[29] The prime minister's office instructed that he be given a temporary permit to remain in the country, and he was taken to Acre. The open files on his case do not indicate what agreement Hawwari reached with Palmon. But to the Communists and Mapam, the left-Zionist Party, it was clear—he had been brought back to found an anti-Communist, pro-Mapai Arab party. The Mapam newspaper, *Mishmar,* reported, "Sources familiar with the complications surrounding Nimer Hawwari report that preparations for the establishment of a 'government' Arab party whose role will be to stop the Arab left are nearing completion."[30]

The exchange of blows (mostly verbal, but also physical) between Hawwari and the Communists was even more fierce. Each side accused the other of association with the mufti in the 1948 war. More important, and perhaps surprising, was the proud declaration of both parties that they had opposed the war. Each proclaimed that it had tried to prevent fighting and had sought a peaceful solution before hostilities began. It was the Communists who first went on the offensive:

> No, it is not a joke. Hawwari, leader of the Najjadah, the well-known anti-Jewish military organization, is in Israel. He is alive and well and enjoys

total liberty. He meets with people and is still threatening his erstwhile enemies in Israel. He fights the Communists and, more than that, enjoys the company of the local police, who visit him at his café from time to time. He has had time to arrange a comfortable corner in Abu-Sa'id's café in Acre. Smoking his water pipe beside the backgammon table, Hawwari is surrounded by friends, one of whom is Ahmad 'Abdu from the Acre municipality, who has been accused of theft by the custodian of absentee property, and Daoud Khuri, a figure from the underworld in the village of Ma'lul. . . . No, it is not a joke or a funny story. It is criminal provocation to allow this murderer to return to a land that has suffered from his provocations and machinations.

He is no longer a danger just to Jews. He also jeopardizes the lives of the Arabs who have survived the national catastrophe, a catastrophe caused by people like Hawwari and his crew. . . . Many still remember the leader of ethnic hatred. We can still find some of the Najjadah people around. These people can still tell us how this man organized his anti-Jewish militia. We can still find also one of the orders of the day he issued then. There are still people who remember the speech he gave at the beginning of 1947 at the Alhambra Cinema in Jaffa, by which he tried to disrupt a meeting of the [Communist] National Liberation League. His words still echo.

In his typical demagogic style, he then shouted, "I have an important announcement for you (the Arab people). I brought it from the lion crouching on the shores of the Nile (the mufti, who was then in Egypt). When I went to visit and congratulate him, I found him teaching his daughter to shoot at a target. When he saw me, he turned his forceful and confident gaze at me and said, 'Tell the people to take up arms. Rifles, Stens, machine guns, and knives. Tell them that the day of the attack on the Jews is approaching.'"

. . . Hawwari is not a man who believes in Jewish-Arab cooperation. He believes in serving his masters. Apparently he has switched masters now. Since he wasted the money of the refugees who sent him to Lausanne, he has come to serve Ben-Gurion.[31]

The Communists did not just write and make speeches in the Knesset.* Two days after the above article appeared, when Hawwari left his café to visit the Acre open-air market, he encountered "a mass demonstration that

---

* A large photograph of Hawwari striding alongside the mufti as they inspected Najjadah and Fu-tuwwa troops in Cairo appeared in the Communist Party's Hebrew newspaper, *Kol ha-'Am,* on April 27, 1950. "Hawwari, champion of racism, feels comfortable in the bosom of reaction in Israel. He is the foster child of the Arab reaction that hopes to place him at the head of its crumbling forces," said the caption.

organized spontaneously," in the words of the Communist Hebrew newspaper *Kol ha-'Am,* during which both Jews and Arabs demanded that he be put on trial as a war criminal. The crowd booed him and cried, "Traitor, you chased other people out of their homes and you returned yourself." Hawwari, according to the newspaper, slipped away with police assistance. A police report offered a different picture—only fifteen people surrounded Hawwari in the market. Neither were security officials convinced of the demonstration's spontaneity. They took severe action that testifies to the unequivocal state support that Hawwari enjoyed; the military governor of the Galilee sent a detachment into Acre's old city "to arrest the two Arabs responsible for incitement against Nimer Hawwari," Ramzi Khuri and Nadim Musa, and issued three-month internal exile orders against them.[32] This was only a short time after the end of the previous order, issued against them after the demonstration described above.

Hawwari left Acre, perhaps because of the attacks, but did not make himself scarce. He settled in Nazareth and spent many long weeks meeting with Arab public figures in an attempt to found a political party. He also tried to buy public support by helping obtain entry permits for Arab officers and fighters from the Nazareth area who had left the Galilee in 1948. He suspected that the Communist Party was weaker than it seemed and speculated about the reasons that Muslims had supported it: "Up until now no one has organized another party and . . . up until now no influential Muslim leader who could serve as its mouthpiece to the authorities has taken up the cause of the Muslim community."[33] This statement, which appears in a police report, testifies to the depth of the fissure between him and the Communists, as well as to his conceptual alliance with the Israeli establishment. Like the authorities, he viewed the Arab community in Israel as a people whose religious identity took precedence over its national identity, rather than as a national minority with a shared identity. Unlike the Communists, he thought that the role of the Arab leadership was to serve as a "mouthpiece to the authorities," not to lead a fight for change.

The Nazareth Communists convened in their local branch to discuss how to fight him. An informer named Salim attended the meeting and reported on it to the police. First, the members surveyed the background to Hawwari's return. The explanation offered was that his goal was to found a party that would support the annexation of the western Galilee to Israel. (That portion of the Galilee was not included in the Jewish state according to the UN partition plan of 1947.) Party activist Saliba Khamis focused on possible courses of action: he was worried about the rising power of the attorney, and he sensed that Hawwari enjoyed no little popularity. His conclusion was that direct confrontation with Hawwari's supporters, some of whom were former Najjadah militants, should be avoided. Confrontation could actually strengthen Hawwari, he maintained. The campaign should be restricted to writing and speeches. Young Communists (led by Hanna Abu-Hanna, who would later become an important poet) did not accept the constraint. They made a practice of shouting expletives at Hawwari when they passed the café where he sat. On at least one occasion this led to physical violence, with the two sides throwing stones, striking each other with sticks, and apparently also using knives.[34]

For a time, the authorities seem to have believed that Hawwari would, after returning, bring about a significant change in the mood of the Israeli Arabs and their attitude toward the country. "Confusion prevails in the ranks of the Communist Party in Nazareth in light of Hawwari's work to found a party. The Communists see an educated man and persuasive speaker like Hawwari as a dangerous enemy who is liable, over time, to entirely undermine their foundations," a police report stated. The author of the report, who seems to have met Hawwari a number of times, noted, "Hawwari does not ignore the fact that many obstacles are ranged before him, because today his circle of supporters is very small and his enemies' camp is large both in people and in ideology, but he gazes optimistically to the future and is certain that he can overcome all obstacles to turning the Arab public living in Israel into a positive and loyal element that will be ready to lay down its life for the country in which it resides."[35]

Both Hawwari's hopes and the Communists' fears turned out to be exaggerated. He never found more than a few supporters, and the Communists kept after him, organizing demonstrations everywhere he appeared, until fears arose that they intended to attack him physically. Many Arabs accepted the Communists' claim that he served the interests of the government, not those of the Arab public,[36] and all that he could do was to try to sway public opinion with his writing. In May 1950, he began publishing his memoirs of the war in the Histadrut- and state-sponsored Arabic newspaper *Al-Yawm*. After describing his attempts to persuade the mufti not to open hostilities, he proceeded to attack the Communists. This offensive was published also in the Mapai Hebrew newspaper *Ha-Dor:* "While I did all I could to stop the fire that was spreading through Jaffa—you, comrades [the word is being used sarcastically to refer to the Arab Communists], worked to spread and fuel the fire." He also named the Communist leaders who, he said, went to visit the mufti in his refuge in 'Alei, in Lebanon—Emil Touma, Emil Habibi, and

Fu'ad Nassar—and received money from him. The newspaper concluded, "None of them joined in with Hawwari's call, which he proclaimed loudly: 'No! No! I don't agree! This is against our interests, it will bring a catastrophe down on us!'"[37]

The points of agreement between the two sides are no less fascinating than the disagreements. Both Hawwari and the Communists maintained that it had been a mistake to oppose the partition decision of 1947 and to start a war. This was diametrically opposed to the position taken by the Palestinian nationalist mainstream before and during the war. Furthermore, both sides presented themselves as advocates of Jewish-Arab coexistence and accepted, whether explicitly or implicitly, Israel's right to exist. Here is how MK Tawfiq Toubi described the Communists' activities during the war: "In their war to found an independent and democratic Arab state alongside the state of Israel, in their war for cooperation between the two sides, the democratic Arab forces [i.e., the Communists] were subject to organized repression and terror by the Arab reaction [i.e., the Arab states and the armies they sent]." This is not how Ben-Gurion and his colleagues in the Zionist leadership saw it. For them, the Communists were the mufti's allies before Israel was established and afterward as well.[38] Hawwari served as the government's spokesman on this, too.

Harassment by the Communists was one of the reasons that Hawwari's political star faded. But pro-establishment Arabs, who ostensibly should have been his natural allies and with whom he tried to form a slate to run in the Second Knesset elections in the summer of 1951, also attacked him, in his moments of crisis, as a former supporter of the mufti.[39] So, less than two years following his return, Hawwari found himself lacking all influence. As a kind of revenge, he disseminated flyers prior to the elections, declaring that none of the Arab slates was worthy of representing the Arab public in the Knesset.[40] He scaled down his political party activity and focused on his legal career. At the end of the 1950s he filed several important suits against land confiscation and continued to represent Arabs who had been victims of government actions. Following the Six Day War, of 1967, he was appointed a district court judge in Nazareth. His name was floated as a candidate for the Supreme Court, but an appointment never came.[41] Later, shortly before his death in 1969, he served as a member of the national commission of inquiry that investigated the arson committed by Michael Rohan at the al-Aqsa Mosque in Jerusalem. The commission absolved the government of all responsibility in the incident.

Mutran Hakim and Hawwari cooperated with the regime against the Communists, in keeping with their own interests. The same was true of the Arab members of the Knesset from Mapai's satellite slates. These latter figures feared that as the Communists gained strength, their own status would decline. They had good reason to think so. Four months following the annexation of the Triangle, a police officer reported, "The consequences of the Communists' activities can be seen in the shaping of the social life of the Arab village. Arab youth believe that Arab MKs like Jarjura and Sayf al-Din Zu'bi have sold out to the Jews, while only Tawfiq Toubi defends the Arab population."[42] At the same time, the authorities had an interest in having Arab organizations and figures participate in the fight against the Communists and having them offer an alternative that accepted Israeli policy. With this in mind, the commander of the military government, Major General Elimelech Avner, met with the military governors and instructed them to take appropriate action: "It is fitting and desirable that, wherever Tawfiq Toubi goes, the locals announce that they do not want him." Go'el Levitzki, who was now governor of the Triangle and attended the meeting, informed him that this tactic was already working: "[During] Toubi's visit in Taybe, while Toubi was speaking to a representative of the governor, the village leaders arrived and in the presence of [Toubi] submitted in writing, with the signatures of the clan heads, a declaration that they wished him to leave." The governor went on to report that the protest against Toubi was spontaneous,[43] but we need not believe him, just as we need not believe the Communist claims that the above-mentioned anti-Hawwari demonstration in Acre was spontaneous.

At the beginning of 1950, tensions between government and Communist supporters in Taybe escalated. In May, Communists disrupted a visit by Hawwari. ("The Communists rounded up children with garbage cans and went out on a street demonstration, banging on the cans and shouting, 'Down with Nimer Hawwari,'" the police reported.) In response, figures in the village who were close to the regime warned Tawfiq Toubi and his associates that they should not dare come to the village. Toubi and his Jewish colleague, Avraham Feigenbaum, made a visit anyway. The local Communists, whose leader was Faysal 'Abd al-Razeq, joined them. The government's supporters, led by Hasan Kamel 'Ubeid, made plans to block them. When the two camps met, a fight broke out. 'Ubeid splattered paint on MK Toubi, three people were wounded, and the police arrived and made arrests.[44]* The military gov-

---

* The Communists assumed, apparently correctly, that the governor had instigated or at least encouraged the demonstration. When Toubi went to Majdal (today's Ashkelon) two months later, he was also beaten by Arabs who shouted, "Long live Ben-Gurion," and vilified the Communist Party. *Al-Ittihad*

ernor banished Faysal ʿAbd al-Razeq and other party activists to Bartaʿa, but the Communists gained support. In the elections of 1951, they won 752 votes in Taybe, a third of those cast.[45] It was the first election in which the inhabitants of the Triangle voted. (The First Knesset elections were held in January 1949, before the area was annexed.) The Communist Party had proved its organizational and ideological strength.

Hasan Kamel ʿUbeid, the paint thrower, was a typical member of a family that belonged to the collaborator class. The event he was involved in testifies to the depth of the rivalry between the Communists and supporters of the regime and, to a certain extent, to the existence of two deep-running currents in the Arab population. His father, Kamel, and his uncle Diab had maintained contacts with Jewish intelligence from the mid-1930s onward. In the mid-1940s, they lived in Jaffa and were in touch with Yehoshua Palmon. Under his direction, they worked against the boycott of the Jewish economy declared by the Higher Arab Committee and were involved in actions against supporters of the mufti. Prior to the outbreak of hostilities in 1947, Kamel returned to Taybe, while his brother Diab remained in Jaffa until just before its capture by Israeli forces. Then, at the request of Zionist intelligence, Diab moved to Tulkarem, then under Iraqi-Jordanian military rule, and continued to pass on intelligence from there. In late 1949, when Diab was arrested by the Jordanian police in Tulkarem on suspicion of espionage (apparently one of his enemies turned him in), relatives managed to get him out on bail. On the evening of his release, in November 1949, he left Tulkarem and crossed the border into Israel. The next day his mother and children also fled Tulkarem and joined him. Diab received a warm welcome from the military government in Taybe and became a close associate of the governor. Israeli police officers made note of rumors that Diab took bribes from Arabs in exchange for using his influence with the governor and other officials in their personal matters.[46]

Thanks to his close relationship with the regime, Diab received gun licenses—he was the only person in the village to receive permits for both a rifle and a pistol—and his nephew Hasan also received a pistol license.[47] Diab was also appointed to the village council when that body was first formed by the governor and the Ministry of Interior in 1951. In 1961, he was elected to the Knesset on the Mapai-associated Cooperation and Brotherhood slate and served three terms. He was scrupulously loyal to his party, and at the

---

(16 July 1950) sneered at the governor of Majdal, "who apparently learned from the governor of Taybe how to organize demonstrations against visits by Toubi" using "the military government's miserable spies."

time of a critical 1963 vote, he (like his Arab colleagues Jaber Dahash Muʻadi and Elias Nakhle) voted with the government against dismantling the military government. Two years later, when Prime Minister Levi Eshkol visited the Triangle, Diab said,

> In our hearts, we the Arabs of Israel, the decisive majority of us, are full of admiration and fondness for the person of the prime minister and unreserved loyalty to our country, which we have proved at times of severe tests. While there is a small minority that displays hatred, the decisive majority of the Arabs of Israel deride and dismiss those hostile individuals who prefer darkness to light. This separatist group is also hostile to most of Israel's Arabs, who prefer to live in peace and brotherhood with the Jewish people in this country.[48]

The Communists, of course, did not take this silently. In a leaflet they issued soon after Eshkol's visit, they wrote, "The masses with consciousness in the Triangle know well who are the representatives of the forces of darkness who voted in favor of the military government, so saving the government, while knifing the inhabitants of the Triangle and the entire public in the back."[49]

These events took place more than a decade after the incident of the paint throwing, and they testify to the continuity of the battle between these currents. The ʻUbeid family's later history is of great interest, even if it does not touch on its rivalry with the Communists. Hasan, the son of Kamel ʻUbeid, also flirted with intelligence and politics. In the 1980s he served as deputy mayor of Taybe and at the same time established contacts in Lebanon. These contacts apparently served at first for intelligence gathering but expanded into drug dealing. In 1989, Hasan and two other family members were sentenced to ten years in prison for trafficking in drugs. Their business partner was Muhammad Biro, one of Lebanon's drug barons, suspected by Hezbollah of collaboration with Israel. Biro was also arrested, dying in an Israeli prison in 2002. (His body was returned to his family in 2004 as part of a prisoner and body exchange with Hezbollah.) Hasan ʻUbeid's son, Qays, changed his orientation entirely from that of his grandfather. In 2000 he left Israel, joined Hezbollah, and there, according to Israeli intelligence, began coordinating activity against Israel. He has been involved in directing armed Palestinian squads in the West Bank, as well as in special missions such as the kidnapping of the Israeli colonel Elhanan Tanenbaum to Lebanon in October 2000.[50]

One last comment on Communist activity during the 1950s and the 1960s. For years, the Communists claimed that Mapai was pressuring and tempting Arab voters to vote for its satellite parties instead of the Communists. "The accusations of pressure made by [Mapai's] opponents have never been proved," wrote the orientalist Jacob Landau in 1971. He referred in particular to the elections to the Third Knesset, held in July 1955.[51] More than thirty years have passed since Landau published his book, and some archives have opened (although the GSS archives, which include sections on civilian and political affairs, contain most of the relevant material and is still sealed). The picture as it looks now supports the Communist charges. The following is what the Nazareth police chief Yitzhak Segev wrote in a "personal, secret" memorandum to the commander of the Yizra'el Subdistrict:

> On 7 July 1955 at 1 P.M., I participated in a meeting with the military governor, Colonel Michael Michael, chief of the GSS northern region Moshe Drori, Mr. Yehuda Bashan [another GSS official, later northern region chief], all the military government's representatives in the villages, and the government's [i.e., prime minister's] adviser on Arab affairs, Mr. Z[alman] Divon. The GSS officials, military government representatives, and I presented an oral report on what is being done in the field and the party's activities in Nazareth and the region, in anticipation of the elections to the Third Knesset. After this report, the governor announced the formation of an advisory council for the city of Nazareth, whose members would include [deputy governor] Major Tepner, a GSS representative, a Mapai representative, and me. He also announced the formation of an advisory council for the villages that would include Captain Yosef Kedem, a representative of the GSS, a representative of the Histadrut, and myself.
>
> The committees were to study the situation in the villages, give an indication to the Arab voter to vote for the Arab slates and not directly for Mapai.
>
> The committees will meet a few times a week. On next Thursday, 16 July 1955, an additional meeting will be held at which the committees will submit reports on actions in the field.
>
> At the end of the meeting, the governor announced that the committees will be given powers to issue permits to go out of the territories [i.e., to the Jewish towns, outside the military-governed areas], and will likewise offer recommendations on granting gun permits as circumstances may dictate. These powers will be in effect until 28 July 1955 [two days after the election].[52]

The report paints a clear picture: public officials from the police, the GSS, the prime minister's office, and the army worked together with the governing party, Mapai, to help it get votes. For this purpose, they were prepared to ease

Figure 7. With some help from friends. MK David Hacohen (left), of Mapai, with Arab MKs from lists affiliated with his party: (from left to right) E. Nakhle, D. 'Ubeid, and A. K. al-Daher, 1961. Photograph by Fritz Cohen; courtesy Israeli Government Press Office.

restrictions on movement and on bearing arms, two temptations that were not easy to resist. It is important to note that the committee encouraged the Arabs to vote for Mapai's Arab slates, not for Mapai itself. There were two reasons for this. First, it did not want to embarrass the satellite parties. If Sayf al-Din Zu'bi, Fares Hamdan, Jaber Mu'adi, and their associates were not elected, they would have severed their ties to Mapai, and the party would have lost more than it gained. The second reason was more a matter of public interest: Israel wanted Arabs in the Knesset. The pro-Zionist speeches these Arabs made in the Knesset, sometimes while wearing Arab headdresses, were a prime propaganda asset for Israel.

How effective these pressures were is difficult to measure. But the report of a collaborator from Tamra indicates that the regime's pressures had some effect on voting patterns. He reported a conversation among several young men in his village. The year was 1958, and these men spoke excitedly about the president of Egypt, Gamal ʿAbd al-Nasser. One said hopefully that Nasser would "sweep away the state of Israel," while another was extremely critical of the military government, saying, "[It] restricts our rights and imposes a curfew on us to prevent us from being free people." The collaborator reported that he asked them which party they supported. The two speakers quickly replied that they favored the Communists. One added, "If they would allow me to join any party I wanted, I would join the Communist Party, and I would become one of its biggest supporters and admirers, and I would become an active member. But what can I do? The military government controls us and robs us of our freedom of thought and forces us to ally with the reprehensible Mapai party."[53] Even if we should not believe every word of this collaborator's report, it can testify to a phenomenon: people voted for Mapai and its Arab puppets not willingly or out of conviction but because they feared that the GSS or military government would hound anyone who voted for the Communists.*

---

* The GSS did indeed prepare lists of the number of Communist voters in each village and tried to identify them. People were certainly afraid of this. For this reason, Arab voting patterns do not, during this period, reflect the real thinking of Israel's Arabs.

THREE

Boundary Breakers
Infiltrators, Smugglers, Spies

ON A SUMMER NIGHT IN 1952, a detachment of policemen arrived in the village of Bi'neh, in the Upper Galilee, searching for infiltrators who had crossed over from Lebanon. The policemen headed for the home of Bulus Hanna Bulus, a veteran Arab nationalist and a member of the Communist Party. Bulus's sister, Ibtihaj, wife of the party secretary in the Galilee, Ramzi Khuri, was also in the house at the time. She herself was a refugee who had recently returned to Israel illegally. The police demanded a search of the house; Bulus and his sister refused to let them in. He argued with the policemen and shouted at them, while she physically blocked their way in. Since a policewoman was not among the search party, the detachment, which was commanded by Yitzhak Shvili, the officer responsible for the Arab villages in the western Galilee, had no choice but to leave empty-handed and humiliated. The security forces' response was not long in coming. Soon after this incident, the military governor issued an order requiring Bulus Bulus to leave his home and reside in the city of Lod for an entire year. This was one of the common punishments meted out in those days to nationalist activists and to Arabs who sheltered infiltrators.[1]

Bulus, like other Palestinian nationalists, maintained that Arab refugees who were uprooted during the 1948 hostilities had the right to return to their homes. The nationalists did not see these refugees as infiltrators but rather as relatives exercising their rights. They were enraged that Israeli forces shot refugees who tried to cross the border at the same time that the new state was handing out these same refugees' land to newly arrived Jewish immigrants. They voiced support for the infiltrators in newspaper articles and speeches and demonstrated it by actively aiding infiltrators. Palestinian nationalists fought obdurately and passionately and were willing to pay a high price for their principles. Their support for infiltrators was an act of political protest, one that sometimes included a personal and a family dimension as well.

Bulus, who ran a local metalworking shop, had been a prominent militant nationalist during the war, four years prior to the incident related above. According to testimony given to the police by inhabitants of his village, he had served as armorer for the Yarmouk Battalion of Qawuqji's Arab Liberation Army, which had deployed in the Galilee. At the end of 1948, when the Upper Galilee was conquered by the IDF in the Hiram operation, Bulus retreated northward with his unit and spent some nine months in Lebanon. He made his way into Israel in 1949 and immediately began promoting social and political solidarity in his village. A Bi'neh storekeeper testified:

> [Bulus] began to organize rallies of the village's inhabitants and to stir them up, [saying that] the Israeli government was only temporary and would not last long [in the territories beyond the partition border]. "You have nothing to be scared of and we need to help each other. Be brave, and every time and at every opportunity that the police or government people come to search for infiltrators, you must resist them at all costs and not allow the Israeli authorities to arrest any one of us or of our fellow infiltrators. If the police want to use legal means against us, I will put a lawyer at your service...."
>
> Ten days ago, in the evening, Bulus Hanna Bulus gathered people from the village of Bi'neh in his home and began to incite them against the police: How can it be that you have let the police arrest Salah 'Ayesh, the infiltrator, with money given to him by the area's inhabitants to take to their relatives in Lebanon, where they are dying of starvation? I see you have lost all your courage to defend our own people. And it's a fact that a short while ago Inspector Shvili came with a few policemen to search my home, and my sister Ibtihaj cursed out Inspector Shvili and the Israeli government, and they were unable to arrest her, and they left the village empty-handed. So why can't you as men do as I did? And from here on out you will always resist.[2]

Bulus, as quoted by the storekeeper, took a nationalist stance, called for active resistance to the injustices of the Israeli regime, and preached against collaboration. This was the approach adopted by the Communist Party, which advocated for refugees seeking to steal over the border and return to their homes. The fact that Bulus's sister, Ibtihaj, was herself a refugee-infiltrator must certainly have made him even more adamant on this issue. But it was not only Communists who resisted turning in returnees. A Bedouin woman from 'Arab al-Khilf, in the Lower Galilee, who was interrogated about a visit that a group of armed infiltrators paid to some relatives of hers, made clear her opinion about collaborating with the authorities. "The Muslim religion does not allow one to betray another Muslim. Most Arabs are traitors. There is only one great man, and he is Hajj Amin al-Husseini. You can tear me into pieces. I will not say a word," she told her interrogators, who were trying to solve a number of murders supposedly committed by infiltrators in the region.[3]

Infiltration was one of the most acute challenges faced by the young state of Israel. The frequent penetration of her borders flouted their integrity and the state's sovereignty; the infiltrators also committed acts of murder and theft. The IDF chief of staff during the mid-1950s, Moshe Dayan, maintained that the infiltrators were motivated by "a sea of hatred and desire for revenge." * Indeed, some infiltrators were out to murder, avenge, and spy. Between 1948 and 1956, infiltrators killed some 220 Israeli civilians and injured another 500. In addition, they caused huge economic damage. Their theft of agricultural equipment and livestock cost farmers the loss of entire growing seasons, and the police and IDF were compelled to divert scarce and valuable resources to prevent infiltration.[4] No other problem so demoralized the Jewish public. Yet only a small minority of the infiltrators were murderers, thieves, and vandals. Most of them had much more prosaic goals—to return to their homes, to harvest their fields, to reunite with family. Others—thousands, perhaps tens of thousands—were motivated by destitution. Some of them lived by robbery and theft in the country that had arisen on the ruins of their villages, and others worked as smugglers. The latter brought in goods that were difficult for the Israeli market to supply but could be found over

---

* These were Dayan's words at the burial of Ro'i Rotberg, a soldier who was killed by infiltrators in April 1956 while stationed at Nahal Oz, on the border with the Gaza strip. In the same eulogy, Dayan also displayed profound comprehension of the infiltrators' motives: "Can we argue with their intense hatred for us? For eight years they have been sitting in the refugee camps in Gaza, and before their eyes we are turning the land and the villages in which they and their forefathers lived into our inheritance." His conclusion was: "This is the doom of our generation, this is the choice [we face] in our lives—to be prepared and armed, strong and determined, otherwise the sword will fall from our hands and our lives will be obliterated." See the IDF journal *Ba-Mahane*, 2 May 1956.

the border (Arab headdresses, meat, drugs, contraceptives, foreign brands of cigarettes), and they returned to Lebanon, Jordan, Syria, and Egypt to sell products that could be obtained less expensively in Israel (kerosene, cement, and dollars).[5] Side by side, smugglers, burglars, and avengers trod on the paths that crossed the border, which was in many spots unfenced and unguarded.

Official Israel viewed all infiltrators, not just criminals, as threats. Arabs who crossed the border with the intention of remaining in the country jeopardized Israel's demographic balance, and smugglers undercut the country's sovereignty within its borders. In viewing infiltration as an act of war, police officer and Arabist Shlomo Ben-Elkana voiced the opinion of many: "The war against us is being conducted, if not in a broad, collective way, then on a large scale, via infiltration. While this war does not have the content and military direction of a headquarters, it is a war that can deplete the Jewish population." He did not mean only murderous infiltration. "Despite all the humanitarian troubles caused by the severing of families, we must treat them with the full force of the law and expel them, and I hardly need state what political and material damage infiltration is liable to inflict on the state," he argued.[6]

It is hardly surprising, then, that the battle against infiltration, both defensive and offensive, was the focal point of IDF operations; the police force and military government also worked hard against it. As a result of the IDF's permissive rules of engagement, thousands of infiltrators were killed on Israel's borders between 1949 and 1956,[7] and the number of Arabs trying to sneak over the borders declined during this period and did so precipitously thereafter.

Between the infiltrators and the state stood Israel's Arab citizens. The infiltrators expected their fellow Arabs to assist and support them. They certainly hoped that their kinsmen would not turn them in. On the other side, Israel's security agencies sought the help of Israel's Arabs, who faced a cruel dilemma. They could help their own people, acquaintances, and sometimes even members of their families, in violation of Israeli law and at personal danger to themselves, or they could collaborate with those who pursued the infiltrators, in violation of their fidelity to their people and families. Many Israeli scholars maintained that the government did not put the loyalty of the Arab population to a test, demanding only that Arabs refrain from violating the law.[8] Now that the archives of a few security agencies have been opened to the public, we can see how inaccurate that statement was. Arab citizens of Israel were expected to turn in members of their own families who had slipped over the borders, and this clearly put them in an untenable situation.

In his reports, police officer Ben-Elkana stressed the aid and support that Israeli Arabs were providing to infiltrators. But the picture was actually much more complex. In practice, the attitudes of the Arabs in Israel toward the infiltrators can be charted along a spectrum. At one end was the classic nationalist position that the refugees had the right to enter the country and that the Arab citizens of Israel were morally bound to assist them. At the other extreme was the collaborationist approach, which advocated unconditional assistance (in operations, intelligence, and propaganda) to the state and its institutions. Most of the country's Arabs found themselves at various points along this spectrum, influenced by personal and family loyalties, by utilitarian considerations growing out of the authorities' policies of reward and punishment, and by ideological and economic factors. Some helped the infiltrators, some ignored them, and some took advantage of their vulnerability to defraud them.[9]

Note that even those who aided the infiltrators did not always do so out of nationalist sentiments, nor did they always explain their resistance to the state and its actions in nationalist terms. Money was an important incentive to cooperate with the infiltrators, as Israel's security institutions were well aware. A participant in a meeting of district police officers in July 1949 acknowledged, "We haven't given the [Arab] population a thing. They are living hand to mouth. They aren't receiving cloth, cigarettes, and flour. So they smuggle what they can into the territory, and the inhabitants are not pleased that we interfere with their smugglers. There is passive assistance to the smugglers." Four years later, another police officer asserted: "[The inhabitants of] Kufr Qara', which had most of its land expropriated, are no longer farmers; instead, ninety percent of them are in practice smugglers, if I can put it that way, because of their inability to find their livelihood in a normal way and because of the conditions they live in."[10]

Another consideration was family—in particular, the desire to reunite families separated during the 1948 war. Those motivated by family did not necessarily voice opposition to the Israeli authorities or the government's policy. Residents of Abu Ghosh, for example, made great efforts to protect relatives who stole over the border and into their village. Even though this was against the law, they continued to foster their image as loyal citizens of Israel, which they had cultivated since the 1948 war. To gain permission for family members to remain after crossing the border, they appealed to the Jewish public through the press and by writing letters to political figures.

They eschewed nationalist rhetoric; on the contrary, in a letter to the Speaker of the Knesset in July 1950, they detailed the aid they had given to the Jewish community during the Mandate period and the 1948 war:

Should the Abu Ghosh clan be repaid for its activities by the expulsion of men, women, and children and their humiliation by the Israeli police and army, only because they came to the village to reunite with their families? The police suddenly changed their policy and began to count the women and children as infiltrators and threw them over the border without respect for the women's honor and without compassion for the little ones. The most recent tragedy happened to our family last Friday (7 July 1950), when the police and the army surrounded the village at dawn and carried out sweeps and searches and took women and children who had no identity cards, even though the police and the relevant authorities know that they have been in the village for more than a year. . . .

We were stunned this time by the way the operation was carried out. This was the first time we have seen them strike a woman and carry her by her hands and feet and throw her into a military vehicle as if she were a sack of barley. It was an awful sight when blood dripped from the women's and children's heads, noses, and feet. The wails of the women and the weeping of the babes were a real horror. . . .

Mr. Speaker and members, we ask for justice. Bring these poor people back to their families. Order the police to keep their hands off women and children. Please treat the Abu Ghosh clan with sympathy. Bring us back our women and children. Long live the government of Israel![11]

The inhabitants of Abu Ghosh declared their loyalty to the state (as did many other Arabs when they wrote to state agencies) and anchored their demand for good treatment in the help they had given the Jewish state-information. In addition, they appealed to basic humanitarian sentiments.* Their illegal activities and their refusal to turn in infiltrators and smugglers coexisted with a patriotic discourse, since they did not view the return of their relatives as a danger to the country. They viewed the state's refusal to allow their refugee relatives to return to their homes as unjust harassment,

---

* They wrote to Foreign Minister Moshe Sharett about a mother who had lost her baby son during an operation in which infiltrators had been deported in January 1950. "The next day some of us went back to search for the child, and found him sleeping his eternal sleep. . . . They took him and buried him while his parents were still under arrest." Muhammad Abdallah and others to Sharett, ISA, MFA files, 2564/22. The letter is undated, but correspondence in the file indicates that it was written in January 1950 and for unknown reason reached Sharett only in July of that year.

and that may have been the reason for their strictly limited cooperation with the security forces in the early 1950s. Even when hand grenades were thrown at a school in the adjacent Jewish settlement of Kiryat Ye'arim in the summer of 1953, the village's leaders did not help the police uncover the perpetrators. (In response, the security agencies exiled four members of the village council to the Galilee.)[12] In any case, on the declarative level and apparently in practice as well, they placed the welfare of their families and community, not necessarily the national interests of either side, at the top of their agenda.

Israeli Arabs thus aided infiltrators for family, economic, and national reasons, and this aid took different forms—participation in smuggling (or intelligence) networks, hiding or providing havens for infiltrators, refusal to provide information about them to the authorities, and the exertion of public pressure to allow them to stay (for example, by petitioning the Supreme Court). The family factor was the most important. At the end of 1949, according to an Israeli government estimate, some twenty-five thousand infiltrators had already entered the country and been taken in by their families. When the government realized that it could not easily deport them, some of them submitted naturalization requests, and the great majority were approved.[13]

Yet, in the very same communities, some collaborators acted as the security agencies expected them to, participating in the effort to halt infiltration. They did so to receive material benefit, because they felt a duty to obey the authorities, or because their jobs and titles (and their desire to keep them) required it. Some feared the authorities, and others wanted to take revenge on a specific person or family. Furthermore, in some circles there was a sense that one should not work against the regime (in keeping with the Arab proverb "Don't bite the hand that feeds you"). It would be hard to estimate how many Arabs worked against the infiltrators, but the practice was hardly marginal. Even if she exaggerated, the Bedouin woman from 'Arab al-Khilf had good reason to say, "Most Arabs are traitors."

SHEIKHS AGAINST INFILTRATORS

An extremely negative attitude toward infiltration—especially when violence was involved—was expressed by Sheikh Saleh Khneifes, a Druze leader from Shefa'amr who aided Jewish forces before and during the 1948 war and who would be elected to the second and Third Knesset (1951–59).[14] His words to a GSS agent at the end of 1949, and even more so the spirit of those words, reflect a view diametrically opposed to the nationalist position:

There can be no doubt that the gangs roaming the western Galilee are aided by the local population, both in supporting people in robberies [as guides or helpers] and in giving shelter and food to the members of the gangs. It simply cannot be that the village of Tamra, in which more than 3,400 Muslims live, did not know who murdered and who planned the attack on Mahmoud al-Aswad two weeks ago. I visited ʿIblin, and I want to tell you that all the village's inhabitants live in indescribable fear of the gangs roaming in their area. I hardly need stress that the police are not displaying any competence for punishing the guilty and their accomplices, just as nothing has changed with regard to the position of the military governor, whose officers are not doing a thing regarding this situation. . . .

Your military regime in the region looks nothing like a military regime, I won't say in an Arab country, but anywhere in the world. A military regime that, instead of putting fear in the hearts of restless inhabitants, as it should, is encouraging them, and I think that the government will in the end face a situation in which the gangs run free and it will not be easy to eradicate them. . . .

The fact that they have stopped searching for infiltrators encourages the gangs' members, and in my opinion they should go back to searching each village, as the army once did, and I mean to search each village no less often than [once] a month. I hope that you will convey my position to those responsible, even though I myself have spoken on more than one occasion to Yehoshua Palmon [the prime minister's adviser on Arab affairs] on the necessity of taking action to eradicate the gangs' lairs, but for the present all I hear are promises.[15]

Khneifes's opposition to the "gangs"—bands of infiltrators—was no less sharp than that of Israeli officialdom. He maintained that Israel should cement its rule in the Galilee's Arab villages, even if that meant governing with an iron hand. He depicted the infiltrators, including those who had no malicious intent, as criminals who wreaked fear and death, and he made concrete proposals to fight them, which were accepted. In the weeks that followed the above conversation, the IDF conducted sweeps through Shefaʿamr and surrounding villages, and in November 1949 it imposed a curfew lasting several days on the town. The purpose was to force the inhabitants to turn in infiltrators who were hiding there. At the time of the curfew, Khneifes declared the local leadership's willingness "to cooperate with the military governor for the benefit of the government and the public." This compelled the town's inhabitants to provide the names of their refugee relatives, some three hundred in number, who had managed to steal back over the border to their homes.[16]

In his conversation with the GSS agent, Khneifes explained that he opposed infiltration because the outlaws imposed a reign of fear on the region's villages. When he spoke to the governor, he remarked that turning in infiltrators was beneficial to both the government and the public. He may have been thinking of his own safety as well. Because of his collaboration with Jewish forces during the war, he was a target of radical nationalist Arabs. But, like the Israeli authorities, he did not direct his ire only at violent infiltrators. Sometimes he also opposed those who sought to rejoin their families. His attitude toward the military government is also interesting. He saw it—or at least so he said—as a toothless body in comparison with other military regimes. In this his rhetoric was quite the opposite of that of the Arab nationalists, who stressed the military government's brutality. Khneifes fit into the prevailing Israeli discourse that celebrated the Jewish state's humanitarian treatment of its Arab minority, in contrast with the harsh treatment that Arab regimes meted out to their own populations.*

Negative attitudes toward infiltrators were also evident among other people who had cooperated with Jewish forces during the war. Sheikh Suleiman Abu-Ghalyun, from the southern Negev, complained that men from rival tribes over the border were trespassing on his tribe's camp. They had, he said, murdered one of his sons and stolen some of his camels. He had also worked for the Jewish forces in 1948, engaging in combat against rival Bedouin tribes. That seems to have been the reason for the attacks on him. Other tribes who had sent some of their men to fight alongside the Jews were also harassed by infiltrators. In many cases, enmity among these contending tribes escalated, leading tribes within Israel to cooperate with Israeli authorities against their enemies. Abu-Ghalyun, for example, organized a camel cavalry that worked alongside the IDF against infiltrators, and in the Triangle, Sheikh Tawfiq Abu-Kishek received gun licenses and reported to the security forces about infiltrators, out of fear that he would be the target of avengers coming over

* At this time, the military government sent Palestinians who had returned to their homes ("infiltrators") back over the border, prevented internal refugees (those who had been sent or had fled from one village or region to another during the war) from returning to their homes, awarded Arab land to Jews, forbade free movement from one village to another, exiled political activists or placed them in administrative detention, and took military action against infiltrators, giving soldiers lenient rules of engagement. Nevertheless, it certainly did not behave like the worst of military regimes. Israel's Arab citizens enjoyed a certain measure of freedom of expression as well as other individual freedoms. This enabled supporters of the military government to portray one aspect of reality while its opponents could condemn another. A question that remains unanswered in reading these reports is to what extent the Arabs quoted really believed what they were saying or whether they were simply seeking the favor of the authorities.

Figure 8. Against infiltration. Many Bedouins helped the IDF prevent infiltration. Here, the son and bodyguard of Sheikh Suleiman al-Huzayyel, who participated in these efforts, 1950. Photograph courtesy Israeli Government Press Office.

the border. He knew that militant nationalists had not yet forgotten his collaboration with the Jews in the Sharon and Tel Aviv regions during the war.[17]

The security forces, for their part, fully exploited the animosity between infiltrators and the local population. The benefit was not only tactical. It was also a way of weakening the nationalist camp, which opposed cooperation with Israel in security matters. At the end of 1952, when the villages of the Triangle suffered from a rash of thefts by infiltrators, the GSS sought to use the situation as an opportunity to initiate a change of consciousness among the area's inhabitants. In a position paper prepared by the chief of the GSS's Arab branch in January 1953, he proposed Arab participation in police ambushes, especially in the winter. His original justification was: "Imposing the burden of guard duty on Arab inhabitants will awaken within them opposition to the infiltration movement and make them feel, if only to a small extent, the suffering caused to Jewish settlements by the infiltrators." Furthermore, he saw this as an opportunity to gauge the true mood of the Arab public: "In this way we can test the population's willingness to fight infiltration, smuggling, and cooperation with the enemy. The moment is right for this, since the inhabitants complain that the security forces and police are, ostensibly, abandoning them." The plan seems not to have been put into action, at least not to any great extent. But it says something about another factor that encouraged Arab citizens to join the fight against infiltration and about the way the GSS thought.[18]

Indeed, Arabs who had suffered at the hands of infiltrators or who were in conflict with a particular group of infiltrators took action against them at times and entered into the official Israeli discourse that categorically rejected infiltration. The state, for its part, encouraged not only action against infiltrators but also the adoption and dissemination of the official rhetoric. On occasion, Arabs played a role in spreading the official Israeli position, in keeping with their jobs, political approaches, or public positions.

In January 1951, two infiltrators were shot and killed near Ramla. Their bodies were brought to the city for burial there. This, according to a police report, "shocked the inhabitants of the Arab neighborhood. Both the Muslims and the Christians silenced their radios as a sign of mourning, and most of the Muslim population put on their best clothes and went out to join the funeral procession. . . . At the end of the funeral, all of them came to the conclusion that it was not worthwhile to risk one's life in order to sneak into Israel and steal." But to be certain that the Arab public really assimilated this message, the authorities sent the imam of Jaffa, Sheikh Khalil al-Fadl, to

Figure 9.   Under the Israeli flag. In Ramla the Israeli authorities succeeded in recruiting the religious leadership to oppose infiltration and to organize Arab workers in Zionist forums. Here, a march in Ramla, 1949. Photograph by Kluger Zlotan; courtesy Israeli Government Press Office.

Ramla a month later. He led Friday prayers in the city's Great Mosque, and at the end of the service he gave a sermon condemning infiltration. He did not direct his address to the refugees living outside the country. His principal concern was the assistance given to infiltrators by the local inhabitants. He "warned the assembled against having any contact with the people coming from outside, if they did not want to find themselves in the same situation as the people of Migdal-Gad [Majdal, in Arabic] who were transferred to Gaza," concluded the report.[19] The transfer (or deportation) of the inhabitants of Majdal to Gaza (in the framework of a government program to send refugees and the inhabitants of isolated Arab settlements over the border) had been concluded a few months earlier. It was still fresh in the minds of Ramla's Arabs, so the threat fell on fearful ears.

Clergymen, especially those who received their salaries from the state (but others as well), were an important conduit for conveying to the Arab population anti-infiltration and anti-nationalist messages. At services the following Sunday, one of the leaders of Ramla's Christian community, Elia Fanous, read passages from the New Testament in which Paul calls on the members of his community to aid the regime. He deduced from this an obligation to help the Israeli government, explaining that it is "a government that was established by the will of God, because if God had not willed it, it would not have been established." The local Orthodox priest, Hanania, added to this an explicit instruction not to come into contact with infiltrators and called on the members of his flock to tell people on the other side of the border to desist from all contact with them. "At the end of his talk [sermon], Hanania announced that the government considered [such contact] a serious crime." The Anglican priest Musa 'Azar and the city's Catholic priest made similar remarks.[20]

The aid provided by these clergymen was verbal, meant to shape people's consciousness. It did not directly injure any particular person but encouraged Israel's Arabs to internalize the notion that they should obey the government's strictures. In the view of the nationalist camp, this was an illegitimate, even treasonous, position to take. That camp was no less censorious of an entirely different kind of verbal assistance—informing on infiltrators, which directly harmed individuals.

When conflict broke out between Hajj 'Abdallah, the imam of the Muslim community in Jish (Gush Halav, in Hebrew), and the village's mukhtar and other notables, the latter sent a letter to the Ministry of Religions demanding that the imam be dismissed and deported to Lebanon. In justification, they claimed, "He is harmful to our interests and the government's interests." Like Khneifes in his conversation with the GSS agent, they deliberately indicated that their interests were identical to the state's. They claimed that members of the imam's family were infiltrating from Lebanon, smuggling goods, and engaging in espionage.[21] Such accusations were not rare; the security forces received hundreds, if not thousands, of reports about infiltrators sent by rivals of those who sheltered infiltrators or by informers who wanted to prove their loyalty and effectiveness. The state benefited from this assistance in its fight against infiltration, and the informers saw it as a means of advancing their personal interests. So such cooperation was a product of mutual interest.

Reconstructing the precise motivations of informers in specific cases is difficult. A refugee who lived in a camp near Tyre, in Lebanon, crossed the border into Israel near M'ilya, in the western Upper Galilee. Before he managed to make his way southward to his family, he was seen by an inhabitant of the village, who sent his son to tell the police. The infiltrator was arrested on the spot. Two other infiltrators, bent on selling contraband, reached Na'ura, one of the Zu'biyya villages east of Afula. The local mukhtar turned one of them over to the police, and the second was captured in a police search conducted with the assistance of the locals.[22] We can only guess why these informers decided to turn the infiltrators in.

In another case, in Qalansawa in the Triangle in 1954, the motive was obvious. That winter, the police received repeated reports about a boy who was sneaking over the border into the village. After several abortive attempts to capture him, a local inhabitant named Qasem—who was himself involved in smuggling—volunteered to turn the boy in, on condition that he himself not be arrested for smuggling. "The promise was made to him," stated a police report, adding that when a fresh report arrived that the boy was in the village, a detachment of six policemen set out to apprehend him. Several inhabitants of the village offered their help.

> And then we commenced a vigorous search of various places with the intent of creating alarm in the village and to get the boy to come out into the street, and indeed a short while later the boy was captured by the said Qasem and handed over to the police. After the infiltrator's arrest it turned out that his name was 'Abdul Karim . . . twelve years old from a refugee camp in Tulkarem, and a search found 66 Israeli pounds in his possession, ten gold Constantine [old Ottoman] coins, six gold coins, eight pairs of gold earrings, a gold-colored wristwatch, and a prayer book (Quran). The boy was incarcerated and the contraband confiscated.[23]

Qasem turned in this small boy for a common reason—the desire to avoid criminal charges. Yet we cannot overlook the assistance that other inhabitants of the village offered, apparently because they wanted to look good to the authorities.

Others were willing to turn in infiltrators so as to mitigate the impact of legal procedures or to disguise criminal activity. When a police detachment captured a well-known smuggler known as Hasan, from Tamra, he was interrogated by the chief of the Acre District's Special Branch. The interrogator reported to his superiors, "I convinced Hasan to supply us with information about smugglers so as to capture them with smuggled goods. In exchange for this information, he suggested that we help him in the matter of his case [in court] and mitigation of punishment." That same day and in the weeks that followed, Hasan submitted reports that the police found valuable—the existence of smuggled kafiyyeh headdresses in the home of a handicapped woman in the village, contraband cigarette papers in the home of another villager, and other such information.[24]

Another familiar motive of informers of this kind was the hope of financial reward. A resident of 'Ara turned in a neighbor who had gone to Barta'a for contraband. An ambush there captured the smuggler and confiscated the goods. The informer's overseer, the chief of the Hadera District's Special Branch, recommended granting the informer a reward in the value of the captured goods, 444 Israeli pounds.[25]

A young Arab from central Israel had a less common motive. He had gotten his girlfriend pregnant, a police officer reported, adding, "She is in danger that her brothers will kill her to preserve the family's honor. Therefore . . . the above-mentioned is prepared to help the police by providing information about infiltrators, so long as the police will intervene in the present case to get assurances from her family to prevent her murder."[26] The police may well have done their duty even if the young Arab had not offered this help, but to be sure that they took matters in hand, he felt it necessary to compensate the police in advance.

Some turned in infiltrators because they expected compensation in the form of a residence permit for a relative or friend. A mukhtar from the Galilee did so with infiltrators who arrived in his village, one of whom was his own son. His purpose was to reach an agreement with the authorities by which the entire group would be deported, except for his son. The Druze MK Jaber Dahash Mu'adi wrote a letter to Minister of Police Bechor Shitrit supporting the son's request to remain in Israel and praising the father:

> The father [of the applicant] is one of the best leaders in the area and the village's mukhtar. On the day the Galilee was liberated, he was among the most important collaborators with the army in collecting arms and such, and he has in his possession documents proving this. From that date to this day, he has aided the security, military, and police authorities in pursuing infiltrators, smugglers, and violators of Israeli law. . . . The police officer in the area asked the mukhtar to provide affidavits against the infiltrators, and since he likes to cooperate with the authorities, he provided the police with important information against thirty-three people in his village, and he is now a witness for the prosecution in such a case in the Supreme Court.[27]

Some infiltrators asked for permission to remain in Israel because of service they had rendered to the state or to the Jews in the past. Others promised such service in the future. One, 'Ali Khalil, a refugee who stole back into the country, petitioned the police through an attorney, requesting an Israeli identity card as well as ration cards for himself and his family. He justified his request by explaining that he had worked for the Israeli government for a considerable time on the other side of the border—apparently tracking groups of infiltrators—and had even been arrested for this by the Jordanians. A similar claim was made by Tawfiq Ahmad, from Wadi ʿAra (the northern part of the Triangle). An infiltrator who had been accused of armed robbery and then acquitted, he asked to remain in Israel with his family in the village of ʿAra and in exchange "offered himself as an informer and [was] prepared, in his words, for any activity . . . required of him." The policeman who received the offer and passed it on to his superiors remarked that, while it was difficult to form an impression from a single conversation, it was clear that he was "bright and prepared to do a great deal."[28]

In many cases, people passed on information they had come across by chance. In other words, they were not necessarily actively collecting information. A man from the village of Turʿan related that when he went to urinate in an olive grove, he ran into a man from his village (by coincidence, an old enemy of his) who was talking with two infiltrators. He gave the information to two of the village's well-known collaborators, one of whom worked for the GSS, the other for the police—in the hopes that the information would reach at least one of these organizations and that measures would be taken against his rival. An inhabitant of Umm al-Fahm was walking close to the border when a woman, mistaking him for someone else, called out to him from the other side. She asked him to pass on a letter to one of his covillagers. He took the letter from her and handed it over to the police (who photocopied it and returned it for delivery and ongoing surveillance). A barber was summoned to a house in his Galilean village to shave the father of the family. He noticed a strange man who spoke in a Lebanese accent and suspected that he was an infiltrator who had come on an intelligence or sabotage mission. He reported this to the police. A cleaning worker from Nazareth visited the village of Muqeible and heard there about an old widow who crossed the border once every two weeks in order to visit her sons in Jenin, and reported this to the Nazareth police.[29]

In other cases, informers conducted interrogations and did detective work to obtain information. Their motives were similar to those of the collaborators described above, but their means were more sophisticated. An informer who preferred anonymity (which may mean that his primary objective was to cause trouble for his enemies) prepared a detailed report, in the autumn of 1953, about smugglers in the Upper Galilee. He wrote about armed smugglers who had arrived in Dir al-Asad and those who housed them, about villagers who owned guns, about a refugee who had crossed the border to smuggle out his friend's fiancée, and others. He supplemented this with a section titled "The Political Situation in the Villages" (he made an effort to write in

Hebrew rather than his mother tongue, Arabic, and the English translation reflects the writer's unidiomatic Hebrew):

> As became apparent to me in my visits to the villages in the area and in my own village, the political village situation is shocking since haters of the state of Israel are the worm that is inside, inciting the inhabitants against the state about every little piece of news heard on the radio or in the newspapers about border incidents or meetings of the Arab League and the Arab army chiefs of staff and more, and they say that we will be the first ones hurt if fighting starts again between Israel and the Arab countries and they glorify the Arab countries and disparage Israel and its army. I suggest opening eyes and being prepared in the Arab villages.[30]

Another diligent informer worked at this time in the Lower Galilee. He reported to his overseers about his visits to villages in the Nazareth region. Among other things, he provided a list of names of infiltrators, an analysis of the situation, and recommendations, in the elementary Hebrew he had only recently learned:

> Their presence in Israel will benefit the Arab countries. They go out to the Arab countries: Syria, Lebanon, Jordan, spy and bring smuggled items with them. These people will do a danger to Israel. These infiltrators in the War of Independence were from the side of the Arabs and worked with members of the Qawuqji army. It is not known for what reason nothing was done against them by the army and the police. Catch them and throw them outside the country because they are here illegally. They are here as spies in the country.[31]

Eager informers worked in a variety of ways. A Lower Galilee villager noticed that another man in his village enjoyed a high standard of living even though he owned no land and did not work. The villager decided, on his own initiative, to keep an eye on him and observed that his well-off neighbor met regularly with a group of other men from the village in one particular house. The wife of the man who owned this house was a relative of the informer's wife, and he took advantage of this connection to invite himself over to her home. When he entered, "he saw everyone sitting around a radio and listening to the Voice of the Arabs [the Egyptian radio, which promoted pan-Arab ideology], and rejoicing at the news." They greeted him coolly, the informer reported, and the group sat quietly for half an hour until he felt uncomfortable and left. But, at the first opportunity, when the wife of his suspect came to visit his family, he interrogated her about her husband's activities. He learned that one of her husband's brothers was a nationalist activist who lived in Lebanon and slipped into Israel every once in a while. This reinforced his suspicions: "This group is acting against the state by gathering information, and their meeting place is Gush Halav [Jish], where they turn information over to the enemy and receive a salary for inhabitants of the state who collaborate with the enemy." The informer's overseer instructed him to continue to shadow the group. Another informer served, at his own initiative, as an agent provocateur. In his village, he talked to people whom he thought were connected with infiltrators, telling them that he intended to run away to Syria because of a family argument. He asked their assistance in making contact with persons who served as guides for infiltrators. Then he shared the information he had gathered from them with the GSS and police.[32]

ISRAEL'S LONG HAND

Hasan al-Fayad was considered one of the most dangerous infiltrators in the Sharon region, the narrow strip along the coast between Tel Aviv and Haifa. He began to infiltrate into Jewish settlements as early as 1948. According to information received by Israeli intelligence, al-Fayad had been involved in at least three murders of Israeli citizens, as well as in kidnappings and robberies. On the night of 7 August 1949, he was visited in his tent near Tulkarem, then in Jordanian territory, by an old acquaintance—a Bedouin named Suleiman, who lived in a tent camp in central Sharon. Suleiman was a guest in al-Fayad's tent for three days. On the fourth night, when they sat drinking coffee, Suleiman asked to see his host's tommy gun. The latter handed him the weapon. Suleiman immediately pulled the trigger and shot al-Fayad point-blank, killing him. Two of al-Fayad's brothers sprang to his aid, but Suleiman shot them in their arms and legs. "The murderer fled to Israeli territory. The area's Arabs and the Jordanian police, who were called in, pursued the criminal, who had in the meantime managed to cross the border.... The outraged inhabitants of Qalqiliya see a Jewish hand in the murder," an Israeli police report stated.[33]

This was how police officer Re'uven Dorenzaft described, without taking direct responsibility, an operation he initiated and carried out with the use of his collaborators. Indeed, beyond verbal collaboration, beyond informing, some collaborators risked their lives to take active roles in such operations and had no hesitation about taking the lives of fellow Arabs. This was perhaps the most blatant form of collaboration, although it had a far smaller effect on the daily life of the Arabs in Israel than did political and intelligence collaboration within the state.

Dorenzaft began forming retribution and liquidation squads in early July 1949, following instructions he had received from the police force's deputy commander-general. The strategy was offensive and involved planting collaborators among the infiltrators in order to wipe them out. The squads were composed of Arabs from both sides of the new border who were qualified in collecting intelligence and moved relatively freely between Israel and Jordan. Like the infiltrators, these collaborators did not attach much importance to border markings and crossed the line routinely. Principally, they liquidated infiltrators with their own hands, as did Suleiman (who had nurtured his friendship with al-Fayad for some time prior to his operation), or they lured the infiltrators into police or army ambushes.

Toward the end of July, the police formed two small armed squads, in coordination with military intelligence. The collaborators chosen for these squads were professionals. One was described as "an accomplice of thieves, a brawler." Another received a more positive evaluation: "muscular, can serve as a sapper, political informer, carries out solo operations."[34] They received a list of targets to be liquidated and were allowed to cross the border to carry out their missions. One member of these squads was named Amin, and he described his recruitment as follows:

> I am from Tira, in the area of the Taybe police station. After Israel received the Taybe area, the military governor, David, who was in Tira at that time, demanded a weapon from me. I went to Naqura, next to Dir Sharaf [near Nablus], and I brought a Canadian rifle and turned it over to the military governor in Tira. A month later, Hasan 'Abdallah and Rafiq Sheikh Najib of Tira were arrested, and two or three days later Officer Riklin showed up with another policeman from the Ra'anana station—I think his name was Yehoshua—and asked me if I could help the Israeli government in the matter of Hasan 'Abdallah and Rafiq Sheikh Najib, who were collaborators with the Iraqi commando force. I told Officer Riklin that I was prepared to help. So I was called twice to the court in Petah Tikva to testify against the two of them. And at about the end of June 1949, when I was at home, I was visited by 'Abed . . . from Taybe, ... and he asked me to go out with him, and there he told me that he would put me together with another strong guy like me so that we could work together for the Israeli government as undercover agents against the Arab commandos, and I told him that I was ready [to do it]. And he told me to come with him to Taybe in two days, and two days later I came to the military government headquarters in Taybe, and I saw 'Abed there . . . and the officers there asked me details about my

family . . . and one of the officers told me that I should be in touch with 'Abed . . . and the latter said before the two officers that we had to kill Hasan Abu-Fayad and Ahmad 'Eid and Mahmoud al-Bahri and others from the Arab commandos. We received instructions and went home to Tira.[35]

Amin was put through a gradual process. At first he was told, as were the rest of his village's residents, to turn in his weapon. Since he did not (or so he claimed) have a gun but wanted to please the governor, he went and brought a Canadian rifle from Jordanian territory and turned it in. After this, he helped by testifying against two prominent men from Tira, 'Abdallah and Sheikh Najib, who were accused of instigating the attack on Rishpon, an Israeli village, at the end of 1948, in which two Jews were killed. Then came his recruitment into the undercover agency against the Arab commandos. Amin did not explain what motivated him in these earlier stages or what prompted him to agree to become an undercover agent. It is clear, however, that 'Abed, a prominent man from the Triangle, had a significant role in his decision. As a result, Amin found himself armed and given a mission to kill some "heavy" infiltrators.

In this case, the mission ran into complications. Amin crossed the border into Jordan with his partner and proceeded to the home of a contact in Qalqiliya, a man named Muslih. Muslih was supposed to be waiting for them, to provide them with assistance, but he was not at home. They waited for several hours in the adjacent olive grove, then returned to Israel with the sense that something was not as it should be. An informer in Qalqiliya told them a few days later that word of their plan had leaked across the border and that the Jordanian police knew about it. Amin decided not to take part in the mission, proposing to an Israeli intelligence officer that his brother Mahmoud carry out the assignment instead. Mahmoud received an IDF rifle and set out. Soon after crossing the border, he was captured in a Jordanian ambush. He was accused of working for Israel and for having come on a liquidation mission. Amin, who felt responsible for his brother, set out with two partners to find out what had happened to him, and all three of them were captured. It turned out that all their contacts on the Jordanian side had given their information to the Jordanian authorities. All four men were brought before a military court in Nablus, where they were given sentences of five to seven years in prison. They were released two years later, at the end of 1951, and handed over to Israel.[36]

Sabotage missions in neighboring countries not only were dangerous, but also exacerbated tensions with Jordan. This may be one of the reasons for the decision, made in 1953, not to use Israeli Arab collaborators to carry out retaliation operations in enemy countries but to use them only as accessories to the central force. Instead, local collaborators from the other countries were used.[37] At the same time, the second kind of operation, in which infiltrators were led into ambushes and killed, became much more common. Two typical examples follow. In the first, a refugee who entered Israel with a group of infiltrators stayed with them in a village in central Israel in July 1951 and then reported to an Israeli police officer that the group was about to set out on its way back to Tulkarem.

> The informer said that he knew exactly what path the smugglers would use. So the informer was taken to a place the smugglers would pass and an ambush was organized at that place to ambush the arrivals.... At 0045 hours, the ambushers, sensing that a group of men was approaching the place, allowed them to get close, and the sergeant ordered them to halt, but the arrivals began to run away. Then [the ambush] opened fire, and three from the group were killed.... The informer's brother knew about the ambush and was last in the group, so he managed to keep himself safe from the gunfire and to get away in the dark. The dead men were photographed, their fingerprints were taken, and they were buried in Jisr al-Zarqa [north of Caesarea].[38]

Another informer was insinuated into a band that rustled draft animals around Binyamina, just north of the Triangle. He reported that the bandits hid out in the abandoned village of Sindianah, which served as the home base for their operations. The informer was told to persuade these infiltrators to ensconce themselves in a particular location within the village, where the police set an ambush. Following a long wait, the informer arrived on his own and said that the band had decided to hide out in a different place in the village. He led the police detachment there. "The three policemen crawled close to the place, and when they had reached a distance of a few meters from the gang, they ordered them to turn themselves in, but the Arabs got up and tried to jump into some nearby bushes. The policemen opened fire on them, and the three [Arabs] were killed on the spot.... They were buried in Faradis."[39]

Another kind of mission that collaborators took on involved leading IDF units to targets over the border, in the framework of Israel's retaliation operations. Like the other kinds of work described above, these operations were dangerous. A mukhtar from the Triangle served as a collaborator with the military government in his community, and his son served as a "combat" collaborator. In 1951, the son and a colleague led an IDF unit into Jordanian territory. Its mission was a retaliation operation in Ras 'Atiah, not far from Qalqiliya. As was the common practice then, two security coordinators from nearby Jewish settlements took part in the operation. When the Israeli force approached its target, it encountered enemy fire. The soldiers returned fire, killing a Jordanian civilian, and withdrew to Israeli territory with no casualties. Two days later, when the Arab guides arrived at their usual meeting place with one of the security coordinators who had taken part in the operation, the coordinator and a colleague shot them and buried their bodies in their settlement. The security coordinator believed that the guides had intentionally led the force into an ambush. The suspicion turned out to be unfounded, and the killers were sentenced to three years in prison.[40]

This was a rare case in which collaborators were killed by Israeli security forces. It is interesting to note that the mukhtar continued to work for the Israelis even after his son was murdered, perhaps because the killers were brought to justice.

Taking part in such military operations was dangerous even inside Israel. Police officer Ze'ev Steinberg was able to recruit an informer from among a band of infiltrators who stole tools from a packinghouse near Karkur. The informer told him that the band was planning to cross the border on the night of 25 January 1951, and he provided information about the route they planned to take. An ambush that had been set up on their path opened fire on the infiltrators. One was killed, two wounded. But the dead man was the informer himself. Steinberg's report of the operation evinces no regret. He blamed the error on the dead man, who, he said, had not followed instructions to keep four meters between him and the rest of the group. Anyway, Steinberg wrote, the deceased was himself a known thief.[41]

An informer code-named Kerem 1 met his death in a minefield near Jerusalem. His name was based on that of his home village, 'Ein Karem, the homes of which were handed over to Jews after the Arabs were uprooted during the war. He was recruited by the police after he crossed the border into Israel at the beginning of 1951, when he was captured and imprisoned. He served actively for fifteen months, during which he went into the field many times with security forces to point out infiltration routes to the Israeli section of Jerusalem. He also exposed bands of counterfeiters of Israeli currency who operated out of Bethlehem. The climax of his service came when he led a paratrooper unit on a retaliation operation in the town of Beit Jala in January 1952, following the rape and murder of a young Jewish girl in

Jerusalem. Kerem 1 investigated the crime and discovered that the murderer was Mahmoud Mansi, a refugee from the village of Walaja. On the night of the operation, Kerem 1 led the force to the Mansi family's home, and IDF sappers blew it up with everyone inside. It turned out, however, that the suspects were not there. The victims included two girls and two women. In the weeks that followed, he continued to meet with his overseers once a week, sometimes more often. At the end of one meeting, a policeman named Yitzhak Asouline drove him to the border. "After he crossed the border there was a loud explosion, and a daylight search conducted on 18 March 1952 made it clear beyond any doubt (by scraps of clothing that were identified) that the informer had stepped on a mine and been killed." The body parts collected by the police were brought for burial on the Israeli side of the village of Beit Safafa.[42]

The collaborators who crossed the border or worked on its far side were not necessarily Israeli citizens. Some were Palestinians who lived in the West Bank or the Gaza Strip, and some were citizens of neighboring countries. In several cases, they were recruited directly by Israeli intelligence officers, but in many others it was Israeli Arab collaborators who enlisted them. For example, an Egyptian intelligence officer in the Gaza Strip was put in contact with an Israeli counterpart by a woman named Halima, from Majdal (Ashkelon), who crossed the border into the Gaza Strip and returned. Another case is of a refugee from Masmiyya who lived in Gaza and was utilized by a well-known Bedouin sheikh from the Negev for army intelligence. This refugee was arrested by the Egyptian military government in Gaza after being fingered by someone there. In his pocket, the Egyptians found a set of instructions given him by his Israeli overseer. In his interrogation, he named other collaborators who worked for Israel in the Gaza Strip, and they, too, were arrested. He was sentenced to ten years in prison.

Jordanian and Egyptian intelligence officials closely followed Israeli activity in their territories. From time to time, they issued lists of Israeli Arabs suspected of espionage, as well as of inhabitants of the West Bank and the Gaza Strip suspected of helping them. Some of these lists reached Israeli intelligence, and an examination of them showed that, in general, they contained reliable information (although there is some irony in the fact that the lists were brought to Israel by the same kinds of agents they purported to expose). Such activity continued until these territories were occupied by Israel in 1967. In 1956, a memorandum circulating among Jordanian security officials stated, "We have learned from a reliable source that the Jews are organizing espionage networks that will operate within Arab countries and in Jordan in particular. They have begun to organize small teams that will carry out sabotage and guerrilla activities, and, in addition, will carry out investigative activities on those responsible for organizing *fedayeen* [Arab guerrilla] groups in Jordan, in order to eradicate them." Attached to this document was an appendix with the names of suspects from the West Bank and Israel. In February 1965 alone, the Jordanian military court in Nablus convicted twenty men on suspicion of collaboration with Israel. The Arab press also addressed the matter and reported on spies captured and brought to trial. The view that the Arabs in Israel were "traitors and spies," common in Arab countries, originated in part because of the deep involvement that some of them had with Israeli intelligence officials.[43]*

In the spring of 1953, Israel endured a run of serious terror attacks. A couple from the farming village of Tsipori was murdered; a bus of teenagers on a field trip was shot at near Meron and a boy killed; Hajj Muhammad 'Omar Qays, a veteran collaborator from the Circassian village of Reihaniyya (who served as a guide for a palmach in Syria in the early 1940s), was shot dead. And several other incidents of gunfire, in which no one was hurt, were directed at Israeli civilians and vehicles. The entire security apparatus addressed itself to investigating these incidents. The assumption was that the attacks were carried out by no more than two or three bands made up of Palestinian refugees, working in coordination with Syrian intelligence. The security forces saw this as a challenge:

> The weak point of our border security is the refugee camps over the border. Fundamental ignorance of what is going on in these camps ... does not allow effective intelligence gathering or certainly action to exterminate the gangs, and does not allow retaliation operations aimed at striking at the guilty and their helpers. It seems to us that no political institution has

---

* An interesting case of recruitment was that of Muhammad, a refugee who had settled in Khan Yunis. He got involved in a brawl in his new home and was arrested. In prison he met a refugee from Jaffa who was commencing a fifteen-year sentence for spying for Israel. This prisoner, named Isma'il, suggested to Muhammad that he work for Israel, and Muhammad agreed. When he was released from prison, he crossed into Israel, presented himself to a contact person Isma'il had named, and began to work for IDF intelligence in the Gaza Strip. The Egyptians discovered his activity, arrested him, and brought him to trial. But Muhammad was acquitted and required only to report to his local police station four times a day. He grew fed up with this after a few months and reestablished contact with his Israeli intelligence officer, who sent him on a mission in Jordan. At some point he fell out with his operator, stole a rifle, and was sent to prison in Israel. In jail, he helped interrogators to get other prisoners to talk. Nazareth PS to SB Jezreel, 22 October 1957, ISA 79, 76/7.

worked hard enough to know who shapes life in each and every camp and what the intentions of their inhabitants are, what the political activities of former Palestine residents [i.e., the refugees] are, and what the details of their plans are.[44]

The decision was to begin to collect intelligence from refugees in Lebanon and to use a method that had been successful in the Triangle—inserting moles into squads of infiltrators who would lead the gunmen into Israeli ambushes. The moles were Israeli citizens who went to Lebanon with a cover story, as well as refugees who were utilized by Israeli Arab relatives. The usual reward was monetary or, in the case of refugees who wanted to return to Israel, the grant of an Israeli identity card.

A twenty-five-year-old man named Zeidan from Shefaʿamr was sent to be such a mole. His mission was to find information about armed infiltrators who were entering Israel. He crossed into Lebanon, and on the other side of the border, in the village ʿAziyya, he met an old friend named Hussein, who was a refugee from the Upper Galilean village of Saʿsaʿ. Hussein told Zeidan that he was lucky to have arrived safely and mentioned that a gang was in the area. Zeidan took advantage of this opportunity and asked for information about the gang's members. His friend had no hesitation about telling him that it was composed of members of the Hamdun tribe and that it was headed by a man named Khaled Sakran. He also knew that the band operated under the protection of Lebanese notables. "I asked Hussein to introduce me to the head of the gang because I wanted to join them to get into Israel from time to time to commit robberies and such. I told him that I was sick of life in Israel and that I had spent time in Israeli prisons." Hussein promised to organize the meeting. In the meantime, so as not to lose time, Zeidan went out to collect information in the Tyre region. He was afraid to go to Sidon because, when he had been in jail in Israel, he collaborated with the prison director, and he feared running into some infiltrators from around Sidon whom he had met in jail. "It's likely that if I fall into their hands, they will take revenge on me," he said.

Zeidan returned to ʿAziyya, where a meeting with Sakran had already been arranged. "I explained to him that I was in a tough situation, that I was wanted in Israel, with lots of enemies in Shefaʿamr informing on me whenever I come to Israel. I want to carry out robberies, and I want them to give me a few men so that I can steal some money. In exchange for the help he [Sakran] gives me, he'll receive part of the loot. On top of that I'll be loyal to him and obey his orders." But Sakran explained to the informer that he

Figure 10. The wild north. An Israeli bus attacked by Palestinian infiltrators in Meron, Upper Galilee, 1953. Photograph by Moshe Pridan; courtesy Israeli Government Press Office.

had prior commitments because of an agreement he had just made with the Lebanese police—that he would stop infiltration in exchange for dropped murder charges against him in Lebanon—and also because of his connections with a member of the Lebanese parliament, Saheb Beq, whom he had helped get elected. The informer returned to Israel with an interim report and told his overseers, "I take it upon myself to set out after the Muslim holiday, on the 22nd of this month approximately, and I will make every effort to join the Hamdun gang. I am determined to bring part of the gang to Israel and to lead them into an ambush, as we spoke of. If you have other proposals, I am at your service."[45]

Another participant in the hunt for the Hamdun infiltrators was a refugee named Sh-hadeh. He lived in 'Aziyya, the gang's home base. He was close to these infiltrators and on occasion provided them with clothing and food when they were hiding from the Lebanese authorities. But at this juncture, his best friend, who had remained in Israel and lived in the western Galilee, began collaborating with Israeli security forces. This collaborator had sent his wife to Lebanon to recruit Sh-hadeh to track the gang that had been murdering Israelis. Sh-hadeh was promised that if he did the job he would be allowed to return to Israel. He accepted the proposal, and since he knew who was in the gang, he went to Sakran's house. He arrived in the middle of a meeting attended by fifteen men. The following is the account he gave to the Israeli police:

> As soon as I came in, the conversation halted. I sat down. Rashid Tarafa turned to me after I asked why they had stopped talking, and he said to me, "We can't go on here because the talk here is top secret, and we are afraid you will inform on us." I replied that I would not be the man to let the secret out. "I am one of you and my son Hasan is one of you." He answered, "If that's the case, you must swear on the Quran that you will keep inside everything you hear here." The Quran was brought in, but when he saw I was willing to swear, he said that whoever has the will is considered as one who has sworn. After that he turned to me and said, "Today you are unemployed and young. Why shouldn't you be one of our men? . . ." My response was, "Perhaps I will sacrifice myself in action, and the Arabs will not beat the Jews." I was answered that it had to be left to God and that He was the one who would help us win. I promised him [Tarafa] that I would enlist in the near future. He asked me whether I would be prepared to go out with them one night on an operation in Israel. I responded that, yes, I was ready at any time. We finished talking and I continued to sit among them. I listened in on a conversation about the last operation they had carried out, which was shooting at a police car on the night of 29 July 1953, near Shomera, in which Nimer Tuhtuh [and others] took part.

Sh-hadeh gave the officer who questioned him the names of those who participated in the meeting, the names of the infiltrators who had shot at cars on Galilean roads, and information on the weapons used in these operations and on the gang's connections to Palestinian organizations and to Syrian and Lebanese intelligence. He promised to try to find out when the Hamduns next planned to cross the border, and he was given a promise that if infiltrators were caught he would receive a prize of six hundred Israeli pounds, adding in his testimony, "And they would induct me into the border police, and I would live a happy life."[46]

There is no good way to evaluate the quality of the information provided by Zeidan and Sh-hadeh and the extent of their sincerity. Neither does an account of the rest of the hunt for the Hamdun gang appear in the files that have been opened to the public. Soon after these events, the gang's members stopped crossing into Israeli territory, perhaps because of their relations with

Lebanese authorities. Or perhaps they reached an agreement with Israeli intelligence. Two years later, four Hamduns who lived in Lebanon took part in an Israeli intelligence operation.[47] Whatever the case, Israeli intelligence organizations obviously fielded Israeli Arab agents in the territory of Israel's neighbors—to prevent infiltration, to gather intelligence, and for any of a myriad other purposes.

The willingness, or readiness, of so many Arabs to collaborate with Israeli intelligence should not be misread. It does not mean that such active collaboration was rampant or that Israel succeeded in recruiting everyone it wanted. The exaggeration of the Bedouin woman's plaint that "most Arabs are traitors" is made obvious with the story of Salah, a refugee from the Lower Galilee.

Salah was born in the village of Tur'an in 1921 and served as an auxiliary policeman in the British Mandatory police force. In December 1947, he was stationed at the Haifa oil refinery and was on the site when dozens of Jewish workers were murdered there.* According to information obtained by the police, Salah helped the Arab attackers get away before the British investigators arrived. Soon thereafter he left the country and settled in the 'Ein al-Hilweh refugee camp in Lebanon—perhaps out of fear of revenge. In early 1950 he made his way over the border into Israel, where he was apprehended and deported to Jordan. From there he went to Syria and began to work for Syrian intelligence. In this capacity, he made contact with two men from his village who were known as collaborators and told them that he was prepared to work for Israel in exchange for permission to return to his home. He reentered Israel under their protection and met, apparently, with an Israeli security officer, who sent him and the other two collaborators on a mission to Syria. When he reached Syria he turned his two partners over to Syrian intelligence, and they were sentenced to ten years in prison on charges of spying for Israel. Salah's motive was that he believed these two men were the ones who informed on him to the Israeli authorities when he arrived in the village in 1950. Salah subsequently reentered Israel a number of times for

* On 29 December 1947, members of the Etzel underground threw a bomb at Arab workers at the entrance to the refinery. They claimed that they sought to avenge the deaths caused by an explosion set off in a Jewish neighborhood a short while before. In the wake of this attack came the murder of thirty-seven Jewish workers that day, and that massacre was followed by a Haganah retaliation operation, carried out by the Palmach's first battalion, against the neighboring village of Balad al-Sheikh on the night of 31 December 1947. See Meir Pa'il, "The Battles," in Yehoshua Ben Arye, ed., *Ha-Historia shel Eretz Yisrael: Milhemet ha-Atzma'ut* [The history of the land of Israel: War of independence] (Jerusalem: Yad Ben Zvi, 1983), 155 (in Hebrew).

personal reasons as well as in the service of Syrian intelligence, without the Israeli authorities being aware that he had turned in his partners.

In 1958, while the two men were still in a Syrian prison, an Israeli intelligence officer from Unit 154, in consultation with the GSS, made another attempt to use Salah. The mission this time was to obtain information on Syrian intelligence, which had intensified its espionage efforts in the Galilee, including the dispatch of agents to scout out the country. The Israeli officer also wanted information on what was going on in the 'Ein al-Hilweh refugee camp. Following the usual practice, the officer tried to make contact with Salah through members of his family who still lived in Israel. The intelligence officer (whose code name was Ghazi) and GSS agent Eliahu M. proposed to a member of Salah's family, a man named Mahmoud (who apparently had a history of collaboration), that he serve as their go-between with Salah. Mahmoud agreed. But that was not sufficient. In order to secure their proposal, Ghazi and Eliahu M. involved another young man from the family, named Yusef, who was at the time incarcerated in the Tel Mond prison on charges of having helped Salah and other infiltrators. Yusef was assigned to write a letter to Salah requesting him to collaborate with Israeli military intelligence in exchange for Yusef's early release. Mahmoud was assigned to travel to Lebanon to give the letter to Salah. The Israeli intelligence operatives hoped that an appeal from Yusef, his relative and friend, would persuade the stubborn Salah to work with them.

Ghazi drove Mahmoud to the Lebanese border. Mahmoud crossed over and handed Yusef's letter to a contact, asking him to convey it to Salah in 'Ein al-Hilweh. To confirm that he did as requested, the contact was asked to bring back a photograph of Salah. Two days later he returned with the photograph, as well as Salah's rejection of the offer. Salah had stated unambiguously that if Mahmoud ever came to Lebanon again on assignment from Israeli intelligence, he, Salah, would make sure that Mahmoud was arrested.

Here was a classic case of refusing to collaborate, including a threat against other collaborators. The fact that Salah had turned in two of his fellow villagers two years earlier underlined how serious he was.[48] This case demonstrates that, however willing some Arabs were to collaborate with Israel, it was hardly a universal practice. In fact, police officers often reported that the Arab population as a whole was hostile to collaborators, who felt isolated and persecuted.

Indeed, the Arab community took action against them. Every so often, Israeli Arabs, either via infiltrators or by crossing the border themselves, conveyed the names of collaborators in their communities to intelligence organizations in Arab countries. According to police and GSS reports, this was done by inhabitants of Baqa al-Gharbiyyeh, Barta'a, Taybe, 'Arrabe, Sakhnin, Kabul, and other places. Others physically attacked collaborators, without outside assistance.[49] 'Abed, a hounded collaborator, described the kind of treatment people like him received:

> I have worked for the government for the last four years. I help the govern-
> ment with everything, and I continued to work until my work expanded
> into Jordanian territory beyond the Israeli border. I helped a lot, and I
> brought the Israeli government what it needed from over the border. . . .
> I was also a spy against the Arab inhabitants near me who were Israeli
> residents to prevent infiltration and smuggling, and as a result of this
> there was hatred between me and the Arabs, and they tried to kill me
> a few times, and I escaped.[50]

So, in Arab villages in Israel, they all lived side by side. There were overt and covert collaborators with Israeli intelligence who worked to seal Israel's borders against infiltrators. There were collaborators with Arab intelligence organizations who conveyed information about Israel over the border, nationalists who sheltered infiltrators, and informers who turned them in. In the big picture, the struggle with infiltration was an important theater of the battle for the Arab population's hearts and minds, a struggle between those who accepted their status as a minority with limited rights and, as a result, enjoyed the support of the security forces, and those who rejected the military rule and sometimes the very existence of the state of Israel itself.

FOUR

The Land

THE MAIN GOAL OF MANY INFILTRATORS was to rejoin their fami-
lies. Thus, Israel's efforts to prevent this became a central bone of contention
between the state and its minority population, impinging on the daily and
family lives of many Arabs. But the Arabs enjoyed no little success. According
to government figures, 20,500 infiltrators who entered Israel between the end
of the 1948 war and October 1953 were allowed to remain and were granted
citizenship. Additionally, some 3,000 Arabs outside the country were granted
entry permits for humanitarian reasons.[1] While these returnees constituted
only a small proportion—fewer than 5 percent—of the refugees who ended up
outside Israel's borders, their reentry was nevertheless no mean achievement.
Nearly every village and community was able to implement a limited "right of
return" for a few of its members, enlarging the country's Arab population by
15 percent. By the nature of the phenomenon, many could claim credit—the
nationalists, who helped conceal and support infiltrators; the people who
aided them for personal and family reasons; and of course the so-called moderate leaders who used their contacts with state agencies to assist members of
their communities, in the process enhancing their own influence.

But two other factors also played a large role. The first was the attitude of
the international community, which pressured Israel to take in refugees; the
second was the Israeli regime's willingness to yield, for humanitarian reasons,
to the Arab population's needs and requests, even during the period of the

military government. The general guidelines the military governors received were to allow only infiltrators "likely to be useful" to them to remain in the country, and the government's policy was that temporary residence permits were to be granted only when they contributed to "enhancing the state organs' power and influence."[2] But these rules were not always observed.

The return of more than twenty thousand refugees testifies to institutional ambivalence and to the fact that the official Israeli policy of "fewer Arabs on less land," to use the phrase coined by the custodian of absentee property, was not always implemented.[3] Yes, special efforts were made to prevent the return of refugees, including a policy of a quick finger on the trigger in border areas, searches for infiltrators in abandoned and inhabited villages, and brutal expulsions of those who crossed the border.[4] On top of all this, the state used pressures and incentives to encourage Arab citizens to emigrate.* However, both because of international pressure and because of the humanist self-image of the state and humanitarian values of some of Israel's leaders, the state on occasion refrained from deporting infiltrators who succeeded in reuniting with their families.

The battle over Arab lands was a different matter. Here the state unquestionably had the upper hand, and the Arab population achieved little (except, perhaps, for illegal construction on state land, which the authorities were unable to prevent for a variety of reasons). Arab lands were transferred to state ownership in a variety of ways, which have been documented and analyzed in many studies.[5] Most effort went into transferring land belonging to refugees—including both those outside the country and internal refugees—to state ownership. The internal refugees were those Arabs who had been uprooted from their homes and villages but remained within Israel and became its citizens.† Jewish settlements were built on their land. In addition,

---

* The Central Council for Arab Affairs established a special subcommittee to explore "options for the exit of Arabs from the country." Its members were GSS chief Isser Halperin (Harel); KKL official Yosef Weitz; the prime minister's adviser on Arab affairs, Yehoshua Palmon; and the head of the military government, Yitzhak Shani (protocol of the council meeting, 3 July 1952, ISA 56, 22/2214). The policy of encouraging Arab emigration continued in the following decade. In 1965, Shmuel Toledano, then adviser on Arab affairs, estimated that about three thousand Arabs had left Israel with the encouragement of the authorities. He recommended that the heads of the security forces "exhaust all possibilities for quiet emigration of Arabs from Israel." PMO-AAA, Shmuel Toledano, to head of the GSS and others, "Blueprint for the Governmental Policy toward the Arab Minority in Israel," 14 July 1965, ISA 79, 2637/5.

† At least 25,000 of the 160,000 Arabs who were granted Israeli citizenship in 1949 were internal refugees, or IDPs (internally displaced persons). Israel's policy was to sever all legal connections between these refugees and their villages and lands. Refugees who resided outside Israel were termed "absentees," and their land was transferred to the custodian of absentee property; those who remained near at hand

lands were expropriated from Arab citizens for various development projects and for the establishment of two new urban centers in the Galilee—Upper Nazareth and Karmiel. The project of "Judaizing the Galilee" commenced when the state was founded and has continued in various guises to the present day (including, more recently, the establishment and enlargement of small exurban commuter communities called *mitzpim*). There were also projects to Judaize the Negev and to expand Jewish settlement in the Triangle.

The transfer of land to the state or to Zionist agencies was accomplished with the help of Arab collaborators. These people acted, generally consciously, in contradiction of their society's norms and against what Arab nationalists perceived as the supreme interest of the Arabs in Israel—keeping their land.

Palestinian Arabs considered the sale of land to the Jews treasonous as early as the end of the Ottoman period. In the 1930s, the Arab national movement conducted a large-scale publicity campaign against land sellers. As part of the campaign, both Muslim and Christian religious authorities issued rulings forbidding the sale of land to Jews. The Arab revolt of 1936–39 and the period leading up to the decisive war (1946–47) were marked by two waves of murders of agents who mediated land deals between Arabs and Jews. Dozens of Arabs involved in land sales to Jews were killed. Particular targets were the *samasira,* the "land sharks," who made such deals their central occupation. Yet this social-national norm also rejected the sale of individual plots by people who needed money. Such sellers were also considered collaborators with the Zionists—in other words, traitors.[6] This view did not change after Israel came into existence. Nevertheless, as they did during the Mandate period, some Arabs agreed to sell their lands to Zionist agencies or to the Jewish state. They now had an additional justification for doing so—the state could expropriate the land even if they did not sell it.

Not only was direct sale to Jews viewed as treasonous by strict nationalist norms, so was any assistance in the transfer of Arab lands to Jewish hands, especially to Zionist institutions or the state. The mainstream nationalist position saw such activity as abetting dispossession of the Arabs and impeding their struggle to survive in their homeland. But Arabs who chose to help Israel politically or militarily generally did not refrain from helping out with land sales as well. This could be done in a variety of ways. Collaborators

within Israel were termed "present absentees," and their land was treated in a similar way. See Hillel Cohen, "Land, Memory and Identity: The Palestinian Internal Refugees in Israel," *Refuge* 21, no. 2 (April 2003): 6–13.

with social standing were often asked to persuade their acquaintances or people considered subordinate to them to sell parcels of land the state was interested in acquiring. Sometimes they mediated negotiations over compensation between the authorities and landowners whose property had been expropriated. (The state preferred that such people receive compensation, so that they could not sue the state or claim it was impoverishing them.) But there were other ways too. One was to report to the authorities about people who owned land in Israel but who had been, during the 1948 war, in areas under Arab control (whether for reasons of work or study or because they had joined the Arab combat forces). Even if such people managed to return to their homes before the first Israeli census and were thus registered as Israeli citizens, the absentee properties law stated that their presence in an enemy state or in an area under Arab rule after 29 November 1947 mandated the transfer of their land to the custodian of absentee property.[7] Information on such people sometimes arrived in the form of anonymous letters seeking to cause damage to the letters' subjects. Here, for example, is a letter sent to the military government in the Galilee: "I would like to notify you that Mukhtar 'Abd al-Majid . . . traveled to Lebanon before the Israeli conquest. He was a member of the 'Center' [of Qawuqji's Arab Liberation Army] in al-Rameh, founded by the commander Ma'mur Bey. The aforementioned mukhtar fought with the Arab Liberation Army in the battle of al-Sajara. After the Liberation Army took an Israeli soldier prisoner, he was brought to trial before him [the mukhtar] and he sentenced him to death. The soldier sentenced to death was sent to Damascus."[8]

Such letters, sent by opportunistic informers, prompted the custodian of absentee property to seek to obtain the property of such Arabs. The custodian also maintained a network of collaborators who reported to him about absentees and their lands. (He and his staff certainly could not have registered all lands belonging to refugees without inside help.) Other collaborators made trips to neighboring countries (principally to Jordan, to either the West or the East Bank) in order to purchase property from refugees on behalf of KKL or the state. The Israeli officials who sent them on these trips sought to minimize the suits that could be filed by refugees in any future settlement, as well as the Palestinian political claim for the "right of return." The material available for researchers contains no information about the dimensions or success of this phenomenon, but there is no shortage of indications that collaborators purchased property in Israel from refugees residing in Jordan.[9]

In Israel, mukhtars played an important role in the state's acquisition of land in those areas where landownership had never been officially registered.

(The British did not complete the registration of all land before they left in 1948.) In such cases, mukhtars had the legal power to sign documents certifying that a given person had possession of a certain tract of land. This procedure originated toward the end of the Ottoman period, continued during the British Mandate, then became part of Israeli procedure. For example, in 1951 the head of the Department of Minorities Affairs in the Ministry of Interior reported on a mukhtar in Faradis who refused to sign documents that would have enabled the transfer of land to the KKL. He was exceptional. Other mukhtars won plaudits from the Israeli authorities for the assistance they gave. One, a mukhtar from Kufr Qara', had begun collaborating with Zionist institutions during the Mandate period, when he and his father had worked against Arab rebels. After the state was founded, he worked with the GSS, the KKL, and the police. The mukhtar of Barta'a did not actually accomplish the transfer of land from Arabs to the state; he worked more indirectly. Barta'a's location on the border between Israel and Jordan (the armistice line of 1949 actually cut through the village, dividing it into Israeli and Jordanian sectors) turned it into an unofficial crossing point between the two countries. The mukhtar on the Israeli side helped Israeli Arabs who had sold their land in crossing into the West Bank. In exchange, he received state support in retaining his position.[10]

Undermining the popular struggle against the sale or expropriation of Arab land was another role of collaborators, which will be discussed below. Still others were told to prevent the return of refugees to their villages. There were also internal refugees who were coaxed into accepting the government's offers to resettle them. Such actions divided the refugee community, and some Arabs viewed those involved as treasonous.

COLLABORATORS AGAINST THE RIGHT OF RETURN

Muhammad (Abu Shafiq) Buqa'i, of the village of Damun, in the Zevulun Valley, was a land dealer who helped the KKL buy land in the north during the Mandate period. His son, Shafiq, assisted him. Back then, they summed up their worldview to their KKL counterpart: "It will be much better for us [the Arabs] with the Jews than without the Jews. We can only learn from them. They have knowledge and they have money and they can develop [the country], and we can learn and live with them and coexist. But there are politicians who incite the people. That's all. That's the source of all our troubles."[11] Such assertions were made by many collaborators. Some sincerely believed what they said. The foundation of their conception was disregard for the conflict between the two peoples. If the national component were removed from the equation, the Arabs would benefit, they believed. The problem with this view was that the Zionists did not share it with them, since the Zionist project was manifestly a nationalist one. In any case, KKL agents appreciated Abu Shafiq's approach and his actions. They believed him to be a man of great dedication, whose help they could rely on and who deserved their help.

Palestinian nationalist activists did not see Abu Shafiq positively, to say the least. In the autumn of 1946, he was one of the victims of a wave of murders of land sharks. He was felled only a few days after meeting Yirmiyahu Feiglin, a KKL lawyer, to provide him with information in connection with a complicated legal proceeding over landownership. Abu Shafiq's son, Shafiq (Abu-'Abdu) Buqa'i, carried on his father's work with the KKL. He also tried to avenge his father but without success.[12]

The war began about a year later. Shafiq Buqa'i abandoned Damun, as did all its other inhabitants. Most of them found refuge in nearby villages within Israel, but when the war ended they were not allowed to return to their homes and their land. Their property was handed over to the custodian of absentee property, as was the property of other Arabs, who became internal refugees, or "present absentees." But Shafiq Buqa'i fared a bit better than his fellow villagers. Because of the assistance he had rendered to the Jews prior to and during the war, the KKL offered him a home and large tracts of farmland, in Sha'ab, a village that had been abandoned by most of its inhabitants (who themselves became internal refugees). Sha'ab's inhabitants were refused permission to return to their village as part of the general policy regarding internal refugees, but in this case the refusal was also a way of paying them back for the militant stand they had taken during the war. The village had been the home base of a unit commanded by a local hero called Abu-Is'af, one of the more effective forces that fought the Jews in the Galilee.

In the first years after the state was founded, many of these refugees refused to be settled on land that was not theirs. They were not only being considerate of the original owners, who were refugees like them, they also feared that accepting resettlement would negate their rights to their own property. Shafiq Buqa'i showed no such concerns. Along with his brother Sami, who was appointed Sha'ab's new mukhtar, he received a lease on most of the village's land. Like other Arabs with close ties to the Israeli regime, the two brothers received arms from the state and were told that their job was to prevent those former inhabitants of Sha'ab who remained in Israel (principally in Majd al-Krum and Sakhnin) from returning to their homes and fields. Since most of the refugees' land was now the brothers', the state's interest—preventing the return of the refugees—became their personal interest as well.[13]

The Buqa'i brothers succeeded only in part. Little by little, Sha'ab's families began to return to their village and were registered by the Ministry of Interior as its residents.* In 1950, about two hundred (out of about two thousand) of the original inhabitants were already living in the village, as were several dozen members of the Buqa'i family (not all of whom were supporters of Shafiq; some were actually closer to the Communists). To halt the ongoing trickle of returnees, in April 1951 the military government declared the village a closed military area, and the Refugee Rehabilitation Authority produced a plan according to which internal refugees from throughout the Galilee would be settled in Sha'ab—with the exception of its original residents. As a result, more refugee families from Damun, Birwe, and Mi'ar were brought in. They were augmented, beginning in 1953, by families evacuated from two villages in the demilitarized zone on the Syrian border, in the Hula Valley—Kirad al-Baqqara and Kirad al-Ghannama. Each family was granted twenty-five *dunams* (6.25 acres) of farmland as well as five *dunams* (1.25 acres) of olive groves.

The original inhabitants of Sha'ab did not sit by quietly when they saw strangers being settled on their land. They pressed the new settlers to abandon the village, making two claims. On the personal level, they said it was their land and they had never abandoned their claim to it, so no one else had the right to live there. On the national level, they argued, the new settlers were being used by Israel to dispossess other refugees, an unacceptable deed. As a result, most of the Arabs brought from the two Hula Valley villages refused to remain in Sha'ab, both because of the pressure and because they wanted to return to their homes.[14] In the meantime, the original Sha'abians took legal action to ensure that those among them who had returned to their village be allowed to remain there. They were represented by none other than Muhammad Nimer al-Hawwari, who was at the time trying to position himself as a representative of Arab interests in Israel. He filed a complaint with the police against the Buqa'i brothers and submitted a petition to the Supreme Court as well. The village itself split into two camps. On one side

---

* This is one example of how Arab citizens in Israel were able to find cracks in the legal and bureaucratic walls erected by the state and to exploit them for their own benefit. These cracks sometimes had their origin in disputes among Israeli officials or in competition among different state actors; sometimes they were merely the product of oversight.

were the original inhabitants and their supporters, including the evacuees from the Hula Valley; on the other were the Buqa'i brothers, part of their extended family, and internal refugees from Mi'ar who settled in the village. Violence broke out in the village. One incident was described by refugees from Damun and Mi'ar (supporters of the Buqa'i brothers) in a letter they sent to the police:

> [It was] a huge mass assault by all the people of 'Arab al-Huli [the Hula Valley evacuees], men, women, and children, on every person they found from the village of Mi'ar, and they beat them senseless. The assault was so fierce and serious that the people from Mi'ar had to flee the village wounded and bleeding and hide themselves among the olive trees.
>
> This mass assault and huge attack was no coincidence but was plotted and programmed in advance with malicious intent. The plotters and incendiaries of the assault and injury of these inhabitants are the former inhabitants of Sha'ab who have returned to their village. These people labor day and night at all kinds of agitation among the different inhabitants of the village to bring about dissension and fighting, using these means to chase out the new inhabitants who settled in the village and get them to leave the place, and by doing so "to purge the village," in their words and to bring back all the old inhabitants. . . . They have had considerable success with this most recent incident, when they created an atmosphere so oppressive for these inhabitants that they have preferred to leave the village rather than inhale the atmosphere of endless conflict and hostility, and in addition their lives are in danger. . . .
>
> One of the people who stands out in this incitement is Nimer Khalil Hussein Ahmad. We believe that the authorities know very well about this man's past, especially during the incidents of 1936–39, together with his extremist brothers in the Galilee. This man is fanning the fires of hatred for everything that is Zionist. This man served as a member of the terrorists' court and afterward was among the leaders of the Movement for the Defense of Sha'ab under the leadership of the notorious Abu-Is'af. In the end this man left the country, went to Lebanon, and enlisted in the Liberation Army. After a long period the Israeli government allowed this man to return to Israel in the hope that he would collaborate with the authorities, but the man remains a rebel and continues to commit his nefarious deeds in secret. . . . He is the man who proclaimed that the Galilee is an Arab area and must remain such.[15]

The letter's authors knew how to get the authorities' attention. They understood how seriously Israel took the refugees' efforts to return to their homes, and they were well aware that officials often treated Arabs in accordance with the level of militancy they had displayed during the Mandate period. The authors made no reference to their own exploitation in the government's land policy. Apparently, they viewed the government's policies as a force majeure.

But the Mi'ar refugees did not wait for the authorities to intervene. In November 1954, another brawl broke out in the village's olive groves, and this time the refugees from Mi'ar had the upper hand. A band of them surrounded Nimer Khalil and clubbed his head and body until he collapsed and lost consciousness. He died two days later at Haifa's Rambam Hospital.

This entire time, Buqa'i controlled most of the village's land and employed the rest of the village's inhabitants in cultivating it. According to complaints they lodged with the police, Buqa'i took advantage of his close ties with the authorities and the dependence of the villagers and exploited them mercilessly. The chief of the Acre police station, Yitzhak Avneri, summed up the situation:

> This Shafiq has taken good advantage of the authorities' confidence in him, has brought into the village various elements who have served him loyally, and he has ruled over the inhabitants without mercy. Among those who have come in are former inhabitants of Sha'ab and refugees from Damun, Birwe, and Mi'ar. Shafiq has employed them in cultivating the land he has leased and paid them an extremely low wage and has treated them like slaves. The people of Sha'ab would not stand for this treatment and began to organize under the leadership of the murdered man, Nimer Ahmad [Hussein] Khalil, who opposed him fiercely and fought him in all ways, both by publicizing what he was doing to the villagers of Sha'ab and by informing the authorities about how [Shafiq] has extorted money from all the village's inhabitants. This open war divided the inhabitants into two. The people from Sha'ab, Birwe, and some of the people from Mi'ar took the side of Nimer Khalil Ahmad, while the people of Damun and most of the refugees from Mi'ar supported Shafiq Abu-'Abdu. At every opportunity the rivals have tried to subdue each other, until in the end it was the lot of the leader of the people of Sha'ab to be killed.[16]

The conflict did not end there. In June 1955, several Sha'abians broke into Shafiq Buqa'i's home, cast him out with his belongings, and took possession of the house. The house's original owner, Rashid Hussein, moved his things in. This occurred while Hussein was conducting a lawsuit against the state for ownership of the house. The director of the Ministry of Agriculture's

Northern District was alarmed and called the police in to evict the squatters.[17] Even though they did not succeed in remaining in the house, the Sha'ab refugees demonstrated their determination, and later other former inhabitants were also allowed to return to the village.

Thus, internal refugees' right of return to their homes was another arena of conflict between the collaborators—and the state, which encouraged them—and the nationalists. The nationalists' victory in Sha'ab was a rare one, owing its success to three factors: the refugees were located not far from their village, they demonstrated exceptional resolve, and their homes had not been razed, as was the case in many other villages whose inhabitants had been displaced. The result was that the authorities, and Buqa'i, eventually had to give in.

Like other people who collaborated with the state, Buqa'i did not limit himself to land issues. In the mid-1950s, the police investigated a serious crime committed in Acre during the 1948 war—the murder of four Jewish employees of the electric company by Arab combatants. The investigation was opened when a resident of a village near Acre told the police that his neighbor had been one of the murderers. The police looked into whether the perpetrators could be brought to trial. The offense was committed during one of the battles over this region, on 18 March 1948, a day after the Haganah ambushed an Arab Liberation Army convoy of weapons and ammunition on its way from Lebanon to Haifa. Arab officers were killed in the attack, and the bodies were taken to Acre by the ALA. That same day, Arab forces in Acre severed the coastal road that connected Haifa, south of Acre, with Nahariya, to its north, thus cutting off Nahariya's Jews from the rest of Jewish-controlled territory. Acre's Arabs also cut the major lines that supplied electricity from the city's power plant to the surrounding region. The British, still officially responsible for maintaining order, called in the electric company to restore the supply of electricity to its nearby bases. A team of workers led by a Jewish technician, Yeshayahu Halevitz, set out for Acre in an armored vehicle, accompanied by two British half-tracks. Halevitz was well-acquainted with Acre's mayor, Husni Khleifi, and assumed that if there were any problems the mayor would help. But ambushers who lay in wait at the entrance to Acre opened fire with rifles and machine guns from several directions. One of the half-tracks managed to break free, but the other one and the armored car were hit. The British soldiers they carried, as well as the electricity workers, were shot to death. Arab guerrillas extricated the bodies (and, according to some witnesses, mutilated them), then drove the armored car around Acre for a victory ride. A British force that arrived a short time later recovered the bodies. An initial investigation was conducted by the Israeli authorities toward the end of the war, but the investigators were unable to identify the murderers. The case was reopened in 1956, after the police received new information. Buqaʻi, as a veteran collaborator who was active in this area during the war, was asked to collect information about the attackers.[18]*

Buqaʻi, who served as a police informer, a KKL agent, and a brake on the return of refugees to their homes, was held in extremely low esteem by some Galilean Arabs. On top of that was his maltreatment of his farmworkers. Yet these circumstances paint only a partial picture of the man and his actions. To complete it, we need to look at what happened in the Galilean village of Majd al-Krum when it was taken by Israeli forces in the autumn of 1948. At the end of that October, IDF forces began moving toward the village as part of the Hiram operation. An Arab Liberation Army unit deployed there retreated to Lebanon. Before their retreat, the unit's commander, an Iraqi officer named Jasem, gathered the village's inhabitants in its central square, around the village well, and proposed that they not abandon the village but instead offer to surrender to Jewish officers whom they knew. Aware of what had happened to Arabs who had left their homes in previous IDF operations, a group of villagers sent word to an Israeli intelligence officer from Nahariya, Haim Auerbach, whom they had known for years. (In fact, a few inhabitants of the village had once defended him when he was attacked near Acre.) The two sides met and reached an agreement, under which the village would surrender and its inhabitants would hand over their weapons. Auerbach, for his part, pledged in the name of the IDF that the villagers would not be harmed. Accordingly, IDF forces entered the village, collected the villagers' weapons, and Majd al-Krum opened a new page in its history.

But a week later, on 6 November, another IDF unit approached the village from the east, not knowing that it had already been taken. After a brief exchange of gunfire between the approaching unit and the one deployed in the village, both forces realized their error. The new unit entered the village,

* The version of the event told by Acre's Arab refugees differs in some respects, as might be expected, and offers an explanation of why the workers were attacked. One of them, Salim Hindi, recounted that the electric company workers were attacked because they tried to drive through Acre on their way to repair the electric line to Nahariya, without doing anything to restore the flow of electricity to the Arab city. This angered the inhabitants, who attacked the convoy. Hindi did not address the mutilation of the bodies and added that two days later the Jews carried out a counterattack, in which six of Acre's Arabs were killed. For details, see refugee interviews, *Journal of Palestine Studies* 18, no. 1 (1988): 162.

relieving the one that had first occupied it. As was the practice in every village after IDF occupation, the commanding officer of the new unit rounded up the inhabitants and ordered them to produce all their weapons within half an hour. Even before this deadline had been reached, the officer ordered the demolition of the home of one villager by the name of Abu-Ma'yuf, in order to demonstrate that he was serious. A short while later, the soldiers picked out five villagers, blindfolded them, and shot them to death. They immediately blindfolded another five. At that moment, Shafiq (Abu-'Abdu) Buqa'i appeared and requested, in the name of Haim Auerbach, that the killing stop. The officer removed the blindfolds from the five men and set them free.

So the "traitor" had also saved the lives of these five men and perhaps of others in the village. The story in Majd al-Krum was that Buqa'i was married to a Jewish woman and that his sons served in the IDF. The Israeli-Palestinian historian 'Adel Manna', a native of Majd al-Krum who heard the story recounted above from his father, added that "the village's inhabitants breathed in relief and never forgot Abu-'Abdu's honorable stand in the spring square, despite his treason and collaboration with the Jews during the war." [19] This same duality is apparent in many collaborators. They frequently took advantage of their power and connections to further their personal interests, but sometimes they also used them for the benefit of their communities or their people.

Sha'ab was not the only place where refugees from the nationalist camp battled for their land against collaborators. Such struggles were a constant feature of the 1950s and 1960s. In 1954, the Ministry of Agriculture began parceling out the land that had belonged to Damun, in the Zevulun Valley, to refugees from other places. Just as Damun's refugees were resettled in Sha'ab while the refugees from Sha'ab had to find shelter in Sakhnin and Majd al-Krum, so was Damun's land leased to other refugees, the condition being that they not be the village's original inhabitants. The Communist Party secretary in Tamra, Ibrahim Fahmawi, himself an internal refugee who had originally lived in the village of Umm al-Zeinat, went out to the fields with a group of refugees from Damun in an attempt to prevent the reallocation of their property. Several of the original owners decided to plow their plots in a gesture of reasserting their rights to the land. Most of them belonged to the Buqa'i family—in other words, relatives of Shafiq, although their politics differed from his. The police arrested ten of them. Furthermore, in order to crush the original landowners entirely, the authorities found refugees who

Figure 11. Displaced. Supper in the village of Iqrit, before the uprooting of its inhabitants: (from left to right) an Israeli soldier, a foreign reporter, and the mukhtar, 1948. Photograph courtesy Israeli Government Press Office.

agreed to accept the Damun lands from the government. Under the circumstances, the Damun refugees had little choice but to give up.[20]

Indeed, finding internal refugees who were willing to act against the positions advocated by the nationalists and against the interests of the refugees as a whole was a fundamental building block of Israel's security agencies when it came to land. When the Galilee Regional Committee on Arab Affairs (comprising senior representatives of the military government, the police, the GSS, and the office of the prime minister's adviser on Arab affairs) met to discuss the refusal of refugees from Saffuri, the largest Arab village in the Lower Galilee, to settle elsewhere, its members proposed pursuing "directed contact with a number of influential refugees, to break their opposition by granting privileges (in the amount or quality of land)." In other words, they sought to buy collaborators. The same tactic was used in other places, such as Kafr Kanna and Shibli, where the police lent support to a resident who agreed to lease land belonging to refugees from the village, in contradiction of the position taken by the rest of his Bedouin tribe. When his opponents uprooted fifty almond tree saplings he had planted on the leased land, the police rushed to his defense.[21]

The authorities had no trouble finding refugees who could be enticed to accept its offers—whether out of weakness, a lack of confidence that the struggle could succeed, an inability to provide for their families without land to farm, or simply because they were unmoved by nationalist ideology. The refugee community had to face up to the problem. For example, the refugees from Bir'am were promised when evacuated by the IDF that they would be allowed to return to their village in the near future. As a result, they refused to accept all offers to resettle permanently elsewhere and appealed several times to the Supreme Court to allow them back. They found shelter in the village of Jish, not far from their homes, but considered their stay in Jish to be temporary. At the end of the 1950s, the state built housing projects for the refugees in Jish, with the aim of resettling refugees from Bir'am and other villages in the upper Galilee there. But the Bir'am refugees refused to occupy the new apartments, so the buildings stood empty for a long time. A refugee from Sa'sa' who also lived in Jish and worked as a teacher (not a trivial fact, since it meant that he was dependent on the government for his livelihood) was persuaded by the authorities to take an apartment in the new project. One night in July 1959, when he came home, he found eight pistol bullets on the stairs. He took this to be a threat against him for having agreed to live in the project. The same thing happened twice more that month. For the police, "it was clear beyond any doubt that the bullets were put there each time by people from Bir'am, and apparently under the direction of the community's leaders, in order to scare the people of Bir'am," so that they would not be tempted to do the same. The police officer who investigated the case knew what was going on in Jish and believed, correctly, that while "leaving bullets [was] an Arab warning of an impending murder," the perpetrators did not actually intend to carry out the threat. They sought only to intimidate the Bir'am refugees by scaring the teacher and would not use violence in the future, either.[22]

Lack of solidarity on the part of the other refugees in Jish and its environs was not the only problem the people of Bir'am had to face. In addition to symbolizing the Palestinian national struggle, they also endured long periods of tension with the permanent residents of Jish, where they now lived. For example, not only did many in Jish feel that the influx of refugees had cramped their living space, but they also frowned on the protest activity pursued by the Bir'am refugees, fearing that it would arouse the authorities' ire against them as well. On top of this, several families in Jish had been given refugee land by the authorities. Once in a while the tension turned into violence. When a valve in the village's water system was vandalized, the Jish natives were convinced that Bir'am refugees were the culprits. The

Bir'am refugees tried to prevent the native Jish villagers from working the refugee land they had received, and a fistfight broke out. The villagers asked the police to intervene, describing the Bir'am activists as "a gang for the disturbance of the peace, inciting the inhabitants of Jish through hostile activities." They went so far as to state, "The Mandate government and Israeli government know us as lovers of peace and very far from being involved in any political problems."[23]

Their statement expressed precisely the attitude that the government wanted to foster among the Arabs—political passivity and granting priority to private interest over the common Arab national interest. It is hardly surprising, then, that the Bir'am refugees viewed some of the Jish villagers as collaborators with the authorities. The extravagant reception that Jish prepared for officials of the Ministry of Minorities only three months after the inhabitants of Bir'am had been forced to leave their village reinforced this feeling. A year later, Bir'am activists sent threatening letters to "the traitors who, for lucre, sold themselves and their people." A particular target of their attacks was the priest Atanes 'Aqel, who maintained good relations with Yitzhak Ben-Zvi and other Zionist leaders. 'Aqel did not cut the figure of a leader ("They see him as a slightly cracked scholar," a police officer commented), but in the depths of their despair, the Bir'am refugees held him almost directly responsible for the disaster they had undergone. 'Aqel had preserved an ancient Jewish tradition that Queen Esther was buried on Bir'am's land, and he encouraged Jewish organizations to promote the gravesite. Some of the refugees believed that this was the reason they were not being allowed to return to their homes. But they also viewed Jish's permanent residents, especially the local leadership, as people who supported the authorities rather than the just claims of their Arab brethren.[24]

As a matter of fact, only a few years later, the people of Jish also grew discontented with their eccentric cleric. 'Aqel had approached Rabbi Zilberman of Safed and reminded him that the tombs of the Tannaitic sages Shem'ayya and Avtalion were located in Jish—which in the Roman period had been a Jewish town called Gush Halav. Zilberman acted quickly. The land around the tomb was expropriated and fenced in, and the tomb was renovated.[25] The original villagers now vilified 'Aqel, but they did not see this as a common cause with the Bir'am refugees. On the contrary.

Just before Israel's fourth national election, in October 1959, tension between the different communities in Jish reached new highs. A group of Bir'am refugees joined Herut, a right-wing Zionist party headed by Menachem Begin. Herut had publicly declared its support for the right of the Bir'am refugees to return to their village, but the refugees also wanted to issue a challenge to Mapai, the ruling party, by supporting Herut, the leading opposition party. Three nights before the election, the Hebrew letter *het,* Herut's symbol, was painted on the village church, on private homes, and on the housing projects that had been built for the refugees, which they had refused to enter. The police were called in. As far as the authorities were concerned, Arabs who supported Herut were almost as dangerous as Arabs who supported the Communists. The investigation found that some of the graffiti had been painted by Bir'am refugees but that the original villagers in Jish had gotten together and painted many of the others, in order to incriminate the refugees. A few weeks later, more graffiti appeared in the village. In addition to the letter *het,* the graffiti now included a swastika and a lengthy invective: "The military government is an ass, down with the military governor, the governor's mother's cunt, we'll fuck collaborators with the police." The police were unable to find out who had painted the slogans,[26] but the tension between collaborators and nationalists could no longer be swept under the rug.

The land issue thus became another arena in which collaborators and opponents of the government constantly fought. In the larger picture, Israeli institutions benefited; tensions within and among communities helped them to enhance the oversight and control system they had instituted, as well as to increase the number of Jews living in Arab areas.

COLLABORATORS FOR EXPROPRIATION

Soon after the war, the Israeli government embarked on a policy of settling more Jews in the Galilee. The formerly mixed cities of Tiberias and Safed became exclusively Jewish. Acre, formerly an entirely Arab city, became a mixed Arab-Jewish city. A new Jewish town, Ma'alot, was built next to the Arab village of Tarshiha (the evacuation of which was not completed); the new town of Kiryat Shmonah was built on the site of the demolished Arab village of Khalsa. These towns, as well as Hatzor HaGlilit, built in the eastern Upper Galilee, and Shlomi, built in its west, were meant to take in the Jewish refugees and immigrants who arrived from Europe and the Islamic world during the 1950s. Most of the land they were built on was that of refugees, including internal refugees. So was most of the land of the moshavim, semi-cooperative farming villages that were established throughout the Galilee during this same period. The state did not, however, make do with just the absentees' land. As part of their master plan for spreading Jewish settlement throughout the Galilee, the authorities also decided to build two additional

Jewish cities, Upper Nazareth and Karmiel. For this purpose, the government expropriated land from Arabs who were not refugees and who lived on their own land in Israel.

In response to the first expropriation of land for the construction of Upper Nazareth, in 1955, the affected Arab landowners sought recourse in the Supreme Court. The government told the court that the land would be used to build a government office center and housing for the civil servants who would work there and that it had the power to choose the location of the office center as it saw fit, even without the consent of the landowners, who would be compensated. The justices accepted this claim; in any case, even before the court ruling some of the landowners had commenced negotiations with the state over compensation.[27] In the second large wave of expropriations in Nazareth, in 1964, most of the landowners, knowing the Supreme Court's fundamental position, negotiated compensation without appeals. Muhammad Hawwari served as their attorney.[28] Protests against the expropriations were relatively limited, and the Hebrew press stressed the minimal damage suffered by the Arabs, as well as the need to "conquer" or "occupy" the Galilee. Nazareth, declared the editor of the daily *Yedi'ot Aharonot,* would no longer be *Judenrein*—the term the Nazis had used for an area with no Jewish presence.[29]

Arab popular attitude toward the land expropriations from the villages of Nahf, Dir al-Asad, and Bi'neh for the purpose of building Karmiel was different. At first the opponents took the same step that their compatriots in Nazareth had. They petitioned the Supreme Court, demanding that the state build the new Jewish city without expropriating private land. But when they saw that the court was not amenable to their plea, they began to organize popular action. They called on all the villages' inhabitants to unite in opposing the program and to reject the government's compensation offer. Some Jewish Israeli groups also joined in the protests.[30]

Here the security forces and KKL entered the picture. Their aim was to undermine the Jewish-Arab front, as well as the solidarity of the villages. As in other places, they ignored the committee set up by the Arab inhabitants and conducted individual negotiations with the landowners. In addition, they leaked reports, some accurate and some not entirely, to the media in order to besmirch the reputations of the struggle's leaders.

A February 1963 article in *Ma'ariv,* written by journalist Shmuel Segev (a former Israeli intelligence officer), is a good example. It began as follows:

In the state of Israel's brief history, a kind of "tradition" has already emerged in the relations between the state and its Arab citizens in the issue of development projects in mixed areas. Immediately after an intention of carrying out a popular development program is discovered, the Communists and the Nasserist National Front commence a fierce propaganda campaign, whose purpose is to make the Israeli Arabs rebel against the country's lawful government. But when the government displays resolve and is not deterred by the threats, the agitators push to the front of the line and take the compensation promised to them even before the incitement campaign began.[31]

This paragraph makes three assertions. First, it depicts the struggle of the Arab farmers against the expropriation of their land as a fight against progress and development. Second, it presents the campaign as a rebellion against the Israeli state under the sponsorship of President Gamal 'Abd al-Nasser of Egypt, the ultimate enemy. Third, it presents the leaders as being the first to ask for compensation, in order to create distrust between the campaign's leaders and their constituencies. Segev went on to interview KKL official Yosef Nahmani, a former member of the prestate Jewish guard force Hashomer and a KKL agent before and after 1948, who was in charge of negotiations with the Arab landowners in this area. Nahmani said that dozens of Arabs had already begun parleying with him, including some from the family of Shukri al-Khazen, one of the leaders of the struggle. Here, too, the implication was clear—the leaders were giving priority to their personal interests. To reinforce this image, Nahmani was depicted as a seeker of justice, in sharp contrast to the disreputable Arab leadership: "The redeemer of the Hula Valley's land, Ein Gev, and the Beit She'an Valley, who has earned a reputation among Israel's Arabs as an honest man, is prepared to fight the authorities, if need be, if he is persuaded of the justice of the claim of any specific Arab citizen.... Despite his gray hairs, he remains strong, galloping daily over the Galilee's mountains, 'sniffing out' land designated for redemption, and tirelessly expanding the land available for Jewish settlement."*

Another of the article's purposes was to undercut the sympathy (limited in any case) that the Arab villagers enjoyed in the Jewish public. The Communists called their effort to enlist Israeli Jews in the protest the Mercy

---

* Nahmani was clearly intent on Judaizing the Galilee. What is less clear is to what extent he won the confidence of the Arab public and to what extent he refrained from excessive use of his powers. Inhabitants of 'Arrabe and Sakhnin complained as early as January 1949 that, when Nahmani tried to purchase land from their villages for KKL, he sent them a warning about refusing to sell, via one of their fellow villagers: "The army will take control of your land and transfer the inhabitants over the border." Inhabitants of 'Arrabe to the Ministry of Minorities, January 1949, ISA 49, 302/114.

Campaign. In response, the newspaper took it upon itself to reveal the party's "true face." "While the Communist Party seeks to preach brotherhood to the Jewish street, it rides roughshod through the Galilean villages, and its activists 'predict' the end of the Israeli regime. . . . The Communist Party also encourages poets to compose murderous, inflammatory poetry," it reported to its readers. *Ma'ariv* informed its readers that the Arab farmers opposed the expropriation only because they were being incited, since their livelihoods would not be harmed. Of the 5,000 *dunams* (1,250 acres) of land designated for the construction of Karmiel, only 2,634 *dunams* belonged to the villagers, and only 300 *dunams* of these were arable, *Ma'ariv* argued.

To top off his propaganda piece, Segev spoke to collaborators, who pronounced the expropriation legitimate and portrayed its opponents as unconscionable agitators. The article quoted one of the mukhtars of Bi'neh to the effect that the establishment of Karmiel would benefit his village. Segev also referred to a man named 'Ali, from the same village, who was stabbed by unknown assailants after reaching an agreement with Nahmani about an exchange of land. "The stabber walks free," proclaimed a subhead to the article, "because the inhabitants of the village refuse to testify against him."[32]

Coincidentally, or perhaps not, a conference on the media was organized by the Communists in Nazareth in July of that same year. The speakers stressed that the Hebrew press "draws its information from the dark apparatus"—that is, the GSS—and that its reports were therefore "the direct opposite of the truth."[33] Whether they had Segev's article in mind is not clear, but it can serve as an archetype of the kind of inaccurate information channeled to the public by elements in the security services and the prime minister's office. (A large part of the piece's claims appeared in a press release put out by the latter.)[34]

A detailed report written for the chief of police of the Northern District casts the events in Bi'neh in an entirely different light. The mukhtar, who in the article appeared as the voice of reason, did not fare so well in the report. It described him as a man who had been "bought as an informer and [who] acted out of a desire for self-aggrandizement." 'Ali, the stabbing victim, was hardly an innocent. The police investigation revealed that his stabbing was not at all clearly related to the land deal. Other possibilities were that he was attacked as part of a family feud or that the land deal was indeed the cause but not attributable to any nationalist issue. Some members of his family preferred to exchange the land the state wanted for other land, instead of money, while others suspected that 'Ali had pocketed all the proceeds rather than splitting them with his brothers. "Doubtlessly a number of factors are mixed up in this quarrel," the report concluded. "Whatever the case, our impression was that 'Ali . . . exaggerates the importance of the land sale and is taking advantage of that to gain the sympathy and assistance of the authorities in his feud." The Galilee Regional Committee also theorized that the background to the stabbing was not necessarily the sale of land to the KKL.[35] But the press—and the public—was given a different story.

One leader of the anti-expropriation struggle was Uri Davis, a Jewish-Israeli pacifist and conscientious objector. In April 1964, he organized a protest march from Acre to the village of Dir al-Asad but was unable to create a mass movement. Only three other people showed up, two of them foreigners. Before they even left Acre they were surrounded by Jewish passersby, who ripped up their placards and beat them up. The demonstrators persisted and reached the village. But their reception in Dir al-Asad was lukewarm at best. Some of the Arabs thought they were government agents who had come to test the village's mood. That is hardly surprising; Israeli intelligence had penetrated the Israeli Arab community deeply, and it made use of journalists, businessmen, and whoever else had contact with Arabs. This created an atmosphere of permanent apprehension that anyone from inside or outside the village might be a spy.

Davis did not give up. He staged a hunger strike in front of the prime minister's office, organized petitions against government takeovers of Arab land, and in the summer of 1964 moved to Dir al-Asad, the village that had lost the most land in this round of expropriation. In October of that year he organized an olive harvest on the expropriated land, inviting Arabs and Jews to take part. The military governor issued an administrative detention order, and a police detachment arrived in the village to arrest Davis. He refused to go, and three policemen had to pick him up and carry him from his house to the police wagon. The arrest seems to have won him the confidence of the villagers. He continued to organize pockets of opposition to expropriations and was arrested again. This second arrest ratcheted up the level of the resistance movement. A group of teenage boys from Nazareth set out on their bicycles bearing banners reading "Free Uri Davis" and "Dismantle the Military Government." The police arrested ten of them and opened criminal dossiers in their names. The police had more trouble dealing with a protest conducted on the expropriated land, which was labeled "Area 9," in February 1965. Hundreds of people participated, including well-known artists, writers, performers, and public figures, such as Uri Avneri, Nathan Yellin-Mor, Yitzhak Danziger, Dahn Ben-Amotz, Uri Zohar, Amos Kenan, Yigal Tumarkin, and Amos Mokdi.[36]

The use of collaborators by the military government and police force to stymie the demonstrators is no less interesting than the protest itself. Collaborators from the affected villages acted in real time to provide the security forces with updates about the protestors and their plans. Their work was especially notable regarding the olive harvest plan, scheduled for Saturday, 17 October 1964. The action was meant to exemplify Jewish-Arab solidarity and to protest the expropriation of the villages' farmland. Davis and his colleagues coordinated their moves with local activists (made up of mostly, but not only, Communists) and planned the activity together with them. Ranged on the other side were the police, military government, and the GSS, which also used their connections in the villages and their informers to keep abreast of developments.

Reports flowed into the police and the GSS as soon as Davis and his colleagues began to organize the olive harvest protest. An informer named Salah told the police that a group of Jews (members of the Young Communist League) was about to arrive in the village and would be staying in his brother's house. Other reports made it clear to the security forces that the event would be much larger than the small demonstrations to which they had been accustomed. They decided to arrest Davis. After the arrest, an informer for the GSS's Unit 149 reported that the joint olive harvest had not been canceled and that several young locals had been sent to the village to track the police presence. On Friday, 16 October, activists began showing up in the disputed olive groves. Collaborators followed them. An informer named Jaber reported to the police that two Jewish teenagers, Emmanuel Bergman and Haim Hanegbi, had arrived in the village, looking for Davis. Jaber knew that after they were told that Davis had been arrested, they walked over to the neighboring village, Bi'neh. A local informer told policemen who went to search for the boys there that they were in the home of Hanna Elias, the village's Communist Party secretary. The police arrested Bergman and Hanegbi.

Informers also joined the group of activists that organized the demonstration, sniffing out plans and passing them on to their operators. An informer named Suleiman overheard a conversation about what routes the harvesters planned to take and passed the information on to the police, who set up barriers. They were unable to seal off the area entirely, however, so about thirty people managed to reach Dir al-Asad. Informers mixed with them as well. One reported to the police about conversations among the arrivals; another, on the speech that the village's Communist Party secretary made to the visitors and their hosts. The demonstrators proceeded to the olive grove, and villagers brought them food, cigarettes, and blankets. One informer prepared a list of the villagers who aided the demonstrators and noted what assistance each one provided.[37]*

In other words, the villagers were not united in the campaign to retain their land. Some protested, either by organizing or by participating or both. Others remained aloof. Still others helped the police arrest protestors. What motivated each of these three groups? There were serious reasons for taking each of these positions. The protestors felt they had been the victims of an injustice. Land had been taken from them, so why should they not protest? The greater part of this group belonged to political organizations that provided support—mostly the Communist Party, but also Mapam and other groups—making it easier for them to take action.

The second group's passivity seems to have grown out of a lack of confidence in the efficacy of protest. They felt that Israel and the security forces that represented the state in the field were so powerful that the Arabs had no prospect for preventing them from carrying out their program. That being the case, the aloof people concluded that it was better not to take part in a protest against the authorities. Such opposition could harm them in the short range (through arrests) and in the long range (by exacerbating their relations with the authorities, making transit and work permits and other such essential papers harder to obtain). The vital role of this sense of helplessness in shaping the political culture of Israel's Arab citizens should not be underestimated.

Although the collaborators did not believe in protest either, they were not passive. Their recognition that the regime had the power advantage was the central motive behind their choice to work with its representatives in the field. One could argue that their work with the authorities was their way of breaking free of their sense of helplessness—a justification that has come up in my conversations with informers. But this was not the only reason. One can also argue that they sabotaged the campaign pursued by their fellow villagers because they supported the expropriations and truly believed, as they argued, that the establishment of Karmiel would bring them benefits.

---

* The informers were not only Arabs. A reporter for the newspaper *Haaretz* by the name of Yehuda Ariel attended Davis's hearing in the magistrate's court in Acre. During a recess he overheard a conversation between Davis and a correspondent for the Mapam party newspaper, *Al ha-Mishmar,* who was a Davis supporter. Davis told the correspondent what the protestors planned to do next. "Yehuda reported this [conversation to the police] after the hearing, and as a result Uri was arrested again and a new file was opened against him in the Acre station," the police report stated. SB Acre to SB Northern District, "Karmiel—Uri Davis's Activities," 19 October 1964, ISA 79, 291/7.

But this was a tenuous belief, given that the loss of land was immediate and the prospect of future profit was hazy at best. Furthermore, the struggle's leaders were not opposed to the construction of Karmiel per se. In fact, they submitted an alternative proposal, according to which the town would be built at an alternative location, where the loss of land to the local Arabs would be minimal. So why did the collaborators undermine the struggle? Some of them opposed Arab nationalist groups for reasons connected to internal politics. They wanted so badly to cause harm to nationalists that they helped the authorities. Others were professional collaborators who viewed themselves as part of the state system. They owed their livelihoods to state organizations, and their relations with their overseers made it difficult for them to say no when they were asked to report on their neighbors and family members. Under these circumstances, they could not pick and choose among the assignments they were given. So they acted to undermine the struggle's leaders and its effectiveness. The result was that Karmiel was built on their villages' lands, rather than on the alternative site proposed by the Committee for the Defense of the Shaghur Lands, only two kilometers from the disputed site.*

"WE WILL CUT OFF THE TRAITORS' HEADS"

Collaborators who helped Israel expropriate land, like collaborators in other fields, were unpopular with the Arab public. Attitudes toward them ranged from contempt to belligerence. Nevertheless, their connections with the authorities, their money, or their family affiliations sometimes allowed them to position themselves as indispensable members of their village communities. Sometimes, it seems, hostility toward collaborators served as a unifying factor (although not a universal one, since the collaborators themselves had sympathizers and allies), especially in times of struggle. This was the case during the great anti-expropriation campaigns in Dir al-Asad, in the neighboring villages, and in the villages of the Lower Galilee, when land belong-

* Some three thousand Arabs from neighboring villages live in Karmiel today (2009) and constitute about 8 percent of its total population. In the municipal elections of 2008 an Arab activist ran for a local council seat for the first time, on a slate called Karmiel for All. The slate did not win enough votes to take any seats on the council, but in response to this slate's creation, a new Jewish slate ran for the council under the title My Home, and its leader declared, "Karmiel is not a mixed city and will not be a mixed city. . . . Open history books to learn the reason for the establishment of Karmiel [Judaization of the Galilee]. If I were to tell this directly I would be denounced as a racist." This slate won three out of the seventeen seats on the local council. See www.nrg.co.il/online/1/ART1/783/238.html (in Hebrew).

ing to them was expropriated for the construction of the National Water Carrier (which would pipe water from the Sea of Galilee down to central and southern Israel). A song sung at a wedding in Sakhnin in July 1962 conveys nationalist attitudes toward "traitors":

> The entire nation has decided to destroy treason.
> Those who sold land will encounter derision.
> They should be destroyed
> With our swishing swords.
> We did not sign—traitors signed.
> The day will come—we will cut off the traitors' heads.
> You who signed—you are the traitors.[38]

As these lyrics show, the nationalists believed they represented the authentic voice of the people, who categorically rejected those who sold land or signed land-swap agreements ("the entire nation has decided"). There is something to this; the general attitude toward land sellers was indeed negative. But two other points should be noted. First, while the rhetoric was fiery with its use of expressions like "swishing swords," taken from the Arabic metaphoric arsenal, collaborators were almost unmolested in practice. In other words, the use of these violent images should not be taken at face value. They were, rather, a way of expressing emotions against the collaborators. Second, in practice, perhaps because they had no choice, many people were persuaded to accept a land swap. Others, fewer in number, helped the security forces neutralize the protests against the expropriations. In other words, the Arabs had no consensus regarding what to do about the land expropriations. Emotionally and politically, a great majority opposed the transfer of land to the state, but within the bounds of what was possible, no few chose to accept compensation or alternative land rather than boycotting all offers made by the state.

Whatever the case, collaborators often attended weddings in their villages and listened to the songs sung by the vocalists. The collaborators certainly would not have felt at ease. Some quickly provided their overseers with the names of the singers, both professionals and those who joined in. Sometimes, as in the case reported here, they also provided a full transcript of the lyrics (and in doing so helped to preserve them for posterity). In many cases the presence of informers among the guests and the knowledge that they would pass on information about the weddings moved the locus of nationalist singing to the women's compound. (Few women served as informers.)

The song that follows was sung at a wedding in Dir al-Asad, the center of the anti-expropriation struggle, in the autumn of 1962. The participants sang it publicly, deliberately defying the collaborators they knew were among them:

Whatever happens
We will not leave our land.
Death to traitors to the nation
And to the lackeys of the military regime.
We will not abandon the Shaghur [the Dir al-Asad area] and the
  Battuf [the Beit Netofa Valley].[39]

This public expression of repugnance toward the land collaborators and their partners was an important means of maintaining sociopolitical norms within the Arab community and of handing them down to the next generation. Ahmad Sa'di, a political scientist, is correct when he states in his study of Palestinian political activity that this form of resistance has not received enough attention.[40] One of the characteristics of this means was that it was generally not directed at a specific person but rather at a type of behavior. This was true of many poems and stories published during this period to attack land sharks (works, for example, by Tawfiq Zayyad, Hanna Abu Hanna, and Nur Salman).[41] In a number of other cases, however, criticism was aimed directly at specific collaborators. One common way of doing this was to send the collaborator a letter containing a threat, a reprimand, or vituperation.

When the route of the National Water Carrier was made public, the affected villages—'Arrabe, Sakhnin, Dir Hanna, 'Eilabun, and Mghar—organized a committee to oppose the land expropriations mandated by the plan and to propose an alternative—a tunnel, instead of a surface canal. The government rejected the proposal and commenced the process of purchasing the necessary land. Here Hasan A. of Dir Hanna entered the picture. He took upon himself the task of helping Mekorot, the Israeli national water company, purchase the land for the canal. In the spring of 1961, Hasan was able to persuade no few landowners in the area to reach an agreement with Mekorot. The opponents of expropriation considered him a traitor and sent him threatening letters on occasion. One of them was written by a group that called itself the Palestine Rescue Organization,* another was signed the Committee for the Preservation of Arab Rights:

* The use of the term *Palestine* was not particularly rare among Arab citizens of Israel at this time, as people sometimes mistakenly think. Arab nationalists used it to refer to the West Bank, which was under Jordanian rule, to the Gaza Strip, and to the territory of Israel. It was used not only by the older generation,

Mr. Hasan, with great sorrow we note your deception, lies, and disregard of the past ... with great sorrow we note that you have joined up with despicable people who lack a past, reputation, consciousness, and Arab identity and blood. No, no, this does not become you. Best that you abandon this path and join the members of your nation in their battle to achieve their rights. ... Do not negotiate over your land, your nation, and your people. ... We hope you will change your ways and become a member of the fighting nation.[42]

This was a relatively mild letter. It was sent the same week that Hasan managed to persuade two of the leaders of the battle against the National Water Carrier plan to reach an agreement with the state. "There is nothing to be gotten out of a lost campaign against the authorities, because the government, which has invested hundreds of millions in this plan so far, will not be deterred from carrying it out," he told them.[43] The letter can be seen as a final attempt to deter Hasan. Frequently such letters used much sharper language, and many collaborators found themselves subject to wild curses and death threats. It seems to have been Hasan's family reputation—his father and grandfather had been active in the national struggle—that led the nationalists to appeal to his sensibilities rather than to attack him directly.

Another way the affected villagers expressed their disgust with land sellers was through graffiti. These did not generally name the sellers. (In this they differed from the graffiti seen in the West Bank and the Gaza Strip during the First Intifada, which were often meant to warn specific collaborators.) A notable case that the police dealt with occurred in Umm al-Fahm in October 1962, in anticipation of the establishment of the site of a new Jewish settlement, Mei-Ami, by the army's Nahal Corps.

According to an evaluation produced by the KKL's agent in the Triangle, Ya'akov Barazani, some forty thousand *dunams* (ten thousand acres) of Umm al-Fahm's land—half of its land reserves—were transferred to state ownership at around the time of Israel's establishment. In addition, the KKL managed, during the state's first decade, to purchase another few thousand *dunams* from their owners.[44] By the end of the 1950s, the vil-

---

which remembered Mandatory Palestine, but also by high school students, who were generally those who wrote the threatening letters.

lage thus faced a real shortage of land, and many inhabitants worked else-where as day laborers. This is the background to the discontent caused by rumors, in October 1962, that Israel was about to take another bite out of Umm al-Fahm's land. One morning that week, the first worshipers who left the mosques in the village's Mahajne and Mahamid neighborhoods encountered placards that proclaimed, "To landowners, do not sell your land. Whoever sells his land to the Jews and speculates with them—will die. And whoever takes down this placard will also die." The placard was signed by "the brothers of Mustafa 'Ashu" (the Palestinian murderer of King 'Abdallah of Jordan in 1951).

A few days later, on the morning of Yom Kippur, when the villagers did not go to work in the nearby Jewish cities, graffiti appeared on more than ten homes in the village. Some of them read, "We will not leave our land"; "We will redeem land with blood and soul"; "Death to the speculators"; "O 'Izz al-Din al-Qassam, we will not leave the Holy Land." This was also a way of staging a public campaign against potential land sellers and the collaboration phenomenon and a way to disseminate national values.

The graffiti scrawled on Umm al-Fahm's homes led to an energetic police investigation, under the command of the district police chief. Informers were put on the case, and handwriting samples were sent to the forensics lab. Paintbrushes were confiscated from people's homes for examination, and vil-lagers were summoned to give testimony. Several were detained as suspects. (They denied the charges against them and declared a hunger strike.)

The goal of the police was to break the spirit of resistance to collabora-tors and to prevent the spread of Arab national discourse. Outwardly, they achieved their goal. Because of past experience and the knowledge that the police would use all the means at their disposal to punish the graffiti writ-ers (the charge lodged against them was vandalism), a ruckus ensued. The Communists, who were sure that suspicion would first fall on them, con-vened a public assembly within a few hours of the graffiti's appearance. They declared that they had not been behind this action. The village council also quickly met, condemned the perpetrators, and offered a five-hundred-pound reward to anyone who helped uncover them. To make their decision public, they published it in the government- and Histadrut-sponsored Arabic daily newspaper *Al-Yawm*.[45]

As far as the police were concerned, these responses were no less impor-tant than discovering the criminals. They were not only working against the resistance to land sales but also sought to influence the Arab-Israeli political discourse. In this context, a blanket condemnation of the graffiti was certainly a success. This was just one example of how the security forces were able to affect the public political discourse in the Arab community in Israel and to shape it into a loyal discourse. This fascinating phenomenon will be presented in the next chapter.

FIVE

The Battle of the Narrative

Symbols, Pronouncements, Teachers

ISTIQLAL/ATZMA'UT, A 1994 DOCUMENTARY FILM directed by Nizar Hasan and named for the Arabic and Hebrew words for "independence," is set in his home village, Mash-had, in the Galilee. In the film, his mother recalls a period when the village, like all other Arab villages in the Galilee, the Triangle, and the Negev, was under military rule. As a schoolteacher, she was expected by the regime to mold her pupils into loyal Israeli citizens. So she taught them about the state's achievements and danced with them on Israel's Independence Day. She was hardly exceptional. Most Arab teachers did the same. Even those who were critical of the Jewish state kept their thoughts to themselves. When Hasan asked his mother why she had yielded to the state's expectations, she explained that times were hard and people feared losing their jobs. Fear and financial pressure also led to informing on colleagues who deviated from the government line. "We were all informers then," she said.

Much has since changed in Israel. People report each other to the authorities less frequently, and state supervision of political speech has lessened. But the Israeli government still exerts control over teachers and political organizations (and control seems to have tightened since the outbreak of the al-Aqsa Intifada and the bloody events of October 2000). This and the memories of the close tracking of political speech and activity in the state's early years have stamped an impression on Israel's Arab citizens. The people Hasan

Figure 12. Education to coexistence. An Arab girls choir welcomes the minister of education, Nazareth, 1949. Photograph courtesy Israeli Government Press Office.

interviewed were notably reluctant to speak their minds. Ibtisam Mara'na's film, *Paradise Lost* (2003), leaves no room for doubt; when the director, born and raised in Faradis (the village's name is an Arabic cognate of the word *paradise*), begins to delve into her village's history, her father tries to deter her. When she begins to take an interest in the events of 1948, he panics:

> "Father, where were you in the 1948 war?"
>
> "I was at home. I was twelve years old."
>
> "And the massacre at Tantura?"
>
> "What about it? I don't know anything about that. I only heard. I don't know anything. Why do you want to get into that subject? It's political. Why do you need all those stories? It's none of our business, girl. Listen to me." *

---

* Dozens of the Arab inhabitants of Tantura, a village that lay on the Mediterranean coast south of Haifa, were killed during (or after) the occupation of the village by the Israeli forces in 1948. Some years ago, historians engaged in a strident and public debate over whether Israeli forces had conducted a "massacre" in the village—that is, whether they had indiscriminately and deliberately murdered dozens of

Later in the film, Mara'na tries to learn about Su'ad, a woman from her village, who joined the PLO during the 1970s, was arrested, and left Israel when she was released from prison. Mara'na shows her own father sitting in a coffee house with an acquaintance. The two men are talking about Su'ad. As Mara'na films, her father tells his friend that he opposes his daughter's political films: "People here don't like trouble. In our village we don't like trouble. I told her not to get involved in politics. Be careful. Be careful." He speaks Arabic but uses the Hebrew word for "problems," *be'ayot*. In the argot of Palestinians in Israel, *be'ayot* means things that the state doesn't like, such as delving into historical events that are better left unremarked. In effect, this wraps two subjects in silence. The first is history and memory—what the country looked like before 1948; what happened in that year; and specific events during Israel's history. The second is current politics—how the country's actions, and how its treatment of its Palestinian Arab citizens, should be understood in the present.

The father's statement would seem to indicate that Israel's policy of silencing the Israeli Arabs has succeeded. After all, it has achieved its purpose—not only to prevent the dissemination of the Palestinian national narrative and to make its Arab citizens wary of political involvement, but also to consign the enforcement of these standards to the hands of the Arab community itself. When she was a girl, Mara'na inked a Palestinian flag on her hand; when she came home, her mother washed it off and slapped her. Her mother's silencing of her political statement is like the Communist Party's disavowal of the graffiti writers in Umm al-Fahm, mentioned above. The background is fear of the authorities. The state employed informers widely. With their help, the government was able to obtain information about what was going on in Palestinian communities and what was said in private. Even when informers were unable to obtain information, they were able to make their fellow Arabs think they knew. A story has it that Paris's chief of police during Napoleon III's regime said he didn't need one out of every three Parisians chatting on the street to be his informer. All he needed was that every three *think* that

---

Arabs after occupying the village. For opposing views (on the case and on the role of the Israeli academy in the debate), see Ilan Pappe, "The Tantura Case in Israel: The Katz Research and Trial," *Journal of Palestine Studies* 30, no. 3 (Spring 2001): 19–39; and Yoav Gelber, "The Status of Zionist and Israeli History in Israeli Universities," in Anita Shapira and Derek Penslar, eds., *Israeli Historical Revisionism: From Left to Right* (London: Frank Cass, 2002), 121–54. The director, Mara'na, joined the liberal-left New Meretz Party in 2008 and was included in its slate for the 2009 parliamentary elections. However, she left the party on the first day of 2009, a few weeks before the elections, because of its initial support of the IDF assault on Gaza.

one among them was an informer. This same principle was adopted by other political police agencies, the GSS included.

FORBIDDEN STATEMENTS AND SELF-CENSORSHIP

One of the tasks collaborators were assigned was to pass on information about people who spoke out against the state, its leaders, or its institutions. Collection of this kind of information began when the country was founded and picked up momentum at the end of the 1950s. Critical statements were recorded in the dossiers of those who made them; the police goal was to have a file on every adult Arab citizen, especially those who were criminally and politically active. The security forces examined the contents of the dossiers when they had to make decisions affecting the life of each Arab citizen.

In the big picture, this collection of utterances had three purposes. The first was to keep tabs on the general mood of the Arab population. In other words, the collection was somewhat like public opinion polling; with it, the authorities could gauge the Arab population's response to government actions and policies and its reactions to specific political developments. The second goal was to identify individuals who might potentially take action against the state. The silent assumption here was that a high correlation existed between the vehemence of utterances against the state and a willingness to engage in covert action against it. The third goal was to establish boundaries for the permitted discourse of Arabs in Israel. By taking retribution against those who spoke against the state and its institutions, the state made clear to the Arabs what kinds of utterances were allowed and what forbidden. In 1960, when radical nationalist statements became routine, the means of control were made public. The prime minister's adviser on Arab affairs, Uri Lubrani, announced that the government would take administrative sanctions against Arabs who slandered the country, sanctions such as dismissal from work and deportation.[1] It is this third goal that is of most interest in the context of this work, since it was a largely overt and forthright means of maneuvering the Arab public to speak in certain specific ways.

I should note that the success of the state in creating an atmosphere in which Arabs feared voicing their opinions publicly does not mean that it succeeded in inculcating the Zionist discourse in the Arab community. Only a handful of Arabs adopted it. Moreover, close supervision of Arab speech engendered resistance in the end, as I will show. In any case, as soon as the state was established it began monitoring Arab speech, and an examination of the huge collection of statements that the police gathered opens a window on the attitudes of Israel's Arab citizens toward the state. (Of course, the sample is not a representative one, since only statements that were perceived as extreme were recorded and reported.) At the same time, these reports also testify to the kinds of statements that interested the security forces and were considered noteworthy by them. As a historian of the Bolshevik political police has noted, intelligence material provides information not only about the population being monitored but also about the agencies that gather the information and about the values and concepts of the state that operates those agencies.[2]

From the start, the security forces took a special interest in collecting statements against collaboration and collaborators. Here, the security forces that oversaw the collaborators shared an interest with the collaborators themselves. The latter were wary that anti-collaboration speech could weaken their social standing and incite physical attacks on them and their property; at the same time, they sought to harm their rivals. Thus, from its earliest days, the collection of Arab speech was a tool for shoring up the position of the collaborator class and neutralizing the influence of its opponents. In 1950, security personnel received reports of verbal attacks on collaborators in a number of villages in the Galilee. They reacted swiftly; the man believed to be the prime agitator in Iksal, a village at the foot of Mt. Tabor in the Lower Galilee, was exiled to southern Israel.[3]* A year later, a report was filed on five men from 'Ein Rafa, in the Jerusalem mountains, who had a conversation in which one of them said, "We, the inhabitants of the village, must be united against this corrupt government. It is interested in setting brother against brother and injects conflict via its agents, both from the police and the army. We are not sitting on our hands. A day will come when we'll slaughter all these despicable Jews."[4]

The collaborator who passed on this report was aware that the villagers knew about his work and that of other collaborators. He also realized that one of the principal reasons he was being employed by the security forces was to undermine social solidarity in the village. But he chose to carry on nevertheless, in part as a way of securing the authorities' support for him against

* The so-called agitator's name was 'Abd al-Rahman Hmeidi, and he was shot to death in July 1952 in his home in Iksal. I have no information about who the murderers were and whether the killing was connected to his opposition to collaborators. It is known, though, that an armed band entered Israel from Jordan to take vengeance against the murderers, but it encountered a police ambush. MG Galilee to OC Northern Command / IDF, "Report of the MG for July 1952," IDFA, 3698/263/66.

public opinion in the village. On this point, his interest coincided with the authorities' interest. They wanted to build up his standing and weaken his opponents, who were also opponents of the regime, and the information he provided helped them do that.

Supporters of the regime were quick to report speech against them and other collaborators as a way of impelling the authorities to put more pressure on their enemies. A man from Taybe was riding a bus "and began to talk, saying, when will Abu-Khaled—he meant Gamal 'Abd al-Nasser—come to Israel, and stated that he wanted Abu-Khaled to finish off the *khawanin* [sic], traitors." Another person on the bus reported this. An Arab from 'Iblin spoke fiercely against a fellow villager who had invited the military governor to a meal at his house. "I'm getting a *khawaziq* [torture pole] for those traitors," he said. A border policeman from the Bedouin al-Heib tribe was killed by a land mine in January 1968, and most of the non-Bedouin inhabitants of his village boycotted his funeral. One of them was overheard saying in the neighborhood general store, "That's how an Arab who fights against the Arab countries ends his life." A Bedouin informer reported it.[5]

But collaborators not only filed reports on statements that touched on them; they also passed on others against the state and recounted political conversations of all types. Police informers in Tira surreptitiously listened through a window to gatherings in the mukhtar's house and reported what the people there said: "Had we fought as we should we wouldn't have gotten to where the Jews rule over us"; "It's not worth getting close to the authorities, because there's no certainty that Israel will rule forever." Informers in 'Ara reported on reactions to reports on Radio Damascus on the outcome of the Sinai Campaign of 1956: "With God's help the Syrians, Iraqis, and Jordanians will come and deal Israel a decisive blow, and we can stop worrying about this criminal country," one villager was reported as saying. Informers in the upper Galilee reported on neighbors who were disappointed by Nasser's defeat in the Six Day War. "It's too bad Nasser didn't finish off the Jews," one man said, and his companion answered, "It really is too bad."[6]

Naturally, political activists were closely watched. The statements of members of the al-Ard movement, which did not recognize the right of Israel to exist and as such was declared illegal, were collected in a special GSS report. In addition to political statements made by Mansour Qardush and other prominent members of the group, statements made by al-Ard's supporters were also quoted. A potter from Nazareth was reported to have said, "A blacker than black end awaits the Jews, in which we will flay them alive." A metalworker from Dir al-Asad said that the Arabs who went to Acre to celebrate the anniversary of its liberation by the IDF "should be mowed down with a machine gun."[7]

Vicious statements against the state were not rare, and they can be seen not only as expressions of concrete political aspirations but also as a channel for venting frustrations and voicing dissent. (Some would say that this is a characteristic form of a weak party's resistance to the regime.) Since the end of the 1950s, when pan-Arab nationalism was on the rise, statements made by Arabs in Israel have displayed emotional, sometimes political, identification with these utterances. It was at this time that the security forces institution-alized their surveillance of Arab speech. Self-censorship—restraint of politi-cal speech by members of the Arab community—also became an established practice. Three examples from 1958, Israel's tenth year, follow. It was also the year of the Egyptian-Syrian union, during which nationalist currents among Israel's Arabs grew stronger—as did the anxiety of the collaborators.

In the spring of 1958, one Tawfiq A. from 'Eilabun, whom security forces had marked as a Communist sympathizer, was married. One of the guests at his wedding was a young Christian from the same village who had volun-teered for service in the IDF's minorities' unit. The music was provided by the Communist Party band in Nazareth. At the request of a guest, the vocalist sang a song in honor of Nasser and Egyptian-Syrian unification. Expressing support for Nasser was considered by the authorities to be tantamount to supporting the destruction of Israel. The soldier went over to the band and to the man who had asked for the song and demanded that they show him their ID cards. He intended to turn them in to the authorities. They cursed him and refused to show their cards. He left the party in anger.[8]

In September of that year, the mayor of Tamra, Yusef al-Diab, was invited to the wedding of a teacher in Kafr Yasif. When the procession that led the bridegroom through the village streets set out, one of the participants called out, "Long live the United Arab Republic!" Another chanted three times, "Long live!" Diab, who was close to MK Yigal Alon (the commander of the Palmach in the 1948 war) and who was himself elected to the Knesset a year later on the Cooperation and Brotherhood slate, "was furious and gave the groom a piece of his mind, telling those present that they should be mortified in front of their guests. He said that had such a thing happened in Tamra, the guests would have cracked some heads open. He refused to go to the bridegroom's house," a GSS report stated.[9]

A few weeks later, a family of internal refugees from Birwe celebrated the wedding of a son, also in Kafr Yasif. "The bridegroom's cousin . . . tried to sing nationalist and Communist songs. . . . An altercation broke out as a result, and the bridegroom and his father demanded that the Communists desist from singing their songs. Several Muslim refugees from Birwe who lived in Jdeideh and Makr (the bridegroom's family came from Birwe) threatened to leave the wedding in protest. Tensions grew high, and in the end the Communist Party members and those who came with them were compelled to take their distance from the procession. They stood far off, sang a few songs, and dispersed."[10]

There is no way of knowing the motives of the bridegroom's father or of Diab and others like them. However, arguing that they fully identified with the state or that they put their own interests before their communities' interests would not provide us with a full explanation for their political behavior. A better, nuanced understanding can be achieved by looking at those few Arab figures who tried to hold back the tide of Arab nationalism. They justified their actions by maintaining that the Jewish public and government would react harshly to manifestations of Arab extremism. In other words, extremism would hurt the Arabs in the end. They thus believed that, as public figures, they should try to moderate the rhetoric in their communities.[11] And there is little doubt that their wish to satisfy the authorities and their confidence that this was the only way to improve Jewish-Arab relations and promote Arab interests in Israel were important components of their worldview.

Of course, they had also personal interests that were taken into consideration, and another motive that can reasonably be ascribed to them is that they sought to maintain good relations with the authorities as individuals. Had it been known that they had listened to nationalist statements and not protested, they would have lost face, and the authorities might have ceased to support them. The members of these circles also had a collective interest. This stratum of "positive persons" in the villages and cities opposed any nationalist awakening. They realized that such a development would cut off the branch on which they roosted. Their working assumption—it was the state's, too—was that the Arabs in Israel could be detached from the rest of the Arab nation. Yet, were Nasserism to capture the public mind, it would undermine this process. In response, many of these accommodationist Arab leaders joined forces with the security agencies to fight Nasserism and pan-Arabism. Some filed secret reports, and others faced off directly with the nationalists. The nationalists' frequent condemnation of Arabs who were close to the Israeli regime ("the government's tails") made the latter all the more willing to take on the task of opposing the nationalists. They sometimes urged the authorities to take action and offered ideas about how to do this, some practical, others less so. For example, a collaborator from Majd al-Krum sent the police a report about popular singers at weddings:

> I have remarked many times already on the danger this practice presents on the social level, and its effect of creating bad citizens, and even more than this, the exacerbation of conflicts and differences of opinion between the Jewish and Arab peoples in this country.... What do you think of when you hear the poet Qasem ... speak in his poem about "the decisive and victorious missile" and "the MIG and Ilyushin planes," given that they are Arab weapons, and he would never think of mentioning anything about Israel, about its arms and power and the good things about it? ...
>
> Why should there not be proper guidance for these poets by one of the government agencies, such as the Public Relations Directorate, or one of the public bodies like the Histadrut's Cultural Department, which can offer guidance to these poets about how to direct their poems toward brotherhood between the two peoples, the good citizen, Israel's beautiful sites, its good actions, its progress, and so on? There is no lack of material on these subjects. In this way these poets will become builders of the state instead of being forces for destruction, conflict, extreme nationalism, and racism.[12]

This is another example of indirect intracommunal supervision offered by an individual who adopted the Zionist discourse of progress and constructiveness. But he and his like were in the minority. In contrast with them stood those who confronted the establishment publicly. Arab weddings thus became arenas of conflict between nationalists and Arabs loyal to the regime. The forces were not equal; in general, as we have seen, the nationalists had the upper hand, and the government's supporters tried to protest against them. In other cases, government loyalists sought to take the initiative, in which case the nationalists responded. One small example of such a clash can be found in a report on a wedding in Tur'an in 1965. When the wedding began, the report states, some villagers began calling out enthusiastically, "'Long live the prime minister of Israel,' 'long live the military governor,' 'long live Moshe Dayan,' 'long live Akiva,' the deputy military governor of the north, 'long live Dov,' the governor's representative in Nazareth, and so on. ... One of the invited guests, named Jamal ... from the same village, responded with these shouts, 'Long live Abu-Khaled' (Gamal 'Abd al-Nasser), 'long live Ben Bella [president of Algeria],' 'long live Amin al-Hafez [president of Syria].' ... The Nazareth police opened an investigation."[13]

To what extent did the paeans to Nasser express a real desire for the destruction of Israel? That question remains open (as does the question of whether the praises of the military governor and Moshe Dayan were sincere and whether the "death to the Arabs" catcalls sometimes still shouted by Israeli soccer fans express a real desire to see the Arabs dead). In any case, this manifestation of Arab nationalism was perceived by the state to be illegitimate. Israelis were also understandably angered when some Arabs voiced support for genocide against the Jews (e.g., "Eichmann didn't finish the job").[14]* Through tight supervision of speech, the state tried to root out all such language. But this was not sufficient for its goals. It sought to create a pro-Israeli Arab rhetoric and to impel its Arab citizens to act as they spoke, at least in public. In other words, Israel wanted the Arabs to accept the state and its values and to assimilate the broad outline of the Zionist narrative. One prime example of this was the security forces' massive encouragement and inducement of Arabs to celebrate Israel's Independence Day and to disregard the day's pernicious implications for them. (Most of Israel's Arabs lived, after all, under military rule, and many had relatives who had become refugees in circumstances connected to the establishment of the state. From being a majority in their country, they had become a minority with limited rights, and the lands of many of them had been expropriated.) The Arab attitude toward Israel's Independence Day thus also became a focus of the struggle between the state and Arab nationalists and between the "loyal" and "militant" forces in each village. It is hardly surprising, then, that a student in Tamra's school who gave a speech congratulating the state and its leaders on Independence Day 1954 received a death-threat letter signed by "the Palestinian underground." Such incidents were not rare.[15]

One of the peaks of tension over this issue was Israel's tenth anniversary, the Decade Festivities of 1958. As noted above, this was the same year that Egypt and Syria merged to become the United Arab Republic (UAR). The Israeli establishment did all it could to enhance the festivities and to ensure massive Arab participation. Collaborators were enlisted in the effort. Arab nationalists called for a boycott of the holiday. A Communist Party leaflet circulated in Tamra offers a good portrayal of this effort:

---

* Suppressing offensive language is a privilege reserved for victors. Israeli leaders could speak of the Nakba and the uprooting of hundreds of thousands of Arabs from their homes as "an unparalleled miracle," but Arabs were expected not to offend Jewish sensibilities.

The Israeli authorities and their lackeys in the appointed local council in our village and other villages are making preparations for the independence celebration. . . . This is part of the government's attempts to fabricate the truth about the sentiments toward the state of its Arab inhabitants. The authorities are trying, in various ways, to portray the Arab inhabitants as pleased with their lot and with the conditions of their lives, as if they are pleased with the military regime, the theft of their lands, and repression, and as if they are pleased by the sequestration of their national rights and the denial that they are part of the Palestinian Arab nation. . . .

Will we dance on the day of mourning for the destruction of our villages? Will we dance on the graves of our martyrs who fell in the many massacres, like the ones at Dir Yasin and Kafr Qasim? Will we celebrate while a million of our compatriots are dispersed in exile and prevented from returning to their homes and their homeland? Will we celebrate when we are stripped of national rights and live under a military regime and national repression? No, we will not celebrate. We are part of a huge nation that is today raising its head everywhere, in Algeria, Oman, Aden, and Lebanon, against the imperialists and their lackeys, and we will pay them back double.[16]

The "integrationists," for their part, worked hard to make sure the celebrations succeeded. Kafr Yasif, for example, was considered a nationalist stronghold. Its veteran mayor, Yanni Yanni, and most of the members of the village council were members of the Communist Party. But the village surprised everyone. The council decided to boycott the celebrations, but villagers established their own special committee to organize the festivities. It succeeded, and they were well-attended. The village secretary of the Israel Labor League (the Arab subsidiary of the Jewish Histadrut labor federation), Ya'qub Hanna Dahoud, made a speech declaring, "Even if there are black spots on the authorities' treatment of the Arab minority in Israel, the path to achieving equal rights is not boycotts and expressions of hostility, but rather seeking understanding and proving to the authorities that the minority is loyal to the state." That was a formulation on which military government officials would happily have signed off: that the Arab public had a continuing obligation to prove its loyalty. The degree of organization surprised the police officers who were invited to the ceremony. "The village was decorated with national flags, colorful ribbons, an abundance of electric light provided by a special generator brought in for this purpose. The stage was festooned with carpets, flags, and photographs of national and Zionist leaders. The technical arrangements, including comfortable seats for the crowd, were not inferior, in my opinion, to the arrangements in Jewish settlements in Israel, whether town or kibbutz," one of the officers effused.[17]

The ceremony in Kafr Yasif was well-attended. In other places, participation was spottier. In Jish, the refugees from Bir'am stayed away, as did many of the local Muslims. The mukhtar, Fawzi Sam'an, was one of the no-shows. "It surprised me," wrote police officer Yitzhak Kravitz. A quick inquiry revealed that Qaisar Ibrahim, the mukhtar of the Bir'am refugees residing in Jish, had persuaded his colleague not to participate, on the grounds that "the inhabitants of Gush Halav [i.e., Jish] are also victims of the current Israeli regime and, among other things, reminded him about the 2,000 *dunams* of fertile, flat land that was expropriated from the people of Gush Halav in 1949 and which was given to Jewish settlements." The mukhtar's absence did not pass without a response. Having benefited from the regime's confidence, he was expected to behave loyally, at least in public. Since he did not do so, he was suspended from the job that the police had arranged for him in the Ministry of Health.[18]

Government officials also wanted Muslim religious institutions and clergymen to take part in the celebrations. They found a simple way of accomplishing this: the celebration of the completion of expensive renovations on Acre's al-Jazzar Mosque was scheduled for Independence Day. Invitations were sent out to Muslim public figures throughout the country, stating explicitly that the ceremony would also honor the Israeli national holiday. Attorney Elias Kusa, a prominent national activist of independent opinions, was furious. "I am convinced," he wrote to the preparatory committee, composed of Muslim clergymen, "that the mention of the second reason [the Decade Festivities] in the invitation letter was made because of pressure applied to you by your persecutors and the tramplers of our people. This is, in my opinion, the greatest denigration of Arab nationalism and human honor that a rational man can conceive of." He continued:

> You are conducting a ceremony not in keeping with the will of the Muslim
> Arabs in Israel and outside it. [You are taking advantage] of a convenient
> time to sing songs of thanks and praise to the same government that is
> harming you and your nation, which has destroyed a large number of
> villages, expelled their inhabitants, who have dispersed in all directions,
> and which has taken control of a large part of your lands, the lands of
> your fathers and grandfathers, and has handed these lands over to Jewish
> immigrants so that they can live pleasant and comfortable lives while
> the Arab owners live in wretchedness, distress, poverty, and need. The
> government has placed a military regime over them that has no parallel

in history, has chained their freedoms as if they were dogs, humiliated them, dishonored them, and turned them into a people lacking in honor and pride. It has also restricted your study, progress, and success and confiscated Muslim religious property of a value, from the founding of the state until 1952, of no less than 180,000 Israeli pounds [$504,000 at the official exchange rate]. . . . After all this, will you celebrate the day of memory that we have no part and share in?[19]

The answer that many Arabs gave to Kusa's rhetorical question was affirmative. They participated in the decade festivities, expressing their desire to be part of the state, even if it did not view them as equal citizens. They were well aware of the conduct of Israel, not only of its dark side, but also of its light. This was not the view of the Arab Front, which was established that same year (and which not long thereafter adopted the name Popular Front—not to be confused with the Palestinian organization of the same name founded by George Habash a decade later).* It not only promoted a boycott of the celebrations, which lauded the achievements of Zionism and the Israeli state, but also launched an Arab nationalist discourse and offered its own narrative of the history of Arabs in Israel. The front's attempt to conduct a memorial ceremony for the victims of the Kafr Qasim massacre in the al-Jazzar Mosque was specifically aimed at achieving this.

The Kafr Qasim massacre took place on 29 October 1956, the day the Sinai Campaign began. Israeli border policemen shot dead forty-seven Arab workers, men and women, who straggled into the village at the end of a day's work, not knowing that a curfew had been imposed while they were away. The policemen killed the workers in obedience to explicit orders from their officers. Soldiers and officers were tried, and the court ruled that the order to shoot the villagers had been "a manifestly illegal order over which a black flag flew." Eight of the soldiers were sentenced to prison terms of between seven and seventeen years (although they eventually had their sentences commuted and were freed before serving out their terms). The commander of the regional regiment, Yiska Shadmi, had handed down the curfew order. When he was asked what to do with a worker who arrived home late, after the cur-

---

* The Popular Front in Israel was established in 1958 at the initiative of the Communist Party and Arab nationalists who did not belong to the party. Its goal was to unite all Arab nationalist forces in Israel. The authorities imposed severe restrictions on it, severely circumscribing its activities. But disputes between the Communists and non-Communist nationalists (who later founded the al-Ard movement) destabilized the front, until it was finally disbanded a year later.

Figure 13. Celebrating independence. Bishop Hakim (front row right) and Druze religious leader Sheikh Amin Tarif (front row center) in Tel Aviv, watching the IDF parade on Israel's Independence Day, 1959. Photograph courtesy Israeli Government Press Office.

few had gone into effect, he replied *"Allah Yirhamu"*—Arabic for "may God have mercy on him." He was fined an agora, Israel's smallest coin.[20]

About two and a half months after the massacre, when the soldiers' trial began in January 1957, the Communist Party organized a partial strike. The purpose was to put the issue—and the military regime as a whole, which according to the Communists had made the massacre possible—on the agenda of Israel's Arab and Jewish citizens. The security forces took a number of steps to prevent participation in the strike. A large contingent was sent into Acre to prevent a planned memorial service in the al-Jazzar Mosque for the victims and to head off public convocations, out of fear that such events would disseminate the view that responsibility for the massacre lay not with the soldiers in the field but rather with the political leadership. Senior security officials met with Arab public figures to clarify the situation: "Anyone who joins this activity is lending his hand to inciters against the state, and he will be treated accordingly in the future." This was one of the methods used to restrict Arab speech, and its goal was to allow current events to be addressed only in the framework of the hegemonic Zionist discourse.

These preventative actions succeeded in limiting the number of participants. Military government officers knew that many Arabs "feared complications with the authorities," but, as the Galilee's military governor commented, it was clear to them that "there was a strike of the heart."[21] For his part, MK Fares Hamdan (the legal cattle smuggler in the service of the security services mentioned in chapter 1), who represented the Agriculture and Development satellite slate of Mapai, quickly adopted the establishment position and presented it as one in which he was emotionally invested. He lauded Ben-Gurion for establishing a commission of inquiry into the events and expressed his confidence that the truth would come to light, as well as his belief that it was a crime committed by individuals rather than a manifestation of government policy. In a letter to the prime minister, he did not forget to remark that the incident took place during the Sinai war: "in those very days on which the state under your honest leadership recorded a glorious page in history with the IDF's massive action in the Sinai Desert and Gaza Strip."[22]

In its fight against the commemoration of the Kafr Qasim massacre, the state was thus assisted by Arabs who worked in its service. So it was on the day of the strike in January 1957, when the Advisory Committee on Muslim Affairs in Acre, which oversaw the al-Jazzar Mosque, opposed holding the memorial convocation in the mosque. And so it was in October 1958, when members of the Popular Front sought to conduct a memorial service in the mosque to mark the massacre's second anniversary. The same committee that had, in April, conducted celebrations in the framework of Israel's Decade Festivities wrote in response, "Mosques were built solely for the worship of the Creator, and there is no possibility of holding lectures, speeches, and general assemblies of extremist committees or parties, since the Creator has said: 'The mosques are dedicated to God, and a man will not call out there except to the Creator.'" This, too, was the result of preparatory talks between military government officers and clergymen.[23]

The person who gave the police the correspondence between the Popular Front and the committee in Acre was Sheikh Musa Tabari, who headed the Advisory Committee on Muslim Affairs in Acre. Tabari was an Israeli loyalist; in 1951 he gave a sermon in the mosque in which he lauded the government for "seeing to the Arabs' comfort." Another member of the committee, Sheikh Muhammad Hubeishi, thanked the government for its "favorable and pleasant treatment of the Arab nation in the state of Israel, seeing to their livelihood and the education of their children."[24] Israel could count on having these men block any attempt to disseminate an alternative discourse publicly. Arabs in Kafr Qasim itself lent a hand in silencing Arab nationalist talk, in part by following and photographing the organizers of and participants in the memorial events held for the victims of the massacre. They turned this material over to the police and the GSS.[25]

The clash between the two political tendencies and between the two narratives reached a symbolic climax in 1964, when the new city of Karmiel was formally dedicated on the very day of the anniversary of the Kafr Qasim massacre. The Mapai camp's Arab Knesset members participated in the dedication ceremony, disregarding the fact that the town was built on land confiscated from Arabs; they absented themselves from the memorial ceremony, however. The opposition Knesset members went to the memorial service but boycotted the Karmiel event. In this way, both sides publicly demonstrated their priorities and loyalties.[26]

Now back to 1958. Independence Day (celebrated according to the Jewish calendar) fell on 24 April that year. May Day came a week later, and tempestuous demonstrations took place in Nazareth and Umm al-Fahm. Hundreds of nationalists and Communists were arrested by the police, some being held for many weeks. This was also an occasion for loyalist Arabs to voice their fealty to the state. MK Hamdan seized the opportunity by submitting a parliamentary question to Prime Minister David Ben-Gurion:

> On May 1, the Communist party organized premeditated disturbances
> in the city of Nazareth and afterward in the village Umm al-Fahm. The
> public has drawn a general and mistaken conclusion from these serious
> riots regarding the Arab population's attitude toward the state. The facts
> prove manifestly that this was a deliberate provocation by the Communist
> Party, which incited its activists in a grave and treasonous way. In view of
> this assault on the state and out of concern for the good name of the Arabs
> of Israel, I would like to ask his excellency the prime minister if it is the gov-
> ernment's intention to use the legal means at its disposal that were intended
> for countering treasonous acts in the country.

Ben-Gurion's response comes as no surprise: "I am entirely in agreement with the honorable questioner, regarding the nature of the treasonous disturbances. . . . Obviously, the government will make use of all means necessary against all acts of rampage and treason in the country."[27] Here Hamdan offered an alternative to the nationalist view: the Arabs in Israel owed allegiance not to the Arab nation or to the Palestinian people but rather to the state of Israel, whose citizenship they held and to whose laws they were subject. The real traitors were not those who were loyal to the state, those referred to derisively as the "regime's tails." The traitors were, rather, those who entered into conflict with the state and its institutions and, in so doing, harmed the interests and good name of the Arabs of Israel. It is no wonder that Hamdan found an ally in Ben-Gurion.

Two weeks after the disturbances came the anniversary of Israel's declaration of independence, 15 May on the Gregorian calendar, thus also the date on which the Palestinians marked the Nakba, the catastrophe their people suffered as the result of the 1948 war. Hundreds of Arab activists were still under arrest. The Arab world marked the tenth anniversary of the defeat of 1948, and the radio stations of the United Arab Republic (Syria and Egypt) called on the world's Arab and Muslim states to hold a symbolic five-minute strike to mourn the establishment of Israel.[28] The call touched the hearts of some of Israel's Arab citizens a lot more than Israel's call to them to go out to watch IDF military parades three weeks earlier. The security forces prepared to prevent the Arabs from following their hearts. The principal concern was what would happen in schools. These fears were hardly groundless.

SECRETS FROM THE TEACHERS' ROOM

In February 1961, the officers of the police's Special Branch gathered for a meeting at the offices of the chief of the investigation division at the police's national headquarters. These officers were responsible for Arab affairs. The major subject on the agenda was Arab nationalism. The investigation chief began by saying, "Arab nationalism has penetrated nearly every minority village and home." He enumerated three channels of this penetration: Voice of the Arabs broadcasts from Cairo, connections with infiltrators and enemy agents, and songs at weddings. He instructed the district and subdistrict officers to take seriously all information they received about nationalist utterances, to bring in suspects for thorough interrogation, to search their homes carefully, and to take deterrent action.

Chief Superintendent Aharon Shlush, one of the police force's most prominent Arabists and chief of the Special Tasks Division, was more modest in his expectations: "There is no way to prevent [Arab nationalism]. We can only restrict and confine it. If people sing paeans in their homes, we can't do anything to them, and if they sing in a public place we can harass them, but we should not take legal action before we know what the results will be. If the punishment is lenient, there is no point in prosecuting. *But if the offender is a government employee, such as a teacher, steps should be taken, because these people have additional obligations, and such behavior is liable to lead them to lose their jobs*" (my emphasis).[29]

Shlush was not presenting a new idea. The practice of severely punishing teachers who expressed opinions opposed to those of the system had been a foundation stone of the security forces' strategy since the state's early days. The authorities also did all they could to choose teachers with loyalist political beliefs.[30]* If this process of elimination could not be done before candidates were granted teaching jobs, it was to be done afterward. In 1952, for example, forty-two Arab teachers were dismissed for having "misused the opportunity given to them as educators of the next generation and shapers of its image," as one military government officer wrote. The number of dismissals amounted to 7 percent of the total of 685 Arab teachers employed.[31] Furthermore, collaborators were appointed to teaching jobs at the recommendation of the security agencies. "Other perquisites we can offer, thanks to our connections with the Ministry of Education, are the employment of teachers and the placement of teaching candidates in courses," said the head of the Special Tasks Division, Superintendent Ziv, in a discussion of ways to compensate collaborators.[32] This was another angle on the story told by the mother of Nizar Hasan, the film director. The military government and the Ministry of Education assumed that the schools could produce a new generation of Israeli Arabs, with but a miniscule link to Palestinian history

---

* Regulations issued in July 1950 stated that applicants for teaching positions had to undergo a "reliability test" by the GSS and police before being accepted. See protocol of the coordination committee [of the security agencies], 19 July 1950, IDFA, 6/243/52. With the establishment of the regional committees in 1954 and the increase in bureaucracy, a new procedure was instituted. It required that "a recommendation [about] the employment of teachers be conveyed to the governors, to be discussed in the regional committee. The governor will convey the committee's decision to the military government department, with copies to the police national headquarters and GSS headquarters, [and] the military government department will convey the agreed-upon decision to the office that applied to it, after additional coordination with the central security agencies." IDF/General Staff/Operations to military governors, "Grant of Security Clearances—Regulations," 6 July 1954, ISA 79, 2314/3.

and a very limited sense of belonging to the Arab nation. Their principal identification would be with Israel.

But the consolidation of a unique Israeli Arab identity—which indeed began to take place at this time as a result of the realities of life as Israeli citizens—did not lead Israel's Arab citizens to abandon their Arab and Palestinian national identities completely. There were several reasons for this. First was the state's ambivalent attitude toward its Arabs, who on the one hand were citizens, yet on the other hand possessed limited rights and were placed under military government. This prevented them from feeling like full-fledged Israelis and helped to preserve their Arab national identity alongside their Israeli one. Second, add to this the effects of external developments—mainly Nasserism—on the Arab public in Israel, effects that were beyond the Israeli state's ability to control. The third factor that prevented the success of this project was the existence of deep undercurrents in which Palestinian national memory was preserved and fostered, not in public, but in family and social frameworks. In addition, the Israeli decision that Arabic would remain the language of teaching in the Arab schools contributed to the affiliation of Israel's Arabs with the rest of the Arab world. All these factors affected both teachers and students and made it difficult to uproot Arab nationalism completely. But the security forces tried, through close supervision of the educational system and the winnowing of teachers, to reduce these factors' influence on the younger generation.

The selection of teachers on the basis of their political opinions had severe consequences for Israel's Arab public school system. First, by disqualifying those teachers with nationalist or Communist leanings, the state significantly reduced the pool of potential educators, especially given the tendency of the educated stratum of Arab society to be more nationalist than the Arab population as a whole. Even more important, the people preferred for teaching positions were not necessarily the most qualified applicants in terms of their education or dedication to their communities. Priority was given to those who agreed to subordinate their opinions to those of the regime or who took it upon themselves to avoid politics. Naturally, this affected the quality of teaching. Even if some of the teachers were good ones, they could not serve as models for their students or engage the young people about the issues that most concerned them. Schools thus became, in many ways, irrelevant. Some nationalists managed to get into the system, but they had to dissimulate; they spoke with one voice to representatives of the government and in another to their students and colleagues. And this double discourse was an educational problem. Furthermore, the GSS and police oversight and surveillance system was meant to find such teachers, as well as the students they enlisted. The result was that the schools turned into arenas where everyone was informing on one another.*

Israel's Decade Festivities and the events commemorating the tenth anniversary of the Nakba served as a test of Israel's success in repressing nationalist sentiments among Israel's Arabs, including those in the schools. Reporting on the events of 15 May 1958, *Davar,* the Histadrut's newspaper and thus the voice of Mapai, stated, "The authorities in Nazareth and the Galilee . . . indirectly conveyed to the Arab inhabitants their decision to use forceful measures against any person who tries to riot or incite against the state."[33] In other words, a threat of punishment hung in the air for anyone who thought of commemorating the Nakba.

But these severe measures were not fully successful. Here and there high school students held ceremonies to mark the day (sometimes with their teachers' consent). Two tenth-grade classes at a high school in Nazareth's eastern neighborhood decided to observe a five-minute silent vigil to mourn and protest the establishment of Israel. The teachers of these classes, who were coincidentally—or perhaps not—Jews, demanded that the students desist from their demonstration. The students refused, and the teachers left the classes. Other students arrived to express their support for the tenth graders. Failed attempts to hold similar events occurred at the high school in central Nazareth and in the city's Franciscan school, where students hung up a picture of Nasser.[34]

The authorities' reaction shows how anxious they were about the commemoration of the Nakba in Arab schools. The measures were typical. First, they threatened the teachers, pitting one against another. This was aimed at preventing the creation of a united front among the teachers and at getting them to supervise their students more intensely. One teacher in the eastern neighborhood school was called in to the police station and told,

---

* In September 2004, Adalah, the Legal Center for Arab Minority Rights in Israel, petitioned the Supreme Court against the GSS's involvement in the appointment of teachers. The Adalah suit stated, "This unseemly regime has produced confused teachers, subservient school principals, and docile school inspectors. Many of them have for many years comprehended their jobs as involving the fulfillment of nonpedagogic imperatives. Fear, a culture of silence, and paralyzing confusion have characterized the conduct of the Arab educational system. The negative consequences of this regime on Arab students was and is still obvious. In practice, the emancipatory role of the teacher, at least according to a certain utopian understanding of reality, has been subordinated to the repression of the spirit of inquiry and the dissemination of knowledge" (Adalah's appeal to the Supreme Court 8193/04).

"The authorities see the teachers as responsible for the student disturbances, and . . . the events of May 15 are liable to be detrimental to the interests of the teachers." The warning brought about the desired results. When the teacher returned to take part in a teachers' meeting to discuss the incident, he demanded that severe measures be taken against the demonstrators in order that "responsibility for this matter not be placed on the teachers, and in order to uphold the school's good name with the authorities." The meeting in the police station also increased tensions among the educational team. The teacher tried to place all the blame on the principal and challenged the principal's claim that he had not been in school at the time.

The second measure was to scare the students. A military government official summoned the school principal and demanded a list of the students in the two rebellious classes, with the names of students receiving state tuition subsidies marked. The official then requested that the principal inform the students "in an appropriate way" that he had given the governor a list of the subsidized students, adding, "It may well be that, two years from now, when they finish school and look for jobs, the officials who have the authority to decide about jobs for the graduates will observe a five-minute silent vigil in memory of the students' lost careers."[35]

This was classic psychological warfare. Such overt and covert threats made parents plead with their children to abjure political activity. Despite this, not a few young people were drawn into political activism because of ideology and belief, or in search of a sense of meaning, or because of the support rendered by the Communists and nationalists. As a result, nationalist activity did not cease, and informers continued to file reports, with the authorities continuing to make threats. This became the routine in many schools.

The mood is evidenced by a report from a school in the mixed Jewish-Arab town of Lod (in Hebrew; al-Lid in Arabic), to the east of Tel Aviv. In one class, students made a practice of singing the song "The High Dam," a paean to Nasser about the construction of the Aswan Dam. In another class, students scribbled on a photograph of Israel's president, Yitzhak Ben-Zvi, and students also defaced Israeli flags that hung in the school. When, in a geography class, they were asked the name of the prime minister, they immediately responded, "Gamal 'Abd al-Nasser." "When [the teacher] corrected them that it was Mr. Ben-Gurion, the students responded that Mr. Ben-Gurion was prime minister for the Jews, but for them, the Arabs, it was Gamal 'Abd al-Nasser." The police received this information from one of the teachers, who was a veteran informer for the Special Branch of the Ramla Police Subdistrict, and from the members of a family of well-

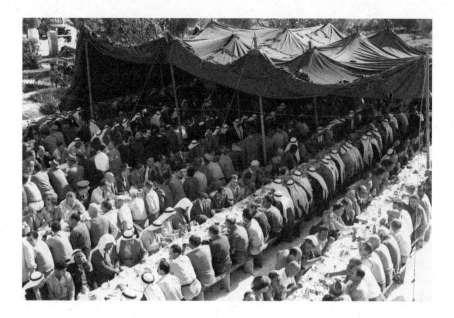

Figure 14. Manipulated *sulha*. In addition to preventing the Arabs from commemorating the massacre of Kafr Qasim, Israel manipulated the inhabitants to participate in a formal *sulha* (forgiveness ceremony) with state officials, 1957. Photograph by Moshe Pridan; courtesy Israeli Government Press Office.

known collaborators who attended the school. Their provision of information to the police exacerbated tensions in the school and sometimes led to fistfights.[36]

This was, then, a violent clash between two ideologies and their symbols: the Jewish state and its emblems versus Arab nationalism and its emblems; Ben-Zvi's photograph versus Nasser's; Nakba Day versus Independence Day; Israeli flags versus Arab flags. The security forces made huge efforts to prevent desecration of Israel's national symbols and to punish the perpetrators. This sometimes reached absurd levels, as in the case of a teacher named 'Ali from an elementary school in the Galilee. According to information that reached the school's principal and was forwarded by him to the police, 'Ali had picked up a picture of Theodor Herzl, the founder of the Zionist movement, from his desk, torn it up, and thrown it into the trash. After hearing about this, the principal took matters into hand. He went with the students to gather up the shreds of paper, giving some of them to the police and keeping the rest. Then he called the teacher in to explain his actions. The principal also sent a report on the incident to the school inspector in the Ministry of Education.

In his defense, the teacher said that the picture had been marked up and torn, so he simply completed the existing tears and threw it away. The police had their doubts. They brought in the students, who ranged in age from nine to eleven, and took testimony from them. One student related that the picture had indeed been marked up. During the course of his testimony he retracted this statement "and said that the picture had been clean and whole and that the teacher had told the students, if asked, to say that the picture had been torn and had lines on it." The rest of the students also testified that the picture had not been torn. The teacher continued to maintain his version of events, even adding that he had tried to find out who had torn the picture. He said he had explained to his students that it was important to respect the symbols of the state and had topped this off with a short lecture on Herzl. He defended his decision to throw out the picture rather than hang it up again, "since it was damaged, so as not to disrespect the late man." The police did not accept his explanation and opened a dossier on him. They charged him with malicious defacement.[37] This was one of the nonpolitical laws enlisted in this political battle. Such a charge would not automatically have been brought against a Jewish student or teacher suspected of defacing property.*

As Shlush said, the police had only a limited ability to monitor private conversations—although they, and the GSS, received some information from family forums. Their efforts were directed, therefore, at the public arena, and their closer supervision of schools, if only partly successful, made educators the state's quasi-representatives in Arab villages. This was clearly evident on Independence Day, when ceremonies were conducted in the schools. During the years of the military government, the police and the GSS carefully noted which inhabitants of Arab villages and cities flew Israeli flags over their homes and which refrained from doing so. They made lists of who attended celebrations and who did not, who went to watch the IDF parade and who reprimanded those who went. Those who wished to prove their

* The use of neutral legal provisions (as opposed to emergency regulations and "security" legislation) for political purposes was accepted practice. For example, the police opened an investigation against people in 'Arrabe who organized a raffle to collect money for a club they had founded. The law violated in this case was one forbidding unlicensed lotteries (see Acre SD to Northern District, "Unlawful Lottery," correspondence from August and September 1966, ISA 79, 318/12). Arabs who opened their places of business on Independence Day were fined (Acre SD to IP HQ, "Independence Day 1961," ISA 79, 174/5). Enhanced enforcement against Arabs was not always directly related to political matters: the police fined Arab farmers who carried passengers on the fenders of their tractors—a common practice in kibbutzim and moshavim (Acre SD to Northern District, 26 March 1961, ISA 79, 318/12). The aim of such steps was to demonstrate Israeli control in the villages.

loyalty to the state had an opportunity to do so, whether by helping organize the events or by making speeches. At the same time, the events also provided an opportunity for opponents to say what was on their minds. Just as some dissented at the time of the Decade Festivities, so too did they in the years that followed. On Independence Day 1961, a teacher in Makr gave a speech on the state's achievements. One of the participants in the ceremony rose at the end of the speech and shouted that everything the speaker had said was a lie. The heckler asked why the speaker had not mentioned the oppression of the inhabitants by the regime and the police. The principal of the local school cut him off and said that the authorities did not bother citizens who obeyed the law and reminded him that he had not even been invited to the event.[38]

As far as the authorities were concerned, the principal acted properly, as did the official speaker. They declaimed what the regime wanted them to declaim and kept silent about what it wanted them to keep silent about. Again, not all the teachers were of this type. Tensions involving political viewpoints surfaced on special occasions. One of these was in the fall of 1961, after five young Arabs were killed on the border with the Gaza Strip when they tried to leave the country surreptitiously.

In the mid-1950s, young Arabs began trying to cross the border into neighboring countries, usually into Lebanon. The number of these attempts— several dozen a year—prompted the security forces to claim publicly that the motives were nationalist. A minority of police officers also maintained that some circles in the Arab community were encouraging these actions. An internal police survey of the border crossings recognized that the matter was more complex than that; it listed five motives for leaving the country in this way. Some of those involved were moved simply by nationalist sentiments— the desire to live under Arab rule or to join the Arab national struggle. A second group was made up of people facing criminal charges. A third functioned as emissaries for their families or for relatives in neighboring countries. A fourth consisted of young people who had fallen out with their parents, and a fifth were some simply out to do something crazy. The anthropologist Emanuel Marx, then working in the office of the prime minister's adviser on Arab affairs, pointed to another cause—failing the national high school graduation exams. "In their despair, some students find an outlet in fleeing the country. . . . Such acts of desperation are a common phenomenon in Arab countries, and each year this leads to a series of suicides," he explained.[39] The border violators were generally arrested by the security forces of Israel's neighbors. Sometimes they were accused of spying (since many Israeli Arabs were in the service of Israeli intelligence); infrequently, they were enlisted for espionage missions by one of the Arab intelligence agencies, trained, and then sent back to Israel. In any case, most were returned to Israel.

This was not the fate of the five young men—three from Haifa, one from Sakhnin, another from Umm al-Fahm—who tried to cross into the Gaza Strip in the early hours of 18 September 1961. An IDF force that noticed them near the border opened fire and killed all five. The IDF claimed that the Arabs had not responded to the soldiers' calls for them to halt. But a rumor spread that the victims had been shot in cold blood and that the soldiers had mutilated their bodies. The Communist Party and Mapam demanded an independent commission of inquiry. The government was opposed, and the demand was rejected. A pathology report found no evidence that the bodies had been mutilated, but the rumors did not cease. The fact that the army and the government took their time to release details about the incident increased tensions.

In the approach of the funeral, set for four days after the shooting, tempers rose in Arab communities. Tempestuous demonstrations took place in many locations, during which protestors condemned the government, shouting slogans like "Ben-Gurion to the grave" and "Palestine is Arab." Municipal governments in many Arab localities issued statements condemning "the crime [against] the five" and demanded a commission of inquiry. In Acre, a mixed Jewish-Arab city, some one hundred Arab students participated in a demonstration organized by Communist activists Ibtihaj Bulus, Jamal Musa, and others. Fistfights between Arabs and Jews broke out there.

As in other events of this type, the security forces made use of their people in the Arab sector to calm things down, as well as to attack the organizers of the demonstrations. The regime's friends in the Arab local councils tried to prevent the acceptance of sweeping resolutions calling for strikes and demonstrations. In Haifa, Arab members of the Histadrut issued a communiqué in Arabic, in which they fiercely attacked the organizers of demonstrations, claiming that they were making capital from the dead men's blood. The placard, drafted by security officials, claimed that the intent of the demonstration's organizers was to further the conflict between Jews and Arabs.[40]

Sakhnin, home village to one of the five, was one focal point of the demonstrations. On the day of the funeral, 22 September, the police reduced the risk of mass involvement by informing the family that the body was on its way only when it was delivered to them. Moreover, the body arrived after the village's laborers had set out for work, in order to ensure minimal attendance at the funeral. (Only about eight hundred people were present; no speeches were made.) But the next day political activists in the village, led by Abu

Subhi, an uncle of the dead man, called a general strike. They demanded that shopkeepers not open their establishments. A couple scheduled to get married that day were told not to hold a *zaffa* (bridal procession) in the village streets. The couple reluctantly agreed. Schoolteachers and students were also told to participate in the strike.

The dilemma faced by schoolteachers and administrators was more difficult than that of private individuals. The schools represented the state, and the government expected loyalty and support from school principals. So, while one principal allowed his students to take part in the strike and the demonstration, another in the village's second school, Raja Sakhnini, declared that he would not allow classes to be canceled. He told students he met on the morning of the strike that the school day would be conducted as planned. He went to his school, assembled the teachers, and instructed them to prevent students from leaving their classes. He told the teachers, "Try to influence [the students] by persuasion, and if that does not work, . . . oppose them and . . . prevent the students from leaving, even at the cost of being exposed to physical harm."[41]

And in fact the school shifted from being an arena of verbal battle to one of physical battle. A group of demonstrating youths arrived and called on the other students to come out and join them. When the principal refused to allow this and argued that the demonstration was not justified, demonstrators from outside broke windows in the classrooms. One began shouting, "Allah yirhamu" (May God have mercy on him), lamenting the dead man, and female students wept. Some demonstrators began dragging girls out of the classrooms. The girls, obedient to the principal, refused to go out. Caught between the prospect of being physically hauled out by the demonstrators, their fear of punishment from the principal, and their own emotions about the killing of the five young men (which can only be guessed at), the girls did nothing.

The activists and the students who joined them continued their demonstration. One of its climaxes came when the GSS regional coordinator, Yehoshua Eckstein, drove his jeep into the village. The demonstrators threw stones at the vehicle, shattering its windshield. Eckstein got out and reprimanded the adults, who in turn rebuked the students for throwing stones. When he got back into his jeep, stones were thrown at him again—this time along with shoes, a symbol of humiliation. The GSS's northern region chief, Yehuda Bashan, was also attacked.[42] The two Israelis bore the brunt of the Sakhnin villagers' anger at the killing of the five and their frustration at life under military rule. This event, like the others described above, proves beyond any doubt that, a decade after the Nakba, many Arab citizens of Israel vigorously demanded their rights, no less and perhaps more forcefully than those in subsequent generations have.

True, some teachers and school principals obeyed the authorities and prevented their students from taking part in the demonstrations. Otherwise the protests would have been even stormier. The position they took was important not just on the practical level—that is, on restraining the extent of the demonstrations—but also in offering a pro-establishment alternative to the nationalist discourse, just as the authorities demanded that they do.

Only a small minority of the Arabs living in Israel adopted the Zionist discourse, and the state's attempt to prevent the majority from publicly voicing other opinions was only partly successful. Even among teachers, who as state employees were more vulnerable than others, many made no attempt to hide their nationalist sympathies. As noted, the GSS kept such teachers under surveillance, and if their politics became extreme, they were warned that if they continued to voice nationalist positions, they would be dismissed. On some occasions, the GSS asked the police to call in and interrogate teachers who had made problematic statements. The purpose was not necessarily to open criminal proceedings but rather to present "a deterrent against such actions in the future."[43]

The GSS's collection of utterances by teachers allows us to understand what this agency was concerned about, what its goals were, and what type of speech it sought to prevent. Detailed periodic reports entitled "Nationalist Activity and Utterances by Teachers and Students" were given by the GSS to the Ministry of Education's security officer.[44] These reports offer a broad picture of utterances that the state considered unacceptable.

The most serious offense seems to have been explicit or implicit support for acts of sabotage, whether voiced by teachers in private to their colleagues or made publicly to their students. "By God, may these forces [al-'Asifa, the armed wing of the newly established Movement for the Liberation of Palestine, known as "Fatah"] destroy this country," said a teacher from Kawkab, and a teacher from Tamra expressed his hopes to his colleagues on the eve of Easter: "We'll all be officers in the Palestinian army when the holiday comes next year." This type of utterance, beyond its symbolic aspect, prompted fear that teachers would allow their students to help terrorist organizations. Utterances with anti-Semitic overtones were recorded and documented: "Better that all the Arabs in this country be killed, just as long as we get rid of this filthy nation [the Jews]," a Nazareth teacher said, and this was recorded in his dossier. Another sensitive subject was speaking out bluntly about the security forces themselves. An important factor in the success of political policing was the public's fear of the seemingly unbounded ability of intelligence services. Casting doubt on their professionalism or merely disrespecting their personnel undermined their very ability to function. "Don't be scared of them. They are low-down dogs," one teacher said to another, referring to the GSS and the police. A report of this was recorded in the appropriate places.

Symbols and ceremonies were also, of course, important. Three teachers spoke about students ripping up an Israeli flag on Independence Day in their village, Kawkab. "The three laughed about desecrating the flag, did not attribute any importance to it, and seemed to be pleased with the event," says a report about them. Another teacher, from Jatt, in the Triangle, wondered, on Independence Day 1965, how Arabs could go to watch the annual military parade; this was recorded. A drunk Arab entered a coffee house in the village and began to lament about how the Arabs were sitting in cafés on such a day, celebrating. "Those present jeered the inebriated man. At that moment a teacher entered the coffee house . . . and when he heard from those present why the drunk they were laughing at was weeping, he said that only the man crying was speaking the truth, while the others lacked conscience." From the point of view of the security services, the problem with such a statement was that the teacher, despite his job, had adopted the Palestinian rather than the Zionist narrative about the 1948 war and was courageous enough to express this in public.

Surveillance was thus intended to restrict the adoption of the Palestinian narrative. So the GSS noted a priest's comment in a religion lesson: "The government stole our land and expelled us from our villages even though the sacred books of the three religions, the Jewish, the Christian, and the Muslim, say that land should not be stolen from a poor man." The names of teachers and students who participated in May Day demonstrations were reported to the authorities, and criticism of the military government's conduct was also perceived as illegitimate and worthy of note. In a conversation about the establishment of a village council in 'Eilabun, a teacher from the village said, "They generally appoint the 'tails' and the collaborators, not the people who are able to work for the village." In Beit Jann a teacher criticized the government's neglect of Arab and Druze education. All these were considered subversive utterances to be reported and documented, and the names of those who made them were added to the list of "problematic" teachers.

The close oversight of Arab speech had a profound effect on the political culture of the Arab community in Israel. Self-censorship (as in the cases cited at the beginning of this chapter), fear of expressing opinions and emotions (such as the protagonists of Nizar Hasan's film or the case of a rhymester who demurred when asked to sing pro-Nasser songs at a wedding on the grounds that he was "a father of children and did not want to go to jail"),[45] and reluctance to get involved politically were characteristic of the sociopolitical milieu of Israel's Arab citizens. Arab public figures' practice of condemning illegal demonstrations and terror attacks also developed. For example, in 1962 the village council of Tira called the Independence Day removal of Israeli flags in the village a "disgrace to the village" and asked that those involved be punished "severely and with an iron hand." The council also condemned a terror attack committed by Fatah militants soon after it launched its armed struggle (in 1965) in the neighboring Jewish farming village of Kfar Hess. Other public figures did the same.[46] Today the Palestinian Arab citizens of Israel are still expected to condemn terror attacks committed by Palestinians. Such condemnations are often issued, whether to mollify the authorities or to express authentic opposition to the attacks.

This conduct was one of the reasons for seeing the generation who lived under Israeli military rule as "the survivor generation," as they were termed by Dan Rabinowitz and Khawla Abu-Baker, who also argued that they were politically passive.[47] But this characterization is only partly true. During Israel's first two decades, Palestinian Arab citizens of Israel fiercely expressed their opposition to the state and its conduct, often more so than they did in later years. The tendency to overlook these acts of opposition has derived principally from the meagerness of historical studies of Arab society in Israel. Examples of such acts are the demonstrations held in Nazareth throughout the 1950s, the events surrounding the tenth anniversary of Israel's independence and the Nakba in 1958, the demonstrations following the killings of the five young men in 1961, and aid extended to infiltrators.

The existing scholarship's overly tight focus on the state's system of oversight and control ignores resistance to it. This approach is based on a tacit assumption that the Palestinians living in Israel were mainly objects to be maneuvered by the state, without any self-awareness or agency on their part. But both those who supported the regime and those who opposed it frequently did so out of a clear view of the world and by seriously weighing the factors involved, whether or not the conclusions they reached were persuasive. Furthermore, this focus ignores the fact that close surveillance was frequently what caused people to resist the state and its surrogates in Arab communities verbally and emotionally. In other words, the product of surveillance was sometimes the opposite of what its enforcers intended. This could be seen in three ways: defiance of the surveilling regime, an increase in hostility toward the collaborators who were the central means of surveillance, and public adoption of forbidden symbols.

The protests were largely verbal. At a wedding in Musmus, in Wadi 'Ara (the Northern Triangle) at the end of 1963, the guests sang nationalist songs. The lyrics of one said, "You can bring in the GSS agents, because I don't give a damn about them." In Tur'an, a group of people in a coffee house listened to a radio address by Nasser on the Voice of Cairo. One of them called out: "Long live Nasser!" Another turned off the radio and warned him that collaborators were present. "Don't turn off the radio, I'm not scared of them," the first man said, and the radio was turned on again.[48]

Increasing hostility toward collaborators was evident, for example, in this letter that a known collaborator from 'Eilabun received:

> Why are you an informer, why are you taking this evil path? How good it will be to crack your head and those of [a list of other collaborators]. You inform and spy against the village of 'Eilabun, and you are the only ones. Turn back from your evil path, which hurts you and our beloved village of 'Eilabun, your beautiful little village. Do what is good for your little village so that you will be appreciated. . . . You have many sisters, so desist. Why do you inform? . . . The inhabitants of 'Eilabun know who the informers are, and the day will come when they will regret their deeds. O informer, what have you gotten out of your tale-bearing? Better for you to be honorable, you big whore, mule, billy goat, spy, and informer.[49]

Poison pen letters of this type were not at all uncommon. In Tur'an, a collaborator received one signed the "Higher Committee of the Association of Palestinian Youth in Tur'an." It said, "Hey agent and traitor. Your day is coming. Haven't you been tracking the people in the village for long enough? Haven't you spread enough hatred and destruction in the village, you tails of the regime? . . . Hey traitors, hey tails, the day is close and the return of the refugees is very close, and the decent people of Palestine will punish you." In general, these letters were not followed by action, but they dealt serious blows to the morale of those who received them. Evidence of this can be found, perhaps, in a report filed by a collaborator in Tur'an to the effect that people were gathering every day at the entrance to the olive press at the edge of the

Figure 15. Who is listening? A resident of Tira brings a radio to his house after electrification reached the village in 1957. Soon the spies would start informing about his choice of broadcast services. Photograph by Moshe Pridan; courtesy Israeli Government Press Office.

village "and look[ing] with derision and scorn at the villagers who are close to the authorities."[50] His self-confidence seems to have been shaken.

The law is not of much help in dealing with looks of derision. But considerable investigative effort was made in trying to locate the authors of threatening letters. The police responded in the same way when letters were sent or posters were plastered on walls denouncing teachers who, from the regime's point of view, had done their job devotedly. Such letters and posters circulated in Kafr Yasif in the spring of 1957. "You traitors, the day will come when your throats will be cut," one of them declared. Letters full of insults and invective were sent to the principal of the local school. The regional school inspector, a resident of Kafr Yasif who had declared his sympathy for the state in songs he wrote and in other forums, received threatening letters a few years later. "To you lowlife, to you tail of the Zionists, to you the traitor to being Arab, to you traitor against Palestine. Serve your masters as much as you want, serve your masters in destroying your homeland, these actions will not bring you any benefit. The day will come when the Arab storm will rise and blow away you and your Zionist masters, in whose mud you sank up to your ears." The obvious suspects were teachers who had been dismissed from their jobs because of reports about their nationalist activity.[51] Nevertheless, it is important to note that only in relatively rare cases did such threats result in assaults or bodily harm.

The third unintended consequence of Israeli coercive policy was an overt use of Arab nationalist symbols by some Arabs. Such behavior was common among people who were able to shake themselves free of the atmosphere of intimidation that government supervision created. We have seen the cases of school students and teachers. In the public at large, some did this by marking the anniversary of the Egyptian revolution while boycotting Israeli Independence Day. Such events are interesting in and of themselves. July 1962 brought with it the tenth anniversary of the free officers' coup in Egypt, and Israeli Arab nationalists viewed it as a holiday. The Hadera Police Subdistrict reported, "In the village [Jatt] it was a day off. Many of the village's young men did not go to work and gathered into coffee houses in which television sets were installed. When Gamal 'Abd al-Nasser appeared on the screen, many cheered, clapped their hands, and called out 'Long live 'Abd al-Nasser.' As reported, the television pictures were blurry; some said that Israel had set off smoke bombs in the Negev, and some said that Israel was blurring reception deliberately with radar devices installed on Mt. Carmel in Haifa and in Givatayyim." These dubious scientific explanations for the reception problems were not important in themselves. What they show is that the people watching television were aware that they were acting against the wishes of the authorities, yet were not deterred. Reports that Arabs had dressed in holiday clothes, stayed home from work, and gathered around television sets came from many villages in the Triangle and the Galilee that year and on the same anniversary in the years that followed.[52]

In other words, the surveillance and control system was not very success-ful. The attempt to instill Zionist ways of thinking was an almost complete failure. And the attempt to prevent public espousal of the Arab or Palestinian national narrative accomplished only part of what it set out to do. Ahmad Sa'di views this as evidence of the success of Palestinian political resistance in Israel. He also, correctly, sees it as proof that the Palestinians in Israel were not only objects manipulated by the state. They were also active players who shaped their own fate. Another scholar, Amal Jamal, has pointed to two parallel, even contradictory, behaviors among the Palestinian popula-tion in Israel during those years. In addition to hosting Israeli leaders and voting for the ruling party, Mapai, the Arabs listened to the Voice of Cairo and admired Gamal 'Abd al-Nasser. Jamal has maintained that this was a survival tactic that became a strategy—the integration of elements of (Israeli) civil identity with elements of (Palestinian and Arab) cultural-national iden-tity. In this, the Arabs in Israel accepted the conventions of public discourse without adopting Zionist ideology.[53] This can be seen as a partial success for the regime, since the greater part of its efforts were directed at making the public space Israeli.

On the other hand, one additional factor cannot be ignored in a discus-sion of the battle over the narrative. Supervision by the state was not the sole author of Israeli Arab accommodation to Zionist symbols and the Zionist discourse. Neither were the Arabs who took this position merely tools of the authorities. Adopting this position involved an authentic political view that had several sources. The first was the estimation that integration of Arabs into the Israeli system, without their openly expressed opposition, was the best way to improve their lot. The second was an uncritical assimilation of the Zionist narrative, after understanding that a part of it was factually correct. The third was giving priority to communal rather than national identity (the approach most common during the Mandate period). These were the major factors that led a variety of people to adopt—and propagate—the Zionist narrative. Even if in some cases one can point to an opportunistic cast to these people's conduct, self-interest was certainly not the only factor.

There is no shortage of examples of the adoption of the official narrative. Some of the Arab writers for the Histadrut Arabic-language newspaper *Al-Yawm* were among the most prominent disseminators of the government worldview, in terms of both fundamental principles and concrete issues. The Arab members of the Knesset from Mapai's satellite parties also adopted part of the Zionist narrative. This was certainly the case with regard to Arab public figures who went on public relations missions for the state, such as Majed al-Fahoum from Nazareth, who made a trip to the United States in 1957.* Zaki 'Aweisat, the mayor of Baqa al-Gharbiyyeh, represented Israel at an international conference of city councils in Berlin in the summer of 1959, and a schoolteacher, Mahmoud Zu'bi, conducted a speaking tour in the United States in 1957. The three of them met with local audiences and also with Arab delegations and public figures. Zu'bi made speeches about the Jewish people returning to their homeland after two thousand years of exile and about the refusal of Arab countries to make peace with Israel. 'Aweisat explained how the participation of "Arabs loyal to the state" in international conferences could contribute to the creation of better relations with Arab countries.[54]

These people were official representatives of Israel. They were part of the system or were paid for their work. Muslim clergymen and functionaries received salaries from the Ministry of Religions, and this may have affected their way of thinking and their sermons. This was the case with Sheikhs Musa Tabari and Hubeishi, who headed the Advisory Committee on Muslim Affairs in Acre. So it was also with Sheikh Taher Tabari, the most senior Muslim cleric to remain within Israel, who served as *qadi* of Nazareth and chief justice of the Muslim Supreme Court of Appeals. Radio Damascus attacked him as a traitor because he called for peace between the Arab states and Israel. But apparently the stories about his willingness to sell his family land to Jews also tarnished his name in Arab nationalist circles.[55]

But again, it was not necessarily the jobs and salaries that made these clergymen celebrate Israel. There were others who did so on their own. The priest Murqus Hanna Mu'allim of 'Eilabun was a good example. At the height of the Sinai Campaign, he gave a sermon in 'Eilabun's church

---

* Fahoum's trip to the United States was supposed to last for two months but was cut short halfway through. Rumors spread through Nazareth that he had returned after suffering a heart attack brought on when he was unable to respond to aggressive questions by Palestinians from the diaspora and Arab representatives. Jezreel SD to SB Northern District, "The Atmosphere in Nazareth," 7 April 1057, ISA 79, 6/80.

Figure 16. A cocktail party. Arab figures from the Nazareth area at a party organized by the military governor, 1950. From this milieu came those Arabs who represented Israel abroad. Photograph by Fritz Cohen; courtesy Israeli Government Press Office.

in which he supported the Israeli offensive and called on the villagers to view the IDF's success as their own. One of the reasons he gave was, "We are inhabitants of the state of Israel and enjoy equality." He seems to have believed what he said.[56]

Belief in the justice of Israel's position and no less a desire to be integrated into Israeli society and to gain its recognition were important motives for the adoption of the Zionist discourse and symbols. An extreme and very concrete expression of this tendency was offered by a number of collaborators who participated in the Sinai Campaign. They demanded to be awarded the war's service pin, just as other IDF soldiers were. Officially, they were not eligible because they had not been formally inducted into the IDF. One collaborator, named 'Abd al-Hamid, had worked for the IDF in 1948 and had afterward settled in Ramla as a refugee. He was called to the flag at the end of 1956. He was attached to an IDF intelligence unit deployed in the Gaza Strip after its conquest. Because he was never officially inducted into the army, he did not receive any medals. Yet he wanted them. On one of his furloughs he went to a store in Jerusalem and bought IDF service pins for some small change and displayed them on his windbreaker. He wanted to show the world that he was not only part of Israeli society but at its vanguard. The irony is that he was arrested by the police on suspicion of impersonating a soldier. He thus symbolized Israeli Jewish society's difficulty in accepting exaggerated manifestations of Arab identification with the Zionist project.[57] *

* That same year, Sheikhs ʿAli Abu-Qrinat and ʿOda Abu-Mʿammar also made official requests to receive the Sinai medal. The military governor of the Negev called their request "crazy" and added, "I see it as a dangerous precedent" (RCAA-South [Negev], 20 June 1957, ISA 79, 2449/31). More on this in chapter 6.

SIX

Minorities within a Minority

Dilemmas of Identity

THE JEWISH STATE'S ARAB SOLDIERS

One morning in February 1956, IDF Corporal Moshe Yefet, who served in the military government, arrived in Yarka, a Druze village in the Galilee. He went by the home of the village's mukhtar, Sheikh Marzuq Sa'id Mu'adi, and the two of them set out together to hand out induction orders to the village's young men. When they reached the home of Suleiman Sirhan Tarif, they asked him whether his son had already reported for service. Tarif shouted at them, "I oppose my son's enlistment. Whoever agreed that the Druze would be drafted into the IDF is a son of a bitch." He then addressed the mukhtar: "If my son is wounded on the border with Egypt or Syria, I will slaughter you in the street." The soldier and mukhtar filed a complaint with the police.

One night a month later, Kamel Salman Tarif, thirty years old, arrived at his home in Julis, another Galilean Druze village. Seven men jumped him, threw him to the ground, blindfolded him with a *kafiyyeh,* and told him, "Now you'll know what it means to sign for us and send us to the army." The previous day, Tarif had given the commander of the IDF's Minorities Battalion the names of several young draft-age Druze. This, he believed, was the cause of the attack on him.[1]

These two incidents were not exceptional. They exemplify the attitude of most Druze toward mandatory military service, first in the reserves (in 1953), and afterward in the regular army (since 1956). They also testify to intrafamily disputes over the issue: like many others, the Tarif family included both proponents and opponents of the draft. Figures from the enlistment department of the IDF's manpower division show that, out of 197 Galilean Druze called up at the beginning of 1956, only 51 voluntarily reported for service. Of the 117 eligible young men from the Druze villages on Mt. Carmel, only 32 reported. In other words, in both regions where Israel's Druze were concentrated, only a bit more than a quarter served willingly.[2]

In opposition to the common wisdom and in partial contradiction to Israel's claim that the Druze asked to be conscripted, they were, to put it mildly, lukewarm about serving in the IDF. Even among the community's leadership, only a handful—led by MKs Jaber Dahash Mu'adi, Saleh Khneifes, and Sheikh Labib Abu-Rukun—voiced enthusiastic support for army service. Their willingness to make a "blood covenant" with the IDF was, it turns out, restricted and conditional. As the security forces understood, opposition to army service had a number of sources, some of them personal (the natural reluctance and worries people usually have about army service), some connected to internal Druze politics (the community's division into factions that took different positions on the issue), some relating to larger political influences (Druze identification with Arab nationalism or concern that service in the IDF would adversely affect their ties with Druze living in Arab countries). In addition, Druze were concerned that Israeli army service would sour their relations with their Muslim neighbors. The officials responsible for Druze affairs in Mapai and in government ministries blamed the community's leaders, who in their view did not do their job and did not sufficiently prepare the ground for army service among Druze youth. As a result, the security authorities decided to take matters into their own hands and to break Druze resistance to enlistment. They used incentives, such as the grant of gun licenses to Druze who encouraged enlistment, as well as force.[3] The enlistment office gave the police the names of some draft dodgers, whom the police arrested. They opened criminal files against these young men and took them to court. The courts released them only after they declared their willingness to enlist. At the same time, the police used legal technicalities to prevent enlistment opponents from holding rallies.[4]

The opponents received support from Druze leaders in neighboring countries, first among them Sultan al-Atrash, leader of the Druze in Syria. In an interview on Radio Damascus, al-Atrash explained that Israel was deceiving and dividing the Druze in order to implement their conscription and that the sheikhs who agreed to the policy were motivated by personal interest and did not represent the community. He promised the Arabs in Israel, including the Druze, "We are building a force in all the Arab countries to liberate you from colonialism." He called on them not to be enticed by Israeli propaganda. In another public statement with three other Druze leaders from Syria and Lebanon, al-Atrash declared that the purpose of mandatory army service was to harm the Druze and ruin their relations with the Arabs. He claimed that Israel would never grant them equal rights and would always consider them disloyal (whether to their own people or to Israel). "Jaber Dahash [Muʿadi], Saleh Khneifes, Labib Abu-Rukun, and others have ruined your good names. Come back to your senses, be aware of your fate, and know that Israel is play-ing with you and making problems for you. Stand with your Arab brothers in the rescue struggle, because the day of victory is not far off. . . . Victory to the Arabs and death to the Zionist regime and to those who collaborate with it," the interview concluded.[5]

To overcome resistance within Israel and from outside it, the police ar-rested Druze who refused to enlist. In March 1957, the police went after draft dodgers in search-and-arrest operations conducted simultaneously in the adjacent Mt. Carmel villages of Daliat al-Karmel and ʿIsfiya. In the latter, they arrested twelve suspects, despite nonviolent resistance by their families. In Daliat al-Karmel, matters were more complicated. With municipal elec-tions approaching, the mayor, who feared losing public support, refused to accompany the police. Instead, he sent with them the city council's messen-ger boy. In the meantime, the suspects were warned that the police were on their way, and most of them made themselves scarce. The police found only three, whom they brought to the municipal building. Most of the village's inhabitants gathered around it "and announced that they would not allow the arrested men to be taken out of the building, even if it meant using force." The police detachment's commander consulted with his superior officer, who ordered that the three men could be released on bail on condition that they report to the police station the next day. The three indeed reported to the police station (in the end agreeing to enlist), but the rest of the village's draft dodgers continued to refuse.[6]

The reasons for resistance to enlistment in the IDF were enumerated by dozens of sheikhs from Shefaʿamr and its surroundings, in a letter they sent to the prime minister and the minister of defense:

1. In light of the difficult and delicate conditions of the time we find ourselves in, we reject finally and absolutely the demand to perform mandatory labor in the Israel Defense Forces.

2. We are Arabs in Israel and have a duty to perform all the obligations that civil law imposes on us, such as paying taxes assessed against us. But it is extremely important to know that we are first of all Arabs, and no Arab fights against his brothers under any circumstances and in any place.

3. Israel does not vitally need the service of us Druze in its army. We the Druze can serve Israel in all kinds of other "civil" ways. . . .

4. The Druze in Israel should be treated just as all the Arabs here. The same body that demanded the conscription of the Druze for mandatory labor in the army thus does not properly represent the Druze.[7]

These were weighty reasons, and many hundreds of Druze (some fifteen hundred, according to one source) signed a petition to this effect. The resisters also expressed their fear that mandatory army service would not only harm the community in Israel but also create hardships for the Druze in nearby countries. Some spoke fiercely against enlistment, such as Sheikh Farhud Qasem Farhud of al-Rameh, who said, according to a report from a gathering held in March 1957 in the *hilweh* (Druze house of prayer) in Kafr Yasif, "The sheikhs who signed their support for the conscription of the community's young men should be liquidated."[8]

For a few months, it looked as if this mass resistance would require the Ministry of Defense to reconsider its position. But this was not the case. The draft resistance movement did not long withstand the arrests and efforts at persuasion. The support it received from the community leadership dissipated, and the protests slowly died out. A few months later the IDF general staff's operations division reported to the Ministry of Defense that the military government's and police force's actions had brought an end to incitement against enlistment, "and the whole thing belongs to the past."[9]

Why did Israel insist on drafting the Druze, and why was the state even willing to use force to compel them to serve? One indication was given by Zalman Divon, the prime minister's adviser on Arab affairs, at a meeting of the parliamentary Committee on Minority Affairs, under the chairmanship of Speaker of the Knesset Yosef Sprinzak. Yigal Alon, a member of the committee, had initiated a discussion of the "draft-dodger hunt," as he called it. Divon said, "At first the Druze unit was composed solely of volunteers. But when difficulties arose in finding sufficient volunteers, they [the unit's commanders] switched—in accordance with the advice of the [Druze] leaders— to mandatory enlistment."[10] This is a practical explanation. The Minorities

Battalion lacked manpower. At first the army tried to increase enlistment through persuasion. Afterward, proposals were made to deny travel permits to Druze who did not serve in the reserves and to make life difficult for them in other ways. But this did not work either. As a result, the draft was extended to the Druze.[11] *

On its surface, this is a sufficient explanation for the Druze draft. But we should not forget that the IDF also had the option of disbanding the unit, which was not in any case an essential part of its order of battle. But that option was rejected. Those responsible for the issue, such as Divon, always took pains to stress that the decision was to maintain the unit, even if it required a draft, at the request of the community's leaders. Ben-Gurion himself, when the draft was instituted, said, "I did not consent to issue an order on conscripting the Druze until I was assured that all those who speak in the name of the Druze, the civil and religious authorities in all the communities, agree to it, and I received assurances that they [the Israeli officials] spoke with all these [community leaders] and that they agree. It is a community with many internal conflicts."[12]

Calling the Druze leaders' request a draft was, in one sense, merely an excuse. The reason Israel persevered in its policy should first be sought in external politics. Al-Atrash's claim that the goal of the draft was to sever the Druze from other Arabs was hardly baseless. Mandatory military service for the Druze was and still is important for much more than their mere fighting power. A document produced by the Minorities Battalion states this explicitly: "The direct effect [of the minorities unit] has been to bring the Druze community closer and to tie it to us, impairing relations between the Druze and Muslims in this country and undermining trust in the Druze outside the country." Israel did not want to relinquish this achievement. In the mid-1950s it sought to broaden the "use" of the Druze, and the Minorities Battalion commander proposed using his unit for interior security and intelligence missions: "Educational and public relations actions will bring the younger generation closer to the problems Israel faces and increase its loyalty, and it will be possible to make use of many of them in internal security, uncovering

* A proposal to disband the minorities' unit and integrate Druze soldiers into other IDF units was rejected in 1957. Ya'akov Tzvia, the Minorities Battalion's commander, wrote, "This human material suffers from feelings of inferiority and suspicion and will not be able to overcome these in a single unit with Jewish soldiers. In my view, also for security reasons, it is desirable that there be separate units, in order to make supervision of them easier." Tzvia to the Operations Division, IDF General Staff, 23 February 1953, IDFA 222/57–1.

foreign agents, infiltrators, smugglers, and so forth. Certain carefully chosen figures will be of great assistance in their contacts with other countries in the form of intelligence and especially from a political point of view."[13]

These, then, were the most significant reasons for persisting with conscription. This is exactly why the basic argument of the resisters—their Arab identity and their desire to maintain their ties to the Arabs inside and outside Israel—made no impression on Israeli officials. Disconnecting them from the Arab world was the central goal of conscription, not a by-product, and Israel had an interest in undermining relations among the different Arab communities in Israel.*

Another important factor in some Druze leaders' consent to conscription was their rivalry with other leaders for primacy among their coreligionists. In the mid-1950s, prominent Druze figures came to the conclusion that they would not be able to gain any significant political clout within their communities without the support of the Israeli establishment or senior figures within it.[14] To gain such support, they had to stress their loyalty to the state and their consent to the conscription of young Druze men. The appointment of Labib Abu-Rukun as mayor of 'Isfiya and the choice of Saleh Khneifes for the Druze slot on a Mapai satellite slate for the Knesset proved the advantages of supporting the draft.[15]

On the opposite side was Sheikh Amin Tarif, acknowledged by most Israeli Druze as their senior religious authority. He opposed conscription because he wanted to avoid causing a break between the Druze in Israel and their coreligionists in the rest of the Middle East. His reservations also related to his fear that the moral values of Druze youth would be compromised. But his opposition was to his detriment. His opponents, who censured him for a lack of transparency in the management of the Nebi Shu'eib trust, which

---

* It was not long, in fact, before Druze increasingly started identifying with the state and with the IDF. As a result, tension between the Druze and other Arab communities increased. This was apparent during the Sinai Campaign, in October 1956. Young Druze from Kafr Yasif reported to the police that a Muslim teacher had spoken to the students about Egyptian battle successes and that the students had broken out in cries of "Long live Gamal 'Abd al-Nasser!" "We notified the principal, Metannes Metannes [a Christian], who told the Druze students, 'You aren't military governors, you have no interest in this matter, and everyone can talk however they want.' The [Muslim] students vilified the Druze students for volunteering to serve in the IDF, as well as for their collaboration with the government.... Since we are young Druze and soldiers in the IDF, we inform you of all these activities" (Druze youth to the commander of Acre police station, 11 October 1956, ISA 79, 78/11). Presumably the Druze students wanted to strengthen their position in the village through adoption of Zionist symbols and participation in the state's surveillance system and felt under attack when their fellow students refused to obey their instructions.

Figure 17. Volunteers? Druze leader Jaber Dahash Muʻadi congratulates a Druze soldier who volunteered to serve in the IDF during the 1948 war. Photograph courtesy Israeli Government Press Office.

oversaw the Druze holy site of that name and was the community's main source of income, took advantage of his opposition to Druze conscription to undermine his position with the Israeli authorities. The families that sent their sons to fight in the IDF's ranks were the first to complain about his position. As early as 1949, Sheikh Salah 'Ali Abu-Rukun, a bereaved father of a soldier who had been killed in the battle of Yanuh, told Ministry of Religions official Ya'akov Yehoshua, "Sheikh Amin Tarif placed a secret ban on men who enlisted in the Israeli army [during the 1948 war], and for this reason, the war dead of the Minorities Battalion in the Yanuh battle [of October 1948, in which ten Druze soldiers from the unit were killed by the Druze of Yanuh] were not buried, and their bodies became carrion for the birds."[16]* In 1953, when the government moved to conscript Druze for reserve duty, Tarif's opponents called a press conference at which they detailed his negative feelings toward the Jews before and during the 1948 war. Tarif's opposition to conscription, they claimed, grew out of his sympathy for Arab nationalism.

Salman Tarif, the sheikh's brother, understood that such an image could be detrimental to Amin Tarif's efforts to obtain Israel's full recognition of his position as the community's political and religious leader. He also presumed, correctly, that his brother's opponents among the Druze were benefiting from the support of senior Israeli security officials, including the commander of the Minorities Battalion, Amnon Yanai. With this in mind, he immediately convened an opposing press conference to refute the charges against his brother and to mitigate the criticism of his opposition to conscription. At the press conference, the two Tarif brothers declared their support for conscription, conditional on the replacement of the commanders of the Minorities Battalion, who, they charged, were involved in *fasad* (intrigues and defamation). In this way, they succeeded not only in mollifying their critics but also

---

* During the Mandate as well as at its end, some Druze saw themselves as part of the Palestinian Arab national movement while others stressed a unique Druze identity. A subset of the latter group advocated ties with the Zionist movement. In the 1948 war, some Druze thus fought alongside Jewish forces while others joined the Arab armies, and many others maintained neutrality. The Druze who assisted the Haganah and the IDF mediated between Jewish commanders and the officers of the Druze battalion of the Arab Liberation Army, and they succeeded in arranging the defection of some of the latter. The defectors, along with a group of Druze from Mt. Carmel, formed a Druze company within the Minorities Battalion, a company manned by volunteers. In the Hiram offensive of October 1948, IDF forces conquered the western Galilee, including a number of Druze villages. In most of the villages, agreements were reached with the inhabitants prior to the IDF's entry, and fighting was avoided. As a result of a misunderstanding, the Druze of Yanuh resisted the Druze unit of the IDF, and ten soldiers were killed in the battle.

in raising questions about Yanai and Yehoshua Palmon, the former prime minister's adviser on Arab affairs, who supported Labib Abu-Rukun and Saleh Khneifes, leaders of the anti-Tarif faction among the Druze. In addition, Tarif acquired a political patron, Abba Hushi, mayor of Haifa, one of the pioneers of Jewish-Druze ties since the 1930s. The alliance was beneficial to both of them. The Tarifs gained a powerful sponsor, and Hushi was able to reestablish his influence among the Druze. He "adopted" Amin Tarif, as well as the Druze member of the Knesset, Jaber Mu'adi, who had also assisted Jewish forces during the war but who was not enthusiastic about conscription. Hushi worked to convince both the Tarifs and Mu'adi that mandatory military service for young Druze would benefit the community.

Sheikh Amin and his brother Salman ceased to voice opposition to conscription, both because of Hushi's lobbying and as a result of a meeting they held with Foreign Minister Moshe Sharett. Now they argued that it was better to draft young Druze men than to expect them to volunteer. A draft would allow them to tell Arabs that they were serving in the army not of their own volition but because the law required it. Such an arrangement was amenable to all sides—the state, the Druze who had supported conscription since 1948, and those who had just recently agreed to endorse mandatory service. Sheikh Amin also withdrew his opposition, on the condition, accepted by the Ministry of Defense, that young Druze who wished to engage in religious studies (as well as 'uqqal—initiates, "knowers") be exempted from service. This created a situation in which no senior Druze leaders dissented from the imposition of the draft. The road to conscription, and to the consolidation of Sheikh Tarif's position as leader of Israel's Druze, was now clear, even though many Druze still opposed the idea of the draft.

Conscription served to set the Druze apart from the other Arabs in Israel and created momentum toward the dissociation of the two communities. In 1957, the Druze were recognized as a distinct religious confession. In 1961, the community's spiritual leadership received the status of a statutory body, and a year later a law was enacted recognizing Druze religious courts and establishing a separate Druze judicial system.* The Nebi Shu'eib celebrations,

* Under Ottoman law, adopted by the British Mandate, then by Israel, personal status affairs, such as marriage, divorce, and burial, are under the purview of religious courts rather than the secular judicial system. The Ottomans did not recognize the Druze as a religious community. As a result, Druze were subject to Muslim religious courts. Legal recognition of the Druze as a community and their religious courts as equal in status to those of other religions was thus aimed at strengthening their separate religious identity, and it was construed by the Druze leadership as correction of a longstanding injustice.

which in the past mainly religious people had attended, became a popular observance. A booklet about the prophet whose tomb was the site of the festivities (whom the Druze identify with the biblical Jethro) was prepared for Druze students. The festivities included displays by Druze boy scouts, and the swearing-in ceremony for Druze conscripts was also held at the site.[17]

All these measures were meant to encourage the Druze to identify themselves as a community distinct from the rest of the Arabs, but without question their service in the army was what "intensified the crisis of confidence between the Druze and the members of other communities," as Aharon Layish, the deputy to the prime minister's adviser on Arab affairs, wrote.[18] Beyond the issue of conscription itself, Arabs grew resentful of the Druze because the Minorities Battalion was used to search abandoned Arab villages to prevent their original inhabitants from resettling in them and to expel refugees who had infiltrated back into Israel.

But, like other Israeli officials responsible for Druze affairs, Layish discerned dissatisfaction on the part of many Druze in the mid-1960s, in particular young ones. The Israelis feared that this would be expressed as refusal to perform military service or as sympathy for Arab nationalism. One important reason for Druze resentment was the community's justified feeling that military service had not brought them equality in Israeli society. Another reason was "the identification of some Druze intellectuals with the Arab national movement."[19] This was clear evidence that the question of whether the Druze should be part of the Arab national movement was still an open one and that it caused tension within the community.

Such tension manifested itself in a variety of ways in the 1960s. Some of it surfaced in interpersonal relationships, some in the press. In March 1964, *Al-Ittihad* published a letter from a Druze man from Hurfeish accusing Sheikh Amin Tarif of seeking to create dissension between the Druze and other Arabs. Later that month, Salah Shufaniyya from Shefaʿamr responded, in the same newspaper, that the government was sowing discord between the Druze and other Arabs, even though the two communities were in fact one. A Druze from al-Buqeiʿa (Peqiʿin) wrote an article in which he asserted, "The Druze are a branch of the Muslim tree and are serving as a tool in the authorities' divide-and-govern strategy, as they are oppressed just like the rest of the Arabs."[20] To make this clear, Quftan ʿAzzam Halabi from Daliat al-Karmel went to court to demand that his identity card label him as an Arab rather than as a Druze.

The response of the prime minister's office offers a peek at how Israeli officialdom operated with the Druze. A public relations official in the office,

Meir Meir, penned a letter responding to Halabi's suit, and asked the adviser on Arab affairs to find a Druze who would sign it and submit it in his own name. The ghost-written letter articulated the Zionist version of the Druze narrative and is worth analyzing in detail (the material in square brackets represents my own additions):

> *Allow me to begin by stating that I am a Druze proud of my descent as one of Bani Ma'ruf* ["people of benevolence," this is how the Druze refer to themselves; Meir, the Jewish author, used internal Druze speech codes to create believability] *and as a member of a community that, after long persecution on the part of our Arab neighbors* [the charge of oppression by the Arabs is the subject of dispute among the Druze; Israel embraced it to produce a unified, anti-Arab Druze history], *has now achieved progress on the high road of independent ethnic existence—for the good of all members of the community* [Druze uniqueness is presented as being good for the community rather than the product of a government strategy of dividing the Arab community]. . . . *A story is being spread through the Druze villages regarding one of the community's notables who fought many years for its rights* [Quftan Halabi was a community leader in Daliat al-Karmel]. *He now covets a position but did not get it the very moment he applied for it. Perhaps he was right that he deserved the post, or perhaps—forgive me if my lips and pen sin—he was not right* [Halabi was not granted the position that he sought, that of *qadi;* Meir portrays Halabi's alliance with Arab nationalists as motivated by his frustration and his personal interests. The implication is that the government's supporters were acting in the interests of the community, whereas its opponents were looking after themselves]. . . . *I think the entire community should condemn such inconstancy* [the community should unite against those who act against its consensus].

The letter Meir sent to Nissim Tokatli, the Haifa representative of the adviser on Arab affairs, completes the picture. "It would be good if the said person [Halabi] were attacked by the Druze," he wrote. "Once the letter is written and published, we can see to a parallel slander [campaign] in the Hebrew press."[21]

The letter was drafted as part of an effort to instill a unique Druze identity and neutralize those Druze who had advocated Arab nationalism. Meir knew that he would have no trouble recruiting a Druze to sign it. There was no shortage of Druze who were anxious to do the government's bidding or of Druze who supported the separatist movement on the basis of their understanding of Druze history. The Ministry of Education also worked to reinforce a separate Druze identity by replacing Muslim and Christian teachers with Druze in schools attended by Druze children. The Histadrut Arabic-language newspaper *Al-Yawm* published a column on Druze affairs (which was criticized by Druze who advocated Arab nationalism, as well as by Mapam's Arabic-language newspaper, *Al-Mirsad*). Despite these efforts, the Druze connection to the Muslims remained a matter of controversy. In 1964, Sheikh Tarif, by then the community's official spiritual leader, was quoted to the effect that he had to consult with the Ministry of Religions about the question of whether the holy month of Ramadan was a Druze holiday. Tarif was widely attacked for this. Letters to the editor expressed anger at the ministry's involvement in Druze religious affairs, and some argued that if Sheikh Tarif were unable to decide for himself what constituted a Druze holiday, he should resign.[22]

The debate over Ramadan's place in Druze religion was a continuation of a decade-old controversy over the status of 'Eid al-Fitr, the holiday marking the end of Ramadan. In 1952, Druze teachers had asked for a vacation for the three-day holiday. This request was accompanied by a desire to have Fridays, the Muslim Sabbath, off. Yehoshua Palmon discerned here the beginning of a tendency of the Druze "to return to getting close to their Muslim neighbors, as in the Mandate." In his analysis, the Druze community had two currents within it, one separatist and one Muslim. The pro-Muslims were led by Sheikh Amin Tarif, who at the time still led the opposition to conscription. "Unfortunately, the ministries have not managed to encourage the Druze faction that has reservations about [identifying themselves as] Muslims, but rather the opposite," Palmon wrote to the GSS.[23] He maintained that the Druze should be encouraged to refrain from observing Muslim holidays, and the Ministry of Religions agreed. In 1964, Tarif no longer opposed this approach. By that time he was confident of his leadership, had made the necessary connections with senior figures in the Israeli establishment, and had adopted a relatively separatist line (like that of the official Israeli position). He had learned to maneuver among his community's power centers, as well as in the corridors of Israeli power centers.

The 1964 calls for the resignation of Sheikh Amin Tarif thus did not get far. Tarif's own political acumen in his community also helped. His conduct in the matter of expropriated Druze property was an example of the caution he exercised with regard to state institutions. In the five years following the establishment of Israel, some thirty thousand *dunams* (seventy-five hundred acres) of land were expropriated from Druze villages in the Galilee, severely impinging on their agricultural capability, which had been their main source of livelihood up until then. Druze service in the IDF did not prevent the confiscation. On the contrary, the loss of farmland actually impelled them to seek employment in the IDF, police, Border Police, and prison administration. In other words, the state made a double profit off the confiscation. The benefit to the Druze is, however, disputable. In any case, the community's leaders, Sheikh Tarif among them, did little to preserve Druze holdings.[24] Here and there petitions against expropriation were organized, here and there Druze took part in Arab protests against expropriation, but the Druze leadership kept silent. At times, the leaders mediated between the state and landowners; in other words, they helped the state obtain ownership of the land it wanted, persuading the fellahin to accept compensation (in money or other land). The Druze leadership's silence stood out in particular in the case of the lands of Mughar al-Kheit.

The Mughar al-Kheit lands, also known as Mughar al-Druze lands, lay on the eastern slopes of the Safed Mountains, next to Hatzor HaGlilit. Before the establishment of Israel, these lands were possessed by inhabitants of Beit Jann, the large Druze village on Mt. Meron. These extensive holdings, more than six thousand *dunams* (fifteen hundred acres), were in part arable, in part rocky. The caves in the area were used as shelter by shepherds, as pens for sheep and goats, and as storerooms for farm tools. The lands were owned cooperatively by all the village's inhabitants (a method known in Arabic as *musha'*). With the establishment of Israel, this tract was closed to Beit Jann's inhabitants and declared a military area. Later, the land was designated for Jewish settlement, at which point the Druze demanded their land back but were met with refusal. In August 1959 a group of them tried to force their way in. "The inciters and rioters were arrested and the attempt to conduct a large-scale demonstration met with failure," a police officer reported. That entire time, state institutions pressured the Druze to accept compensation for the expropriated land, but the Druze were united in their opposition to the offer. At the beginning of 1960, the united front began to come apart. One family in Beit Jann consented to accept payment. Little by little, other families followed suit. Tension grew in the village between those who received compensation and those who refused to accept it. Inhabitants of the eastern neighborhood, in particular the Qabalan family, who led the struggle, announced that they would not allow the "traitors"—those who had ceded rights to the land—into their neighborhood. People from families that had accepted compensation were attacked verbally and physically. In August 1960, a brawl broke out between the two factions. A large police contingent arrived and ended the fighting. The police arrested an equal number of people from each side and brought them in for interrogation.

The village went through tough times. The opponents of compensation asked Druze religious leaders to ostracize the land sellers and declare them traitors and heretics. To reinforce the religious aspect of their claims, they asserted that the village's inhabitants had made an oath in their local *hilweh* not to give up their land. Thus, anyone who broke the oath was violating a religious prohibition. On 15 August 1960, the *'uqqal* convened under the leadership of Sheikh Amin Tarif and decided that ceding the Mughar al-Kheit lands did not constitute a violation of Druze religious law, that each individual could act as he saw fit.[25]

This ruling was diametrically opposed to the Muslim religious rulings issued by Hajj Amin al-Husseini and others during the Mandate period, to a parallel Christian ruling issued at the same time as al-Husseini's, and to the traditional Druze position on the land issue.[26] This is hardly surprising, of course, in light of the Druze religious leadership's interest in differentiating its faith from Islam (and certainly from the political aspects of Islam) and in light of the leadership's desire to maintain good relations with state institutions. But by conducting itself in this way, the leadership acted against what seemed to many Druze to be their fundamental basic interest—keeping their land. The leaders departed from this line only at the end of that year, when anger flared in the Arab and Druze communities over proposed legislation on agricultural land ownership. Arabs and Druze feared it would be used to take more land away from them, and many Druze took part in the protests. Only then did Sheikh Tarif indicate that he would convene sheikhs from all Galilean Druze villages to discuss what steps were necessary, perhaps even to approach foreign diplomats and ask for their intervention. As far as is known, such a convocation was never held; in any case, the bill never came up for a vote.[27]

As a general rule, then, the Druze leadership fell in line with the authorities even on the sensitive subject of land expropriations and sales. When there was tension between the need to satisfy the authorities and the desire to demonstrate unity with their Christian and Muslim neighbors, the Druze leadership chose the first option. The same was true when, in 1962 and 1963, the Knesset voted on proposals to eliminate military rule over Israel's Arabs. The Druze MK Jaber Mu'adi voted no; in exchange, Prime Minister Ben-Gurion announced that Druze living in areas under military government would be granted relief from some strictures.[28] The disparity between the Druze and other Arabs increased, as did recognition of their distinct identity and their identification with the state in central questions of security and lands.* This was a classic case of a confluence of interests between a minority within a minority (which feared being overwhelmed by the larger minority community) and a majority group (which also viewed the large minority as a threat). It also demonstrated the fluidity of national identities. In a different political situation, the Druze of the Galilee and Mt. Carmel, like their coreligionists in Syria and Lebanon, would no doubt have viewed themselves as part of the Arab nation and would have considered themselves bound by Arab values.

To a certain extent, Israelis involved in Arab affairs could count the development of a separate Druze identity as an achievement. But they also realized how fragile a gain it was. Beginning in the 1960s, security authorities conducted heated discussions about the future of relations with the Druze. At a meeting of the Central Committee on Arab Affairs, composed of representatives of all security agencies and headed by the prime minister's adviser on Arab affairs, the police force's representative, Aharon Shlush, said that the Druze could not be granted fully equal rights, because this would lead to confrontation between the Druze and the Jews. The chief of the GSS's Arab branch, Avraham Ahituv, proposed "carrying on with efforts to intensify Druze distinctiveness and separatism from the Arabs, especially among the younger generation." But he also expressed his awareness of this policy's limitations: "Despite all our political declarations, they will remain a minority group and will feel discrimination and disadvantage." His forecast was: "There is no way of preventing a process of the Druze being swept up by the nationalist current."[29] Some forty years have passed since then, and when young Druze are asked about their identity today, they may not ignore its Arab component. But they are not necessarily Arab nationalists, in the sense that the GSS defines them, and only a very small number view themselves as Palestinians, although the great majority of Israel's Arab citizens do view themselves as such.[30]

ENTRAPPED COMMUNITIES

Soon after it was established in 1952, the Central Council for Arab Affairs (on which representatives of the security agencies and relevant ministries sat) began discussing the treatment of different communities. A position

---

* MK Diab 'Ubeid, a Muslim from Taybe, also voted to retain the military government. But, unlike Mu'adi, he did so out of duty to Mapai and was unable to demonstrate any gain to his voters.

paper prepared in advance of this discussion, in the summer of that year, enumerated five distinct religious and national groups among Israel's non-Jews: Arab Christians (further divided into different sects); non-Arab Christians (Armenians and Greeks), Arab Muslims (the majority among the minorities), non-Arab Muslims (Circassians), and non-Muslim Arabs (Druze). The principal claim of the author of the paper, confirmed by Foreign Minister Sharett, was that the British had sought to create a single nation out of this jumble of communities:

> As will be recalled, in Palestine at the beginning of the British Mandate there were different national and religious communities and groups, each of which lived its own life and fostered its unique religious and social values. The Mandate government did much, in a variety of ways and to a large extent by artificial means, to eliminate the unique nature of each community and to blend and unite them as an Arab nation, with the clear purpose of granting the Muslim community supremacy over the other communities. This drive and these actions were resented by many inhabitants because of the absence of free will and the repression that these activities involved.
>
> It is unnecessary to state that the state of Israel is not interested in the continuation of the Mandate government's policy in this area. It is the right of every collective to foster freely, as it wishes, its religious, national, and social values. The government, for its part, must help, assist, and grant such possibility for development.[31]

The document's author argued that Palestinian Arab nationality was created by coercion. The claim is not entirely unfounded, but the same is also true of many other national groups. The author also contended that the British regime stood behind the establishment and consolidation of the Arab national movement. In other words, the paper's author was of the opinion that Palestinian identity was inauthentic. In his view, the grant of maximum autonomy to religious communities, as well as the state's differential treatment of each one, was an act of liberation, the correction of a distortion, and a way of preventing the largest community, the Muslims, from exploiting its power and exerting control over the others. This view was enshrined in the term still used by Israeli officialdom and also by mainstream scholarship at that time to refer to the country's non-Jews—*bnei ha-mi'utim,* the minorities. This term defines the Arabs in Israel not as a single unit, with a common national identity despite internal variation, but rather as a collection of distinct minority communities. As such, each community is supposed to conduct its affairs with the state independently. This has made possible achievements such as persuading the Druze leadership to endorse the conscription of its community's young men, not to oppose the military government, and to allow the sale of community land.

The Druze were not the only ones who had to formulate positions on controversial issues touching on Jewish-Arab relations. The Circassians also found themselves caught in the middle, between the state and the Arab Muslims, who were the majority within the minority. They also chose to serve in the army, first as volunteers, later as conscripts, and they hoped that their status as veterans would grant them greater rights. They also sought, in general, to distinguish themselves from the Arabs around them and were encouraged by the state to do so. The way they portrayed themselves to themselves and to those around them is illustrated by the following anecdote.

Salah Hasan Hakku, a Circassian from Kufr Kama in the Lower Galilee, was considering in 1957 the possibility of leaving Israel and moving to Turkey. He owned 140 *dunams* (35 acres) of land in the village, and in preparation for his move he entered into negotiations with a Bedouin of the nearby 'Arab al-Sbeih tribe who was interested in buying his holdings. The prospect of the sale roused vociferous opposition in the village. The village council and the local army veterans' association sent a letter to the commander of the Minorities Battalion asking him to prevent the sale. "The veterans cannot allow these Arabs to enter the village and build new nests of infiltrators here. 'Arab al-Sbeih is well-known to the authorities for their hostile attitude toward the state," they wrote.[32] To whom might the Circassian army veterans have turned had Hakku sought to sell his land to Jews?

Like other such letters we have seen, the appeal to patriotism was meant to prod Israeli officialdom into action. The Circassian villagers did not want to give the Sbeihs a foothold on their land, not necessarily because they feared the entry of hostile agents into their village. More important were the tense relations between the two communities, dating to the Circassians' arrival and settlement in the Galilee in the nineteenth century. The close relations the Circassians developed with Jewish settlers in the Lower Galilee before the establishment of Israel and their decision to serve in the IDF grew out of their sense of being a minority in an Arab environment. Both Israel and the Circassians hoped to benefit from the community's consent to the conscription of its young men into the Israeli army. The inhabitants of Kufr Kama expected to enhance their standing in the eyes of the authorities and to gain the benefits that accrue to those who are close to the centers of power. The state, for its part, would win the allegiance of the Circassian minority, as well as deepen the division among Israel's non-Jews—a fundamental tenet of the state's system of control.

Figure 18. Encouraging ethnic traditions. A Circassian language course, sponsored by the state, in the cultural center of the Circassian village of Kufr Kama, 1966. Photograph by Moshe Pridan; courtesy Israeli Government Press Office.

Army service was an important factor in setting the Circassians apart from the Arabs, both in their own view and in that of those around them. So when the agricultural cooperative formed by army veterans in Kufr Kama sought financing to purchase a tractor, they approached Israel's president, Yitzhak Ben-Zvi, and reminded him of their contributions: "We fought shoulder to shoulder alongside the Israel Defense Forces against the forces of evil and against the Arab countries deliberately, devotedly, and loyally, to reach our goal, which is to create a secure source of livelihood in our place of residence in Kufr Kama, under democratic and free Israeli rule." They also explained that their alliance should give them priority over the country's other minorities: "We have done much and will do much for Israel, not in speech but in action."[33] Their concern at that time was that the Arabs far outnumbered the Circassians, and thus Israeli institutions might give priority to the Arabs.

It was not hard to raise the dividers between the Circassians and their Arab neighbors. The Circassians, after all, are not Arabs, and, unlike the Druze, they did not share a mother tongue with the Arabs. They thus had no connection at all to Arab nationalism. Their strained relations with their Arab neighbors reinforced this difference.

On the other hand, they did share something important with the Arab villages and tribes around them; they, too, were Sunni Muslims. And indeed, at the beginning of the 1960s it seemed to government officials that the Circassians were assimilating into the Arab Muslim population. In response, the state took action to strengthen awareness of Circassian culture. It issued Circassian school textbooks ("a stimulus to the Circassian minority that is being swallowed up by its Muslim neighbors," as the prime minister's office put it) and started broadcasting programs of Circassian music on the national radio station, the Voice of Israel. ("We want to reinforce their national consciousness," the station explained.)[34] This same logic was applied to the Druze as well.

The Circassians are a tiny minority in Israel. Today there are about three thousand of them; in the period under discussion there were fewer than a thousand. In addition to Kufr Kama in the Lower Galilee, where two-thirds of the community lives, only one other Circassian village exists in Israel, Reihaniyya, in the eastern Upper Galilee near the Lebanese border. (An IDF plan, approved by Ben-Gurion, to uproot this village's inhabitants, along with the Arabs of M'ilya, Fassuta, Tarshiha, Jish, and Hurfeish, and resettle them farther into the interior was stymied at the end of 1949 by Moshe Sharett.)[35] The relations between Reihaniyya and the authorities were a bit more complex than those in Kufr Kama. Reihaniyya's proximity to the border, the fact that some of its inhabitants became refugees during the 1948 war, and the presence of intelligence officers from Syria's Circassian community operating in the sector prompted some of Reihaniyya's inhabitants to work for the Syrians. On the other hand, one of the village's leaders, Hajj Muhammad 'Omar Qays, who, as mentioned earlier, had served as a guide for Palmach forces in the 1940s, maintained his relationship with Moshe Dayan and other senior Israeli figures. The result was the division of the village into warring camps. "One faction collaborates with the authorities, while the second faction tends not to collaborate," as Israel's Supreme Court put it. Tensions between the two groups reached an acute point in June 1953, when Qays was assassinated by unknown assailants. The police presumed that the murder had been ordered by some of the village's opponents of Israel and arrested six of them. But the police were unable to prove the suspects' involvement. The military governor of the Galilee then issued an order banning one of them, Isma'il 'Ali, from the village for a year, and the order was confirmed by the Supreme Court.[36] In the years that followed, the tension in Reihaniyya dissipated. Perhaps recognition that Israel had no intention of returning to the borders of the 1947 partition proposal helped reduce opposition to the state.

The two camps in Reihaniyya were marked by the tension created by the question of whether the Circassians, who stood on the sidelines of the conflict, should ally with the Jews or with the Arabs. One dimension of the cultural-national strain they found themselves in was the decision the two villages made about which language should be the principal language of instruction in their schools. In the 1970s, the parents in Kufr Kama decided to switch to Hebrew, whereas in Reihaniyya Arabic remained the principal language.[37] In addition to this dilemma, small minority communities had to face many others, all of them involving the question of whether to deal with the state directly or to see themselves as part of a larger minority community in which the Muslim Arabs were the majority.

The state, as noted, encouraged communities to be independent and found people within each community who preferred independence. The humanist justification for this was presented above. But the strategy also made it easier for the state to exert its control. The honest report of January 1958 of the Galilee's military governor, Colonel Michael Michael, is illustrative in this regard. That month, military government officers discerned a shift in the population's attitudes toward the state and its institutions. They perceived that collaboration with the authorities was declining, and they sensed the expectation of a war, led by Nasser, in which Israel would be defeated. The cautionary report written by the governor cited another disturbing change. "Relations among the [minority] communities have improved considerably, and the differences that in the past led to schism and conflict have recently grown smaller. External attempts [by the security forces] to exacerbate these relations have not enjoyed the same success as in the past. The commonality stands out more than the division. Various Arab bodies are now more in contact in mutual sympathy. These phenomena have become everyday affairs," he wrote in concern.[38]

Israel created divisions among its minority communities by treating them differently. One example was the privilege of allowing refugees to return, as in the previously discussed case of the Greek Catholic community led by Bishop George Hakim. Another was permitting the Druze to possess a relatively large number of weapons. From the 1950s onward, these differences were institutionalized in the military conscription imposed on the Druze and Circassians and in the official recognition of the Druze as a separate religious community. Naturally, these moves exacerbated relations between the groups. The policy continued in the 1960s and 1970s, when the prime minister's adviser on Arab affairs, Shmuel Toledano, wrote, "The communal frameworks of religious and linguistic groups should be fostered, except for the Muslim, and the individuality of each and every separate community should be consolidated."[39] Indeed, as far as the Muslims were concerned, the policy was the "prevention of opportunities (or means) to form a Muslim community in Israel," because they constituted a majority among the minority groups, as the chief of the GSS's Arab division remarked in the summer of 1957.[40]

These moves to divide the minority communities return us to the Israeli claim that Palestinian Arab nationality was imposed by the British on all Palestine's non-Jews. The importance of this claim lies not only in the policies it engendered but also in the kernel of truth it contains.* It is important to remember that Palestinian nationalism did not come out of nowhere. Like other nationalisms, it was shaped by interested parties. The fissures exploited by Israeli security agencies were not invented by them; they were part and parcel of the sociopolitical landscape of the non-Jews in Israel, and in Mandate Palestine beforehand. Neither was the opposition of smaller minorities to the Palestinian national movement a figment of the Israeli intelligence community's imagination. They took note of such opposition, encouraged it, and amplified its importance (sometimes disproportionately). Moreover, in each of these minority communities, there were some whose worldview and analysis of their political, social, and religious situation were similar to those of the Israeli establishment. This was the case among the Circassians, the Bedouin, and some of the Christians as well.

A letter sent by the secretary of the Haifa municipality during the Mandate, Jiryis Khuri (a Christian originally from the village of Taybe, near Ramallah), to Foreign Minister Sharett in November 1948 illustrates the nonnational Christian position. Khuri formulated a plan to establish an organization of Christian Israelis who would disseminate pro-Zionist propaganda among Christians in the Middle East and in the West. His letter went into great detail, and he asked for Sharett's support for his initiative. Khuri

---

* This is not to argue that the British invested all their energies in Palestinian nation-building. In fact, their main concern was maintaining their control over the population, and in order to achieve that they also used divide and rule methods. Thus, they established separate Muslim institutions (the Supreme Muslim Council was the most important of them); they gave Christians priority in employment; the categories used in their population censuses were based on religion (Muslim, Christians, and Jews) rather than on nation (Arabs and Jews); and so on.

explained the conflict of interest between the oppressive Muslim majority in the Middle East and the oppressed Christian minority, and described Israel's War of Independence as an event from which the Christians should learn that they need not bow their heads before the Muslims. They were not in any way compelled to adopt Arab nationalism in its "Muslim" version.[41]

The most blatant expression of disassociation from Arab nationalism was military service in the IDF. Among the Christians, who were not conscripted, a minority advocated military service and viewed it as incontrovertible proof of their loyalty to the state. They hoped that serving would grant them equal rights. At the beginning of the 1950s, Elias Matar, a Greek Catholic from 'Eilabun, convinced about thirty young men from his family and others close to him to enlist. They were placed in a separate platoon in the Minorities Battalion, but no more than a few of them completed their full term of service. Only a handful of Christian Arabs followed in their footsteps. (Most members of the community thought army service was "total insanity," a police officer remarked.) Mutran Hakim endorsed the initiative; "his hostile appearance on the outside is friendlier on the inside," said the prime minister's adviser on Arab affairs. But his support was deliberately not publicized, and the initiative faded away.

In the mid-1960s, Matar tried to persuade Mutran Hakim to declare that young Christians should enlist in the IDF. But he was in any case a lone voice. Hakim was too smart to place himself in direct conflict with the entire Arab world. In 1970, an initiative came from the grass roots; ten young Christian men from the Galilee wrote to Minister of Defense Moshe Dayan and requested that he conscript Christians. They argued, "All the Christian boys will enlist, because this is their hope—this is our native soil and our homeland, and we must defend it with our blood." They explained what they feared about volunteering for service, as some of their fellows had: "The Muslims will point to us, as we walk down the street, as Arab traitors." The Galilee Regional Committee on Arab Affairs, which discussed the request, understood that this group did not really represent the community, but the issue of the conscription of Christians was handed over to the IDF general staff. Military service was not imposed on Christian Arabs in the end, but Christian volunteers were welcomed and continue to be. Since the beginning of the 1990s, an upsurge in Christian volunteers has occurred. Precise figures are not available, but some claim that, in the first decade of the twenty-first century, a higher proportion of Christians than Bedouin are volunteering. This may be attributable not only to their identification with the state and their desire to detach themselves from the Muslims but also to the desire of these young men to receive military training and weapons, in part because of the Druze-Christian tension that sometimes flares up in Galilean villages.[42] A similar phenomenon, if on a smaller scale, is evident also in Muslim villages. Thus, the state experiences other beneficial results from the conflict among minority groups—enhancement (even if tiny) of the IDF's manpower and a reinforcement of minority communities' allegiance to it.

THE NOBLE SAVAGE AND BREACHED BOUNDARIES

In May 1950, IDF chief of staff Yigal Yadin paid a visit to Sheikh Suleiman al-Huzayyel, chief of one of the large Bedouin tribes that remained in the Negev. A reporter from the popular daily newspaper *Yedi'ot Aharonot* accompanied him. The headline on the resulting newspaper account was "A Royal Feast in the Heart of the Desert." The subhead was: "The Chief of the Tiyaha Tribe Welcomed the Chief of Staff with [a Display of] Gunfire and Galloping." This was an error of identification, boosting the sheikh's status, since Sheikh Suleiman headed only one of the tribes in the Tiyaha federation. And the journalist continued: "'Bring the food in honor of his excellency, the illustrious commander of the armies of Israel.' These were the words that ended the ceremony and began the royal meal in the heart of the desert. Even before the echoes of the gunshots and of the riders' galloping had faded, the speeches ended and the feasting began. . . . The feast ended with the presentation of the sword of the desert to the chief of staff."[43]

The motifs of royal feasting and gunfire salutes fit well with that period's common portrayal of the Bedouin as hospitable noble savages, an image that persisted for quite some time. The "sword of the desert" also fit the image. Eight years later, when Haim Laskov, general of Israel's southern command, was appointed chief of staff, he was invited to a meal hosted by Bedouin sheikhs, and again a reporter for *Yedi'ot Aharonot* was present. He didn't know the names of the sheikhs, but he licked his lips: "The chief of staff and his entourage dined to their hearts' content on roasted hens and rice and on the rest of the delicacies piled before them by the Bedouin."[44] But these meals were only one aspect of the relationship between the Bedouin and the IDF. Two other important elements were the constriction of Bedouin living space by the military government and the enlistment of Bedouin in the army. Both of these processes began at the end of 1948. In that year, a committee appointed by Prime Minister and Minister of Defense David Ben-Gurion, among whose members were KKL official Yosef Weitz, General Yigal Yadin, and General Yigal Alon, approved a plan to leave friendly Bedouin tribes

Figure 19. Tradition continues. Sheikh 'Oda Abu-M'ammar grants the "desert sword" to Prime Minister Yitzhak Shamir, 1988, as he had done to many prime ministers and IDF officers since 1949. Photograph by Maggi Ayalon; courtesy Israeli Government Press Office.

in the "Hebrew Negev." The stated conditions were: "The Bedouin will be concentrated, by tribe, in three centers, at least ten kilometers [six miles] from one another. . . . Most young men of military age will be enlisted in an appropriate combat unit . . . the tribes will be required to commit themselves to a particular policy, as well as to obligations regarding their land."[45] This policy was based on the assumption that despite their being Muslim Arabs, the Bedouin had not been fully integrated into the Palestinian national movement in the Mandate period and would be ready to cooperate with the Israeli authorities in all fields, including the most sensitive ones, land and security. To obtain Bedouin land and encourage enlistment, the military government's officers were assisted by local sheikhs. Suleiman al-Huzayyel was one of the best known of these.

Al-Huzayyel had been a sheikh for a long time. Unlike others who held the title, he had belonged to the Bedouin ruling class in the Mandate period as well. At that time he opposed the militant political line led by the mufti of Jerusalem, Hajj Amin al-Husseini.[46] He and his tribe thus did not engage in combat against the Jewish settlements in the Negev in the war of 1948. As a result, they were allowed to remain in Israel. After 1948, he was one of the only sheikhs who had standing throughout the region. He tended to be scornful of other sheikhs, such as 'Oda Abu-M'ammar (mentioned in chapter 1), who was granted the position of sheikh solely because of his collaboration with the Jews. The sheikhs of today are not sheikhs but rather *nawatir kumbania* (guards of kibbutz fields), al-Huzayyel liked to say archly. Indeed, as a military intelligence report noted, "the Israeli authorities also appointed sheikhs without any real noble lineage, out of realistic considerations and various considerations." Some of these were drunkards, others sold land to Jews, and some had, even before 1948, indeed been informers and guards of kibbutz fields rather than tribal chiefs.[47]

Security officials sought to keep the sheikhs as submissive as possible. So when the police heard that al-Huzayyel was spreading rumors that some police and military government officers had taken bribes, he was summoned to police headquarters and reprimanded by an officer named Singer. The officer's description of the encounter is telling:

> I warned him . . . that if he continued in this way he would find himself outside Israeli territory. He made strenuous excuses and claimed that such things against Officer Frisch or the military governor had never crossed his lips, since he knew them well and had good relations with them. He is prepared to accept any punishment if someone will prove to him the truth of the accusations leveled against him, and he claims that rumors are being spread about him by his enemies, who are members of the al-'Atawna tribe, and he had more than once proved, ostensibly, by his deeds that he is loyal to Israel and that back then the men of his tribe had fought alongside the IDF. In my estimation the warnings have made a strong impression on him, and I saw tears welling up in his eyes, to which I responded that tears would not persuade me and I demanded that he prove it with his actions.[48]

The policeman's approach was more than a bit patronizing. The same attitude prevailed in the military government, which frequently treated the sheikhs like children. "We live in a country where everyone has equal rights with everyone else," said Colonel Shani, chief of the military government, at a meeting with the sheikhs of the Negev in 1951. "But in addition to rights there are obligations. And if you fulfill the obligations like everyone else, you will be equal and we will want you. Because a country is happy when its inhabitants are happy," he declared. It was important for him to persuade the sheikhs to acknowledge that the state was just, not only strong. He also

Figure 20. Summit in the desert. "Loyal" Arab leaders used to host visitors from abroad. Here, Eleanor Roosevelt with Sheikh al-Huzayyel and the Negev MG, 1952. Photograph by Fritz Cohen; courtesy Israeli Government Press Office.

wanted them to be docile. Al-Huzayyel and other sheikhs tried to stand their ground. "We have tied our fate to Israel, and we must receive everything, just as our neighbors the [Jewish] settlements do," al-Huzayyel said at the same meeting. He also demanded that he be given all his land back, after being confined, like the rest of the Bedouin tribes, to restricted areas set aside for them.[49] His demands of the military governor may be seen as an attempt to maintain his prestige, which in his particular case derived not only from the size of his tribe but also from something that was known to Bedouin and also printed in the Hebrew press. "The Jews know principally the fact that he has thirty-nine wives."[50]

The Jordanian authorities, for their part, focused on other information that came their way about al-Huzayyel's actions. According to what seems to have been well-founded intelligence reports, the sheikh operated an Israeli intelligence network on Mt. Hebron, in the southern West Bank, involving his sons 'Ali, Muhammad, and Jadwa', and others. The Jordanians presumed that he was not the only sheikh who ran such a network. Another one, they suspected, was Abu-M'ammar, who sent his men to Egypt and Jordan on Israeli intelligence missions.[51] This was a relatively invisible aspect of Bedouin involvement in Israeli security. Another, more overt, one was enlistment of Bedouin into the Minorities Battalion toward the end of the 1948 war (most of them were demobilized a year later) and longstanding involvement in IDF sweeps aimed at expelling Bedouin families who had crossed the border back into the country. Often, the Negev Bedouin had their own interest in getting rid of the infiltrators, who frequently attacked Bedouin who had remained in Israel. Members of the Mas'oudin al-'Azazmeh tribe, as well as the tribes of Abu-Ghalyun and Abu-Sbeitan, were attacked more than once by Bedouin who had crossed the border into Israel. Since they had a motive to help Israel, the Bedouin placed their unique skills at the service of the war against infiltration. In April 1950, for example, the IDF learned that many Bedouin had infiltrated into the area of Mamshit, in the Negev, and had set up camp in areas inaccessible by motor vehicle. The IDF sent a force of fourteen Bedouin mounted on camels, "which patrolled the area for three days running and expelled dozens of infiltrators," the military government reported.[52]

Their animosity toward infiltrating Bedouin, collaboration prior to 1948, fear of deportation, and the desire to improve their image with the authorities were among the important factors that led Bedouin sheikhs to collaborate with Israel during the first years after the 1948 war. A comparison with the leaders of the Druze community shows a number of points of similarity but also notable differences. The principal similarity is that the groups' leaders generally had more interest in having their young men serve in the army than, perhaps, the community as a whole had. As a result, they encouraged enlistment by various means and used their clout to sway their subordinates. The Bedouin, however, did not view themselves as a united community, as the Druze did. Therefore, different sheikhs made different decisions about military service. Another difference was that the Bedouin did not live in a nationalist environment, as the Druze in the Galilee did (in particular those who lived in religiously mixed villages). The system of pressures they acted in was linked, by and large, to the members of their tribes who lived over the border. Either way, the Bedouin were never conscripted into the army. At most, sheikhs reached agreements with the authorities regarding how many combat soldiers or trackers would be made available to the security forces.

Not all sheikhs were inclined or prepared to collaborate, and readiness to collaborate was not limited to the sheikhs alone. Here is a minor but representative story of a small-time collaborator.

Akram, a Bedouin from a family that had joined the Abu-Rbei'a tribe, became an intelligence operative at the beginning of the 1960s. He told his story to police interrogators who had arrested him when he returned from Jordan. They did not know that he had been sent by the officers of IDF Intelligence Unit 154—the unit responsible for overseeing agents in countries bordering Israel—and he tried to conceal this from them. After several days of incarceration, he broke, told them his story, and asked them to call in the intelligence officer he worked with to corroborate it. He had no great adventures to tell, only about the life of a border-crosser:

> It all began a couple of years ago, more or less. I thought to myself that I'd had enough of being a simple shepherd, and here other people like Abu al-Sheikh, for example, had made themselves contacts with Israeli intelligence and that way became people with status. At that time I went one day to the home of 'Ali . . . , who is a friend of mine, and both of us went outside the tent and we sat to talk alone. I told 'Ali that I wanted to make connections with Israeli intelligence in order to work with them. 'Ali responded by telling me that a short while ago, Sheikh A had come to him and proposed that he collaborate with intelligence officers. . . . About ten or fifteen days later 'Ali came to my home and told me that he had met at A's home with the officers "Musa" and "Yusef" from intelligence and told them about me; in other words he told them that I was prepared to go to Jordan to recruit people for the job.[53]

As in the Galilee and the Triangle, one of the tasks assigned to Arab collaborators was recruiting agents from over the border for military intelligence there. The officers of Unit 154 sent Akram to Jordan. He left his tent camp and walked a few miles northward, in the direction of the camp of the 'Arab al-Saray'a tribe, in what was then Jordan. This tribe's members lived on the eastern slopes of Mt. Hebron, spanning the border between Israel and the West Bank. He did not choose this destination by coincidence. He knew a member of the tribe who frequently crossed into Israel as a smuggler. When he met this man, Akram asked him to bring a certain person into Israel with him—a person he wanted to recruit. A week later, the al-Saray'a smuggler returned to Israel with Hamdan, the man whom Akram had specified, and brought him to the camp of the Abu-Rbei'a tribe in Israel. The smuggler returned to Jordan; Akram took Hamdan to a cave near the Dead Sea to wait for a meeting. Akram had no telephone, so he went to 'Ali's home, and 'Ali went to Beersheva the next day to report to the intelligence officers that a potential agent had arrived. The day after that the intelligence officers met with Hamdan. Akram was not present and could not tell the police interrogators what happened there. A few months later, Akram set out for Jordan again, this time heading for the East Bank. On this trip, which lasted several weeks and covered several hundred kilometers (mostly on foot), his mission was to recruit a Jordanian Bedouin who served in the Arab Legion, Jordan's armed forces.[54]

The story of Mahmoud 'Issa al-Battat, who operated in the Negev even though he was not a Bedouin, is much more convoluted and complicated than Akram's. Mahmoud's father, 'Issa, commanded an armed band in the Mt. Hebron area during the Arab rebellion of 1936–39. He was killed by the British in 1938. Mahmoud was an eleven-year-old schoolboy in the town of Dahariyya at the time. He stayed in school for another three years and then began to work at paving roads and construction. When the 1948 war broke out, he volunteered for combat so as to carry on his father's legacy. His older brother did the same. Mahmoud's first assignment was to guard the arms caches of the Palestinian forces in Dahariyya. When the Egyptian army reached Hebron, he served as a bodyguard for one of the Egyptian officers. When his orienteering skills were recognized, he was sent to guide camel caravans laden with arms and food from Mt. Hebron to the Egyptian force besieged at Faluja. Egyptian officers appreciated his work, and he was awarded the rank of master sergeant.

After the Egyptians evacuated the region, the al-Battat brothers were arrested by the Jordanians on suspicion of having murdered 'Abd al-Rahman al-'Azzi, who, the al-Battat family claimed, had turned their father over to the British ten years earlier.* Mahmoud was acquitted, and his brother convicted. Soon thereafter, Mahmoud began to engage in smuggling. For the most part, he transported sugar from Mt. Hebron to Bedouin sheikhs in the Negev. That was how he got to know Sheikh Jaber. Here is his account: "In 1952, Sheikh Jaber introduced me to a Jewish officer named Yehuda and the deputy military governor, Freih. The Jewish officers asked me to provide them with information about infiltrators, smugglers, and the Jordanian army. I agreed to work for them and arranged meetings with the officers via the sheikh. Once every two weeks I would produce for them the information they requested from me. They would pay me five, ten, or fifteen [Jordanian] dinars, in accordance with the work I did."[55]

In his testimony, Sheikh Jaber described how he recruited al-Battat:

> I inquired of the Ibn Bari family if they could connect me with Mahmoud al-Battat because I needed him. . . . They said that they could do that, because he engaged in smuggling with the Bedouin in the area, but that he might well be afraid to come. So I told them to convey to him that it was in his interest. Two or three weeks later, 'Abd [Ibn Bari] appeared at my home with a young man and introduced him as Mahmoud al-Battat. I spoke with Battat and told him that officers wanted to meet with him about work matters, and he told me that he was scared to meet them. I told him that he had nothing to be frightened of and that I was responsible for what would happen to him. The next day I sent for the officer Yehuda, and Battat slept that night at my house. When the officer Yehuda arrived, I introduced him to Battat, and they spoke between themselves about work matters. And so the officer Yehuda continued to meet with Battat, always in my tent.[56]

The sheikh's key role in recruiting and overseeing al-Battat is salient in both testimonies. Without the sheikh's influence, al-Battat would not have agreed to meet with "the officer Yehuda," who was a GSS operative. Al-Battat worked with the GSS for about six months, and afterward responsibility for

---

* The al-'Azzi family were the strongest family in the Beit Jibrin and Tel al-Safi area. During the revolt of 1936–39, they swung between participating in the rebellion and helping the British and Zionists suppress it. Some members of the family were involved in land sales to the Jews, and in 1948 they tried to prevent fighting in their area. In general, they were considered to be close to the Hashemite regime in Jordan and to the opponents of Hajj Amin al-Husseini (which is why the Jordanians quickly opened an investigation of the murder). Their connections with the Jews did not always help them. With a few individual exceptions, the entire extended family, like the rest of the inhabitants of the area, were uprooted from their villages. The family's leaders established the al-'Azzi refugee camp in Bethlehem, where some of the refugees from their villages still live today.

him was handed over to Unit 154, whose commander in the south was Major Ya'akov Nimrodi (later Israeli military attaché to the Shah of Iran and after that the owner of the Israeli daily newspaper *Ma'ariv*). There, al-Battat was assigned to recruit Jordanian soldiers to work as informants. He succeeded. Three soldiers provided him with information, which he conveyed to his overseer, who met with him in Omer, a town outside Beersheva.

But not content with his income from his intelligence activities, al-Battat kept up his smuggling. He became friendly with a couple of Omer's residents; there was a girl he'd have breakfast with, and he bought rifle bullets from a young man to sell in Dahariyya. So his overseer switched the venue of their meetings. Al-Battat nevertheless continued to run a large smuggling operation, worth thousands of dollars.

In the meantime, al-Battat was also recruited by Egyptian intelligence officers, who were aware of his virtues and knew that he was still active. As a starter, they asked him to buy Israeli newspapers and magazines inside Israel and to hand them over to a man in Hebron who worked for them. Another Hebron resident who served as a Syrian intelligence agent asked al-Battat to bring newspapers for him as well, and al-Battat complied. He thus worked simultaneously for the intelligence agencies of Israel, Egypt, and Syria and as an independent smuggler as well. At the end of 1953, the Egyptians asked him to gather intelligence for them in Jordan—the location of military installations, roads, and airports. He was discovered and arrested by the Jordanians, who accused him of spying for Israel. The Egyptian consul in Amman intervened, admitted that al-Battat had been an Egyptian operative, and obtained his release. At this stage, the consul sought to use al-Battat for mining and sabotage missions in Israel, but this initiative was never acted on. The Syrians were also interested in using him for similar purposes, but this idea, also, never came to fruition.

Not long after this, al-Battat, who had gained quite a reputation among both smugglers and intelligence officers, was recruited by Jordanian intelligence. The governor of Hebron and the West Bank's chief intelligence officer asked him to kidnap Yusef Quteina, who worked as an informer for Israel. Quteina was kidnapped, and the Jordanians executed him. According to one source, Glubb Pasha himself, the British commander-in-chief of the Arab Legion, met with al-Battat and his associates to thank them for a flawless execution of the mission. (Al-Battat denied direct involvement in the abduction.) At the end of 1955, al-Battat devoted most of his time to gathering intelligence for the Jordanians. Among other things, he scouted out IDF bases in the Qastina area and along the Negev's railroad line. By that time he had stopped meeting with his Israeli operators and gave the Jordanians the names of Bedouin collaborators who worked with Israeli military intelligence.

During those months al-Battat began to suspect that Israeli intelligence was aware of his actions and was planning to take revenge against him. The pressure grew when a Palestinian from Hebron confessed to him that he had been ordered by his Israeli overseers to liquidate al-Battat, showing him the pistol he had received from an IDF officer for the purpose. Additional information reached Jordanian intelligence, which warned him against entering Israel. Al-Battat decided to meet with his GSS and Unit 154 overseers "to explain his position to the Israeli intelligence officers and ask them to begin working with him again." In November 1955 he went to two such meetings. At the second he was arrested for questioning. The interrogators discovered that he had been involved in breaking into and stealing from Omer's armaments cache. Al-Battat provided the names of Israeli Bedouin who worked for Egyptian and Jordanian intelligence.[57] Just as some Israeli Bedouin worked for Israeli intelligence, others, or sometimes the same ones, worked also for the intelligence agencies of neighboring countries.

Al-Battat was sentenced to a long prison term, but his end came sooner than expected. Toward the end of July 1958, he was transferred to the Shatta prison in the Jezreel Valley, in northern Israel. At that time, the prisoners incarcerated there for security offenses (among them a group of Egyptians) were planning an escape. According to some testimonies, al-Battat was brought into the plan and contributed his talents. The prisoners succeeded in overcoming a guard in their wing, cut the telephone line, severed the electricity supply, reached the main gate of the prison, and broke through it. But other prisoners being held on criminal charges—Jews and apparently Arabs as well—tried to keep them from getting out. The plotters fought the other inmates and prison guards who rushed to the scene. Two guards were killed, and many prisoners escaped. They headed up nearby Mt. Gilboa with the intention of reaching the village of Faqua, across the border in the Jordanian West Bank. Large IDF, police, and border guard forces arrived to hunt them down. They killed thirteen of the escapees. A handful managed to get over the border. Al-Battat was not one of the lucky ones. He had managed to grab an Uzi submachine gun and led a group of eight prisoners. But a member of the border guard spotted them and opened fire, killing al-Battat.[58]

Al-Battat was exceptional in his daring and for his tangled network of contacts with intelligence operatives and Bedouin sheikhs in several countries. But for no few Bedouin, crossing the border on intelligence missions was a

Figure 21. Al-Battat's colleagues. The Arab prisoners who were captured and returned to Shatta prison after their failed attempt to escape, 1958. Photograph by Hans Pinn; courtesy Israeli Government Press Office.

fairly routine matter. Many of them had relatives on the other side. Some also engaged in smuggling. Others were involved in cross-border drug networks. Unit 154 had no compunctions about recruiting them. So, for example, one police report mentions a prominent collaborator from the Abu-Rbei'a tribe who stayed in Jordan and wanted to return. "After the intervention of the special tasks officer [of intelligence Unit 154], said person was returned to Israel a few months ago, and since then serves as contact man for the special tasks officer. Said person is known from the Mandate period as a large-scale drug smuggler, and it is said that in the past he transported drugs via airplane to Egypt."[59] *

This entire system was orchestrated by the sheikhs of those tribes that

---

* In his interrogation, al-Battat asserted that Israeli intelligence officers were involved in drug dealing. He said that from one officer he had received "four *oqia* [a Turkish unit of weight equal to 240 grams, about half a pound] of hashish composed of sixteen pieces." (See his confession to the police, 27 November 1955, ISA, 213/8.)

remained in Israel. They became prominent members of the collaborator class. Their relatively large measure of control over their people, which was encouraged by the military government, reinforced their power all the more. The security services' coordination with one another hardly prevented the sheikhs from playing off one against another. In the mid-1950s a military government officer, Sasson Bar-Zvi (who was mentioned above by his Arab nickname, Freih), analyzed the balance of power between the tribal chiefs and the authorities:

> Over the years, the sheikhs necessarily became the center of affairs in the field. All the principal smuggling lines go through them, most of the arable land is divided up for the tribe by the sheikh, food rations are apportioned in the tribe by the sheikh or his representative, and this without effective and full supervision by the authorities. In the intelligence area, the sheikhs and a few notables have become, in a manner, professional collaborators who have not made a secret of their work, and those who frequent their homes were and continue to be visible and everyone around knows, meets, and sees them. In addition, they have taken advantage of this work of theirs to buttress their position economically and to bolster their status in the tribe and in the area as a whole.
>
> These collaborators have reached an extremely high level in the field, which should not be belittled. They constitute a force with influence over the authorities, and their camps constitute secure centers of smuggling and infiltration, the richest and largest in the Negev....
>
> These sheikhs have already learned not to display too much love for and assistance to Israel. They try not to get involved in providing information of value, [or] in turning in spies, infiltrators, and so forth.
>
> In contrast, the stratum of collaborators with the enemy is growing and getting stronger. This has been helped in no small measure by the excessive backing and support given, in my opinion, to collaborators by the intelligence services, which in addition to salaries see to arms and pastures, and release them [collaborators] and their people from detainment, and have even halted prosecutions of serious crimes. And after all this they have continued to employ them and they remain respected. This situation has created an awareness among them that their work is vital to intelligence and that they will not be given up easily. They thus make conditions and demands that the intelligence services fulfill for them.[60]

The Bedouin sheikhs in the Negev thus knew well how to exploit the neediness of the Israeli intelligence apparatuses. They became classic examples of collaborators who, in practice, also manipulated their overseers rather than being only subordinate to them. In this way they tried to gain perquisites for themselves and sometimes also for their tribes. They avoided voicing support for Arab nationalism, certainly on the symbolic level. Their major concerns were their tribes or, in other cases, their personal welfare.

Of interest is the displeasure that the military government expressed when Bedouin collaborators wanted to display explicit loyalty to it. This happened after the Sinai Campaign, of 1956, in which Negev Bedouin assisted the IDF in various ways. Two of the most prominent collaborators were Sheikhs ʿOda Abu-Mʿammar and ʿA., who sent men of theirs on military missions. The two sheikhs asked for a symbolic reward; they wanted to be granted the Sinai medal that was awarded to all IDF soldiers who participated in the war. But the military governor of the Negev called the request "madness." "I see it as a dangerous precedent. Not just [in regard to] ʿOda and ʿA., but in principle. The main reason is that it is serious and dangerous," he wrote, not offering any real justification for his position.[61]

In the years that followed, the sheikhs continued to maneuver among conflicting interests: their own, those of the state, those of the parts of their tribes in Israel, and those of the tribal parts who lived over the borders. ʿOda Abu-Mʿammar was in an especially sensitive position. On the one hand, he was one of the leading proponents of collaboration with Israel. On the other hand, many members of the ʿAzazmeh tribal federation, to which his own tribe belonged, were expelled by Israel during the 1950s. This tension reached a climax at the end of 1959, when Jordan complained about the deportation of several hundred members of the tribe into its territory and demanded that Israel allow them to return. The armistice commission decided to permit three tribal leaders to travel through Israeli territory in the company of United Nations representatives in order to convince the latter that all these ʿAzazmeh deportees had indeed lived in Israeli territory. That should not have been a difficult task, but Israel's state institutions outmaneuvered them. "The three Bedouin, with the UN observers, entered Israel via Aqaba, spent four days [in Israel], and traversed 1,250 kilometers but were unable to prove a thing. Even Sheikh ʿOda Abu-Mʿammar, the sheikh of the ʿAzazmeh, who live legally in Israel, denied that he knew them (he was warned and acted accordingly)," the Foreign Ministry reported.[62]

The political conduct of the Negev Bedouin was thus different from that of the Arabs of the Galilee and the Triangle. Despite what joined them—all lived under the military government—the Bedouin discourse was largely devoid of political and nationalist rhetoric. The Communist Party did not establish itself in the Negev, and the sheikhs retained their influence. Their strategy was to play both sides. Sometimes they chose disobedience and noncooperation; at other times collaboration granted them room to maneuver. They remained relatively distant from national politics. The first Bedouin candidate for the Knesset was Sheikh 'Oda Abu-M'ammar, who was recruited for the number-two spot on a satellite Arab slate, called the Peace Slate, for the elections to the Sixth Knesset, in 1965. (The Peace Slate was put together by Rafi, a party that had split from Mapai and was under the leadership of Ben-Gurion.) The slate, however, did not receive enough votes to win Sheikh 'Oda a seat, and not until 1973 was the first Bedouin elected to serve in the Knesset, Sheikh Hamed Abu-Rbei'a. Bedouin voter turnout was relatively low compared with the rest of the Arab population—66 percent versus 87 percent in 1965, and even lower in previous years.[63] The Communists remained a negligible force among the Bedouin throughout this period, receiving no more than 5 percent of the Bedouin vote in the Negev and usually much less. Nevertheless, the party's members tried to politicize the Bedouin community. Communist teachers who were exiled from their villages in the Galilee and Triangle to the Negev organized protest actions sponsored by the party. They conducted home meetings, passed out anti-military government badges and leaflets, and organized demonstrations. But when the security forces realized what was going on, the teachers were dismissed.[64] That decision was made by the Negev Regional Committee on Arab Affairs, which coordinated the actions of the security forces in the area. Indeed, the regional committees were at the fore-front of the battle against the Communist Party, in the Negev and elsewhere, and were assigned to further the Israeli policy of divide and rule among the Arab population, as will be seen in the next chapter.

SEVEN

Circles of Control, Circles of Resistance

THE "SECURITY AUTHORITIES" AND THE SHAPING OF LOCAL LEADERSHIP

In May 1921, Arabs from the villages on the Sharon plain, north of Tel Aviv, attacked the surrounding Jewish settlements. In Palestinian historical literature, this offensive is considered the beginning of organized Palestinian resistance to Zionism. Hundreds of villagers and Bedouin from the Sharon and Bani Sa'b area mustered in 'Azzun, a village on the western slopes of the Samarian highlands, divided themselves into detachments, and struck at Jewish farming communities. They had only limited success because of the meager arms they had at their disposal (only a few dozen had guns), because of advance warnings received by the Jews, and because of a sharp British response. But their initiative and resolve made the attackers paragons of Palestinian nationalism. One of the three commanders of the campaign was Sheikh Najib 'Abd al-Hayy, of the village of Tira.[1] From that time onward in local Palestinian memory—as well as Jewish—his name was a synonym for adamant, active Arab nationalism.

His son, Rafiq 'Abd al-Hayy, followed in his footsteps. Fifteen years after the 1921 attacks, he led a unit of rebels who fought under the command of 'Abd al-Rahim Hajj Muhammad, one of the commanders of the Great Rebellion of 1936–39. Rafiq participated in a number of actions in the area of

Netanya. He continued his nationalist and combat activity in 1948, when he served as a member of his village's Committee of National Defense. During the brief period of Iraqi occupation of the Triangle, at the end of 1948 and beginning of 1949, he was considered by Israeli intelligence the principal organizer of attacks on neighboring Jewish settlements, such as Rishpon and Ramat HaKovesh. After the annexation of the Triangle to Israel, he was (unusually) put on trial in Israel on several counts of murder. Although he was acquitted, some intelligence reports from 1952 implicated him in a number of criminal and hostile incidents.[2]

Yet, by 1954 Rafiq seemed to have undergone a total conversion. He desisted from all nationalist activity and established ties with figures in Mapai. In exchange, he was appointed to the post of his village's secretary of the Histadrut, the national labor federation.* This was a powerful position that allowed him to hand out jobs to those he favored and deny them to those he did not.[3] From the point of view of the security authorities, it was a real coup; the village's nationalist symbol now represented the party of government. What brought about Rafiq's change of heart is not entirely clear, but it was certainly a good deal for both sides. So good that Rafiq's son Tareq 'Abd al-Hayy followed in his own father's footsteps. It helped him in life. At the beginning of the 1960s he was given a teaching job in the village, and in 1964 he headed a slate that competed in elections to the village council and won two of its eleven seats. A police report noted laconically: "The GSS was interested in the success of Tareq 'Abd al-Hayy in the elections, because he is connected to them." Despite his slate's decent showing, 'Abd al-Hayy remained in the council's opposition block (the mayor, Ibrahim Khalil Qasem, was also defined as "loyal to the authorities," so the local politics had to do with local clan rivalries, not attitudes toward Israel). In the meantime, the security authorities continued to promote him, and in advance of the 1965–66 school year he was appointed assistant principal of the village school. This roused opposition from several directions, including from the principal: "Principal Ibrahim Shbeita fears that Tareq will try to undermine him in order to take over his position, with the help of the authorities," the same police intelligence report stated, sympathetically.[4]

In mid-February 1966, a resident of Tira named 'Abd al-Rahim 'Iraqi

---

* In 1953 the Histadrut decided for the first time to accept Arabs to its trade unions, but they were not considered full members of the Histadrut. Only in 1966 were Arabs granted full membership and the right to participate in the elections for the Histadrut. Yair Bauml, *A Blue and White Shadow: Israeli Establishment Policy and Actions among Its Arab Citizens, 1958–1968* (Haifa: Pardes, 2007), 118 (in Hebrew).

Figure 22. Loyal men. Ibrahim Qasem (right), the head of the local council of Tira, near the local mosque with Sheikh Sultani from the village, 1966. Photograph by Moshe Pridan; courtesy Israeli Government Press Office.

discovered that his vineyard had been vandalized; 138 vines were completely uprooted and another 60 damaged. 'Iraqi's background was similar to 'Abd al-Hayy's. Before Israel's birth he had been a nationalist activist. After 1948, he joined the Communist Party and in 1956 was exiled from his village for two months. When he returned, he sought to establish good relations with the authorities and served as director of the local Histadrut club. Although he was considered one of the leaders of the larger 'Iraqi family, his relatives did not approve of his new politics. Some of them numbered among the village's nationalist hard core: Husni 'Iraqi was one of the founders of Tira's Culture and Sport Club, a target of GSS espionage; other members of the family were on the club's board. 'Abd al-Rahim 'Iraqi went to the police and filed a complaint about the attack on his property, and a police force was sent to the site. The force's tracker found footprints that led to a point close to the home of Tareq 'Abd al-Hayy. He became the principal suspect. He had an apparent motive—a desire to take revenge on members of the 'Iraqi family who had signed a petition to prevent his appointment as assistant principal.[5]

A similar incident occurred in April 1967. A vineyard belonging to Tareq 'Abd al-Hayy's uncle, Tawfiq, was almost entirely torn up. The financial damage was estimated at 20,000 Israeli pounds ($6,667 at the official exchange rate then). Again, footprints led in the direction of Tareq's house, and this time they were identified as being similar to those of Tareq's younger brothers, Basem and Bassam. There was, again, an ostensible motive; Tareq and his uncle had quarreled over the demarcation of the boundary between their adjoining plots. Given the footprint evidence and the motive, the police arrested Tareq's two brothers. But just a few hours later, GSS agent Yair Khamus contacted the police and asked them to release the men on bail. Khamus feared that the arrest would damage Tareq's prestige and status. But no less important a reason was the possibility that the destruction of the vines, in both cases, had been carried out by provocateurs whose real target was Tareq 'Abd al-Hayy. Under the circumstances, the police complied. "Forces hostile to the state are interested in tarnishing the name of Tareq 'Abd al-Hayy and inflicting suspicion and guilt on him, so that the police will arrest him and in doing so indirectly hurt others who collaborate with the authorities," wrote the chief of the Special Branch of the Southern District. And the head of the same branch in Petah Tikva noted, "It is no secret that members of the 'Abd al-Hayy clan help Tareq carry out the missions given to him by the service [the GSS], especially in the matter of the Communist Party and the Sport Club, so hostile elements seek to besmirch his honor."[6]

Assistance in the struggle against the Culture and Sport Club and the Communists was one of the principal missions that the GSS assigned to 'Abd al-Hayy. One of the GSS's major activities among Israel's Arabs has been an ongoing attempt to undermine and dismantle anti-establishment political frameworks. It thus viewed institutions like Tira's Culture and Sport Club and similar clubs established elsewhere as dangerous. Tira's, headed by 'Iraqi, was thought to play a central role among the clubs in the Triangle, so the GSS made a special effort to obstruct it. The club had been established in 1961 (after two previous attempts, the first in 1957, had been halted by the GSS). 'Iraqi slowly set up other such clubs in the villages of the Triangle. When one was opened in Kufr Qara' in August 1963, it was 'Iraqi who gave the keynote speech. His remarks explain why the authorities targeted him. A GSS report states that he explained that the clubs were being established "because the Arab representatives in the Knesset and local councils do not act for the good of the Arabs. He denounced the treason of the Arab members of the Knesset in voting to retain the military government and attacked the Ministry of Education for disqualifying teachers as a result of talebearing." Nationalist theater performances, the support of some of the club members for the nationalist al-Ard movement, and the playing of the United Arab Republic's anthem at club meetings were further proof, for the GSS, that the clubs were subversive organizations.[7] The major concern seems to have been the crystallization of political groups that would offer an active alternative to the path of collaboration taken by Arab mayors and Knesset members, in the spirit of al-Ard and the Communists. It is hardly surprising, then, that the GSS decided to wage battle against the culture and sport clubs, nor is it surprising that pro-establishment Arabs took part in the fight.

In the spring of 1964, the clubs organized sports days. The security agencies reacted sharply, deciding to fight the clubs with all means at their disposal. The existence of a military government and emergency decrees, along with the lack of judicial review, made the obstruction possible. The first sports day was scheduled for 25 April. Two days before that, the police placed five central figures in the Tira and Kufr Qara' clubs under administrative detention. In addition, Kufr Qara', where the competitions were to take place, was declared a closed military area, its access roads blocked. Dozens of young people who nevertheless managed to enter the village and take part in the events were arrested, tried on charges of entering a closed area, and fined. The second sports day was to take place a week later in Tira. On that day, this village was also declared a closed military area, and the event was canceled. A GSS report notes, "The arrest of the club members caused panic, and many parents ordered their children to avoid any involvement in the club and in the sports day."[8] The creation of such an atmosphere of fear was one of the security forces' principal tactics, often prompting concerned parents to make sure that their children steered free of any political involvement.

The responses of the Triangle's municipal governments to these events shows the extent to which the tactic of creating a pro-establishment leadership succeeded. The Tira village council appealed to the military governor and the prime minister's adviser on Arab affairs to revoke the local club's license and shut it down immediately. The council also held a press conference at which it condemned the club's "negative activity" and announced its request to shut the club down. The day before the second sports day, the mayor of Kafr Qasim told the police that, in his opinion, the inhabitants of his village who went to the event should be arrested "so as to deter them from any nationalist activity." The Baqa al-Gharbiyyeh council, headed by Mayor Fares Hamdan, decided to set up a competing club that would be "under the full oversight of the village council."[9]

This was the type of leadership that the security forces sought to nurture, which is one of the reasons why the GSS wanted to promote Tareq 'Abd al-Hayy. We do not know exactly what actions Tareq took against Tira's sport club*—the relevant GSS documents are still classified—but it is clear that the support he received in exchange for his work quickly bore fruit. A decade later, he was mayor of Tira. In this capacity he continued to fight the nationalist spirit in his village. On 30 March 1976, when the nationalist leadership of Israel's Arab citizens declared a general strike to mark the first Land Day, he tried to break the strike in Tira. "When shopkeepers tried to resist him, 'Abd al-Hayy called the police, which sent in a force of hundreds of policemen, who used great power, fired live ammunition, injured several demonstrators, and arrested about forty people," the Communist newspaper Al-Ittihad reported.[10] This was, without a doubt, one of the high points of 'Abd al-Hayy's collaboration. In nationalist circles, it turned him into a symbol of all that was bad about the local leadership of Israel's Arabs.

But this was also the swan song of his close relationship with the security

---

* The actions of another collaborator against the Kufr Qara' club are detailed in a warning letter sent to him by the club's officials: he tried to persuade club members to organize by clan, attempted to get unfit people elected to run the club, and strove to sow discord among its members. SB Hadera to SB Northern District, 1 November 1963, ISA 79, 316/17. Such actions were typical tactics used by the security agencies.

forces. Following the events of Land Day, he realized that his position was alienating him from the public. He also felt that the authorities were not providing him with sufficient backing. "We took upon ourselves a huge responsibility, and in the end they embarrassed us. They left us with nothing at all. We are empty people. We made a mistake, and we will not repeat it. . . . It's enough that [the authorities] used us. We represent a policy that has caused harm to Israel's Arabs for thirty years," he said. He drew the appropriate conclusions, and like others at that time he left the Labor Party and joined Hadash, a political front with the Communists at its center but also including people of other political persuasions.[11]* Perhaps he was guided by considerations of profit and loss, or perhaps the spirit of his late grandfather, who had carried the flag of rebellion in 1921, again beat within him.

Land Day of 1976 was in many ways a turning point in the political conduct of Israel's Arab citizens. It was followed by significant changes in the structure of the community's local and national leadership (changes that lie outside the scope of this discussion). Although the security agencies did not cease to intervene in Arab politics, their efforts grew less effective. The story of Tareq 'Abd al-Hayy illustrates the nature of the GSS's activity and the measure of its success during Israel's first two decades, but this was, of course, only one example of many such instances of GSS interference and success. The GSS also worked to place people it trusted in leadership positions in other villages and towns and to shunt to the margins those it did not like.

By and large, this was done in coordination with the other security agencies via the Regional Committees on Arab Affairs. I have referred to these groups in previous chapters, but, as they were central to the state's oversight and control system and served as its long arm into Arab politics and society, they and their methods are key to understanding state-Arab dynamics and need to be addressed in more detail.

---

* This does not mean that 'Abd al-Hayy cut all his ties with the GSS. As late as 1992 'Abd al-Hayy supported a former GSS official, Yossi Ginossar, when the Supreme Court discussed an appeal against Ginossar's appointment as the general director of the Housing Ministry because of his involvement in unlawful activities during his service. 'Abd al-Hayy wrote the court that Ginossar was known for supporting equality between Jews and Arabs in Israel and should receive the post (see appeals 6177/92 and 6163/92). 'Abd al-Hayy passed away in 1993, and in the elections of that year another member of the family, Tha'er, was elected mayor. Then the mayorship passed on to Khalil Qasem (whose family was described as "loyal to the authorities"). Qasem remained in his post for ten years despite police investigations against him, thanks to the support he received from the Labor Party and the security agencies (on this matter see *Haaretz* online, 17 October 2008, in Hebrew). In the 2008 elections, Tareq's son, Ma'mun 'Abd al-Hayy, was elected mayor with the votes of the Communists and the Arab National "Balad" Party.

The Central Committee on Arab Affairs was established in 1954. Its permanent members were at the helm of the GSS's Arab Branch and the offices of the prime minister's adviser on Arab affairs, the supreme commander of the military government, and the chief of the Special Branch of the police force's central command. Subordinate to the Central Committee were three regional committees, in the Galilee, the Triangle, and the Negev, comprising the parallel regional chiefs of the same security agencies, sometimes with the addition of a representative of the adviser's office and a representative of military intelligence (Unit 154). The Galilee Regional Committee (northern) also included the commander of the Minorities Battalion or his deputy. The committees met at least once a month. They synchronized the fieldwork of the different agencies and sought to prevent competition and lack of coordination among them. They also established common positions on issues, individuals, and events.

The first meeting of the Galilee Regional Committee was held in September 1954. It defined two principal missions: "strengthening the regime and preventing the consolidation of the Arab minority." As far as the committee members were concerned, these were two sides of the same coin. They maintained, probably correctly, that controlling unorganized individuals would be easier than controlling a self-aware and politically organized public. The crystallization of Arab communities and proper relations among families were causes for concern to the security agencies. ("Families appear united before us on the question of their relations with the Israeli authorities, and this makes our work very difficult," one police officer reported to his superiors in 1950.)[12] As a direct result of this working assumption, the Galilee Regional Committee decided to prevent the establishment of organizations and public institutions within the Arab population.[13] For the same reason, the regional committees opposed the demand made by many villages to establish village councils and conduct municipal elections. As the Galilee Regional Committee put it, "In principle, the committee does not favor the appointment of municipalities in the Arab settlements, certain as it is that this will make it difficult for the security forces to control these settlements and will lead to the rise of undesirable elements within the Arab minority."[14] The committees preferred to maintain the system of rule by appointed mukhtars. They could dismiss mukhtars and appoint new ones at their pleasure. This was also a way to strengthen figures who collaborated and to shove opponents of military rule to the sidelines. In the words of the Galilee Regional

Committee: "The room for maneuver in making and revoking appointments is one of the foundations of the work of security agencies in the field."[15]*

The security agencies' working methods and the attitudes the committees' members displayed to the population they oversaw can be learned from the minutes of the regional committees' meetings. At the end of 1954 a session of the Triangle Regional Committee focused on heads of clans and mukhtars in 'Ara and 'Ar'ara. It began with a discussion of one of these men. (I will cite only his first name, Muhammad.) The committee members agreed that he was "erratic by nature, with a pathological ambition for high public position. Is prepared to attach himself to any movement that will promise the fulfillment of his ambitions." They concluded, "The committee does not see him as a person who should be supported and promoted. Our attitude toward him will be tied closely to his actions; in other words, any negative manifestation on his part will be answered with a negative reaction on our part. We will take no initiative toward him." The committee members moved on to talk about the next person. "Muslih . . . of 'Ar'ara can and should be used with the intention of restraining and prodding the current mukhtar, since Muslih wishes to obtain the position of mukhtar. We should display a favorable attitude toward him in order to avert his inclination to establish ties with negative groups. As a counterweight to the current mukhtar, he needs additional support, so he should be strengthened to a certain extent. These relations with Muslih will lead the current mukhtar to cooperate more, out of fear of losing his position to Muslih." With regard to another mukhtar, Khalil, the committee noted, "He does his job as best he can but his ability and influence are very limited. He acquired his position because of our desire to reduce the influence of the Yunis family in 'Ar'ara. His [appointment] as mukhtar has not led to any significant change in the power relationships in the village. His personality is not adequate to take advantage of his post and his position, which is a product of his post. He will continue to do his job; at this point our attitude toward him will not change."[16]

This discussion displays the internal logic of the security agencies. Three

---

* Jacob Landau claimed, "No one in Israel seriously intended to prevent the Arabs from electing local councils in their settlements and to take part in [the] local government system throughout the country." The material presented in this discussion indicates that this was either dissemblance or wishful thinking. Landau, who probably based his analysis on information provided by state officials, goes on to explain the delays in the establishment of local councils by referring to "Israeli experts, like Yehoshua Palmon, [who] warned that the introduction of local government would lead to rivalries in Arab villages." *The Arabs in Israel*, 157–60. He did not address the conflicts and rivalries that in some cases the security forces deliberately created, as we will see below.

modes of action regarding the appointment of mukhtars are discernable. The first was the use of such appointments to neutralize the influence of other people, as was done in the case of Khalil. The Yunis family was considered nationalist (although it included some individuals who were inclined to collaborate); some of its members had fought in command positions alongside the Iraqis in 1948. The security agencies thus decided to undermine the family's standing by appointing a mukhtar from another family.

A second mode of action was the use of people as spurs to prod others to collaborate. An explicit or implicit threat to replace them, the members of the committee assumed, would induce serving mukhtars to be more cooperative with the authorities. (In one case, the committee used the following words in regard to a certain mukhtar: "Contact should be established with his opponents in order to keep him in suspense." In another case they wrote similarly of a man who wanted to be appointed mukhtar: "With shrewd and firm treatment, he can serve as a card against the mukhtar.")[17]

The third mode was supporting or appointing specific individuals with the goal of drawing them away from "negative groups." This was co-optation in its most basic form. The analysis of personalities that members of the committee offered should not necessarily be taken as truth. Keep in mind that they were looking in from the outside and that their purpose was control. We cannot be certain that their evaluations represent the way these people were seen by their own communities.

The power to appoint and dismiss mukhtars used by the security agencies (a power they wielded, apparently, without sanction—legally, the appointments were made by the Ministry of Interior) also served to aid intelligence penetration of the villages. In 1954, for example, some of the inhabitants of Umm al-Fahm demanded that one of the village's mukhtars be dismissed on the grounds that he had impregnated a widow from another family who had worked in his house as a maid. It was a complicated story that had preoccupied the police even before the request. When the mukhtar's deed was revealed, a fight broke out between his family and the widow's, and the police arrested some one hundred people from both groups. A *sulha* (reconciliation ceremony) was held, and the mukhtar married the widow. A short time later she fell ill and died, and the fetus was lost as well. Some claimed that the mukhtar had killed them, but this was disproved. Despite this, his critics continued to demand his dismissal, and the police and the military government had to make a decision. In the process, they looked into the mukhtar's politics and his past; the information they received was not unambiguous. On the one hand, they found, he "was one of the witnesses against the head of the armed bands active in the area, Yusef Abu-Durra," in 1938; that is, he opposed the Arab nationalists. On the other hand, in 1948 he had been an accomplice in the murder of three electric company workers in Wadi 'Ara. He took the pistol of one of the murdered men and presented it as a gift to 'Abd al-Qader al-Husseini, the commander of the Palestinian Holy Jihad militia. The military governor was inclined to take the post of mukhtar away from him and even notified him of this. But the police suggested that the dismissal be suspended for a few months. The reason they offered was "a desire to create an 'uproar' on both sides in order to produce maximum benefit for the police." Their suggestion was taken.[18]

The considerable benefit that the security authorities received from their power to dismiss and appoint mukhtars reinforced their opposition to the establishment of municipal governments in the villages. The result was a fierce struggle against the Ministry of Interior, which sought to further the municipalization process. To prevent the entry of ministry officials into territory controlled by the military government, the latter used its power to require a permit of any person who wanted to travel to these areas—a measure never before enforced against Jews, and certainly not against state officials. The head of the military government, Colonel Yitzhak Shani, instructed his subordinates, "Interior Ministry officials working in the area must carry entry permits, and they should be told this. If they are caught again without permits, they should be treated like any other offender"—in other words, put on trial.[19] The fact that these officials were operating at the behest of the interior minister and under legally issued regulations was irrelevant, as far as Shani was concerned.

The establishment of the regional committees institutionalized the security community's traditional opposition to local elections. At one of the first meetings of the Northern Regional Committee, its members resolved to act against the establishment of village councils in M'ilya and Tarshiha, in opposition to the Ministry of Interior's decision and counter to what the government had announced officially. The committee also recommended against the establishment of local governments in two other villages—al-Buqei'a (Peqi'in) and al-Rameh—for which a similar order had already been issued.[20] The military government backtracked on its intention of establishing a village council in Tamra, and the Galilee Regional Committee discussed how this reversal could be effectuated. When it turned out that the decision to set up the council could not be countermanded, the committee decided to cooperate with the Interior Ministry to put together what was seen as the least dangerous appointed village council. (The procedure was first to install an appointed village council, and after four years, usually, elections would be held.)[21] Such a solution was also adopted in other cases in which the ministry successfully pursued its plans. But to stay in control, the regional committees continued to appoint mukhtars, even after village councils were formed. "Increasing the authorities' ties with these mukhtars will serve as a counterweight to the negative activities and lack of sufficient collaboration by the local councils," the members of the Northern Regional Committee wrote to justify this policy.[22] This, apparently, was the reason for the committee's decision to boost the status of the mukhtars by giving them special travel permits that allowed them to move freely, not just throughout the Galilee, but also to Haifa and Tel Aviv. Likewise, the same committee decided that mukhtars would "enjoy special treatment during military police searches and may enter the offices of representatives of the military government and licensing officials without waiting in line. This special treatment should be given visibility," the military governor ordered. The committee also decided to hold meetings of mukhtars in the military government's offices, to invite them to lectures and field trips, and to provide them with public relations material.[23]

The security agencies sought to uphold the traditional leadership or, more accurately, to support those members of the traditional leadership who favored collaboration. They did not limit themselves to mukhtars; other figures were also promoted in order to "bring the population together around them in accordance with the policies of the security agencies" and to create power centers that would be alternatives to nationalist circles. The policy in question was that of fostering religious and ethnic division. In the winter of 1955, the Galilee Regional Committee prepared a community-based list of individuals with leadership potential. The intention was to make these figures models to be emulated by members of their communities and to use them as liaisons between the communities and the authorities. The purpose was to reinforce communal identities so that they would overshadow Arab national identity. "These figures will be fostered and built up by the activities of all the services (GSS, police, Special Branch officers, minorities, [military] government) and other government agencies," the committee determined. Some of these people were appointed to advisory committees set up by the military government, and others to committees that addressed specific issues (agricultural development, education, labor, income tax, etc.).[24] In the Negev, people whom the authorities favored were given a different kind of privilege; the Negev Regional Committee decided that only sheikhs would be able to provide personal guarantees for the release of suspects pending police investigations and trials. At one of this committee's meetings, the military governor of the Negev criticized the grant of this privilege to other Bedouin, not sheikhs, as a way of enhancing their status and power within their community. This was "unacceptable and open[ed] the door to ugly actions." This privilege, he maintained, should be reserved solely for tribal leaders. Indeed, a certain amount of self-criticism can be seen in the internal discussions of all the regional committees.[25]

Both the committee and the men it wished to promote made sure to flaunt the ties between them, especially in calm times. One way of doing this was to conduct visits to these figures' homes on holidays, by representatives of all the agencies, alone or together. Such visits enhanced the prestige of the hosts, who at times competed with one another for the honor of welcoming government delegations. Such joint visits were also meant to show the public at large that all of Israel's governing agencies worked in step with one another.[26]*

The committees' policy was, then, to do all they could to prevent the establishment of village councils. But when they realized that the battle was lost, they pursued alternative courses of actions. When the inhabitants of Mghar demanded establishment of a municipal government, some members of the Galilee Regional Committee wanted to spur collaborators in the village to oppose the move. But the idea was rejected after a discussion. Such a move "would be very difficult and costly," committee members explained. They also feared that it would strengthen ties between the Ministry of Interior and the village's advocates of the change. Consequently, the committee decided to support the establishment of a village council—and to appoint its members. Representatives of the various agencies met with figures in the village, drawing up a list of appropriate candidates.[27] But they were still uneasy about it; they would be able to control the makeup only of the first, appointed council. The law required elections thereafter, which would considerably reduce the security agencies' influence. So they continued to block the establishment of councils wherever they could.

The regional committees' rearguard battle against the Interior Ministry impelled the minister, Yisrael Bar-Yehuda, of the Ahdut Ha-Avodah party, to appoint a committee to study the subject. Its preliminary report, submitted in April 1956, recorded the military government's three reasons for opposing the establishment of local governments: some elected officials did not collaborate with the military government; the military government feared that the establishment of public bodies in the Arab sector would undermine

---

* Security officials also maintained lists of uncooperative figures, including those who were to be arrested in times of emergency. For an example of a 1955 list, see RCAA-Central [Triangle], protocol of 1 December 1955, ISA 79, 2314/8.

its ability to control the population; local governments' control over master plans would thwart the military government's wish to continue its control over Arab building and settlement activity. The ministry's committee, for its part, noted that in any case all midsized and large villages already had official and unofficial committees overseeing areas that were generally the responsibility of a local government, such as education, road improvement, and water, and that these committees collected money from the inhabitants. It also noted that overseeing a local government that operated within the framework of the law was easier than risking rebels who operated outside the law. Its recommendation was unambiguous: to instruct the military government "to desist from its hard-line opposition to the establishment of [local] councils."[28]

It was no coincidence that the initiative to expand the number of municipal governments came from a member of Ahdut Ha-Avodah (which had recently split from Mapam and competed with both Mapam and Mapai over Jewish and Arab votes). The sense of the public at large, including the parties that were members of the ruling coalition, was that the military government served the specific interests of Mapai. Its personnel, they suspected, encouraged Arabs to vote for the ruling party and its satellite slates, at the expense of other parties. The interior minister forwarded the report to David Ben-Gurion, the prime minister and minister of defense, and asked to discuss the matter with him. The prime minister's adviser on Arab affairs, Zalman Divon, wrote to the prime minister that there was no need for a fundamental change in the military government, because it had rescinded its opposition to the establishment of local governments and requested only that their establishment be coordinated with it in advance.[29]

However, the military establishment maintained its opposition to local governments for many more years. In July 1965, Shmuel Toledano, then the prime minister's adviser on Arab affairs, wrote a detailed memo with the title "Guidelines for Government Policy toward the Arab Minority in Israel." It stated unambiguously, "The municipalization of the Arab and Druze sector should not be encouraged." In the same spirit, he argued that the state should support the development of each religious community separately and "nurture the communal frameworks of all religious and linguistic communities except the Muslims."[30] But, as we have seen, the process of establishing local governments picked up steam, and security officials could not always stop it. By 1966, Israel had two Arab cities (Nazareth and Shefa'amr, both of which had been granted this status before 1948) and thirty-eight villages with local governments. (Of the Arab villages that remained inhabited after the 1948 war, only one, Kafr Yasif, had had a local government under the Mandate.) Seventeen other villages were integrated into regional councils, which were dominated by Jewish settlements.* A total of two hundred thousand Arabs, two-thirds of Israel's Palestinian citizens at the time, lived under local governments of one sort or another.[31] This was one more area in which Israel's Arab citizens, aided by other civil bodies (in this case the Interior Ministry, which was usually not controlled by Mapai), were able to prevail over the defense establishment. As a result of this change, the GSS began to concentrate its efforts on neutralizing the Communists and other nationalist forces in the local councils, in particular by trying to prevent their inclusion in local ruling coalitions. (As in the Knesset, local council candidates were elected proportionally by party slate; the council then named one of its members, usually the leader of the largest slate, as mayor.) A minidrama that took place in 'Iblin, in the Zevulun Valley, in 1966 illustrates the great importance that the security agencies, in particular the GSS, attached to the composition of city and village councils.

'Iblin's mayor was 'Ursan Salman, whom the security forces considered a "positive force." The village council, which numbered eleven members, included three elected on the Communist slate and two Mapam sympathizers who had been voted in on nonparty clan slates. In March 1966, these five councilmen were able to turn themselves into a majority when another council member crossed over to their side. They called a special meeting of the village council to topple Salman, electing their own candidate in his place. The GSS intervened, "taking a number of preemptive steps, after which one of the council members resigned, and his replacement voided the danger of [Salman's] dismissal." We don't know what those steps were or how the council member was persuaded to resign, but in June the two Mapam sympathizers and three Communists again persuaded a sixth council member to join them in order to unseat Salman. The GSS was tense. They wanted to keep the Communists out of the ruling coalition, so they asked for an urgent meeting of the Galilee Regional Committee. "Communist control of the 'Iblin village council means not only a political victory for them but also control of a local government with large sources of income unparalleled among the minorities. Today the local government received a monthly income of fifteen thousand

---

* Kibbutzim and moshavim and some Arab villages are organized with regional councils that supply services (such as refuse collection and schooling). These councils also have statutory authority over planning and construction. Some small Arab villages with populations too small for a local council have also been included in this system.

Israeli pounds from its slaughterhouse alone," the GSS reported to the committee. (The 'Iblin slaughterhouse was, at the time, Israel's major source of pork.) "In addition, the slaughterhouse already employs nine Communists," it added. The GSS immediately commenced a series of intensive meetings with members of the village council. The intelligence officials quickly realized that the motive for the attempt to remove Salman was not political. The Mapam sympathizers and independents who were in the coalition with Salman declared that they opposed the Communists politically. But they were not prepared to commit themselves to supporting Salman. The Galilee Regional Committee members realized at an urgent meeting that they had no chance of keeping Salman in office. So, to maintain their rule that the Communists should not be allowed into governing coalitions, they decided to sacrifice him. The task now was to build a coalition of at least six council members that excluded the Communists. The strategy was simple: they offered the mayor's chair to Hawash al-Hajj, one of the "rebellious" Mapam sympathizers, on the assumption that the other Mapam member would support him. They enlisted a third council member by promising him the post of deputy mayor, which came with a salary. (Village council members served without compensation.) Another member was also offered a paying job. The fifth was easily dealt with; "we can assume that [as a teacher] he will be amenable to positive persuasion," the committee reasoned. Now all they needed was a sixth member for the new coalition. "All the loose ends must be tied before the meeting to unseat [the mayor], which has been set for the end of this week," the members of the regional committee agreed.[32]

One of the villages in which the GSS had repeatedly—but unsuccessfully—tried to install a coalition without Communists was Kafr Yasif, in the western Galilee. This village had a municipal government in place before 1948, headed by Yanni Yanni, who also headed the Communist slate. In the 1962 elections the Communists won four seats, Mapam two, a slate associated with Mapai two, and a Histadrut-sponsored slate one. Nevertheless, after some intrigues, the Communists were able to reelect their leader mayor. First, however, the Mapai and Mapam members agreed to form a Mapai-led coalition, in exchange for Mapai's support for the Mapam candidate in the village of M'ilya. As a result, Elias Jibris, the Mapam candidate in M'ilya, was chosen mayor. But when the Kafr Yasif council met, personal feuds kept the Mapai candidate from receiving the support of all the non-Communists. Four months passed; military government and GSS officials cajoled and pressured but were unable to establish a coalition. In the end, the Communists were able to persuade council member Fawzi Khuri to support them, after promising him the deputy mayor's post. (Khuri's wife, Violet, would later be elected mayor—the only woman ever to preside over an Arab village or city in Israel as of this writing. The police believed that she had been instrumental in persuading her husband to support the Communists.) The coalition agreement was signed in January 1962, and Yanni remained mayor. The event was celebrated with a large rally. One of the speakers was MK Emil Habibi, who "called on the Arabs not to be afraid of the [military] government and its lackeys and called on the inhabitants of Kafr Yasif not to fear Yaʿakov Eini and Boaz [security agents], who are wandering around the village," the police reported. The intrigues of security officials were a subject of intense interest during and after the village elections. Even before the effort to topple Yanni began, his slate had put up posters warning against "[military] government, GSS, and Mapai lackey plots to unseat the democratic leadership of Kafr Yasif."[33]

Some tried to portray the Communists as paranoid, but the documents of the regional committees show that such interventions in local government were a significant part of the GSS's day-to-day activity in the Arab sector in Israel. Sometimes these interventions were more successful than at other times. In Tira, the GSS tried to dismantle a coalition that included a Communist; in Umm al-Fahm it tried to persuade the mayor to appoint as his deputy a council member who was thinking of resigning. The reason was that the resignation would give the Communists the balance of power. In ʿArrabe, security forces sought to postpone local elections because the Communists were getting stronger. In Nazareth, the Galilee Regional Committee worked for many years to maintain the city's ruling coalition so that the Communists could be kept out. The Central Committee tried to postpone the 1966 local elections because they were scheduled for 2 November, the anniversary of the Balfour Declaration. Security officials feared that the occasion would rouse nationalist sentiments and grant the Communists an advantage. These are only a few examples.[34]*

The Galilee Regional Committee also concerned itself with the national leadership—that is, the Arab members of the Knesset. At the committee's inception, it made several decisions: "We will continue to encourage Sheikh Saleh Khneifes and Sayf al-Din Zuʿbi, and we will maintain proper relations with Sheikh Jaber Dahash [Muʿadi]. With regard to Masʿad Qasis, we have

---

* The determined effort against the Communists in Nazareth bore fruit—not until 1975 was a Communist mayor elected there, the poet and member of the Knesset Tawfiq Zayyad.

determined that the attitude toward him will be lukewarm, but on the other hand no special measures will be taken against him." Encouragement was given to Knesset members primarily by granting requests they submitted on behalf of members of their communities (family reunification, work permits, gun permits). At the same meeting, the committee recommended granting identity cards to "veteran infiltrators" who were close to Zu'bi and Khneifes. Qasis's requests were rejected.[35] The consequence was to reinforce the status of the first two men, who were seen as having influence with the authorities. This helped them get reelected. Qasis, in contrast, lost standing. (In 1956, however, the committee felt that it had cold-shouldered him beyond what was reasonable. It recommended approving a family reunification request he had submitted, because, "given the state of relations with MK Mas'ad Qasis, all his requests have of late been rejected.")[36] Nevertheless, the committee seems to have given most of its attention to local leadership.

This focus on the local is hardly surprising. The Arabs in Israel did not succeed in uniting and establishing a national leadership—and, except for the Communists, hardly tried to. So Israeli officials viewed control of local figures as the basis for controlling the entire population. The method proved effective. The "positive" figures who served as mayors demonstrated again and again that they were prepared to fight the nationalists. This was evident in responses to the sports clubs in the Triangle and to protest songs at weddings. The same was true when the Communists tried to persuade village councils to act against the military government. A representative case was one in Tur'an, in the period leading up to the Knesset's 1962 debate on dismantling the military government. A Communist member of the village council, Amin Sam'an, demanded that the council pass a resolution condemning the use of emergency measures and calling for an end to the military government. The mayor, Mahmoud 'Adawi, refused to allow discussion of the issue, on the grounds that it was a political matter not within the village council's purview.[37] This was the kind of mayor the GSS liked; he kept away from politics and ignored the Communists. They also liked the mayor of Tamra, Mustafa al-Diab, who reported to the police on his meetings with other mayors and on many occasions thwarted attempts by his colleagues to organize militant activities.[38]

These mayors were not just pawns moved around by the GSS. In many cases they were figures with well-defined worldviews that differed from those of the Communists and militant nationalists. They advocated integration into Israeli society, accepting the dominance of the Jewish population. From their perspective, accentuating Arab nationalism would only alienate the

Figure 23. Beneficial contacts. The mayor of Tamra, al-Diab (left), visits his brother, who was accepted into the much-desired tractor course, 1957. Photograph by Moshe Pridan; courtesy Israeli Government Press Office.

Arabs from the country's other citizens. They believed that direct ties to the establishment could produce a better response to Arab needs than could confrontation.

INTIMATE CONTROL

Shaping a local leadership was a cornerstone of Israel's system of controlling its Arab population. But this leadership had limited influence and powers, so other bureaucratic means of control were also necessary. An undated document that circulated among members of the regional committees enumerated twenty-six activities for which Arab citizens of Israel needed permits from the security authorities—that is, from the regional committees. Over time, procedures were established regarding which security agency would oversee each of these areas and in which areas they would have an advisory role, which agency would open a case file, which would write a recommendation, and which would grant final approval. It was a bureaucratic control system that constituted (and still constitutes) a large part of the work of the GSS and the police. Some of the subjects touched on public life. For example, the sensitive issue of approving the establishment of organizations and associations fell to the military governor (in areas under military government) or the district chief of the Ministry of Interior (in the rest of the country), in collaboration with a police officer. Before granting a permit, these bodies had to receive a recommendation from the GSS's regional chief. The charged area of religious life was divided among several agencies. The renovation and upkeep of mosques was coordinated by the prime minister's adviser on Arab affairs, in consultation with the military government, the GSS's Arab Branch, and the police. The GSS was responsible for the appointment of clergymen, in consultation with the police and the military government. All this reinforced Israeli control over Arab communal, religious, and political life.

Personal matters also required permits from the security agencies. A person who wanted to move from his village or city to another needed a permit from the military government. That government was supposed to approve or reject the request only after consulting with the police (the district minorities officer) and the GSS's district chief. An Arab who wanted to take out a mortgage to purchase or build a house could not do so without GSS and police approval. In areas subject to the military government, the governor coordinated the processing of these requests. The Histadrut did not accept Arab members without the approval of the adviser on Arab affairs. The adviser, for his part, was not authorized to approve such a request without first consulting with the military government, the police, and the GSS. Tour guide licenses, in contrast, were processed by the GSS, which requested a recommendation from the police. To be accepted into vocational training programs that led to work in public institutions, Arabs also required a permit from the GSS's Arab Branch. An Arab who sought a job in a bank needed a permit from the adviser on Arab affairs, and the adviser could issue it only on the basis of a recommendation from the police and the GSS (and from the military government as well in areas under military rule). Possessing a motorboat and fishing also required the permission of the security agencies.[39] A person whose file contained negative statements about Israel or evidence of nationalist activity generally did not get what he wanted.* It was a way of educating the public in good behavior.

---

* Special permits were also required in matters not included on this list, and sometimes discussions of these requests included harsh findings. A man named Fawwaz from Tur'an applied to open a corner grocery store. He submitted an official request. The military governor was opposed; according to information he had received from security agencies, Fawwaz had fought against the Israeli forces in the Galilee

Figure 24. Arab fishermen in Acre, 1960. Photograph by Fritz Cohen; courtesy Israeli Government Press Office.

The regional committees' discussions generally involved individual cases, but the committees' members also addressed matters of principle. Their decisions indicate that their absolute top priority was the preservation and enhancement of their control. The most blatant example might be the Triangle Regional Committee's decision, in November 1954, to bar Arabs from colleges. The decision was made as part of a discussion of "Arab students at the [Hebrew] University and the Technion." The summary was: "The committee does not view with favor higher education for inhabitants of the region [the Triangle]. Since there is no way of preventing their entry into these institutions after being accepted as students, the committee proposes to contact the

in 1948. More critically, intelligence material indicated that he had been involved in the battle of Beit Keshet, in which seven Jewish guards had been killed, and right after the battle had turned up in his village with gold teeth extracted from the mouth of one of the victims. A police investigation had not succeeded in proving his guilt, so the case was closed. In opposition to the governor, the commander of the Jezreel Police Subdistrict maintained that there was no legal basis for denying Fawwaz a store permit. Jezreel SD to chief of SB Northern District, "Fawwaz . . . : Application for License for a Grocery Store," 5 May 1959, ISA 79, 318/4. This case involved an account from the past and was not aimed at channeling political behavior.

administrations of these institutions to prevent their acceptance. The contact will be made by the military governor of the central region via the Ministry of Defense, Military Government Department."[40] The wording of the decision indicates that the committee was aware of the limitations on its power and that other bodies, such as the university admissions offices, were independent and not subordinate to the security agencies. On the other hand, the decision displays a sense of confidence in the agencies' ability to maneuver behind the scenes via social and political networks. The working assumption was that the Hebrew University and the Technion would consent to reject Arab candidates if the security agencies asked them to. Three years later the decision to bar Arabs was revoked.

The committee did not offer any reasons for denying higher education to the inhabitants of the Triangle. But the motive was clearly an interest in preventing the creation of an educated class that would develop political-national consciousness, organize itself, and make demands of the state. In this sense, the decision was part of the committees' general policy of thwarting the creation of independent Palestinian Arab institutions. The same logic was used with regard to organizations formed on religious, local, or nationwide platforms.

When a request was made by Arab activists to transfer control of *waqf* (Muslim religious trust) lands to a Muslim religious body, the GSS was inalterably opposed. It insisted that the authority to decide how *waqf* money would be spent should be retained by a state body (the Office of the Prime Minister). To keep up an appearance of Muslim involvement in decision making about their community's property, the GSS suggested the establishment of regional *waqf* committees but also the assurance that they would have advisory status only. The GSS justified its position by claiming that granting significant financial resources to Muslim figures or to an Islamic body would give them the potential for organizing the entire Muslim community. Division within the Muslim community, in the analysis of GSS officials, was a product of the absence of leaders with personal standing and institutions with the means needed for mobilizing the population—a situation that should be maintained.[41] *

---

* When the Nebi Saleh celebrations in Ramla gained popularity and metamorphosed from a modest event into a mass festival (in May 1967 about five thousand Muslims took part), the police recommended that ways of reducing participation be sought. The police were not impressed by the participation of Ramla's Jewish mayor among the official speakers and the ceremony's and audience members' display of Israeli flags alongside flags of the Israeli scouts movement. A police officer from the subdistrict assessed

A similar approach was taken on the local level. When members of the Greek Orthodox community in 'Iblin wanted to establish a committee to represent them in the summer of 1964, the Galilee Regional Committee expressed its fear: "If such a body is established it will be subject to Communist influence and will serve [that party's] goals." Field agents for the security agencies were instructed to exert their influence on potential members of the proposed body to persuade them not to join it.[42] When a similar initiative was taken in Acre a year later, the security agencies again feared that the Communists would take control of the proposed body. Indeed, most of the candidates were Communist sympathizers and activists, some having been convicted of nationalist activities. The Galilee Regional Committee decided as follows:

1. The committee views negatively this effort to organize.

2. The military commander [of the region] will meet with the district commissioner [of the Interior Ministry] to use his powers to delay granting a permit for the establishment of this council.

3. The representative of the [prime minister's] adviser on Arab affairs in Haifa will meet the notables of the Orthodox community in Acre with the intention of getting them to rid themselves of undesirable elements among them and only later, in light of the results of this treatment, to examine the possibility of establishing a community council.[43]

This decision derived from the regional committees' general policy of preventing the establishment of Arab organizations (point 1 of the decision), as described earlier in this chapter, and displays the two major methods employed by committee members. The first was using powers granted to them by emergency regulations or other legislation (point 2), and the second, using the influence of field personnel from governing institutions to exert their influence on elements in the Arab community (point 3). They knew from experience that personal conversations could have considerable influence on people involved in projects of various kinds. This influence derived from per-

---

that the religious awakening would, in the end, lead to the promotion of extremist nationalism. He continued, "We must take into account that the city of Ramla is inhabited by members of different communities. . . . If measures are not taken in time to reduce the number of participants in these processions and all related activities, it will lead over the years to an outbreak of violence between Jews and Arabs." Ramla SD to the SB Central District, the IP HQ, and the GSS, 11 May 1967, ISA 79, 274/20.

sonal relations created over the course of years between representatives of the state and Arab citizens, even more so from the power that security officials possessed and their ability to channel the Arab population's day-to-day and political life.

The employment of emergency regulations (originally enacted by the British Mandatory government to counter Jewish and Arab resistance and integrated into the Israeli legal system in 1948), together with the use of figures who were inclined to collaborate with the authorities, became the winning formula for the regional committees. It worked in the battle against the sports clubs in the Triangle, with the assistance of 'Abd al-Hayy, as well as in the measures taken in 1964 against political clubs in the Galilee. In that year, al-Ard activists led by Muhammad Mi'ari established such a club in the village of Makr, in the western Galilee. The security agencies took it upon themselves to undermine the club, and the Galilee Regional Committee employed its characteristic pincer tactic. First, it issued orders restricting the freedom of movement of al-Ard's leaders. (Mi'ari traveled to Haifa in violation of the order and was brought to trial.) In addition, it called Arabs with close ties to the authorities into action. The committee located inhabitants of Makr who were prepared to set up a rival, "positive" club and asked the prime minister's adviser on Arab affairs to provide an appropriate budget.[44] The committee also took action against the Culture and Sport Club in Sakhnin. Its members sought to prevent the owners of buildings in the village from renting them to the club. It also tried to persuade the club's president "to keep his promise to police officers that he would halt all nationalist activity," a promise made when al-Ard activists were arrested on the night of 23 November 1964.[45] An independent club was founded in Nahf, in the western Galilee, and the Galilee Regional Committee feared that it would fall under the sway of the Communists or al-Ard. Security officials saw a way out: "Among the club's founders are a number of people who are willing to divert its activities into positive channels."[46]

This kind of intimate acquaintance with the population was a necessary condition for the regional committees' work against the nationalists. It enabled them to receive assistance from what they termed "positive elements"—those Arabs who accepted the authority of state agencies and the military government—as well as from others. Sometimes they had to work hard to achieve the results they sought. Such was the case at the time of Israel's Decade Festivities in 1958, an especially turbulent year (as described in chapter 5). As will be recalled, stormy demonstrations took place in the Galilee and the Triangle on Independence Day, Nakba Day, and May Day, and many nationalists were arrested. But the unrest had begun at the start of the year, when Egypt and Syria merged to establish the United Arab Republic. At the time, members of the Central Committee on Arab Affairs feared wholesale rebellion by Israel's Palestinian citizens in support of Nasser.[47] The security forces took a variety of steps, which included calling in nationalist activists one by one, on the basis of a list prepared by the committee, and issuing each one an admonition: "We have been ordered by the military authorities to call you in and warn you with all due severity that you must not be dragged into these plans and actions, because if you are, the most severe measures will be taken." Recipients of these warnings knew that the military government had broad disciplinary powers under the emergency regulations. The military government knew that they knew this. The reaction of the activists, as reported by a military government officer, evidenced their apprehension about entering into a confrontation with the authorities. The committee reported that one of them had portrayed himself as "a destroyed, exhausted man, sick of it all. He sits at home and is not involved in anything. All the claims that he ostensibly operates against the state are lies." A second activist, Mansour Qardush, was not allowed to respond, but the officer sensed that "he was dumbfounded and agitated." A third was quick to stress that he could not possibly cooperate with the Communists "because he and his family are known as haters of the Communist Party." A fourth announced that he was "prepared to collaborate with the authorities."[48]

In this case, the information about the intentions of the people called in seems not to have been accurate. Not all of them were active in the national cause. But only a few weeks later a wave of nationalism swept over Israel's Arab neighborhoods, villages, and cities. The tenth anniversary of the Nakba was commemorated in many places, and parades on May Day, which followed soon after, turned into mass demonstrations, during which dozens of people were arrested. The Communist Party was quick to respond. It established the Public Committee for the Defense of the Prisoners and Deportees, and forty-five Arab public figures signed a petition calling for the release of the May Day arrestees and their return to their homes. The security agencies were surprised to see among the signatories many "who had all the time maintained close ties to the authorities." The Triangle and Galilee Regional Committee on Arab Affairs convened emergency meetings to decide how to treat "positive figures" who had been coaxed into signing the Communist-sponsored petition. People were again called in for clarifications and threats. This time the GSS took one step forward and, fired up to cause the signatories to revoke their signatures, drafted an alternative petition that denounced the "government's malevolent plan" but in language milder than the original petition. Authoring anti-government posters in the name of real or imaginary opposition groups is accepted practice by intelligence agencies around the world. In this case it was intended to sever these Arab figures from the Communists. But the ploy was unsuccessful. The vast majority of the signatories to the Communist petition refused to revoke their signatures. Other means of seduction were put in action, such as releasing imprisoned family members of signers who were willing to rescind their signatures. But this also proved insufficient; many of the signers still refused to accede to the authorities' wishes. The committees decided to take harsher measures, but only against signatories who were considered positive (since it wanted to return them to the right path), not against Communists (who were considered lost causes). First, the police opened files on the former and, in the case of "especially prominent figures," decided to gradually institute "other measures such as the revocation of licenses and other perquisites."[49]

It was a delicate game played by the security forces. Their goal was to reinforce the pro-establishment camp and suppress nationalist feeling. They were not satisfied with action in the public space. On the contrary, they put a special emphasis on the personal and the intimate. They knew that in one-on-one exchanges they had the upper hand. Many Arabs who sat with them face to face would naturally be "dumbfounded and agitated" and might well offer to collaborate. They created a wide-ranging network of obligations. To this end, security personnel did not wait for times of emergency, such as the demonstrations of 1958. They worked at it on a daily basis. Some of this was done in their offices, through bureaucratic measures; some, in individual meetings. The policy was one of reward and punishment, the accounts sometimes petty—who said what to whom, who talked back, and who did as the military government asked. This was the source of the security agencies' power. At many meetings of the Regional Committees on Arab Affairs, these were the principal items of business.

Routine punishment and retribution were imposed in two principal areas, employment and gun licensing, but the committees did not refrain from inserting themselves into other areas of life as well. At session after session the members spoke of people, individuals whom most of those present knew personally or had at least read reports about. Majed al-Fahoum of Nazareth "proved the extent of his collaboration in the Nazareth municipal election campaign and in the framework of the current city council. Is in severe financial distress and without work," the Galilee Regional Committee noted, concluding that an appropriate job should be found for al-Fahoum, perhaps as director of the local Social Security Institute office. The committee took up his plight again a year later. He had not received the sinecure and had been "going around without a livelihood for years." The committee members recommended granting him compensation for land expropriated from his family, which had not been paid out so far. Their principal concern was that he not wander around the city in his penury and serve as a living example of the unpleasant fate that awaited people who cast their lot with the ruling party.[50] The sons of collaborators from Jish and Dir al-Asad were also looking for work. The committee recommended hiring them as teachers. It arranged a job as a guard for another collaborator.[51] One collaborator from Mghar submitted a request to the minister of transportation to be granted a cab license. The committee decided, "Since the man is a long-time collaborator, it seems to the members of the committee that there is reason to recommend the grant of the application."[52] They were also inclined to help at times with matters of illegal construction. Another collaborator from Wadi Hamam erected some shacks without a license. The director of the GSS's northern region told the Galilee Regional Committee about the man's history as a collaborator in the past and present. The committee decided to ask the Ministry of Interior to cancel its legal proceedings against him.[53]

Support for collaborators, even if limited, was one side of the coin. The other was the use of the committees' authority to restrain nationalist activity. The committees wielded their powers in particular against civil servants. A veterinarian by the name of Jamil Qutub worked for a public agency. The Northern Regional Committee received information that he had fought with the Arab forces in 1948 and that, among other actions, he had organized the attack on Kibbutz Afek. The committee also had more up-to-date information to the effect that he continued "to be a nationalist Arab who slanders the Israeli government." It recommended dismissing him from his position.[54] Four teachers in the Negev were involved in Communist activity. The Negev Regional Committee had them fired. At the same time, it demanded of the Ministry of Education that it send teachers with positive backgrounds to the Negev, rather than using the South as a Siberia for troublemakers.[55]

The conduct of teachers was a sensitive subject, as we have seen. It became all the more sensitive in the case of Druze teachers who adopted the Arab nationalist line or who joined the Communist Party and publicly opposed the Druze leadership that accepted the Zionist hegemony. This happened in Mghar at the beginning of the 1960s. The Galilee Regional Committee saw ways to bring them under control. "The village of Mghar, which was known in the past for standing out in its loyalty to the state, has recently evidenced nationalist activity and incitement against the authorities. At the center of this activity is a group of teachers who have come out openly against the authorities. . . . The village notables and collaborators are helpless in the face of this activity and are convinced that a small strike at these teachers will largely still the winds and return the situation to what it was before," the committee heard in a survey of the situation. It decided "to fire or transfer the following teachers from their current place of employment in Mghar: Salman Qasem Qaʻwar, Qasem Farid Ghanem, Farhan Jiryis ʻArtul." The GSS representative reported that the Ministry of Education had yet to respond to his directive on the matter. The committee decided that if the ministry would not accede to the request, provisions in the emergency regulations would be invoked against the teachers, and they would be forbidden to work as teachers or would be exiled from their village. It is interesting to note that the committee believed its approach was acceptable to the village's notables and that its role was to intervene in a struggle between two parallel currents in the Arab public.[56]

At times, disciplining disobedient Druze soldiers was necessary. Here military regulations entered the picture. A demobilized soldier from Mghar who was close to the nationalist teachers published a letter in the Communist Arabic newspaper *Al-Ittihad* decrying the army's treatment of its Druze soldiers. The military authorities viewed this behavior severely. At the beginning of the 1960s, Druze opposition to conscription had not entirely died down, and going public with the difficulties and discrimination the Druze recruits faced was liable to hinder the delicate work of creating a "blood covenant" between the Jews and the Druze. The Galilee Regional Committee decided on an interesting response, one that exerted a fair amount of pressure on the veteran in question. They arranged for him to be called up for active reserve duty, "so that any disciplinary violation on his part would result in his being brought to trial." This seems not to have been a frequent recourse; after a wave of anti-conscription Druze letters to the editor appeared in the first half of 1964, milder measures were used. The protestors were summoned to talk with a representative of the military governor or the GSS coordinator; sometimes soldiers were promised gun licenses as an incentive to get them back on track.[57]

A more complex case of exerting control via the workplace was that of Leila Jad Habibi, a relative of the author and parliamentarian Emil Habibi. She worked as an inspector for the Ministry of Welfare. Her husband was Shafiq Shalhut, a Communist activist. In 1962, the ministry decided to redraw its district boundaries, and Leila Jad Habibi was in line for a promotion. The Galilee Regional Committee was not happy about this, explaining, "She is liable to be under the influence of her husband." It recommended that "the Office of the Adviser on Arab Affairs contact the Welfare Ministry and ask that the redrawing of district boundaries be postponed for about a year, and likewise that the Welfare Ministry indicate [to Ms. Habibi] that the delay in her appointment is the result of her husband's hostile activity and that the final decision will be made in light of her behavior."[58] This, too, was a typical action. Pressure was brought to bear on the relevant government ministry, even at the price of delaying the ministry's reorganization plan. In addition, information was leaked in order to pressure the worker and impel her to restrain her husband's political activity.

Conveying information, whether officially or unofficially, was a common way of inducing people to reconsider their nationalist activity. A resident of Nazareth worked in the state tourism office. When information indicated that he had begun to evince nationalist sympathies, his advancement at his job came to an end. Someone made a point of letting him know why. Only after the GSS and the military government provided information "pointing to a considerable improvement in the said man's behavior and his willingness to collaborate" was his promotion allowed.[59] A priest from the Galilee submitted an application for a permit to teach religion. The Galilee Regional Committee had information that the priest was a Popular Front sympathizer. A representative of the military government met the priest, who declared his loyalty to the state and his willingness to collaborate. The committee decided that the governor should have him in for another interview and, if he made a positive impression, approve his application to be a teacher.[60] The imam of the Muslim community in 'Iblin, like all who held this post, received his salary from the Ministry of Religions. But the Galilee Regional Committee, after examining his activity, stated, "He is one of the agitators in the village. There is information about his negative history." The committee decided to designate a military government official to attempt to set him on the right path, "and if this does not succeed, the committee will recommend his dismissal."[61] After the deputy mayor of Nazareth, Nadim Bathish, gave a "nationalist" speech to a group of foreign priests who had come on a visit to Israel, he was summoned by the head of the northern office of the adviser on Arab affairs to explain his actions.[62] The committee received information about the nationalist activity of Yihia Dabbah of Acre, who served as a probation officer. He was summoned to Jerusalem for a talk with the management of the Welfare Ministry, and the GSS began to track him.[63] In other words, the regional committees routinely discussed and ruled on the fates of civil servants, mukhtars, even vocalists; for instance, the committees decided which vocalists would be invited to sing for the Minorities Battalion, in accordance with their involvement in singing nationalist songs at weddings.[64]

Poets who represented and shaped the Palestinian national narrative or the local Arab national discourse were also discussed by the Galilee Regional Committee. In December 1962, Mahmoud Darwish participated in a Popular Front conference in Nazareth, where he read a poem entitled "Our Beloved Soil." Intelligence sources related that the poem "fired up the participants." The committee asked the GSS to examine the precise wording of the poem, to ascertain whether its author could be prosecuted under the emergency regulations.[65] Two weeks later, the committee decided that a confining order could be issued against Darwish but that it would be best to wait first for further information about his negative activity. GSS agents were assigned to track him and report on his movements.[66] This was the beginning of the process that led Darwish to leave Israel in 1971 and join the Palestinian national movement in exile; in 1988 he authored the Palestinian Declaration of Independence. Darwish visited Israel only after the Oslo agreement (which he opposed), by which time he had achieved the status of Palestinian national poet. When he passed away in the summer of 2008, he was buried in Ramallah, the temporary capital of the Palestinian Authority, not in his village of origin in the Galilee.

Darwish had never been a civil servant and did not receive a salary from the state, so the authorities could take only administrative measures against him. But that was not the case with another poet, Samih al-Qasem, on whom the Galilee Regional Committee trained its sights a year later. At that time, al-Qasem was a teacher and was also linked to two state-sponsored Arabic-language media outlets—the newspaper *Al-Yawm* (which published his work from time to time) and the Voice of Israel radio station—favors usually granted only to people who agreed with and were good at expressing the government line. But al-Qasem began displaying nationalist inclinations in his poetry. After publishing a poem in *Al-Ittihad* supporting the refugees' right of return, the regional committee decided that the Ministry of Education would call him in and warn him, "If he carries on with his nationalist activity they will no longer be able to employ him."[67] Al-Qasem stuck to his principles and, in the years that followed, attained the status of an important national poet whose books are sold throughout the Middle East.

Threatening a person's livelihood was one, often successful, way of constraining his or her behavior. Another was granting or revoking gun licenses. In 1962, the Galilee Regional Committee was informed that the secretary of the Tamra municipality had made nationalist comments. The committee decided to suspend his gun license. The goal was to deter him, so the license was not fully revoked. "Since the intention is to bring him back from the nationalist path he has begun to walk down, the governor will judge, in accordance with his future behavior, if there is cause for reinstating his license."[68] The full sanction was used against the deputy mayor of al-Bqei'a, who had begun to show Communist sympathies. The Galilee Regional Committee wanted to hurt him in order to demonstrate that he would lose out by joining the Communists. The best way was to revoke his gun license.[69]

The son of a collaborator from Makr insulted an Arab member of the Knesset, Jaber Dahash Mu'adi, because he had voted to retain the military government. The military governor called in the young man's father for clarification and was taken by surprise when the collaborator, instead of bowing his head and apologizing for his son's behavior, "impudently" stood up for him. When the man applied to renew his gun license, the regional committee decided not to deny his application. Apparently the committee members believed that the collaborator could be gotten back on track. A man named 'Abdallah, from Sakhnin, was not treated with such indulgence. He had been among the leaders of the fight against routing the National Water Carrier through his village's lands in the Beit Netofa Valley, so his application was denied.[70]

In other cases, the considerations were more complex. A man from 'Iblin, named Najib, fired shots into the air during a wedding celebration (a time-honored practice at Arab celebrations), with a rifle for which he held a license. A criminal investigation ensued. The police maintained that his license should not be renewed, especially since "the extent of his past collaboration was extremely small." The GSS saw things otherwise: "Since his family, which up until now had kept its distance from the authorities, has recently displayed a certain willingness to collaborate," it would be better to let him keep his license. It would be a mistake to anger an entire family at such a sensitive stage, the GSS's representative on the Galilee Regional Committee argued. The committee agreed. Here, as in many other cases, the family factor was important. Security agencies related to Arabs not only as single persons but also, in keeping with their understanding of the social structure of Israel's Palestinian community, as members of families. For that reason, the military's cost-and-benefit policy and its manipulations were often carried out vis-à-vis entire families rather than individuals.[71]

On occasion, this was extended to entire ethnic or religious groups. Such was the case, for example, when the military government and the GSS received reports of nationalist pronouncements by the priest Salim Mu'allim, from Dir Hanna. The first impulse was to confiscate his gun. But the regional committee feared that such an action would be seen by Mutran Hakim, the leader of the Catholic community to which Mu'allim belonged, as a deliberate attempt to impair the community's status in the village. It came up with a creative solution. A representative of the governor would notify the priest that his gun was being confiscated, but the threat would not be carried out, and it would not be given legal standing in the form of an official notification to the Ministry of Interior. If Hakim protested, the confiscation procedure would be canceled, with the cancellation to be presented as a gesture to Hakim. If no reaction came from Hakim within a month, the official notice would be given to the ministry, which would then confiscate the gun.[72]

On the other side of the equation, granting a weapon or a license was one of the most salient rewards the authorities could accord to Arabs they wished to favor. Agents for the GSS and Unit 154 generally received gun licenses. The Negev Regional Committee considered the request of a Bedouin named Salim for a license for a hunting rifle. At first, the police opposed the request: "The man's file testifies to this day about smuggling and contact with infiltrators." But Salim was a Unit 154 agent, and the GSS's representative on the committee, Aryeh Ben-Ya'akov, stated what everyone knew: "I don't know any Bedouin who carries a gun and is not suspected on one of these counts. . . . It is unreasonable for us not to give a gun to a man employed by Unit 154. This man has been of great service, and, in my opinion, he should be given the weapon he requests." His recommendation was accepted.

In the mid-1950s, Shoshana Har-Zion, sister of Unit 101 commando Meir Har-Zion, went on a hike in the then Jordanian part of the Judean Desert with her boyfriend, Oded Wagmeister. The two of them were murdered by Bedouin. The security forces sent Bedouin from Israel to locate the bodies; the Israeli Bedouin received assistance from Bedouin on the other side of the border, in the West Bank. One of the latter brought the bodies back to Israel and asked to remain in the country. The Negev Regional Committee recommended approving his request, also recommending that he be awarded a cash payment and a gun license.[73]

A Druze man named 'Ali requested a gun license. The application was treated favorably; he had helped Yosef Nahmani purchase land around the village of Kisra, in the western Upper Galilee.[74] At times the grant of a license or a delay in granting one was used as an inducement for getting people to obey the authorities. A veteran named Mahmoud Hasan requested a license. In his favor was his military service. (He belonged to the al-Heib Bedouin tribe in the Galilee, many of whose young men volunteered for the IDF.) But he lived illegally in an area that the army used as a firing range and, until submitting his application at the beginning of 1964, had refused to vacate. "Decision: as long as the offender lives in Firing Range 110, he will not receive a gun license. If he moves out and submits a new request, Colonel Dotan [the military governor] will recommend that his request be granted."[75]

Beginning at the end of the 1950s and increasing in the 1960s, the military government's power waned. Israel's Arab citizens won greater freedom of movement, and the restrictions on their everyday life diminished. There were many reasons for this. On the economic front, Israel needed more laborers in its Jewish cities. On the Israel-Arab front, the United Arab Republic fell apart in 1961, and Israel grew less fearful of an Arab offensive in which its own Arab citizens would participate. Politically, opposition parties pressed for an end to the military government, which they viewed as an instrument used by Mapai to perpetuate its hold on power. Furthermore, extraparliamentary organizations campaigned for granting full and equal rights to Arab citizens. On 1 December 1966, the military government apparatus was officially dismantled. However, the emergency defense regulations remained in force, and the police force was assigned to enforce them. Six months later, the Six Day War broke out.

During the waiting period before the war—May–June 1967—the security forces expanded their control of the Arab population. It turned out that the military government was not at all necessary in order to exert control and collect information. Reports about anti-Israel utterances arrived from all over the country. A woman from Nazareth said that there was no reason to hoard food because the Arab armies would soon arrive and there would be plenty of food. A man from Sulam voiced his hope: "Nasser [will] eliminate the Jews, and then I'll be able to travel through the country without a license." A man from Nazareth told his friends, "This time it's not 1948 and not Sinai [1956]. This time Egypt is more powerful, and it will show them." A resident of Shefa'amr told a neighbor whose truck had been requisitioned by the army, "'Abd al-Nasser will come and slaughter you." Arabs who spoke this way were called in for interrogation as a warning. Most of them promised to change their ways. Those who persisted were arrested. Some tension was evident between Muslims and Druze, resulting in a few fistfights.

At the same time, the daily reports compiled by the police and the GSS documented many manifestations of identification with the state. In other words, both of the prevailing approaches pursued by Israel's Arabs over the previous two decades were taken to their extremes as war neared. The Druze, who had for a decade been drafted into the IDF, organized rallies in support of the state. But similar events occurred in Christian and Muslim villages as well. One hundred residents of Umm al-Fahm signed a petition of support for the country, and in Jish six thousand Israeli pounds (some two thousand U.S. dollars then) were collected for the Friends of the Israel Defense Forces. Muslims and Christians in Haifa signed a joint statement of support, and people in M'ilya and Tarshiha told Israeli officials of their willingness to share the burden of war with the rest of Israel's population. Notables from Kufr Qara' met with representatives of the nearby Jewish settlements and offered their assistance as farmhands while Jewish men were called up for military service. Youths from Sulam volunteered to help out at Kibbutz Merhavya, automobile mechanics in Nazareth put their garages at the disposal of the IDF, and members of the Umm al-Fahm village council donated two days' salaries to the state. People from 'Eilabun volunteered to work at Kibbutz Ginosar, the workers of Kafr Kanna sent a telegram of support to the police, as did teachers from Kabul. And these are only a few examples.[76]

A week after the war, Nissim Tokatli, the northern representative of the adviser on Arab affairs, summed up the position of Israel's Arabs toward the state's adversaries: "They identified, by and large, with the state and its defense and economic struggle."[77] A GSS survey at the beginning of 1971 took a more nuanced view. Support for Israel came not out of love but out of the sense of powerlessness Israel's Arabs felt—the view that they had no realistic alternative. This was what kept them from aiding and abetting terrorist acts or developing separatist tendencies.[78] The adviser and the GSS had two different viewpoints on this. According to the former, the Arabs in Israel authentically identified with the state. In other words, the program of instilling patriotic values in the Arabs had succeeded, or, alternatively, the Arabs acknowledged the advantages of life in the Jewish state. The author of the GSS report, in contrast, did not view the manifestations of support as sincere. The principal factor that kept Israel's Arab citizens from working with the enemy was, according to the GSS, the finely honed system of control developed by the security agencies, which made the Arabs feel helpless.

These two systems of control, the carrot and the stick, or better, persuasion and coercion, complemented each other during the years under study. They each formed an arm of the security agencies' pincers, one arm being severe administrative measures; the other, persuasion, propaganda, and education. But it is important to remember that not everything Israel's Arab citizens felt was a product of manipulation by the Israeli establishment. Some Arabs identified with Israel (or at least with the positive components of Israeliness) as a product of their own independent thinking and their life experience. They did not need to be persuaded or coerced to adopt an identity as loyal Arab citizens of Israel. On the other hand, Israel's ability to coerce and persuade was limited. The nationalist camp among Israel's Arab citizens never ceased to express its opinions and to challenge the state and its agencies. In doing so, it disseminated a unique variety of Palestinian Arab nationalist discourse that became pervasive among Palestinian Israelis. Just as it did this before 1967, so it continued to do thereafter, when the social and political environment changed utterly.

The outcome of the 1967 war led the security forces to change their tactics. Their attention was diverted from the Palestinian citizens of Israel to the Palestinians in the territories occupied during the war. While supervision of Arab citizens within Israel proper did not cease, the security forces were busy spreading a net of informers and collaborators through the West Bank and the Gaza Strip. The GSS was able to do so in short order, and these collaborators, in the territories' villages, cities, and refugee camps, helped neutralize the activity of Fatah, the Popular Front for the Liberation of Palestine, and other Palestinian organizations. The experience gained during nineteen years of work within Israel helped the security agencies carry out their new mission, as did the network of informers who had worked for Israel in the West Bank and the Gaza Strip even while those territories were under Jordanian and Egyptian control.

In the more than forty years that have passed since 1967, collaborators have served as Israel's most important tool against Palestinian guerrilla and terror activity, as well as in the political arena. Yet there is one obvious difference between the security agencies' work in the Palestinian community in Israel and that in the territories. Unlike the Israeli aims in dealing with the Palestinians in the territories discussed in this book, Israel has made no attempt to change their consciousness or to imbue them with an alternate identity. The principal goal in recruiting collaborators has been to use them to defeat the Palestinian national struggle.

Arab collaborators who were Israeli citizens, and whose consciousness and identities had been shaped by the means described here, served in various Israeli agencies in the territories occupied in 1967 and played an important role in the Israeli occupation system, especially during its first years. However, the Communist Party and other Arab movements in Israel have participated in the political struggle against occupation since its very first months. Hence, the contesting political worldviews that have existed among the Arabs in Israel were expressed by them also in the context of the Israeli occupation of the territories.

Conclusion

THE LIVES OF ISRAEL'S ARAB CITIZENS—a national minority in a Jewish state—have involved the dilemma of how to relate to the state of Israel and its institutions, a dilemma that still faces each one of them. This is not just a question of identification, in the standard formulation of Israel's public opinion pollsters: "Do you feel more Israeli or more Arab/Palestinian?" or in its theoretical formulation: "Do I owe loyalty to a state that has granted me citizenship but discriminates against me?" or in its theological formulation: "What is the proper attitude toward a non-Muslim ruler who has established a regime on Muslim land?" These abstract questions indeed hover in the background, but in the period under discussion they had very concrete manifestations—as they still do today, if in different ways. Should I accept the request or demand of a KKL agent to hand over land in exchange for compensation? Should I accept an intelligence officer's request to provide information on strangers who have appeared in my village? Should I tell my children what happened in the Galilee during the 1948 war? Should I encourage them to engage in oppositional political activity? Should I curry favor with officials of the Histadrut or the military government in order to obtain a teaching job? None of these questions has a single answer, and, quite naturally, different people have made different decisions regarding each of them. Some Arabs have also changed their minds. In the background, bitter contention often existed between national sentiments and personal needs (e.g., to support a family).

On the political level, two camps faced off within the Palestinian community in Israel, representing the two sides of the dilemma. One camp, led by traditional leaders supported by the establishment, maintained that Israel's Arab citizens should accept the state's sovereignty and, over and above that, acquiesce to its deeds. Vociferous protest against actions by the authorities or the presentation of an alternative to the regime was illegitimate as far as this accommodationist camp was concerned. Its leaders formulated an analysis of the situation that justified their approach. In their view, only support for and collaboration with the authorities would induce the state to grant more rights to its Arab population. It is vital to emphasize that the members of this camp viewed themselves as loyal and committed members of the Arab nation, acting in the best interests of their communities. In elections to the Knesset during the 1950s and 1960s, the leaders of this group, who headed Mapai's satellite parties, won the votes of a majority of Israel's Arab citizens. This does not necessarily prove that their principles were accepted by the Arab public at large. The assistance these leaders were able to render to their communities induced people to vote for them, as did pressure from the state, family connections, and social structures.

On the opposite side was the nationalist camp, led during most of this period by the Communist Party. The party's stance differed from the classic Palestinian nationalist line of the Mandate period, since it defined itself as a Jewish-Arab party and accepted the legitimacy of the Israeli state as early as the United Nations partition decision of November 1947. It thus became an integral part of the Israeli political system. At the same time, the Israeli establishment placed it outside the pale. (Ben-Gurion did not view it as a legitimate coalition partner.) Yet it was the only legal political framework in which Arab nationalist sentiments could be expressed, and it sometimes joined forces with more radical elements that rejected the legitimacy of the Jewish state. In any case, soon after the establishment of Israel, the Communist Party positioned itself as a nationalist alternative to the traditional, accommodationist leadership and launched the struggle that it pursued during this entire period—as Mapai's rival for the leadership of the Arab citizens of Israel.

The struggle between these two views was not limited to the election campaigns or even to the political sphere in general. The two camps faced off in almost every village and neighborhood. They differed on nearly every issue: how to treat infiltrators (refugees who tried to return to their homes), how to relate to the military government, how to react to the imposition of military conscription on the Druze. Their different stances could also be seen in their attitudes toward state symbols and ceremonies. Members of the accommodationist camp participated in Independence Day ceremonies and flew Israeli flags, and at their weddings vocalists sang the praises of the military governors. The Communists and their supporters had only contempt for such behavior (although the Israeli flag flew at Communist Party congresses). The Arab public at large stood in the middle, maneuvering between the two approaches.

As is typical of national minority communities, Israeli intelligence and security agencies entered into this tension. Like Histadrut and Mapai officials, these intelligence and security agents were the representatives of the Jewish-Israeli society within the Arab society. They sought to reinforce the accommodationist camp, to maximize the Arab population's collaboration with state agencies, and to encourage Arabs to work against the nationalists. In the absence of clear instructions and policy set by the Israeli leadership, field agents became decision makers (on matters of principle, in consultation with the Central Committee on Arab Affairs). The three Regional Committees on Arab Affairs, composed of representatives of the security agencies, thus determined the fates of communities, villages, and individuals. The broad range of powers granted to these committees, along with their deep penetration of the minority population, made them the real masters of the Arab sector. The means of control over the Arab population described by Ian Lustick in his book *Arabs in the Jewish State* (written without access to recently declassified documents) take on flesh and blood when one reads the minutes of the regional committees' meetings. Through them, the state exacerbated distinctions and discord among different parts of Israel's Arab population, played off one religious and ethnic community against another, used pressures and incentives to co-opt nationalist figures into the establishment, and exploited the financial dependence of Arab civil servants and teachers on the state to enhance its control over the Arab population.

The pressure exerted by state agencies, along with the circumstances under which the Arabs in Israel became citizens of the state, also helped shape this population's identity. This was the superstructure of the control project—changing the consciousness of Israel's Arab citizens and turning them from members of the imagined Palestinian community/nation, with all the political significance that membership bore (including inbuilt opposition to the Jewish state), into members of Israeli civil society. Indeed, creating this new Israeli Arab identity was one of the state's tacit goals. Formally, this combined identity presented no problem, since the population was Arab in ethnicity and Israeli in citizenship. But on a more fundamental level, it turned out to be problematic because of the state's inability (and unwillingness) to create a common ethos and narrative. Jews' and Arabs' perceptions of recent history (Zionist settlement, the Mandate period, and the 1948 war), as well as of earlier history, were sharply contradictory. Furthermore, the two publics did not agree on the role of the state and the definition of the common good, because state institutions and the Jewish public as a whole viewed the state as the actualization of the aspirations of all the Jewish people, including the Jewish Diaspora, rather than of all the state's citizens as a whole. This impinged on Arab interests. The most concrete expression of this was the state's expropriation of Arab land for the purpose of building settlements for Jewish immigrants.

Since it found no way to integrate the two conceptions, the state simply disregarded the Palestinian narrative, the Arab population's aspirations, and Palestinian history. These elements made no appearance in the Israeli curricula produced for Arab schools (let alone for Jewish ones). The hope was that the new generation born after 1948 would not tie itself to the Palestinian past. To achieve this shift, the state sought to silence voices that offered Arab nationalist glosses on current events, such as the Kafr Qasim massacre of 1956. Also silenced were voices that sought to revive Palestinian heritage, connect the younger generation with the Palestinian national movement, and recount the events of the Nakba.

This tension reached one of its climaxes in 1958, the tenth anniversary of the founding of Israel—and of the Nakba. Israel hosted its Decade Festivities. Arab countries conducted ceremonies marking the Nakba. The Arabs in Israel were divided. Some willingly accepted invitations issued by state representatives to participate in the festivities. Others raged, "Will we dance on the graves of our martyrs?" The radio station of the United Arab Republic called on Israel's Arabs to commemorate the Nakba. Some Arab schools in Israel marked it with a moment of silence. In contrast, a celebration of Israel's decade of independence was held in the al-Jazzar Mosque, in Acre. Arab nationalists protested. Just a year before, the mosque's sheikhs (who were appointees and employees of Israel's Ministry of Religions) had refused to conduct a memorial service in honor of the victims of the Kafr Qasim massacre on the grounds that mosques were not supposed to host political activities. Yet here they were celebrating the establishment of the Jewish state.

The nonconfrontational Arab accommodationists indeed played an important role in suppressing the Palestinian nationalist narrative and creating an Israeli Arab identity. Arab public figures participating in state-sponsored events were not the only ones to adopt the Zionist discourse. So did the informers, minor and major, who operated in all of Israel's Arab communities. One of their central missions, as we have seen, was to report all nationalist sentiments they heard expressed in their villages and cities. They were expected to keep a special eye on schoolteachers, who were supposed to educate the younger generation to be devoid of nationalist feelings, but they were told to report on others as well. The result was a comprehensive system of reports from informers. As in all bureaucracies, copies were sent to all interested agencies—the GSS, the military government, the police, the Ministry of Education, and the office of the prime minister's adviser on Arab affairs. Security agencies found ways to strike at Arabs who took nationalist positions, especially by blocking their professional advancement. It was a carefully calculated system through which the security agencies tried to "educate" Arab citizens in what they were permitted and what they were forbidden to say. In other words, the system established the boundaries of Arab discourse in Israel.

Control of speech by the security agencies was Israel's primary tool for shaping the political consciousness of Israel's Arabs. Land agents made their own contribution, if indirectly and in an entirely different way. The willingness of local and national leaders to serve as middlemen in land deals between their communities and the state or the KKL involved a conscious renouncing of one of the cornerstones of Arab nationalism—not allowing the Jews to acquire Arab land. In serving this way, they putatively weakened this tenet's status as a supreme value. Ethnic, local, and religious leaders who placed their community's identity above Arab national identity (often with the support of the Israeli establishment) served as a counterweight to the advocates of Arab nationalism, which was based, on the ideological level, on the equality and brotherhood of all Arabs.

The Arabs who worked with state and Zionist institutions did so not just because their analysis led them to believe that this was best for Israel's Arab population, although the contribution of this motive to Palestinians' collaboration with Israel since the Mandate period should not be understated. Two other factors were also involved. The first was the state's dual character. Despite the imposition of military rule on Arab areas and blatant discrimination against Arabs, even during the 1950s and 1960s Israel possessed certain traits and took certain actions that made it attractive, or valuable, to some of its Arab citizens. I do not mean just the extension of the state's electricity and water grids to Arab villages, mandatory public education, and other development projects; the very nature of the state was attractive. Israel's democratic ethos established red lines that its security agencies could not cross and also allowed Arabs to petition courts to protect their rights (sometimes even successfully). Together with the perception of the state as modern and "Western," this ethos led Arabs to develop a complex attitude toward the Jewish state, neutralizing nationalist components. Indeed, perception of the positive aspects of the state (or Zionism) was an influential factor in the decision to collaborate during the Mandate and after the Jewish state came into being.

A second factor of accommodation that should not be ignored is the system of compensation. Even though the roots of this system lie in the period before 1948, it was the establishment of the state that granted Zionist and state institutions the power to determine the fate of every one of its country's citizens. Leases for abandoned land, gun licenses, career promotions, licenses to move around in and outside of military government zones, permission to engage in legal smuggling, payment for information, and, no less important, assistance in building up political standing were all accepted means of compensation during the period under discussion. Quantifying the influence of such compensation on the political, social, and economic lives of Israel's Arab citizens is not possible, but the significant effect of the state and its security agencies on Arab social structures in Israel and their contribution to the creation of political and economic power centers are obvious.

No wonder, then, that it was not hard for Israel to find Arabs who saw it to their advantage—or who were impelled—to collaborate with state institutions. But, by the end of the period surveyed here—that is, up until the Six Day War of 1967—the two principal currents in Israel's Arab community faced off without either side achieving dominance. Moreover, the state and its Arab supporters did not have the power to eradicate the nationalist view. Indeed, opposition to the military government and to state discrimination against Arabs was the greatest and most vociferous when the control was most blatant and when state supervision of the Arab community was tightest.

An important facilitator of Arab national activity, to which I alluded above, was the system of red lines that constrained Israel's security agencies. True, the state took a hard line against Arab nationalist activists, who were often exiled from their villages or placed under administrative detention. And also true, the state's network of collaborators severely constrained freedom of expression. Yet the security agencies did not possess unlimited power. The existence of a system of checks and balances (both on the parliamentary level, in the form of opposition Knesset members, Communists, and others, and on the legal level) constrained the Regional Committees on Arab Affairs and the military government. Furthermore, Israeli officials—at least in part—were imbued with a socialist-humanist worldview that countered their hawkishness. Even if those who fought the military government did not always perceive this in real time, we cannot ignore it in analyzing the system in retrospect.

Palestinian Arab national activity in Israel blocked the adoption of the Zionist discourse by Arabs. But there was another important reason for the absence of Zionist discourse among Arabs: the Zionist movement—and the state it produced—did not offer Arab citizens a real path to participation in the state, influence on policies, or involvement in its public life. The consequence was that the state actually reinforced Arab identity among its Arab citizens. Just as the Palestinian refugees were not absorbed into the Arab countries where they resided, and they suffered discrimination in most of these countries, thus preserving their unique Palestinian identity, neither did the Arabs in Israel become an integral part of the country they lived in. Israel found no place for them in its polity, so they preserved their national discourse and identity.

Here is another way of putting it: the Nakba could not be eliminated from the memory of Palestinians in Israel, even if schoolteachers were forbidden to talk about it, because the Nakba was not just an event in history but also a part of daily life. Land expropriations, military rule, discrimination in the allocation of government funds, a national anthem that made no reference to the Arabs in Israel (and these are only some examples) perpetuated a situation in which the Arabs were, in their own term, *mankubin,* or "Nakba-ed"; that is, they were a community that lived the Nakba on an ongoing basis. Even those who did not belong to any nationalist organization could not disregard that. To a certain extent, the more the authorities beat down the public, the clearer it was to each individual Arab that he belonged to a community with a national identity. In turn, the desire to express those nationalist sentiments grew among part of that public.

Another factor that helped preserve national identity among the Palestinians in Israel was the backing they received from Arab countries. Even though certain Arab circles viewed the Arab citizens of Israel as traitors, both because some of the Israeli Arabs spied for Israel during and after the 1948 war and because they consented to live under Israeli rule without taking part in the armed struggle against it, that view coexisted with another that considered them an integral part of the Arab nation. Thus Nasser's pan-Arab ideology, his vocal support for the restitution of Palestinian rights, and his charisma lent, during the decade prior to 1967, important support to the Arab nationalists in Israel. It gave them self-confidence, helping them expand their ranks and establishing them firmly in the Arab community. This does not necessarily mean, however, that these Palestinian citizens of Israel also identified with Nasser's boast that he would destroy the Jewish state. Yet that rhetoric did serve to boost Arab nationalist feeling. Ties to Arab countries were also abetted by Israel's decision to maintain a separate Arabic-language school system in which only Arabs studied. The result was that, even during the period when they were physically isolated from the rest of the Arab nation, Arabs in Israel, including those born after 1948, retained cultural ties to the Arab world.

The 1967 war changed the map of the Middle East and also the geography of identity for Israel's Arab citizens. Those changes lie outside the scope of this work. But the fundamental duality between Palestinian Arab national identity and integration into Israel's civil society did not change, even as it metamorphosed with the development of relations between Israel and official representatives of the Palestinian people. After 1967, Palestinians on both sides of the Green Line, in Israel and in the occupied territories, established cultural, economic, and social ties—but rarely political and military ones. Generally speaking, the Palestinians in Israel supported the struggle of the Palestinians in the West Bank and Gaza for an independent Palestinian state but from a distance, and their participation was on the declarative level. They focused instead on their own campaign for equality with the Jewish citizens of Israel. These two segments of the Palestinian people did not establish joint political frameworks.

This divide between Palestinians in Israel and those outside its borders can be seen as a success of the Israeli security agencies, yet the Israeli establishment is clearly not satisfied with the current state of affairs. The demand of the Palestinian Arab citizens of Israel to define Israel as a state of all its citizens is perceived as a strategic threat to Israel. Israel's view of its Arabs as a threat was reinforced by the events of October 2000, when violent demonstrations of Arab citizens broke out (and thirteen demonstrators were killed by the Israeli police). Thus, recent years have seen funds and efforts redirected to surveillance and control of the Arab minority in Israel by the General Security Service. While the methods used today are presumably not the same ones used in the 1950s, the political activity of Palestinians in Israel, even when legitimate, is still under surveillance, and the level of involvement of the security services in Arab local and national politics is still significant.

NOTES

ABBREVIATIONS

AAA	adviser on Arab affairs
ACC	assistant chief constable
ALA	Arab Liberation Army
CC	chief constable
CZA	Central Zionist Archives
DCC	deputy chief constable
GSS	General Security Service (Shin Bet)
HA	Haganah Archives
HQ	headquarters
IDFA	Israel Defense Forces Archives
IP	Israel Police
ISA	Israel State Archive
MFA	Ministry of Foreign Affairs
MG	Military Government
OC	officer in command
OHD-HU	Oral History Division, Harman Institute of Contemporary Jewry, Hebrew University of Jerusalem
PMO	prime minister's office

PS	police station
RCAA	Regional Committee on Arab Affairs
SB	Special Branch
SD	subdistrict

Note: The Israeli police, during the first half of the period under discussion, followed the British system in both structure and ranks. Thus the highest ranks in each district were chief constable (i.e., the district's police commander), deputy chief constable, and assistant chief constable.

Israel's police force was organized in three to five districts—with a few changes throughout time—and each of them was divided into subdistricts. Thus we can find certain villages that were under the Southern District then under the Central District, or first under the Haifa District then under the Northern District, and so forth.

It also should be noted that the terms for the geographical divisions among the police, the IDF, and the MG were not exactly the same. The terms were the most confusing in regard to the Triangle, in the center of Israel, where the military government had its "Central Region"; the police had its "Central Subdistrict (SD)" *(nafat tikhon)* but also its "Central District" *(mahoz merkaz),* which included the Central SD *(tikhon* and *merkaz* both mean "center"); while the southern Triangle was under the IDF "Central Command."

INTRODUCTION

1. *Mapai* is actually an acronym for Mifleget Po'alei Eretz Israel (Israel's Labor Party).

2. Dan Rabinowitz and Khawla Abu-Baker, *Coffins on Our Shoulders: The Experience of the Palestinian Citizens of Israel* (Berkeley: University of California Press, 2005).

3. Ahmad H. Sa'di, "Minority Resistance to State Control: Towards a Reanalysis of Palestinian Political Activity in Israel," *Social Identities* 2, no. 3 (1996): 395–412.

4. Shira Nomi Robinson, "Occupied Citizens in a Liberal State: Palestinians under Military Rule and the Colonial Formation of Israeli Society, 1948–1966," Ph.D. dissertation, Stanford University, 2005.

5. Elie Rekhess, *Ha-Mi'ut ha-Aravi be-Israel: Bein Komonisem le-L'umiut Aravit* [Between communism and Arab nationalism: Rakah and the Arab minority in Israel, 1965–1973] (Tel Aviv: Hakibutz ha-me'uhad, 1993), 16 (in Hebrew). For a similar opinion, see also Yohanan Peres and Nira Davis, "On the National Identity of the Israeli Arab," *Ha-Mizzrah he-Hadash* 18 (1968): 108–9 (in Hebrew). Sammy Smooha has written, "The demands made of the Arab citizen are minimal—to

abide by the law and maintain public order. It is sufficient that he be an unhostile citizen and he is not pressured to be a devoted and patriotic citizen. . . . He has the freedom to voice nationalist ideas as long as he remains within the law." Sammy Smooha, "Arabs and Jews in Israel: Minority-Majority Relations," *Magamot* 22 (1976): 415 (in Hebrew).

6. Hillel Cohen, *Army of Shadows: Palestinian Collaboration with Zionism, 1917–1948* (Berkeley: University of California Press, 2008).

I. BEGINNING A BEAUTIFUL FRIENDSHIP

1. Unreferenced details are from an interview with ʿAbd al-Raʾouf by Haviv Knaʿan, published in four parts in the daily newspaper *Yom Yom,* beginning 19 June 1949.

2. On Black Saturday, 29 June 1946, the British army raided Jewish settlements, confiscated weapons, and arrested some twenty-seven hundred Haganah members and Zionist political leaders.

3. On the meeting of 14 September 1947, see CZA, S25/3300; for the meeting of 17 December 1947, see CZA, S25/9208; and on a meeting dated 13 January 1948, see HA, 105/215.

4. "ʿAbd al-Raʾouf ʿAbd al-Razeq: Personal Questionnaire," 15 June 1950, ISA 79, 8/21.

5. On the warm welcome, see Israeli police, Ha-Sharon SD to Tel Aviv District HQ, "Operation 'To the Mount,'" 8 May 1949, ISA 79, 95/64.

6. Activity of Arab collaborators in the Triangle before, during, or after the war is mentioned sporadically; see, for example, Zikhron Yaʿakov PS to Hadera SD, 28 December 1950, ISA 79, 138/10; Haim Hermesh to Hadera police commander, 2 January 1950, ISA 79, 138/10. Other examples can be found in the personal sheets of mukhtars and other local figures in ISA 79, file 2183/10.

7. Ben-Elkana to ACC Hadera, weekly report, 31 May 1949, ISA 79, 152/12; [Ben-Elkana], "Umm al-Fahm: A Report," May 1949, ISA 79, 120/1.

8. [Ben-Elkana], "Umm al-Fahm: A Report," May 1949, ISA 79, 120/1.

9. An undated report written by an informer tells of the harsh conditions under the Iraqis and Jordanians and the pleasant surprise from the new Israeli rulers: ISA 79, 2183/8; see also Umm al-Fahm PS to ACC Hadera, "Report on the Triangle within the Borders of Hadera SD," 28 August 1949, ISA 79, 4/8.

10. Report on the activities of the military government in Nazareth, October 1948, ISA, MFA files, 2564/11. On collaboration of Arabs from Nazareth area during the war, see IDFA, report of 15 June 1948, 1950/2384-7. On the phenomenon as a whole, see Cohen, *Army of Shadows.*

11. For a list of villages that surrendered and those that were conquered, see "List of Villages," Ministry of Minorities, Nazareth Bureau, to Ministry of Minori-

ties, Tel Aviv, ISA 49, 302/114. In some of these villages, there were clashes before the first truce but no resistance during the decisive battles, from July onward.

12. On the role of collaborators in the surrender of villages, see Cohen, *Army of Shadows,* chapter 9. Not mentioned in that book were other villages that also surrendered in a similar fashion—Dir al-Asad and Kafr Kanna; for these see "Clearance Test" of Ahmad Qasem of Dir al-Asad, 5 December 1950, Acre PS to Haifa District HQ, ISA 79, 1/17; and Ahmad Yusef of Kafr Kanna to minister of police, 30 October 1966, ISA 79, 285/18.

13. "Figures of the Bedouins in the Israeli-Controlled Area of the Negev," 15 November 1948, ISA, MFA 2567/10.

14. 'Oda Abu M'ammar to MG–Beersheva, December 1948, ISA, MFA 2567/10. A translation of the letter was distributed by the MFA's research division to the prime minister, foreign minister, minorities minister, and senior officials.

15. Nazareth PS to Tiberias District, "Weekly Report," 4 July 1949, ISA 79, 57/3.

16. Ibid.

17. Weekly reports of Haifa District HQ and Karkur PS, 22 September and 7 October 1949, ISA 79, 138/6.

18. Reports of 12 and 24 November 1949, ISA 79, 138/6. The sense of neglect by the government increased gradually, as can be learned from the biweekly report on Arab affairs, the Central SD to Haifa District, 5 January 1951. This very report also leveled criticism at the MG for the failure to resolve the problem of the supply of flour and bread to Kufr Qara' and for the corruption in the leasing of lands in the Triangle as a whole, ISA 79, 2/2.

19. [Ya'akov Sapir to Haifa CC], 14 July 1950, ISA 79, 2183/29; Muhammad Najib's testimony, 28 July 1949, ISA 79, 138/9; Israeli Police HQ to CC Stavi, "Reports from the Triangle," 25 January 1950, ISA 79, 2183/8; Haifa District to Acre PS, "Collaborators with the Enemy," 6 November 1950, ISA 79, 1/17. Transmitting information to the security services was considered problematic before this but not to the same extent.

20. Ze'ev Steinberg, Central SD, "Summary of Arab Affairs," 28 July 1950, ISA 79, 138/6.

21. General Staff—Division of Operations, "Biweekly Security Report," 30 November 1949, IDFA, 580/1956-169.

22. Meeting in the Southern District HQ, 25 July 1949, ISA 79, 95/10.

23. Shlomo Ben-Elkana, "The Activity of the Southern Triangle in Past and Present (a Political Report)," submitted to head of Investigation Department, IP HQ, by Sharon SD, 31 May 1950, ISA 79, 121/18.

24. Quoted in Uzi Benziman and 'Atalla Mansur, *Dayarei Mishne: Arviyei Yisra'el, Ma'amadam ve-ha-Mediniyut Klapeihem* [Subtenants: The Arabs of Israel, their status and the policies toward them] (Jerusalem: Keter, 1992), 34–35 (in Hebrew).

25. On the activity of Sheikh Salameh during the war and the leaflet distributed against him in December 1947, see HA, file 105/154. On his activity in the 1950s and his relations with other sheikhs, see "Protocol no. 2 of the Special Branch Officers' Meeting," 10 February 1959, ISA 79, 398/1.

26. British police report, 15 October 1947, ISA 17, 2456/359/47.

27. Sayf al-Din Zu'bi, *Shahed 'Ayan: Mudhakkarat* [Eyewitness: Memories] (Shefa'amr, 1987), 10 (in Arabic).

28. Tsori to Tene, "On the Happenings in Nazareth and the Region," 4 July 1948, HA, 105/154; "On the Arab Refugee Problem," 8 October 1948, IDFA, 121/50-178; Arab Liberation Army, Yarmuk Battalion/Intelligence to Lebanese Battalion HQ, August 1948, IDFA, ALA documents, 1/57-279. The involvement of Sayf al-Din with the Shai is mentioned also in his official biographical note in the Knesset web site; see http://www.knesset.gov.il/mk/heb/mk.asp?mk_individual_id_t=251 (last accessed 30 December 2008).

29. See, for example, "Report on the Visit of the Military Governor in Muqeible," 28 July 1949, IDFA, 721/72-842.

30. For a detailed list of mukhtars in the western Galilee, see Zevulun SD, "Mukhtars," 15 August 1950, ISA 79, 1/18; for the eastern Galilee, see Nazareth PS, "Coordination with the MG," 1 February 1951, ISA 79, 57/22.

31. "Memorandum of the Coordination Meeting of the Agencies Active in the Central Region," December 1949, ISA 79, 138/6.

32. Safed PS, 22 June 1950, ISA 79, 84/2. On the family history of this man, who assisted the Jews in other ways as well, see Safed SB to SB IP-HQ, 24 March 1960, ISA 79, 162/29.

33. Karkur PS to Central SD, 12 February 1951, ISA 79, 2/23; IP HQ/Investigations to Central Region military governor, "Permits of Movement from the Administrated Area," 19 October 1951, and reply from 4 November 1951, both in ISA 79, 316/17; Taybe PS to Central SD, 14 September 1951, ISA 79, 2/23.

34. Barukh Yekutiely, deputy of PMO-AAA, to Yitzhak Cohen, of the Department of Land Leasing, 17 July 1951, ISA 102, 17097/48.

35. Protocol of the Committee on Leasing Land in the Triangle, 6 November 1953, ISA 99, 2199/3126 gimel. Recommendations to lease land to collaborators appear in protocols of other meetings in the same file.

36. Protocol of the Higher Committee on Land Leasing, 30 December 1953, ISA 99, 2199/3126 gimel.

37. Protocol of the Committee on Land and Orchard Leasing, 19 March 1953, ISA, MFA 1989/3.

38. Taybe PS to Central SD, "Intelligence and Agents," 14 September 1951, ISA 79, 2/23; Tiberias District to all PSs and SDs, "Import from Arab Countries," 15 May 1950, ISA 79, 4/26; IP HQ to CC Stavi, "Special Report," 5 February 1950, ISA 79, 2183/8 (on Hamdan); PMO-AAA to IP, "Importing from Arab countries," undated, ISA 79, 2/19; IP, "Biweekly Report," 19 June 1950, ISA 79, 138/6. For

leaking information to the Jordanians about Hamdan's activity, see Hadera SD, "Information from '229,'" 22 October 1949, ISA 79, 3/16; on antagonism toward Hamdan in the Triangle because of his tight control over land and his contacts with a leader in the Arab revolt of 1936–39 who was known for "killing dozens of Arabs," see Haifa District to IP HQ, "Atmosphere," 22 July 1951, ISA 79, 2175/15.

39. For examples of security officials' recommendations to allow refugee-infiltrators to remain in Israel and the reasons given, see "List of People Brought from the Triangle," 12 January 1950; "Summary of [Meeting of the Committee on] Temporary Residence Permits," 5 September 1950; "List of Those Who Were Permitted to Stay in Israel," undated; all in ISA 79, 138/10.

40. Letter drafted by Palmon for the mutran to sign, undated, ISA 102, 17114/20. This file includes the lists of Christian Arabs who were allowed to return to Israel thanks to the mutran, as well as his correspondence with the authorities.

41. Giora Zeid, Ministry of Minorities, to Haifa District CC and minister of police, "Collaboration between the Druze and the Police Forces," 11 April 1949, ISA 79, 2146/30.

42. Protocol of the secondary coordination committee, 12 April 1950, IDFA, 834/53-293. Among the participants: Palmon of the PMO, Ilani of the Shin Bet, Go'el Levitzki of the MG, and a representative of the police (and probably the MFA as well).

43. Jerusalem District CC to Villages Department, 29 September 1949, ISA 79, 37/19; Karkur PS to Central SD, "Rewarding Informers," 11 May 1952, ISA 79, 81/8; Karkur PS to Central SD, "List of Informers and Agents in the Districts," 13 September 1951, ISA 79, 2/23.

44. Intelligence 10-west to Hadera SD commander, 17 July 1954, ISA 79, 81/7.

45. Karkur PS to Central SD, "List of Informers and Agents in the Districts," 13 September 1951, ISA 79, 2/23.

46. SB Jezreel SD to SB Northern District, "The Atmosphere in Nazareth," 15 February 1952, ISA 79, 80/6.

47. On 'Awad's activity during the 1948 war, see Cohen, *Army of Shadows,* 241–43.

48. See 'Awad's appeal to the Israeli Supreme Court of Justice, 19/50; and Hillel Cohen, *Ha-Nifkadim ha-Nokhehim* [The present absentees: The Palestinian refugees in Israel] (Jerusalem: Institute for Israeli Arab Studies, 2000), 128–29 (in Hebrew).

49. 'Awad to Ben-Gurion, 4 March 1952, ISA 79, 30/8.

50. Hadera SD, "List of Persons in Baqa Area," 3 October 1954, ISA 79, 138/16.

51. Steinberg to Hadera SD, 28 August 1949, ISA 79, 4/8; "Summary of Reports for the Week Ended on 22 September 1949," ISA 79, 38/6.

52. For some more details on Samwili, see Benny Morris, *Israel's Border Wars, 1949–1956: Arab Infiltration, Israeli Retaliation and the Countdown to War* (Oxford: Clarendon Press, 1993), 62.

53. Sergeant Friesling to OC Lod PS, 18 September 1954; Goldberg to OC Ramla SD, 27 October 1954; OC Ramla SD to CC, 31 October 1954; all in ISA 79, 6/35.

54. Rafi Sitton and Yitzhak Shushan, *Anshei ha-Sod ve-ha-Seter* [Men of secrets, men of mystery] (Tel Aviv: Idanim, 1990), 130–31 (in Hebrew); Josef Argman, *Ze Haya Sodi be-Yoter* [It was top secret] (Tel Aviv: Ministry of Defense Publishing House, 2003), 167–80 (in Hebrew).

55. ACC Aharon Shlush, IP-HQ/Investigations, to Jerusalem police and GSS-3, 15 May 1951, ISA 79, 373/9. The letter was sent following tension among the various agencies in the villages west of Jerusalem.

56. Dorenzaft to ACC Southern District, "Report on a Tour in the Triangle," 4 July 1949, ISA 79, 95/20.

57. Dorenzaft, "Information from the Triangle," 18 December 1949, ISA 79, 2183/8.

58. It is interesting to note that the first cabinet decision in this matter (decision 249, of 9 March 1952) did not include the GSS among the organizations participating in the Supreme Committee. The GSS appealed this, and subsequently the cabinet decided, on 27 April of that year, to include a GSS representative as well. The representative was Isser Halperin (aka Harel). See the decisions of the cabinet on the above-mentioned dates and also the correspondence on that matter in ISA 79, 2246/10 and 2246/11. It is not that the GSS lacked responsibilities. According to a decision of the cabinet, dated 3 May 1949, a representative of the GSS was appointed as a chair of the committee in charge of entry permissions to Israel, and this authority was reaffirmed in the reorganization of 1952. See ISA 56, 2218/1.

2. COMMUNISTS VS. THE MILITARY GOVERNMENT

1. Some of the elders of 'Eilabun to commander of Nazareth PS, 22 August 1955, ISA 79, 82/19.

2. Sa'id M. to police minister, "The Communists in Makr," 7 April 1952, ISA 113, 3313/2/13.

3. For figures on the Arab vote to the Knesset in the period under discussion, see Jacob Landau, *The Arabs in Israel: A Political Study* (London: Oxford University Press, 1969), chapter 5.

4. Some, like Lutfi Mash'our, editor of the Arabic-Israeli newspaper *Al-Sinnara,* have argued that Arab Communists also helped convey arms to the Jewish forces. He made this charge in his newspaper in 1988, in response to which the Communist writer Emil Habibi sued him for libel; see court cases 388/88 (Nazareth district court), in which Habibi won, and *Al-Sinnara*'s legal appeals to the Supreme Court (civil appeals 808/89 and 1370/91), which did not lead to changing the decision.

5. "The National Liberation League," 26 August 1948, IDFA, 2384/50-8. The document is not signed, and its author is not known, but even if it was not a person associated with the military government, he must certainly have been close to it. The author may, perhaps, have been a member of the left-wing Mapam party.

6. See also Arye Gelblum, *Haaretz*, 19 November 1948.

7. Ben-Gurion Diaries, entry of 20 December 1948, Ben-Gurion Archive; Sede Boker, quoted in Sara Ozacky-Lazar, "The Military Government as a Control Mechanism over Arab Citizens: The First Decade, 1948–1956," *Ha-Mizrah He-Hadash* 43 (2002): 107 (in Hebrew).

8. Memorandum of a meeting of the military governors with the commander of the MG, 28 March 1950, IDFA, 834/53-293.

9. Ozacky-Lazar, "The Military Government as a Control Mechanism over Arab Citizens," 107–8, 126.

10. *Divrey ha-Knesset* [the Knesset protocols] 2 (1949): 1190 (in Hebrew).

11. *Divrey ha-Knesset* 4 (1950): 858–61.

12. Israel Police, Tiberias District, "Weekly Intelligence Summary," 3 April 1950, ISA 79, 2293/15.

13. *Divrey ha-Knesset* 17 (1954): 228–30.

14. SB Safed to SB Northern District, "The Village of 'Eilabun: A Report," 9 December 1954, ISA 79, 82/19.

15. Ibid.

16. Benny Morris, *The Birth of the Palestinian Refugee Problem, 1947–1949* (Cambridge: Cambridge University Press, 1987), 229–30.

17. Ministry of Minorities, "On the Happenings among the Minorities," 16 March 1949, IDFA, 1308/50-485; AAA briefing to MFA, "Bishop Georgious Hakim," 24 May 1964, ISA, MFA 3782/23. The latter file includes reports on Hakim's talks with Israeli officials over the years.

18. Hakim to Ben-Gurion, 18 July 1949, ISA 102, 17109/14.

19. Haifa District HQ, "Arab Affairs," 1 July 1949, ISA 79, 2162/37.

20. Shefa'Amr PS to Zevulun SD, 17 October 1949, ISA 79, 1/19.

21. Nazareth PS to Haifa CC, 18 September 1950, ISA 79, 57/13.

22. *Al-Ittihad*, 28 May 1950, reported on Hakim's position in regard to Iqrit.

23. H.M. to MG of Shefa'amr [1962], ISA 79, 316/5.

24. Ibid.

25. *Al-Yawm*, 8 December 1954, quoted in SB Safed to SB Northern District, "The Village of 'Eilabun: A Report," 9 December 1954, ISA 79, 82/19.

26. Hakim's speech was published in *Davar*, *'Al ha-Mishmar*, and *Al-Yawm*, 7 July 1963. The response was published in *Al-Ittihad*, 12 July 1963.

27. Briefing on al-Najjadah and al-Futuwwa, CZA, S25/9066; Shem Tov to Delphi, HA 105/325; Cohen, *Army of Shadows*, 233, 255, 257.

28. IP, "Summary of Information on Arab Affairs," April 1950, ISA 79, 57/3;

Muhammad Nimer al-Hawwari, *Sirr al-Nakba* [The secret of al-Nakba] (Nazareth, 1955), 41ff. (in Arabic).

29. Eilon PS to Zevulun SD, "Nimer Hawwari," 16 January 1950; Zevulun SD to Haifa District, "Nimer al-Hawwari," 7 February 1950; both in ISA 79, 1/17.

30. *Mishmar,* 23 January 1950.

31. *Kol ha-'Am,* 15 January 1950; and see also *Al-Ittihad* of the same week (both organs of the Communist Party).

32. MG, "Report on the Security Situation in the Areas under the MG, 8 January–23 January 1950," IDFA, 834/53-293; Acre PS to Zevulun SD, "M.N. al-Hawwari," 19 January 1950, ISA 79, 1/17; *Kol ha-'Am,* 18 January 1950.

33. Tiberias District, "Weekly Intelligence Summary," 3 April 1950, ISA 79, 2293/15.

34. IP report, "A Communist Gathering," 28 March 1950, ISA 79, 57/13; *Ha-Herut,* 10 April 1950; *Kol ha-'Am,* 10 April 1950; [Nazareth PS], "Intelligence Summary," 15 April 1950, ISA 79, 57/3.

35. IP, "Intelligence Summary until 15 April 1950," ISA 79, 57/13.

36. Hawwari maintained that the Communist Party's Central Committee instructed party branches to demonstrate against him everywhere he went. He said this to figures he met with in Taybe—Diab 'Ubeid, 'Abd al-Ra'ouf 'Abd al-Razeq, and Kamel al-Tibi, all close to the regime; see "Biweekly Report on Arab Affairs," 13 May 1950, ISA 79, 121/31; and see also the same report for negative reactions to Hawwari's presence in Iksal.

37. The article of *Ha-Dor* is quoted in "media summary" for the police, May 1950, ISA 79, 2162/30.

38. Knesset meeting on 9 March 1949, *Divrey ha-Knesset* 1 (1949): 84–85; protocols of government meeting, *Divrey ha-Knesset* 14 (1954): 34. The Communists' position on partition was not uniform. On the disputes among different persons, see Elie Rekhess, "Jews and Arabs in the PCP," *Ha-Tsiyonut* 15 (1991): 175–86, especially 182–84 (in Hebrew).

39. Nazareth PS to Haifa CC, "Elections to the Second Knesset," 24 June 1951, ISA 79, 2175/1.

40. Nazareth PS to Tiberias District, "Operation Yatsiv (Stable)—the Elections to the Second Knesset," 3 August 1951, ISA 79, 2175/16.

41. See the biographical introduction to Muhammad Nimer al-Hawwari, *Al-Hawariyun* (Acre: n.p., n.d.), 11–17 (in Arabic).

42. Dorenzaft to Southern District CC, "Information from a Tour in the Villages of the Triangle," 16 August 1949, ISA 79, 95/21.

43. All exchanges reported in MG HQ, "Memorandum and Decisions of the Meeting of the Military Governors with the Head of the MG," 28 March 1950, IDFA, 834/53-293.

44. Taybe PS, "Weekly Report," 14 May 1950, ISA 79, 121/20; Central SD to Haifa District, "MK Tawfiq Toubi," 23 June 1950, ISA 79, 138/10.

45. On al-Razeq's exile, see Central SD, "Biweekly Report on Arab Affairs," 31 August 1950, ISA 79, 138/6. For the results of the elections, see Landau, *The Arabs in Israel,* 114–16. Landau argued mistakenly (116) that the Communist Party was strengthened from no voters in Taybe in the first general elections to 752 in the second, but actually the people of Taybe were not Israeli citizens on the date of the first general elections in Israel and did not participate in these elections.

46. "Diab Hasan 'Ubeid: Personal Sheet," written by Ben-Elkana, 15 June 1950, ISA 79, 8/21; IP, "List of Personalities in the Triangle," 3 November 1954, ISA 79, 121/11.

47. Summary of the meeting of the coordinating committee, 21 October 1954, ISA 79, 121/10.

48. Unsigned IP document, "The Speech of MK 'Ubeid," ISA 79, 274/20.

49. RCAA-Central [Triangle], August 1965, ISA 79, 453/21.

50. Yossi Melman, "To Lebanon by a Car, a Shipping Container and a Fishing Boat," *Haaretz,* 5 July 2002, b-4.

51. Landau, *The Arabs in Israel,* 120.

52. ACC Segev to Jezreel SD, "Meeting of the Advisory Committee on Elections," 11 July 1955, ISA 79, 29/14.

53. "Report from Tamra" [1958], ISA 79, 234/25.

3. BOUNDARY BREAKERS

1. The details are from testimony to the police given by a neighbor of Bulus, identified simply as "H." (to protect his privacy), 15 June 1952; and from the exile order for Bulus; both in ISA 79, 4/38.

2. H. testimony, ISA 79, 4/38.

3. IP, Tiberias District HQ to SDs, MG Galilee, and GSS/North, "Murder and an Attempt to Murder in the Galilee," 16 July 1953, ISA 79, 1/16.

4. Morris, *Israel's Border Wars,* chapters 2 and 4.

5. Jezreel SD, undated report, ISA 79, 152/6.

6. Ben-Elkana, "The Activity of the Southern Triangle in Past and Present (a Political Report)," IP HQ/head of Investigations Department, by the Sharon SD, 31 May 1950, ISA 79, 121/18; see also his review "The Infiltration Problem," 7 March 1951, Minorities Branch, IP HQ, in the same file.

7. For assessment of the number of the infiltrators who were killed, see Morris, *Israel's Border Wars,* 135–38.

8. Rekhess, *Ha-Mi'ut ha-Aravi be-Israel,* 16. For a similar view, see Peres and Davis, "On the National Identity of the Israeli Arab."

9. IP, "Biweekly Report on Arab Affairs for the Period Ending 25 April 1950," ISA 79, 121/31. A report of the anti-infiltration unit of the Villages SD, Jerusalem District, describes a group of villagers from Abu Ghosh who pretended to be

Israeli soldiers, frightened infiltrators, and took the goods they had smuggled; see "The Village of Abu Ghosh—a Survey," 14 September 1953, ISA 79, 379/2.

10. Meeting in the Southern District HQ, 25 July 1949, ISA 79, 95/10; ACC Ziv, "Kufr Qara'—Complaint against Policemen," May 1953, ISA 79, 30/25.

11. Residents from Abu Ghosh to Speaker of the Knesset, [July 1950], ISA 79, 260/2.

12. The Israeli Supreme Court discussed the question of whether refusal to collaborate with the authorities legitimates an exile order and decided in the negative. However, the court approved this specific exile on the basis of a claim of an IDF officer, according to which there were additional concrete security reasons for the exile. See the decision dated 29 October 1953, Supreme Court file 188/53, copy preserved in ISA 79, 379/2.

13. "The Minorities' Population," ISA, MFA files, 1966/2, 1955, based on figures updated in October 1953.

14. For the activity of Sheikh Khneifes before the establishment of the state, see Cohen, *Army of Shadows*, 226–27, 246–47.

15. Quoted in a letter sent in the name of the head of the GSS to PMO-AAA, to IP HQ, and to MG HQ, "Bands in Western Galilee," ISA 79, 1/19.

16. MG western Galilee to MG HQ, "Imposing Curfew of Shefar'am," 16 November 1949, ISA 79, 1/25 (note: "Shefar'am" is the Hebrew spelling for the Arabic village Shefa'amr); see also Morris, *Israel's Border Wars*, 146 n. 111.

17. Suleiman Abu-Ghalyun to MG Negev, 26 July and 25 August 1950, IDFA 834/53-267. For handing over infiltrators by Bedouin sheikhs, see Avraham Shammash to MG Negev, 8 July 1949, IDFA, 834/53-177. For cases of collaborators who were murdered by Bedouin infiltrators, see: "Inventory of Murder Cases for 1951," ISA 79, 2198/17; "Inventory of Murder Cases for 1953," ISA 79, 2278/53; and Kfar Saba PS to Sharon SD, "Weekly Report," 26 October 1949; all in ISA 79, 91/41. On the activity of Abu-Kishek during 1948 according to Arab intelligence reports, see Cohen, *Army of Shadows*, 245.

18. GSS/3 to SB IP HQ and to MG Department in the Ministry of Defense, "Deterioration of the Security in the Southern Triangle," 12 January 1953, ISA 79, 2246/21.

19. Ha-Shfela SD to Jerusalem District and GSS/south, "Biweekly Report: Arab Affairs," 24 February 1951, ISA 79, 8/17.

20. Ibid.

21. "Hajj 'Abdallah ... ," report of the SB officer of the Northern District, Yitzhak Segev, 3 February 1953, ISA 79, 84/12.

22. MG Central Region, "Security Report," August 1962, ISA 79, 290/8.

23. Deputy OC of Taybe PS to OC Sharon SD, 24 November 1954, ISA 79, 121/11.

24. Acre SB to Northern District SB, "Smuggling in Tamra," 28 January 1959, ISA 79, 205/2.

25. Minkowski of Hadera SB to Northern District, 18 September 1959, ISA 79, 182/12.

26. Crime Investigation Bureau, Hadera PS, "Information," 16 December 1949, ISA 79, 138/6.

27. Jaber Mu'adi to Minister of Police Shitrit, 25 July 1953, ISA 119, 3314/3/276.

28. Attorney firm Hoter-Yishai and Ben-Haviv to Officer Mittleman, of Zikhron Ya'akov PS, 20 August 1952, ISA 79, 30/11; Tawfiq Ahmad to MG Triangle, 19 October 1951, ISA 79, 2/23; memo to OC Hadera SD, 13 May 1954, ISA 79, 81/7.

29. Jezreel SB to Northern District SB, "Intelligence Report," 18 October 1956, ISA 79, 120/2; Jezreel SD to Northern District, "Suspicion of Infiltration into Tur'an," 28 January 1962, ISA 79, 318/4; the barber testimony, 13 February 1960, ISA 79, 312/20; Nazareth PS, "Report on a Meeting," 25 November 1962, ISA 79, 183/6.

30. "Secret Report on Smugglers and Infiltrators," September 1953, ISA 79, 4/37.

31. "Trustworthy Informer to the Head of the IDF Intelligence," 23 February 1952, IDFA 263/66-3936.

32. Corporal Ben-Hanan, Nazareth PS, to OC Nazareth PS, 1 March 1963, ISA 79, 204/16; SB Jezreel SD to GSS/149, 25 February 1962, "Infiltration into Tur'an," ISA 79, 318/4.

33. Dorenzaft to Southern District CC, "Information from Tours in the Villages of the Triangle," 16 August 1949, ISA 79, 95/21; Ben-Elkana, "Summary of Figures," [1950], ISA 79, 8/21.

34. Dorenzaft to Southern District ACC, "Report on a Tour in the Triangle," 4 July 1949, ISA 79, 95/20. See also Dorenzaft to Southern District CC, "Recruitment of Informers," 26 July 1949; and Dorenzaft to Sharon DCC, "Recruitment of Arab Informers"; both in ISA 79, 95/21.

35. Amin's testimony, Kfar Yona PS, 23 December 1951, ISA 79, 2/23.

36. According to Amin's and his colleagues' testimonies, ISA 79, 2/23.

37. Deputy OC of IP, Amos Ben-Gurion, to all district CCs, 19 May 1953, ISA 79, 1/23.

38. OC Petah Tikva SD to Central District HQ, "Report on Ambushes," 1 July 1951, ISA 79, 2/23.

39. Ibid. One might doubt whether the policemen had ordered the infiltrators to turn themselves in and opened fire only after the latter tried to escape, or alternatively the policemen opened fire without warning but reported that they warned them first for legal reasons.

40. Petah Tikva SD to Central District HQ, 25 June 1956, ISA 79, 121/9.

41. Ze'ev Steinberg of Central SD to Haifa District HQ, "Operations Initiated by Central SD," 2 February 1951, ISA 79, 2/23.

42. Villages SD to IP HQ/Anti-infiltration Branch, 11 April 1952, ISA 79, 2446/18; see also Sitton and Shushan, *Anshei ha-Sod ve-ha-Seter*, 124–27.

43. Cases of the collaboration of Palestinians from the West Bank and the Gaza Strip with Israeli agencies are numerous and are mentioned in the following documents (among others): Dorenzaft to ACC Southern District, 4 July 1949, "Report on a Tour in the Triangle," ISA 79, 95/20; Dorenzaft to CC Southern District, "Information from Lydda, Ramle, and Migdal Gad," 7 September 1949, ISA 79, 95/21; and Central SD to Haifa District HQ, "Retaliation Operations," 25 December 1950, ISA 79, 138/5. Lists of Arabs suspected of spying were prepared by the Jordanian intelligence and reached Israel; for those, see the following: Jerusalem SB to GSS and police units, 21 January 1952, and all related correspondence, ISA 79, 2446/18; Jerusalem District to Jerusalem Police Border and Negev SB, 22 August 1956, ISA 79, 336/12; and MG Triangle, "Security Report April 1965," 5, ISA 79, 358/20. The state-sponsored newspaper *Al-Yawm* randomly quoted Arab media that reported on trials of spies (e.g., *Al-Yawm,* 27 August 1950). For the Arab states' perception of Arab citizens of Israel as traitors, see Gideon Shilo, *Arviyei Yisrael Be-'einei Medinot Arav ve-Ashaf* [Israel's Arabs in the eyes of the Arab states and the PLO] (Jerusalem: Magnes, 1982), 30–31 (in Hebrew).

44. ACC Tiberias District to CC Tiberias, 16 July 1953, ISA 79, 1/16.

45. Zeidan's testimony, 16 August 1953, ISA 79, 1/16.

46. Sh-hadeh's testimony, 10 August 1953, ISA 79, 1/16.

47. This was revealed when the magistrate's court in Nazareth issued arrest warrants for all four men for their involvement in a kidnapping. They were released on bail paid by Bedouin sheikhs from the Galilee but did not appear in court because they were on a special mission outside the area. That same month they attended the wedding of a friend in the village of Naqura, in Lebanon, dressed in IDF uniforms. An arrest order was issued, mentioning all these details, on 29 November 1955, and is in ISA 79, 29/14.

48. Jezreel SD to Northern District SB, "Fedayeen Cell," 22 February 1956, ISA 79, 148/5; Jezreel SD to Northern District SB, "Yusef . . . ," 28 May 1958, ISA 79, 318/4.

49. IP HQ/Investigations to GSS—"The Qassamites," 12 May 1951, ISA 79, 2175/12; IP HQ to CC Stavi, "Information from the Triangle," 25 January 1950, ISA 79, 2183/8; testimony of Muhammad Najib, 28 July 1949, ISA 79, 138/9; 'Ara PS to Afula PS and to Jezreel SB, 18 February 1957, ISA 79, 77/8.

50. 'Abed . . . to minister of police, [1952], ISA 79, 81/8.

4. THE LAND

1. "The Minorities' Population," ISA, MFA files, 1966/2, 1955, based on figures updated in October 1953.

2. Operation Department/MG to military governors, 5 September 1950, IDFA, 243/52-6; AAA Palmon to MG and Ministry of Interior, 28 September 1949, ISA 56, 2214/21.

3. Mordechai Shatner, the custodian of absentee property, during discussion in his office, ISA, Labor Ministry files, 6178/2924.

4. On the policy of expelling infiltrators, sometimes brutally, see Morris, *Israel's Border Wars,* 144–53.

5. The assessment is from Benziman and Mansur, *Dayarei mishne,* 165; see also the sources mentioned there, as well as the presentation of the main laws used by the state for transferring Arab land into state ownership. It should be noted, though, that a fundamental debate exists between the state and its Arab citizens over the definition of "state land" and "*miri* land": the Arabs see uncultivated land in the environs of villages as public land of the villages (i.e., Arab land), whereas the state sees it as state land.

6. On the sale of land and attitudes toward land sellers from the dawn of the Arab national movement in Palestine, see Cohen, *Army of Shadows,* 44–55, 68–71, 189–96, 214–22.

7. The Absentee Properties Law (1950), article 1.b.

8. From "trustworthy informer," undated, IDFA 263/66-3698.

9. For example, see Abd al-Latif's and Baruch Hen's testimonies to the police, 9 and 11 November 1966, ISA 79, 398/10; see also head of SB Jezreel to Nazareth PS, "Israeli Spies in Jordan," 29 November 1955, ISA 79, 29/14.

10. For the case of Faradis, see Minorities Affairs Department, in the Ministry of Interior, to Haifa district officer, Ministry of Interior, 22 July 1951, ISA 56, 2216/32; on the mukhtars of Barta'a and Kufr Qara', see letter of the Triangle MG to MG Department in the Ministry of Defense, 9 October 1952, in the same file.

11. Quoted in the testimony of Sha'ul Mandelman, OHD-HU, 57/34, interview of 1 January 1974.

12. Testimony of Yirmiyahu Feiglin, OHD-HU, 57/21, interview of 31 March 1972.

13. Yitzhak Shvili of Majd al-Krum PS to SB Northern District, "Arms Licenses—Minorities," 18 December 1953, ISA 79, 4/37.

14. Eventually, with the help of the United Nations, the villagers from the Hula Valley were allowed to return home (although they were soon evacuated again). For more on this, see Suleiman Shteiwi Khawaldi, "Changes in the Tribe of Kirad al-Kheit in the Galilee, 1858–Present," *Notes on the Bedouins* 27 (1995) (in Hebrew).

15. Refugees from Mi'ar and Damun to Acre police, 17 August 1953, ISA 79, 78/1.

16. Avneri, OC Acre PS, to head of Investigation Department, "Murder in the Village of Sha'ab," 14 November 1954, ISA 79, 78/1. For a detailed account of the events, see report of MG Galilee to Northern Command, "The Village of Sha'ab," 26 January 1956, ISA 79, 78/1.

17. Yosef Dagan, head of Land Department to Officer Sabag of Acre PS, 9 June 1955, ISA 79, 78/1.

18. CO Acre PS to CO Acre SD, "Summary of Investigation on the Murder of the Workers of the Electric Company," 27 April 1956; testimony of Buqai, undated; and anonymous letter to CC Northern District, "R.A.'s Criminal Biography," 28 April 1956; all in ISA 79, 174/7.

19. The events in the village were described by Dr. 'Adel Manna', originally from the village, who collected written and oral testimonies on the village before, during, and after the 1948 war.

20. MG Shefar'am [Shefa'amr] to MG Galilee, "Disturbances to Land Allocation in Damun," 20 January 1955, ISA 79, 2314/6. On the policy not to lend land in the abandoned villages to their original inhabitants, see protocol of the meeting of the RCAA-North [Galilee], 2 September 1954, ISA 79, 2314/6.

21. RCAA-North, first meeting, 2 September 1954, ISA 79, 2314/6; RCAA-North, protocol of meeting 10 February 1955, ISA 79, 2314/6; Jezreel SD to SB Northern District, 3 January 1958, ISA 79, 119/5.

22. Y. Kravits, CO SB Safed, to SB Northern District, 30 July 1959, ISA 79, 183/1.

23. The mukhtars of Jish and others to PMO, "Complaint of Some Residents of Jish on Former Residents of Bir'am," 12 May 1952, ISA 79, 84/12.

24. Ibid.; Hanna Daher to CO Safed PS, 5 September 1950, ISA 79, 84/2; Ministry of Minorities, "On the Happenings among the Minorities," 16 March 1949, IDFA 1308/50-485; 'Aqel to minister of the interior, "The Hatred of Bir'am's Refugees in Jish," 1 May 1956, ISA 79, 183/1; Safed SD to SB Northern District, 13 June 1956, "The Priest Ettanas Yusef 'Aqel of Jish," ISA 79, 183/1.

25. Ibid.

26. Safed SD to MG North, "Slander Graffiti on the MG Building in Gush Halav," 4 December 1959; and Safed SD to Northern District and GSS 950, "Slogans against the MG and a Swastika on the MG Office in Gush Halav," 8 January 1960; both in ISA 79, 183/1.

27. Supreme Court of Justice, appeal 30/55.

28. See appeals to the Supreme Court of Justice, 12/64, 110/64, and 111/64. See also monthly security reports of MG North for March and April 1964, ISA 79, 287/20.

29. H. Rosenblum, *Yedi'ot Aharonot,* 24 November 1957.

30. Monthly security report, MG North, February 1962, ISA 79, 290/8; leaflet signed by the Committee for the Defense of the Shaghur Villages, March 1963, ISA 79, 291/1.

31. Shmuel Segev, "The Hatred Keepers in Karmiel," *Ma'ariv,* 8 February 1963.

32. Ibid.

33. *Al-Ittihad,* 16 July 1963.

34. PMO—press releases of 17 and 30 January 1963, ISA 73, 6337/1653.

35. H. Ben Yitzhak, SB Acre, to CC Northern District, "Conflicts in . . . Fam-

ily in Bi'neh," 21 February 1963, ISA 79, 200/37; summary of meeting of RCAA-North, 16 October 1962, ISA 79, 240/7.

36. MG-North, security reports, March 1965, ISA 79, 358/19, and April 1964, ISA 79, 286/20; Uri Davis, *Crossing the Border* (London: Books and Books, 1995), 69–85.

37. SB Acre to SB Northern District, "Karmiel—Uri Davis's Activities," 19 October 1964, ISA 79, 291/7.

38. SB Acre to Shefar'am PS, 1 August 1962, ISA 79, 202/1.

39. SB Acre to Krum PS, 17 October 1962, ISA 79, 291/1. The dossier also contains other anti-expropriation songs sung at weddings.

40. Sa'di, "Minority Resistance to State Control."

41. On this literature, see Amal Jamal, "The Ambiguities of Minority Patriotism: Love for Homeland versus State among Palestinians in Israel," *Nationalism and Ethnic Politics* 10, no. 3 (2004): 433–71.

42. The Committee for the Preservation of Arab Rights to Hasan . . . , 24 March 1961, ISA 79, 202/5; and Hasan's testimony to the police in the same file.

43. Acre SD to IP HQ/Investigations, "National Water Carrier—Netofa Valley," 28 March 1961, ISA 79, 318/12.

44. Raziel Mamat and Avi Bleir, *Me Nikrot Tsurim* [From the clefts of rocks: The amazing story of Ya'akov Barazani] (Tel Aviv: Ministry of Defense Publishing House, 1979), 337 (in Hebrew).

45. Hadera SD to CC, Northern District, "Events in Umm al-Fahm," 25 October 1962; "Memorandum," CC Northern District, 25 October 1962; both in ISA 79, 200/37.

5. THE BATTLE OF THE NARRATIVE

1. Tsvi Zimmerman, *Bein Patish ha-Knesset le-Sadan ha-Memshala* [Between the Knesset's rock and the government's hard place] (Tel Aviv: Institute for Studying Israeli Society and Economy, 1994), 34–35 (in Hebrew). MK Zimmerman was critical of the governmental approach, as was clear from his speech in the Knesset on 16 November 1960.

2. Peter Holquist, "'Information Is the Alpha and Omega of Our Work': Bolshevik Surveillance in Its Pan European Context," *Journal of Modern History* 69, no. 3 (1997): 415–50.

3. Tsvi Sapir to IP, 14 July 1950, ISA 79, 2183/21; MG eastern Galilee to IP, Tiberias District, 31 May 1950, ISA 79, 57/1.

4. Chief of the General Division—Jerusalem District, to IP HQ and GSS Jerusalem, 27 September 1951, ISA 79, 15/3.

5. Taybe PS to SB Sharon SD, 6 December 1965, ISA 79, 453/21; SB Petah Tikva PS to SB Southern District and GSS, 7 December 1965, ISA 79, 453/21;

MG Galilee to GSS 149 and IP Northern District, 30 November 1964, ISA 79, 319/23; SB Tiberias to SB Northern District, IP HQ, and GSS 149, 30 January 1968, ISA 79, 469/10.

6. Tel Mond PS to ha-Sharon SD, "Tira: Weekly Summary of Events," 21 September 1949, ISA 79, 91/41. On men from 'Ara discussing Israel as a criminal state a few days after the massacre in Kafr Qasim, see SB Jezreel SD to SB Northern District, 6 November 1956, ISA 79, 152/12. Ascertaining whether this statement was a response to the massacre or to the war as a whole is difficult, but it is not certain that the news about the massacre had reached Wadi 'Ara at that time because of the Israeli censorship. For the response to the Arab defeat in the 1967 war, see SB Acre to SB Northern District, 10 December 1968, ISA 79, 469/10.

7. GSS, "The Minorities in Israel: The Attitude of the al-Ard Movement toward the State and the Jewish People," 9 June 1964, ISA 79, 233/21.

8. GSS 950 to MG North and IP Northern District, "Poems Praising Nasser in a Wedding in 'Eilabun," 23 April 1958, ISA 79, 316/5.

9. GSS 950 to MG North and IP Northern District, "Poems Praising Nasser in Wedding in Kafr Yasif," 31 September 1958, ISA 79, 183/2.

10. Northern District to OC Acre SD, "Nationalistic Songs," 15 October 1958, ISA 79, 183/2.

11. David Oren [Histadrut leader, Nazareth] to Reuven Bareket, 11 August 1958, Labor and Pioneer Archive of the Pinhas Lavon Institute, IV 219/157.

12. Unsigned letter written by a resident of Majd al-Krum, "A Report on the Popular Poetry," 12 August 1964, ISA 79, 236/17.

13. SB Jezreel SD to Northern District, "Nationalist Expressions in Tur'an," 27 July 1965, ISA 79, 318/4.

14. See MG North to GSS, 30 November 1964, ISA 79, 319/23.

15. MG North to IP Northern District, 11 August 1954, ISA 79, 119/11.

16. The leaflet, translated into Hebrew, is in ISA 79, 205/2.

17. Acre SD to SB Northern District, "Celebrating the Tenth Anniversary in Kafr Yasif," 27 May 1958, ISA 79, 183/2.

18. Safed SD to SB Northern District, 6 June 1958, ISA 79, 183/1.

19. Elias Kusa to Islamic Advisory Committee, 19 April 1958, ISA 79, 174/5.

20. Yigal Eilam, *Memal'ey ha-Pkudot* [The executors] (Jerusalem: Keter, 1990), 53–70 (in Hebrew).

21. MG North to OC of IDF's Northern Command, 14 January 1957, ISA 102, 13904/7.

22. MK Hamdan to David Ben-Gurion, 11 November 1956, ISA 102, 13904/7. For a detailed analysis, see Shira Robinson, "Local Struggle, National Struggle: Palestinian Responses to the Kafr Qasim Massacre and Its Aftermath, 1956–1966," *International Journal of Middle East Studies* 35, no. 3 (2003): 393–416.

23. Popular Front to Islamic Advisory Committee, 21 October 1958, and committee's reply the following day; see also Acre SD to Northern District, "Com-

memoration of Those Who Were Killed in Kafr Qasim," 27 October 1958; all in ISA 79, 174/7.

24. Acre PS, "Biweekly Report on Arab Affairs," 16 June 1951, ISA 79, 4/38.

25. SB ha-Sharon to SB Southern District and GSS, October 1966, ISA 79, 373/1.

26. Maki's leaflet of September 1965; ISA 79, 236/17.

27. The parliamentary question of 21 May 1958 and the answer of Ben-Gurion of 2 June that year appear in ISA 112, 6275/536.

28. *Davar,* 18 May 1958.

29. Memo of the SB and heads of investigation departments, 28 February 1961, ISA 79, 393/1.

30. Report of the head of the Minorities Department in the Ministry of Education in a meeting of military governors, 22 March 1953, ISA 102, 17109/41. For the total number of Arab teachers, see military governors meeting, 11 October 1953, ISA 102, 17109/41.

31. Protocol of SB officers' meeting, Acre, 6 October 1963, ISA 79, 398/1, 9.

32. GSS to Ministry of Education—security officer, "National Activity and Talks of Teachers and Pupils," 19 July 1965, ISA 79, 236/17. On recruiting teachers as informers, see the proposal of Yosef Mizrahi of Safed SB in the meeting of SB officers, Northern District, 16 October 1960, ISA 79, 393/1.

33. *Davar,* 18 May 1958.

34. Jezreel SD to SB Northern District, "Arab Pupils Went on Strike on 15 May … ," 28 May 1958; MG North to SB Northern District, "Expressions of Nationalistic Feelings among Pupils," 28 May 1958; both in ISA 79, 174/5.

35. MG North to SB Northern District, "Expressions of Nationalistic Feelings among Pupils," 28 May 1958, ISA 79, 174/5.

36. Ramla SD to IP HQ/Investigations, "An Arab School in Lydda," 5 June 1960, ISA 79, 162/29.

37. Safed SD to IP HQ/Investigations, "Ali … ," 24 March 1960, ISA 79, 162/29.

38. Acre SD to IP HQ/Investigations, "Independence Day [1961]," 27 April 1961, ISA 79, 174/5.

39. Acre SD, [background and summary of activity], [1961], ISA 79, 436/12; Emanuel Marx to Luria, 21 September 1955, ISA 102, 17020/13.

40. The leaflet and its draft are in ISA 79, 174/1. More details can be found in GSS, "The Minorities in Israel: Items from the Press," no. 245, 15 October 1961, ISA 79, 174/1; Acre SD to Shefar'am PS, "Events in Sakhnin, 23 September 1961," 10 October 1961, ISA 79, 202/1; and Acre SD to OC Northern District, "Events in Acre and the Neighboring Villages—Summary Report," 3 October 1961, ISA 79, 200/36.

41. Acre SD to Shefar'am PS, "Events in Sakhnin, 23 September 1961," 10 October 1961, ISA 79, 202/1.

42. Acre SD to Shefar'am PS, "Events in Sakhnin, 23 September 1961," 10 October 1961, ISA 79, 202/1; Acre SD to OC Northern District, "Events in Acre and the Neighboring Villages—Summary Report," 3 October 1961, ISA 79, 200/36.

43. GSS 950 to MG North and IP Northern District, "Poems [by teachers] Praising Nasser in a Wedding in Kafr Yasif," 31 September 1958, ISA 79, 183/2.

44. The quotes in the remainder of this section all come from GSS to Ministry of Education—security officer, "Nationalist Activity and Utterances by Teachers and Pupils," 19 July 1965, ISA 79, 236/17.

45. Jezreel SD to IP HQ/Investigations, "Poems Praising Gamal 'Abd al-Nasser in a Wedding at Tur'an," 28 August 1961, ISA 79, 318/4.

46. IP, "A Meeting of Tira's Notables with the SD OC," 25 May 1962, ISA 79, 274/12; MG Central Region, "Security Report: March 1965," ISA 79, 358/20.

47. Rabinowitz and Abu-Baker, *Coffins on Our Shoulders.*

48. MG Central Region, "Security Report for December 1963," ISA 79, 287/22; MG North to GSS, "Nationalistic Expressions: Tur'an," 22 December 1963, ISA 79, 185/12.

49. An undated letter [January 1958], and testimonies of suspects to the police, January 1958, ISA 79, 82/19.

50. A letter dated 22 October 1963, ISA 79, 318/4; SB Safed to SB Jezreel, "info," 25 May 1967, ISA 79, 318/4.

51. Acre SD to Northern District, "Leaflets That Include Threats and Insults," 11 March 1957, ISA 79, 119/9; Acre SD to Northern District, "Threat Letter," 13 September 1965, ISA 79, 288/16.

52. Hadera SD to IP HQ, "General Atmosphere: The Tenth Anniversary of the Egyptian Revolution," 29 July 1962, ISA 79, 316/17; Acre SD to Northern District, "General Atmosphere—Egypt's Revolution Day," 26 July 1964, ISA 79, 236/17; Acre SD to Northern District, "Egypt's Revolution Day," 27 July 1966, ISA 79, 288/14.

53. Jamal, "The Ambiguities of Minority Patriotism"; Sa'di, "Minority Resistance to State Control."

54. Zaki 'Aweisat to Local Councils' Center, "Report on the International Congress of Local Councils," [August 1959], ISA, MFA files, 3772/46; Education attaché, Israeli consulate in New York to public relations officer, MFA, "Mahmoud Irsheid Zu'bi," 9 January 1962, ISA, MFA files, 3768/22.

55. The broadcast from Damascus is quoted in IP HQ, "Biweekly Report on Arab Affairs," 20 July 1950, ISA 79, 121/31; about the land issue, see Nazareth PS to Tiberias CC, "Sheikh Taher Tabari," 14 November 1950, ISA 79, 57/9; and memo on the talk of the head of the Development Authority with the finance minister, 18 July 1955, ISA 99 [Israel Land Authority], 3097/25/4. It seems that despite Taher Tabari's profound knowledge of Islam and his being a Muslim scholar, he did not regard selling land to Jews as a sin.

56. Safed SD to SB Northern District, "'Eilabun," 15 November 1956, ISA 79, 82/19.

57. 'Abd al-Hamid's testimony to the police, 2 January 1957, ISA 79, 78/26.

6. MINORITIES WITHIN A MINORITY

1. Northern District, "Threat of Violence," 7 March 1956; Northern District to MG North, "Attack on Kamel Salman," 6 April 1956; both in ISA 79, 2449/9.

2. IDF General Staff/Operations to deputy chief of staff, "Recruitment of Druze," 11 March 1956, ISA 79, 2449/30.

3. For the incentives, see ibid.; see also Minorities Battalion to MG North, "Arms Licenses," 23 February 1955, IDFA, 1-22/57.

4. Haifa District to IP HQ/Minorities, "Resentment among the Opponents of Recruitment in Daliat al-Karmel," 25 March 1956, ISA 79, 2449/9.

5. An interview with al-Atrash in Syria, 28 August 1956, and his undated declaration, both in ISA 79, 2449/12.

6. Haifa District to IP HQ-SB, "Compulsory Reserve Service of Druze in the IDF," 19 March 1957, ISA 79, 2449/9.

7. Druze sheikhs to prime minister, 18 February 1957, ISA 79, 2449/28.

8. Acre SD to Northern District SB, "Meeting in the *Hilwe* of al-Khader, Kafr Yasif," 12 March 1957, ISA 79, 119/9. For the open letter, see ISA, MFA, 3751/21.

9. IDF General Staff/Operations to Colonel Argov, Ministry of Defense, "Salman 'Alian—Shefar'am," 7 May 1957, ISA 79, 2449/9.

10. Committee on Minority Affairs, 16 March 1957, ISA 102, 17001/15.

11. OC Minorities Battalion to MG North, "Encouraging Recruitment to the Reserve and Regular Service," 24 February 1955, IDFA, 1-222/57.

12. Cabinet meeting, 22 April 1956, *Cabinet Meetings,* 1956, 10 (in ISA).

13. Minorities Battalion HQ, "Summary of a Meeting," 20 October 1952, IDFA 52-7/54.

14. Kais Firro, *The Druzes in the Jewish State* (Leiden: Brill, 1999), 104–27. Background information in this section is from Firro's book, unless other sources are mentioned.

15. A placard issued by Labib Abu-Rukun, 6 November 1956, left no room for doubt about where he stood. "Enlist en masse, members of my community, and make your contribution to the Defense Fund," he declared. "Druze youth, prepare for struggle and be steadfast in your efforts to defend your free country, blooming Israel. Do not hesitate to do your duty to your beloved country.... Long live freedom, long live Israel, long live Israeli independence." ISA 79, 242/18.

16. Ya'akov Yehoshua (citing Abu-Rukun) to H. Z. Hirschberg, 26 October 1949, ISA 102, 17011/29.

17. "The Druze Youth: Background for Discussion," the PMO-AAA to MG

North, GSS North, Minorities Battalion, and others, 9 August 1966, ISA 79, 288/19.

18. Ibid.

19. Ibid.

20. *Al-Ittihad*, 3 and 17 March 1964, quoted in MG North, "Security Report: March 1964," ISA 79, 287/20.

21. Meir Meir to Nissim Tokatli, 8 April 1964, ISA 43, 6337/1653.

22. Amal Nasser al-Din to Aharon Layish, 29 August 1963 (on the teachers); Salman Falah to Layish, [1964], "The Activity of the Column of Druze Citizens" (an assessment of the Druze column in *Al-Yawm*); both in ISA 102, 13905/2. For the debate on the holiday, see *Al-Mirsad,* 10 April 1964; *Al-Ittihad,* 2 April 1964; and *Al-Musawwar,* 26 February 1964.

23. Palmon to GSS, IP, and MG North, "Druze Holidays," 9 July 1952, ISA 79, 2244/10; on the internal disputes in the Druze community and Tarif's opposition to recruitment, see Northern District SB to IP HQ-SB, 2 November 1953, ISA 79, 78/1.

24. Firro, *The Druzes in the Jewish State,* 127, 135.

25. The events are described in a police report, "Quarrel in Beit Jann," 30 August 1960, ISA 79, 200/36.

26. On Muslim and Christian religious verdicts, see Cohen, *Army of Shadows,* 49–50.

27. "Unrest among the Minorities in Regard to the Legislation Proposal on Concentration of Agricultural Land," 28 February 1961, ISA 79, 7226/26.

28. On the debate in the Knesset, see Yair Bauml, "The Military Government and the Process of Its Abolition," *Ha-Mizrah he-Hadash* 43 (2002): 142–47 (in Hebrew). On Druze satisfaction from the relief, see MG North, "Security Report, February 1962," ISA 79, 290/8.

29. Central Committee, meeting of 7 November 1966, ISA 102, 13905/2.

30. Rabah Halabi, "Heibetim Psikhologiyim-Hevratiyim shel ha-Zehut ha-Druzit be-Yisrael" [Sociopsychological aspects of Druze identity in Israel], Ph.D. dissertation, Hebrew University of Jerusalem, 2003 (in Hebrew).

31. "The Non-Jewish Minority in Israel—Governmental Policy and Practices toward It," with approval of the minister of foreign affairs, 29 August 1952, ISA 102, 17115/11.

32. Mas'ud Shabso to OC Minorities Battalion, 20 August 1957, ISA 112, 17035/8.

33. The Circassian Union to President Ben-Zvi, 25 May 1955, ISA 112, 17035/8.

34. [Meir Meir] to Gad Frenkel, "Circassian Textbooks," 4 July 1962; Meir Meir to Hanokh Hasson, Israel Broadcast Service, "Circassian Music," 2 July 1964; both in ISA 43/02, 6337/1653.

35. Walter Eitan to Moshe Sharett, December 1949, ISA, MFA files, 2402/29; Palmon on the position of the prime minister, CZA, KKL 5/18876.

36. Safed SD to Tiberias District SB, 10 February 1953, ISA 79, 35/26; "Murder Cases 1953: Muhammad Hajj Omar," ISA 79, 2278/33; Hajj 'Ali against IP and MG Galilee, *Piskei din* [Supreme Court verdicts], 8, 1953, 914 (in Hebrew).

37. Yuli Khromtsenko, "People Speak Many Languages Here," *Haaretz,* 22 March 2005.

38. MG North, Michael Michael, "Atmosphere among the Arab Population in the Area of MG North," 25 January 1958, ISA 2314/6 and 2449/30.

39. PMO-AAA Toledano to head of GSS, head of military intelligence, MFA— general director, IP OC, and others, "Guidelines for Government Policy toward the Arab Minority in Israel," 14 July 1965, ISA 79, 2637/5, 5.

40. GSS Unit 50 to PMO-AAA, 21 June 1957, ISA 79, 2449/28.

41. Khuri to Sharett, 17 November 1948, ISA, MFA files, 2567/10.

42. Committee on Minority Affairs, meeting of 16 March 1957, ISA 102, 17001/15; SB Haifa District to Northern District, "Responses to Bishop Hakim's Speech," 22 July 1966, ISA 79, 429/22; OC Minorities Battalion to OC Northern Command, "Proposal for 'Voluntary' Army Service," 24 December 1970, ISA 102, 17079/7; AAA Haifa Bureau to RCAA-North [Galilee], "Recruitment of Druze to the IDF," 1 February 1971, ISA 102, 17079/7. On the violent Druze attack on Christians in Mghar in 2005, see U.S. Department of State, *Country Reports on Human Rights Practices for 2005* (Washington, DC: U.S. Government Printing Office, May 2006), vol. 2, 1877–78.

43. *Yedi'ot Aharonot,* 3 May 1950.

44. Ibid., 30 January 1958.

45. Yigal Alon to Weitz, Yadin, and MG Negev, 1 December 1948, IDFA 834/53-390.

46. Muhammad Yusef Sawa'ed, "Yahasei Bedvim-Yehudim in Eretz Yisrael ha-Mandatorit" [Bedouin-Jew relations in Mandatory Palestine], Ph.D. dissertation, Bar-Ilan University, 1998, 229 (in Hebrew), based on documents of the Haganah intelligence service.

47. IDF General Staff/Intelligence, *Bedviyei ha-Negev bi-Mdinat Yisrael* [The Bedouin of the Negev in the state of Israel] (IDF: Tel Aviv, 1954), 26.

48. Shfela SD to Southern District, "Sheikh Suleiman al-Huzayyel," 22 December 1949, ISA 79, 91/41.

49. IDF General Staff/Intelligence, *Bedviyei ha-Negev bi-Mdinat Yisrael.*

50. MG Negev, "Joint Meeting with the Sheikhs," 8 November 1951, IDFA, 834/53-133.

51. IDF military intelligence officer—Jerusalem to IP and GSS, "Names of Arabs Suspected of Espionage [for Israel]," 21 January 1952, ISA 79, 2446/18; "Israel's Sabotage and Espionage Activity in Jordan," 22 August 1958, ISA 79, 336/12.

52. Security report, April 1950, IDFA, 834/53-293.

53. Akram's testimony to the police, 6 February 1961, ISA 79, 336/11.

54. Ibid.

55. Mahmoud al-Battat's testimony to the police, 27 November 1955, ISA, 213/8 (where he also tells his personal history).

56. Sheikh Jaber's testimony, 27 May 1957, ISA 79, 213/8.

57. Reports from the investigation, 20 and 24 November 1955, [GSS?], ISA 79, 213/8. See also SB Jerusalem to SB Negev, "From the Mischiefs of a Habitual Infiltrator: Mahmoud al-Battat," ISA 79, 336/12.

58. Jihad Aqel, "Shatta 1958: The Israeli Abu Ghrayeb?" [*Al-Ittihad*], 25 September 2004, online at www.aljabha.org/q/print.asp?f=-3305258156.htm (accessed January 2008).

59. SB Jerusalem District to IP-HQ, "Abu-Rbei'a Tribe," 5 July 1954, ISA 79, 2312/9.

60. Sasson Bar-Zvi to IDF General Staff—MG HQ, 30 June 1956, ISA 79, 2449/13.

61. RCAA-South [Negev], 20 June 1957, ISA 79, 2449/31.

62. Arye Lavia, MFA, "The 'Azazmeh Problem," 6 November 1959.

63. See Landau, *The Arabs in Israel*, 127–28 (tables of Arab vote in 1959), 133 (Arab vote in 1961), and 147 (Arab vote in 1965).

64. RCAA-South, 20 June 1963, ISA 79, 262/24.

7. CIRCLES OF CONTROL, CIRCLES OF RESISTANCE

1. Nimer Sirhan and Mustafa Kabha, *'Abd al-Rahim Hajj Muhammad: Al-Qa'id al-'Am li-Thawrat 1936–39* ['Abd al-Rahim Hajj Muhammad: The general commander of the 1936–39 revolt] (Ramallah, 2000), 11–12 (in Arabic).

2. Tene to Tiroshi, "Defense Forces in the Arab Settlements in the Central Region," 22 January 1948, HA, 105/227; SB ha-Sharon SD, "Testimony of an Iraqi Soldier Who Surrendered to the Israeli Forces," 8 March 1949, ISA 79, 95/64; Taybe PS to Central SD, "Five People Wounded in Tira," 18 August 1952, ISA 79, 137/11; *Al-Yawm*, 26 July 1950.

3. Hadera SD to Central District, "List of Personas in the Triangle," 3 November 1954, ISA 79, 121/11.

4. Southern District HQ, "Intelligence Briefing—the Village of Tira," 22 February 1966, ISA 79, 274/20.

5. Ibid.

6. Ibid.; and also Petah Tikva SD to SB Southern District and GSS, "Uprooting of an Orchard in Tira," 11 April 1967, ISA 79, 373/2.

7. GSS, "The Minorities in Israel: The Sport and Culture Club in Tira—a Special Report," 12 February 1964, ISA 79, 233/22.

8. GSS, "The Sport and Culture Club in Tira," 4 June 1964, ISA 79, 233/22.

9. Ibid.

10. *Al-Ittihad*, 31 March 1976.

11. Rekhess, *The Arab Minority in Israel*, 106.

12. Superintendent Ze'ev Steinberg to Haifa District/Investigations, "Intelligence Summary of Arab Affairs," 28 July 1950, ISA 79, 138/6.

13. RCAA-North [Galilee], summary of meeting of 2 September 1954, ISA 79, 2314/6.

14. RCAA-North, summary of meeting of 21 December 1955, ISA 79, 2314/6.

15. Ibid.

16. [RCAA-Central (Triangle)], coordination meeting no. 7 of 7 December 1954, ISA 79, 2314/8.

17. Summary of RCAA [Triangle] meetings, 27 January and 19 May 1955, ISA 79, 2314/8.

18. Northern District to IP HQ—Minorities, 30 November and 31 December 1954, ISA 79, 120/1.

19. Protocol of meeting of military governors, 4 March 1954, ISA 102, 17109/41.

20. RCAA-North, summary of meeting of 26 August 1954, ISA 79, 2314/6.

21. RCAA-North, summaries of meetings of 10 March and 12 May 1955, ISA 79, 2314/6.

22. RCAA-North, summary of meeting of 31 March 1955, ISA 79, 2314/6.

23. Jezreel SD to PS, "Mukhtars," 29 May 1955, ISA 79, 29/14.

24. RCAA-North, summaries of meetings of 5 October and 7 November 1955, ISA 79, 2314/6.

25. RCAA-South [Negev], summary of meeting of 20 June 1957, ISA 79, 2449/31.

26. Summary of coordination meeting [Triangle], 18 November 1954, ISA 79, 2314/8.

27. RCAA-North, summary of meeting of 12 May 1955, ISA 79, 2314/6.

28. "The Committee for the Municipalization of Arab Localities," a report submitted to the minister of the interior, 17 April 1956, ISA 102, 17031/8.

29. Minister of interior to minister of defense, 22 April 1956, ISA 102, 17031/8; PMO-AAA to prime minister, "Local Councils in Minorities Localities," 14 May 1956, ISA 102, 17031/8.

30. PMO-AAA, Shmuel Toledano, to head of the GSS, head of IDF/Intelligence Branch, MFA director-general, Ministry of Defense director-general, OC IP, and others, "Guidelines for Government Policy toward the Arab Minority in Israel," 14 July 1965, ISA 79, 2637/5.

31. Landau, *The Arabs in Israel*, 157–58.

32. RCAA-North, summary of meeting of 6 June 1966, ISA 79, 398/9.

33. Acre SD to IP HQ/Investigations, 20 January 1962, ISA 79, 183/2.

34. RCAA-Central [Triangle], summary of meeting of 27 October 1970, ISA 79, 411/3; RCAA-North, summary of meeting of 13 December 1967, ISA 79, 429/17. On Nazareth, see RCAA-North, summary of meeting of 5 October 1955, ISA 79, 2314/6; and Central Committee meeting of 4 August 1966, ISA 79, 373/14.

35. RCAA-North, summaries of meetings of 2 September and 14 November 1955, ISA 79, 2314/6.

36. RCAA-North, summary of meeting of 9 February 1956, ISA 79, 2449/30.

37. Jezreel SD to Northern District, "The Activity of the Local Council in Tur'an," 8 February 1962, ISA 79, 318/4; see also *Al-Ittihad*, 19 January 1962.

38. Acre SD to IP HQ, "Heads of Arab Local Councils—Activity," 15 March 1962, ISA 79, 236/17.

39. Undated table in ISA 79, 173/5.

40. RCAA-Central [Triangle], summary of meeting of 18 November 1954, ISA 79, 2314/8.

41. GSS Unit 50 to PMO-AAA, 21 June 1957, ISA 79, 2449/28.

42. RCAA-North, summary of meeting of 3 June 1964, ISA 79, 319/23.

43. RCAA-North, summary of meeting of 8 April 1965, ISA 79, 356/1.

44. RCAA-North, summary of meetings of 3 June and 8 July 1964, ISA 79, 319/23.

45. RCAA-North, summary of meeting of 18 December 1964, ISA 79, 319/23.

46. RCAA-North, summary of meeting of 8 July 1964, ISA 79, 319/23.

47. Bauml, "The Military Government and the Process of Its Abolition," 138–39 and n. 34.

48. RCAA-North, summary of meeting of 13 February 1958, ISA 79, 2449/30.

49. Report of RCAA-North, 8 June 1958; and memo of its meeting of 13 June 1958; both in ISA 79, 236/1.

50. RCAA-North, summary of meeting of 10 February 1955, ISA 79, 2314/6; RCAA-North, meeting of 9 February 1956, ISA 79, 2449/30.

51. RCAA-North, summary of meeting of 16 October 1962, ISA 79, 290/7.

52. RCAA-North, summary of meeting of 10 January 1963, ISA 79, 393/1.

53. RCAA-North, summary of meeting of 24 April 1961, ISA 79, 289/9.

54. RCAA-North, summaries of meetings of 10 February and 14 November 1955, ISA 79, 2314/6; see there also for information on his Jewish colleague who tried to refute the accusations.

55. RCAA-South, summary of meeting of 23 June 1963, ISA 79, 262/24.

56. RCAA-North, summary of meeting of 17 December 1962, ISA 79, 290/7.

57. Ibid.; see also the discussion in the meeting of 10 January 1963, in ISA 79, 393/1. In addition, see RCAA-North, summary of meeting of 3 June 1964, ISA 79, 319/23.

58. RCAA-North, summary of meeting of 16 October 1962, ISA 79, 290/7.

59. Ibid.; and summary of meeting of 17 December 1962, also in ISA 79, 290/7.

60. RCAA-North, summary of meeting of 17 December 1962, ISA 79, 290/7.

61. RCAA-North, summary of meeting of 27 January 1955, ISA 79, 2314/6.

62. RCAA-North, summary of meeting of 14 December 1964, ISA 79, 319/23.

63. RCAA-North, summary of meeting of 3 June 1964, ISA 79, 319/23.

64. RCAA-North, summary of meeting of 16 October 1962, ISA 79, 290/7.

65. RCAA-North, summary of meeting of 17 December 1962, ISA 79, 290/7.

66. RCAA-North, summary of meeting of 10 January 1963, ISA 79, 393/1.

67. RCAA-North, summary of meeting of 2 March 1964, ISA 79, 319/23.

68. RCAA-North, summary of meeting of 16 October 1962, ISA 79, 290/7.

69. RCAA-North, summary of meeting of 24 April 1961, ISA 79, 289/9.

70. RCAA-North, summary of meeting of 24 January 1964, ISA 79, 319/23.

71. Ibid.

72. Ibid.

73. RCAA-[Negev], summary of meeting of 15 March 1955, ISA 79, 2314/7.

74. RCAA-North, summary of meeting of 2 March 1964, ISA 79, 319/23.

75. RCAA-North, summary of meeting of 24 January 1964, ISA 79, 319/23.

76. "Summary of Reports from the Arab Sector," from various dates between 24 May and 5 June 1967, ISA 79, 431/3.

77. N. Tokatli, head of AAA bureau in Haifa, to PMO-AAA, [15 June] 1967, ISA 79, 429/17.

78. GSS, "Possible [Future] Changes in Political Stances of, and Internal Security Problems among, Israel's Arabs in 1980," February 1971, ISA 79, 412/3.

BIBLIOGRAPHY

ARABIC PRESS

Al-Ittihad
Al-Mirsad
Al-Musawwar
Al-Yawm

HEBREW PRESS

'Al ha-Mishmar (previously *Mishmar*)
Ba-Mahane
Davar
Haaretz
Kol ha-'Am
Ma'ariv
Yedi'ot Aharonot
Yom Yom

BOOKS AND ARTICLES

Argaman, Josef. *Ze Haya Sodi be-Yoter* [It was top secret]. Tel Aviv: Ministry of Defense Publishing House, 2003 [in Hebrew].
Bauml, Yair. "The Military Government and the Process of Its Abolition." *Ha-Mizrah he-Hadash,* 43 (2002): 133–56 [in Hebrew].

———. *Tsel Cahol Lavan: Medinyut ha-Mimsad ha-Yisraeli, 1958–68* [A blue and white shadow: Israeli establishment policy and actions among its Arab citizens, 1958–1968]. Haifa: Pardes, 2007 [in Hebrew].

Benziman, Uzi, and ʿAtallah Mansur. *Dayarei Mishne: Arviyei Yisraʾel, Maʿamadam ve-ha-Mediniyut Klapeihem* [Subtenants: The Arabs of Israel, their status and the policies toward them]. Jerusalem: Keter, 1992 [in Hebrew].

Cohen, Hillel. *Army of Shadows: Palestinian Collaboration with Zionism, 1917–1948.* Berkeley: University of California Press, 2008.

———. *Ha-Nifkadim ha-Nokhehim* [The present absentees: The Palestinian refugees in Israel]. Jerusalem: The Institute for Israeli Arab Studies, 2000 [in Hebrew].

———. "Land, Memory and Identity: The Palestinian Internal Refugees in Israel." *Refuge* 21, no. 2 (April 2003): 6–13.

Davis, Uri. *Crossing the Border.* London: Books and Books, 1995.

Divrey ha-Knesset [the Knesset protocols], 1949–54 [in Hebrew].

Eilam, Yigal. *Memalʾey ha-Pkudot* [The executors]. Jerusalem: Keter, 1990 [in Hebrew].

Firro, Kais. *The Druzes in the Jewish State.* Leiden: Brill, 1999.

Gelber, Yoav. "The Status of Zionist and Israeli History in Israeli Universities." In Anita Shapira and Derek Penslar, eds., *Israeli Historical Revisionism: From Left to Right,* 121–54. London: Frank Cass, 2002.

Halabi, Rabah. "Heibetim Psikhologiyim-Hevratiyim shel ha-Zehut ha-Druzit be-Yisrael" [Sociopsychological aspects of Druze identity in Israel]. Ph.D. dissertation, Hebrew University of Jerusalem, 2003 [in Hebrew].

Hawwari, Muhammad Nimer al-. *Al-Hawariyun.* Acre: n.p., n.d. [in Arabic].

———. *Sirr al-Nakba* [The secret of al-Nakba]. Nazareth, 1955 [in Arabic].

Holquist, Peter. "ʿInformation Is the Alpha and Omega of Our Workʾ: Bolshevik Surveillance in Its Pan European Context." *Journal of Modern History* 69, no. 3 (1997): 415–50.

IDF General Staff/Intelligence. *Bedviyei ha-Negev bi-Mdinat Yisrael* [The Bedouin of the Negev in the state of Israel]. Tel Aviv: IDF, 1954 [in Hebrew].

Jamal, Amal. "The Ambiguities of Minority Patriotism: Love for Homeland versus State among Palestinians in Israel." *Nationalism and Ethnic Politics* 10, no. 3 (2004): 433–71.

Khawaldi, Sleiman Shteiwi. "Changes in the Tribe of Kirad al-Kheit in the Galilee, 1858–Present." *Notes on the Bedouins* 27 (1995) [in Hebrew].

Khuri, Elias. *Bab al-Shams.* Beirut, Dar al-Adab, 1998

Landau, Jacob. *The Arabs in Israel: A Political Study.* London: Oxford University Press, 1969.

Lustick, Ian. *Arabs in the Jewish State: Israel's Control of a National Minority.* Austin: University of Texas Press, 1980.

Mamat, Raziel, and Avi Bleir. *Me-Nikrot Tsurim* [From the clefts of rocks: The amazing story of Ya'akov Barazani]. Tel Aviv: Ministry of Defense Publishing House, 1979 [in Hebrew].

Morris, Benny. *The Birth of the Palestinian Refugee Problem, 1947–1949.* Cambridge: Cambridge University Press, 1987.

———. *Israel's Border Wars, 1949–1956: Arab Infiltration, Israeli Retaliation and the Countdown to War.* Oxford: Clarendon Press, 1993.

Ozacky-Lazar, Sara. "The Military Government as a Control Mechanism over Arab Citizens: The First Decade, 1948–1956." *Ha-Mizrah he-Hadash* 43 (2002): 103–32 [in Hebrew].

Pa'il, Meir. "The Battles." In Yehoshua Ben Arye, ed., *Ha-Historia shel Eretz Yisrael: Milhemet ha-Atzma'ut* [The history of the land of Israel: War of independence], vol. 10, 151–271. Jerusalem: Yad Ben Zvi, 1983 [in Hebrew].

———. "The Fighting Forces." In Yehoshua Ben Arye, ed., *Ha-Historia shel Eretz Yisrael: Milhemet ha-Atzma'ut* [The history of the land of Israel: War of independence], vol. 10, 109–50. Jerusalem: Yad Ben Zvi, 1983 [in Hebrew].

Pappe, Ilan. "The Tantura Case in Israel: The Katz Research and Trial." *Journal of Palestine Studies* 30, no. 3 (Spring 2001): 19–39.

Peres, Yohanan, and Nira Davis. "On the National Identity of the Israeli Arab." *Ha-Mizrah he-Hadash* 18 (1968): 106–11 [in Hebrew].

Piskei din [Israel's Supreme Court verdicts], 1953 [in Hebrew].

Rabinowitz, Dan, and Khawla Abu-Baker. *Coffins on Our Shoulders: The Experience of the Palestinian Citizens of Israel.* Berkeley: University of California Press, 2005.

Refugee interviews. *Journal of Palestine Studies* 18, no. 1 (1988).

Rekhess, Elie. *Ha-Mi'ut ha-Aravi be-Israel: Bein Komonisem le-L'umiut Aravit* [Between communism and Arab nationalism: Rakah and the Arab minority in Israel, 1965–1973]. Tel Aviv: Hakibutz ha-me'uhad, 1993 [in Hebrew].

———. "Jews and Arabs in the PCP." *Ha-Tsiyonut* 15 (1991): 175–86 [in Hebrew].

Robinson, Shira Nomi. "Local Struggle, National Struggle: Palestinian Responses to the Kafr Qasim Massacre and Its Aftermath, 1956–1966." *International Journal of Middle East Studies* 35, no. 3 (2003): 393–416.

———. "Occupied Citizens in a Liberal State: Palestinians under Military Rule and the Colonial Formation of Israeli Society, 1948–1966." Ph.D. dissertation, Stanford University, 2005.

Sa'di, Ahmad H. "Minority Resistance to State Control: Towards a Re-analysis of Palestinian Political Activity in Israel." *Social Identities* 2, no. 3 (1996): 395–412.

Sawa'ed, Muhammad Yusef. "Yahasei Bedvim-Yehudim in Eretz Yisrael ha-Mandatorit" [Bedouin-Jew relations in Mandatory Palestine]. Ph.D. dissertation, Bar-Ilan University, 1998 [in Hebrew].

Shilo, Gideon. *Arviyei Yisrael Be-'einei Medinot Arav ve-Ashaf* [Israel's Arabs in the eyes of the Arab states and the PLO]. Jerusalem: Magnes, 1982 [in Hebrew].

Sirhan, Nimer, and Mustafa Kabha. *'Abd al-Rahim Hajj Muhammad: Al-Qa'id al-'Am li-Thawrat 1936–39* ['Abd al-Rahim Hajj Muhammad: The general commander of the 1936–39 revolt]. Ramallah, 2000 [in Arabic].

Sitton, Rafi, and Yitzhak Shushan. *Anshei ha-Sod ve-ha-Seter* [Men of secrets, men of mystery]. Tel Aviv: Idanim, 1990 [in Hebrew].

Smooha, Sammy. "Arabs and Jews in Israel: Minority-Majority Relations." *Magamot* 22 (1976): 397–423 [in Hebrew].

U.S. Department of State. *Country Reports on Human Rights Practices for 2005.* Washington, DC: U.S. Government Printing Office, May 2006.

Zimmerman, Tsvi. *Bein Patish ha-Knesset le-Sadan ha-Memshala* [Between the Knesset's rock and the government's hard place]. Tel Aviv: Institute for Studying Israeli Society and Economy, 1994 [in Hebrew].

Zu'bi, Sayf al-Din. *Shahed 'Ayan: Mudhakkarat* [Eyewitness: Memories]. Shefa'amr, 1987 [in Arabic].

INDEX

(The Arabic definite article "al" has generally been omitted from names in order to make search easier.)

'Abd al-Hayy, Basem and Bassam, 198

'Abd al-Hayy, Ma'mun, 201n

'Abd al-Hayy, Rafiq, 83–4, 195

'Abd al-Hayy, Sheikh Najib, 195–96

'Abd al-Hayy, Tareq, 196–201, 218

'Abd al-Hayy, Tawfiq, 198

'Abd al-Razeq, 'Abd al-Ra'ouf, 11–13, 22, 23

'Abd al-Razeq, 'Aref, 12–13

'Abd al-Razeq, Faysal, 59–60

'Abdallah, Hasan (of Tira), 83–84

'Abdallah, king, 16, 22, 121

'Abdallah, Muhammad (of Abu Ghosh), 70n

'Abdu, Ahmad, 55

'Abdu, Yusuf, 40

absentee property, 16, 20, 26–27, 29, 55, 96, 96–97n, 98, 100–4, 110. *See also* land; refugees

Abu Baker, Khawla, 4, 151

Abu-Durra, Yusef, 205

Abu-Fayad, Hasan (aka Fayad), 82–84

Abu Ghalyun (tribe), 73, 185

Abu Ghalyun, sheikh Suleiman, 73

Abu Ghosh (village), 69–71

Abu-Hanna, Hanna, 57, 119

Abu Is'af, 100, 102

Abu Khaled. *See* Nasser

Abu-Kishek, Tawfiq, 73

Abu-M'ammar, 'Oda, 18, 22–23, 25, 158n, 182 (fig.), 183, 185, 193–94

Abu Ma'yuf, 106

Abu-Qrinat, sheikh 'Ali, 158n

Abu-Rbei'a (tribe), 186, 187, 191

Abu-Rbei'a, Hamed, 194

Abu-Rukun, Labib, 160–61, 164, 167

Abu-Rukun, Salah, 166

Abu Sbeitan (tribe), 185

Acre, 43, 54–6, 59, 103, 104, 105, 105n, 110, 114, 116n, 128–29, 134, 137–38, 147, 156, 215 (fig.), 217, 223

Adalah (legal center), 142n

'Adawi, Mahmoud, 212

Aden, 131
administrative measures. *See* emergency
    regulations
Advisor on Arab Affairs, PM office, 8, 27,
    36, 40, 54, 62, 72, 96n, 107, 126, 146, 162,
    167, 168, 169, 173, 179, 180, 200, 202, 208,
    214, 217, 218, 223, 228, 235
Advisory Committee on Arab Affairs, 137–
    38, 156
Afek (kibbutz), 221
Afula, 77
'Agur, 34
Ahdut Ha-Avoda (party) 207
Ahituv, Avraham, 173
Ahmad, Tawfiq, 80
'Alei, 57
Algeria, 131, 133
Al-Hamishmar, 54, 116
Alhambra (cinema), 55
'Ali, Isma'il (Reihaniyya), 177
Alon, yigal, 129, 162, 181–82
Aloni, Reuven, 27
Amir, Pinhas, 27
Amman, 189
Anglo-American Committee of Inquiry, 47
'Aqel, Atanes, 109
al-Aqsa intifada, 123
al-Aqsa Mosque, 58
'Ara (village), 15, 79, 80, 128, 203
Arab Front. *See* Popular Front
Arab intelligence activity, 2, 71, 80, 94,
    146–47, 189–90; in 1948, 23; Egyptian,
    87; Hezbollah, 61; Jordanian, 36, 87, 185;
    Lebanese, 91; Syrian, 88, 91, 92–93, 177
Arab League, 13, 47, 81
Arab Liberation Army, 13, 16, 43, 46, 66, 81,
    98. *See also* Qawuqji, Fawzi
Arab nationalism, 129–30, 131, 132, 134,
    139–41, 144, 179–80, 195, 216–17n, 219,
    235; among Bedouins, 193; and Ciracas-
    sians, 177; among Druze, 160, 166, 168–
    70; Jewish possible reactions, 212–13,
    216–17n
Arab revolt, 1936–9, 11–2, 19, 20, 21, 22, 46,
    97, 187, 188n, 195–96, 244n38
Arab Slates: affiliated with Mapai/Rafi, 3,
    41, 52, 58–59, 62–63, 164; Agriculture
    and Development, 28, 137; Cooperation

and Brotherhood, 60, 129; Peace Slate,
    194
Arabic, 81, 123, 136, 141, 178, 238
Arabs in the Jewish State, 233
'Ar'ara, 15, 203
archives, xi, 62, 68
al-Ard (movement), 4, 128–29, 135n, 199,
    218
Ariel, Yehuda, 116n
armistice agreements (1949, Rhodes), 1, 11,
    13, 16, 20, 99
Army of Shadows, 7
'Arrabe, 17, 94, 112n, 119, 145n, 211
'Artul, Farhan Jiryis, 222
'Ashu Mustafa, 121
Asouline, Yitzhak, 87
Aswan Dam, 143
'Atawna (tribe), 183
al-Atrash, Sultan, 160–61
attitudes towards the state among Arabs,
    2, 4–5, 18–21, 25, 37–38, 57, 109, 111–12,
    127–139, 175, 178, 196, 231–33, 236; after
    the nakba, 16, 18–20; and relations with
    Jews, 31–32, 41, 58, 111, 115, 130, 175; social
    aspects, 4–5, 35, 119, 140–41, 148–49, 151,
    163–4, 173, 234, 235
Auerbach, Haim, 106
Avner, Elimelech, 59
Avneri, Uri, 114
Avneri, Yitzhak, 103
'Awad, Rabbah, 31–32
'Aweisat, Zaki, 156
'Ayesh, Salah, 66
'Azar, Musa, 77
'Azazmeh (Bedouin Tribes), 18, 22, 25, 185,
    193
'Aziyya (in Lebanon), 89
'Azzi, 'Abd al-Rahman, 187–88
'Azzun, 195

Baghdad, 12
Bahri, Mahmoud, 84
Balad (Party), 201n
Balad al-Sheikh, 92n
Balfour Declaration, 211
Bani Sa'b (region), 195
Baqa al-Gharbiyyeh, 14, 18, 28, 33, 104, 156,
    200

Bar-Yehuda, Yisrael, 207
Bar-Zvi, Sasson (aka: Freikh), 188, 192–3
Barazani, Yaakov, 120
Barta'a, 15, 60, 79, 94, 99
Bashan, Yehuda, 62, 148
Bathish, Nadim, 223
Battat, Issa, 187–190
Battuf (Beit Netofa) Valley, 119, 225
Bedouin, 6, 10, 17–18, 22, 67, 71, 73, 74
    (fig.), 82, 87, 107, 128, 175, 179, 180, 181–
    88, 190, 192, 193–94, 195, 207, 226–27
Beersheva, 18, 187, 189
Begin, Menachem, 109–10
Beit Jala, 86
Beit Jann, 150, 171–72
Beit Jibrin, 188n
Beit Keshet, 215n
Beit Netofa Valley, 119
Beit Safafa, 87
Beit She'an Valley, 112
Ben-Amotz, Dahn, 114
Ben Bella, 131
Ben-Elkana, Shlomo, 15–16, 20, 68–69
Ben Gurion, David, 32, 42, 43, 47, 55, 58,
    59n, 137–39, 143, 147, 163, 172, 177, 181,
    194, 208, 232
Ben-Natan, Efrayim, 15
Ben-Ya'akov, Aryeh, 226
Ben Zvi, Yitzhak, 109, 143, 144, 176
Bergman, Emmanuel, 115
Berlin, 11, 12, 156
Bethlehem, 86, 188n
Bi'neh, 65–67, 111, 113, 115
Binyamina, 85
Bir'am, 108–10, 134
Biro, Muhammad, 61
Birwe, 101, 103, 129–30
Bolshevik police, 127
border crossing. See infiltrators
British mandate, 1, 9, 12, 14–15, 17, 22, 23,
    25, 26, 28, 31, 35, 42, 45–6, 53, 70, 92, 97,
    99, 103, 104, 109, 120n, 155, 166n, 167n,
    170, 172, 174, 179, 182, 187–8, 191, 195,
    209, 218, 232, 234, 235, 236
Bulgaria, 12
Bulus, Hanna Bulus, 65–67
Bulus Ibtihaj, 147
Buqa'i family, 100–4

Buqa'i, Muhammad, 99–100
Buqa'i, Shafiq, 100–6
Buqei'a (Peqi'in), 168, 205

café, 34, 150; Abu Sa'id's, 55, 57
Central Committee on Arab Affairs, 8, 36,
    173, 202, 211, 219, 233
Central Council for Arab Affairs, 96n
Czechoslovakia, arms deal with, 41–42
Christians, 3, 10, 47–8, 52, 75, 76–77, 97,
    129, 150, 156–57, 164n, 169–70, 172, 174,
    223, 228; and nationalism, 179–81; and
    volunteering to the IDF, 180–81. See also
    religious identities
Ciracassians, 10, 28, 88, 174–79
citizenship. See identity cards
clubs: Cultural and Sport (Nationalistic),
    198–200, 212, 218; "loyal," 198, 200, 218
collaborators: abandonment of, 25–26, 38;
    agency of, 36, 37, 106, 116, 192–93; compe-
    tition among, 35–6; Druze versus Bed-
    ouin, 185–86; killed, 23, 86, 87, 94, 97;
    motives, 7–8, 21, 30, 31, 33, 40, 71, 45, 77–
    80, 116–17, 130–31, 157, 160–61, 185, 235;
    personality assessments of, 25, 30, 83, 113,
    203–4; pre-state, 7, 11–13, 14, 17, 18, 21–
    23, 26, 28, 31–32, 60, 99–100, 188n, 204–
    5; refuse to collaborate, 92–94; relations
    with the authorities, 37, 52, 60, 117, 130,
    177, 183, 198, 200–1, 203, 211–12, 217–18;
    rewards to, 25–32, 207, 213, 220–21, 226,
    236; society and collaborators, 7, 19, 37–
    38, 81–82, 117–18, 127–28; worldview of,
    4, 7–8, 31, 33, 35–37, 45, 99–100, 106,
    116–17, 130–31, 192–93, 212–13, 234–35.
    See also letters
Communist Party, 4, 6, 8, 23, 29, 31, 38,
    39–64, 65–66, 101, 106, 112–3, 115–6, 121,
    129–30, 132–33, 135n, 136–37, 138, 141, 143,
    147, 193–94, 198, 199, 200, 201, 209–12,
    217, 218, 219, 220–22, 225, 230, 232–33,
    236
condemnations, 151
control and surveillance, 195–230. See also
    education; emergency regulations

Dabbah, Yihia, 223
Daburiyya, 17

Dahariyya, 187, 189
Daliat al-Karmel, 5, 161, 168–69
Damascus, 53, 98, 128, 156, 160
Damun, 99–107
Danin Aharon, 23, 47n
Danin, Ezra, 15
Darwish, Mahmoud, 224
Davar, 142
Davis, Nira, 7
Davis, Uri, 114–16
Dayan, Moshe, 28, 67, 67n, 131, 132, 177, 180
Decade Festivities, 132, 134, 137, 142, 146, 218, 234
demonstrations, 5, 41, 44, 55–6, 57, 59, 114–16, 138–39, 142–3, 147–49, 150, 151, 171, 194, 200, 218–19, 220, 238
Development Authority, 31
Diab, Mustafa, 212
Diab, Yusef, 129–30, 213 (fig.)
Dir al-Asad, 6, 80–81, 111, 114–15, 117–19, 128–29, 221
Dir Hanna, 17, 119, 226
Dir Sharaf (Nablus), 83
Dir Yasin, 133
discourses and historical narratives, 3, 9–10, 70, 149–50, 155–56, 234–35; Arab discourse and its control, 3, 10, 121–22, 123–31, 138, 151–55, 195, 224, 234–35; clash of, 9, 94, 132, 138, 143–44, 150, 232; double discourse, 141–42; Zionist narrative, 31, 73, 75, 126, 131, 137, 149, 158, 169, 237
Divon, Zalman (Shmuel), 62, 162–3, 208
Dorenzaft, Reuven, 35, 82–83
Dotan (colonel), 227
drug dealing, 61, 68, 191
Druze, 3, 5, 10, 29–30, 71, 79, 136 (fig.), 150, 173, 174, 176, 177, 178, 181, 185, 186, 208, 221–22, 226, 227, 228, 232; and conscription, 159–66; identity of, 163–64, 166n, 167–70, 173; land, 170–72; and Muslims/Islam, 163, 164n, 167n, 168, 170, 172, 227; relations with Christians, 181. *See also* Minorities Battalion; religious identities

Ecksteinm Yehoshua, 148
education, 3, 6, 120n, 124 (fig.), 228, 237, 238; Ciracassian, 177–78; and control, 3, 7, 9–10, 37, 108, 123, 138, 139–46, 148,

149–50, 154, 156, 163, 164n, 194, 196, 210, 223, 233, 234, 235, 236; Druze, 164n, 169–170; ministry of, 140–41, 144–45, 149, 169–70, 199, 221–2, 224, 235; prevention of higher education, 215–16; as site for Arab national activity, 132, 148–49, 154
Egypt, 2, 9, 18, 47, 55, 66, 68, 81, 87, 88n, 112, 129, 132, 153, 154, 159, 164, 185, 187, 189, 190, 191, 219, 227, 229
Eichmann, 132
'Eid, Ahmad, 84
'Eilabun, 5, 39–40, 45–47, 50–52, 119, 129, 150, 152, 156–57, 180, 228; burning of the Communist club, 50–51
Ein Gev, 112
'Ein al-Hilwe, 92–93
'Ein Karem, 86
'Ein Rafa, 127
Eini Ya'akov, 211
elections, 3; general elections, 4, 41, 43 (fig.), 52, 58, 60–62, 109–10, 194, 196, 232; involvement of security agencies, 62–63, 205–11, 220; local elections, 24 (fig.), 117n, 125n, 161, 201n, 202, 211. *See also* Arab Slates; Knesset and MKs; local councils and municipalities
Elias, Hanna, 115
emergency regulations, 4, 31, 36, 44, 65, 71, 73n, 114, 126, 145n, 177, 194, 198, 199, 207, 212, 217, 218, 219, 220, 221, 222, 224, 227, 229, 236
Eshkol, Levi, 61
Even Sapir, 34

Fadl, sheikh Khalil, 75
Fahmawi, Ibrahim, 106
Fahoum, Majed, 156, 220–21
Fahoum, Yusef, 16–17
Faluja, 187
Fanous, Elia, 76–77
Faqua, 190
Faradis, 85, 99, 124–25
Farhud Qasem Farhud, 162
Fassuta, 177
Fatah (movement), 149, 151, 222
Fayad, Hasan, 82–84
Feigenbaum, Avraham, 59

[Feinstein], Akiva, 131

flag, 144; display of the Israeli, 15, 49–50, 76 (fig.), 133, 145, 216n, 233; removal of Israeli, 143, 150–51; Palestinian, 125; Vatican, 49

French mandate, 12

Gaza, 5, 29, 67n, 76, 87, 88n, 119n, 120, 125n, 137, 146, 147, 157, 229, 238

Geffen, Hayyim, 25–26

General Security Service (GSS, shabak), xi, 5, 6, 8, 33, 38, 52, 73, 75, 77, 80, 82, 93, 94, 96n, 99, 113, 115, 128, 138, 140, 142, 145, 148, 149, 150, 152, 170, 173, 179, 188, 190, 198, 199, 200–1, 202, 219, 226, 228–29, 235; and elections, 62–3, 64n, 196, 198; in the RCAA, 107, 206, 209–14, 216–27; relations with police, 33–36

Germany, Third Reich, 11–12, 28, 111

Ghabsiyya, 31–32

Ghanem, Qasem Farid, 222

Ginosar (kibbutz), 228

Ginossar, Yossi, 201n

Givatayyim, 154

Goebbels, 12

Golani junction, 46

Goldberg, Ezra, 34–35

graffiti, 110, 120–22, 125

Greek Catholics, 29, 47, 49 (fig.), 49–50, 52, 178, 180, 226. *See also* Hakim, George

Greek orthodox, 217

Gush Halav. *See* Jish

Haaretz, 116n

Habibi, Emile, 43–44, 57, 211, 222, 245n4

Habibi, Leila Jad, 222–23

Hacohen, David, 63 (fig.)

Hadash (party), 201. *See also* Communist Party

Ha-Dor, 57

Hafez, Amin, 131

Haganah (prestate Zionist military organization), 11–12, 22, 31, 41–42, 54, 92n, 104, 166n. *See also* Shai

Haifa, 29, 47, 50, 92, 103, 104, 147, 154, 167, 169, 179, 206, 217, 218, 228

Hajj, Hawash al-, 210

Hajj Muhammad, 'Abd al-Rahim, 195

Hakim, George (Bishop), 8, 29, 47–53, 58, 136 (fig.), 178, 180, 226

Hakku, Salah Hasan, 175

Halabi, Quftan 'Azzam, 168–69

Halevitz, Yeshayahu, 104

Hamdan, Fares, 28, 28n, 63, 137, 138–39, 200

Hamdun (tribe, band), 90–92

Hanegbi, Haim, 115

Har-Zion, Meir and Shoshana, 226

Hasan, Mahmoud, 227

Hasan, Nizar, 123–24, 151

Hashomer, 112

Hatzor HaGlilit, 110, 171

Hawwari, Muhammad Nimer, 8, 53–59, 101, 111

Hebrew, 1, 81, 110, 125, 178

Hebron, 53, 185, 187–88, 189–90

al-Heib tribe, 128, 227

Herzl, Theodor, 144–45

Herut (party), 109–10

Hezbollah, 61

Higher Arab Committee, 47, 53, 60

Higher Committee of Palestinian Youth in Tur'an, 152

Himmler, 12

Hiram Operation (1948), 17, 66, 105–6, 166n

Histadrut, 44, 57, 62, 121, 131, 133, 142, 147, 156, 170, 196, 196n, 198, 210, 214, 231, 233

Hmeidi, 'Abd al-Rahman, 127

Hubeishi, Muhammad, 138, 156

Hula Valley, 101–2, 112

Hurfeish, 168, 177

Hushi, Abba, 167

Hussein Rashid (of Sha'ab), 103

Husseini, 'Abd al-Qader, 205

Husseini, Amin, 12–13, 21–22, 23, 28, 47, 63, 172, 182, 188n

Husseini, Jamal, 47

Husseini party, 28n, 53

Huzayyel, sheikh Suleiman, 74 (fig.), 181–85

Huzayyel 'ali, Jadwa', and Muhammad, 185

'Iblin, 48–49, 72, 128, 209–10, 217, 223, 225

Ibrahim, Qaisar, 134

identities, xi, 2, 3, 4, 10, 38, 56, 97n, 120, 141, 155, 174, 178–79, 206, 229, 233–35, 237, 238. Ciracassian, 175–78; Druze, 164, 166n,

identities *(continued)*
168–70, 172–73. *See also* Palestinian identity; pan-Arabism
identity cards (and citizenship), 6, 29, 47, 70, 79–80, 89, 95, 96n, 139, 168, 212, 231
IDF (Israeli army), 8, 13, 16–17, 18, 19, 22, 23, 25, 26, 29, 32, 84, 85–86, 105–6, 108, 125, 129, 136 (fig.), 137, 139, 145, 147, 157, 159, 177, 181–82, 185, 189, 190, 228; Arabs in the service of, 73–74, 85–87, 129, 159–67, 171, 175, 180, 183, 193, 227, 228; intelligence, 15, 28, 30, 36, 42, 46, 49, 66, 67, 68, 72, 73, 88, 186. *See also* Minorities Battalion; Unit 154
Iksal, 17, 127
Independence Day, 48–49 (figs.), 123, 132–34, 136 (fig.), 138, 144–6, 150–51, 154, 218, 233
infiltrators, 2, 5, 6, 7, 9, 18, 30, 34–35, 36, 38, 40, 65–82, 139, 151, 164, 188, 192, 212, 226, 232; from Israel to Arab countries, 146–47; operations against, 82–91, 93, 94, 168, 175, 185; return of, 95–96. *See also* identity cards; refugees
informers, 2, 3, 10, 14–15, 21, 23, 28, 30, 33, 34, 35, 41, 56, 77–78, 78–90, 94, 98, 105, 113, 115–18, 121, 123, 125–26, 128, 143, 152, 183, 189, 229, 235. *See also* collaborators
intelligence activity, 2, 7, 11, 13, 15, 17, 22, 23, 26, 27, 28, 30, 31, 32, 114, 127, 146, 157, 163–4, 204, 224, 233; Israeli in Arab countries, 2, 5, 13, 61, 82–94, 98, 185–87, 189–91, 226, 229, 251n3. *See also* Arab intelligence activity; General Security Service; Shai; Unit 154
Intifada, 120
Iqrit, 50, 107 (fig.)
Iraq, 12, 13, 16, 19–20, 60, 83, 105, 128, 196, 204
'Iraqi, 'Abd al-Rahim, 196–98
'Iraqi, Husni, 198, 199
'Isfiya, 161, 164
Israel Labor League (of the Histadrut), 133
Istiqlal/Atzma'ut, 123
Al-Ittihad, 45, 49, 53, 59n, 168, 200, 222, 224

Jaffa, 12, 53, 54, 55, 57, 60, 75–76, 88n
Jaljulia, 14

Jamal, Amal, 155
Jarjura [Amin, MK], 59
Jatt (Triangle), 154
al-Jazzar Mosque, 134–37, 234
Jerusalem, 34, 58, 86–87, 157, 182, 222
Jethro, 168
Jewish Agency, 12, 22
Jibris, Elias, 210
Jish, 77, 108–10, 134, 177, 221, 228
Jisr al-Zarqa, 85
JNF. *See* KKL
Jordan, 16, 18, 28n, 35–36, 60, 68, 80, 81–88, 92, 94, 94, 99, 121, 127n, 128, 185–90, 191, 193, 226, 229
Judaization and settlement, 21, 22, 27, 96–97, 110–11, 112, 117n, 120, 134, 171, 234
Julis, 159

Kabul, 17, 94, 228
Kafr Kanna, 17, 107, 228
Kafr Qasim, 13–14; massacre, 135–38, 144 (fig.), 200, 234
Kafr Yasif, 129, 133–34, 154, 162, 164n, 209, 210–11
Karkur, 86
Karmiel, 5, 97, 111, 113, 116–17, 138
Kawkab (Abu al-Hija), 149, 150
Kedem, Yosef, 62
Kenan Amos, 114
Kerem 1 (alias), 86–87
Keren Kayemet Leyisrael. *See* KKL
Kfar Hess, 151
Khalil, 'Ali, 79
Khalsa, 110
Khamis, saliba, 56
Khamus, Yair, 198
Khan Yunis, 88n
Khazen, Shukri, 112
Khilf, Arab al- (Bedouin tribe), 67, 71
Khleifi, Husni, 104
Khneifes, Saleh, 29, 71–73, 77, 160–61, 164, 167, 211, 212
Khuri, Daoud, 55
Khuri, Fawzi, 210–11
Khuri, Jiryis, 179–80
Khuri, Ramzi, 43, 56, 65
Khuri, Violet, 211
Kilani, Rashid 'Ali, 12

Kirad al-Baqqara, 101
Kirad al-Ghannama, 101
Kiryat Shmonah, 110
Kiryat Ye'arim, 71
Kisra, 226
KKL (Keren Kayemet, JNF, 17, 21, 22, 23,
    26, 27, 47, 96n, 98, 99–100, 105, 111, 112,
    120, 181–82, 231, 235
Knesset and MKs, 3, 4, 5, 8, 24 (fig.), 28,
    41, 43, 44, 45, 46, 55, 58–59, 60, 62–63,
    70, 71, 128, 138, 156, 162, 164, 167, 172,
    194, 199, 209, 211–12, 223, 225, 232, 236.
    See also elections; *names of individual
    members*
Kravitz, Yitzhak, 134
Kufr Kama, 175–76 (fig.), 177
Kufr Qara', 14, 15, 69, 99, 199, 200n, 228
Kusa, elias, 134–35

Labor Party. *See* Mapai
land, 95–122; Arab assisstance in transfer-
    ring to Jews, 22–23, 26, 47, 97–98, 113,
    115–16, 119, 188n, 226, 235; Bedouin, 182–
    84; Ciracassians, 175; Druze, 170–72, 175;
    expropriation and resistance, 3, 5, 9, 14,
    19–20, 31–32, 37, 40, 42, 52, 58, 67n, 69,
    73n, 97, 98, 111–16, 117–21, 133, 134, 138,
    150, 156, 234, 236; in Palestinian ethos, 9,
    97; registration, 98–99; reward to inform-
    ers, 16, 26–27, 36, 100, 221; waqf land, 216;
    in Zionist ethos, 12, 67n. *See also* absentee
    property
Land Day, 200–1
Land Leasing Committee, 27
Landau, Yaakov (Jacob), 62, 203n
Laskov, Haim, 181
Lausanne Conference, 54, 55
Lavon, Pinhas, 44
Layish, Aharon, 168
leaders and leadership, 25–27, 29, 37, 45, 47,
    52–53, 54–55, 56, 59, 71–72, 76–77, 79,
    95, 108, 109, 111–12, 130, 136 (fig.), 177,
    184 (fig.), 188n, 195–213; Druze, 160–72,
    174–75, 185, 221, 226, 232–33, 235. *See also*
    Knesset and MKs; local councils and
    municipalities; mukhtars
leaflets, 43 (fig.), 61, 132–33, 194
Lebanon, 5, 26, 29, 46, 47, 57, 61, 65, 66, 68,

77, 81, 82, 89–93, 98, 102, 104, 105, 133,
    146, 161, 173
letters, 77, 80–81, 93, 102–3, 134, 137, 179; to
    the editor, 168, 170, 222; fabricated, 168–
    9; by informers, 39–40, 77, 81, 98; lobby-
    ing, 18, 29, 46–47, 69–70, 79, 161, 175, 176;
    threats to collaborators, 109, 119–20, 132,
    152–54, 200n
Levitzki, Go'el, 26, 59
Al-Lid. *See* Lod
Liftzin, Yaakov, 27
Lod, 34, 65, 143
local councils and municipalities, 3, 23,
    27, 33, 60, 61, 71, 117n, 121, 129, 133, 147,
    150, 151, 156, 161, 164, 175, 196–97, 199–
    212, 213 (fig.), 220, 223, 225, 228. *See also*
    elections
loyalty (and loyalists), 3, 7, 9, 13–14, 17, 18,
    19, 22, 23, 28n, 42, 57, 60–61, 68, 69, 70,
    77, 95, 109, 122, 123, 131, 132, 133, 134, 138–
    9, 140, 145–46, 148, 156, 161, 163–4, 176,
    180, 183, 184 (fig.), 193, 196, 197 (fig.), 200,
    201n, 222–3, 229, 231, 232, 234–35
Lubrani, Uri, 126
Lustick, Ian, 233

Ma'alot, 110
Ma'anit (kibbutz), 15
Ma'ariv, 111–13, 189
Mahajne neighborhood, 121
Mahamid neighborhood, 121
Majdal, 59n, 76, 87
Majd al-Krum, 100, 105–6, 131
Maki. *See* Communist Party
Makr, 40, 130, 146, 218, 225
Ma'lul, 55
Mamshit, 185
Ma'mur Bey (ALA), 98
Mandate period. *See* British mandate
Manna', 'Adel, 106
Mansi, Mahmoud, 87
Mapai (labor party), 3, 28, 31, 40, 41, 44, 52,
    54, 57, 60, 61–63, 63 (fig.), 64, 110, 137, 138,
    142, 155, 156, 160, 164, 173n, 194, 196, 201,
    208, 209, 210, 211, 227, 232, 233. *See also*
    Arab Slates
Mapam (party), 54, 116, 147, 170, 208,
    209–10

Mara'na, Ibtisam, 124–25
Maroun, 46
Marx, Emmanuel, 146
Mash-had, 17, 123
Masmiyya, 87
Mas'oudin (Bedouin tribe), 18, 22, 185
Matar, Elias, 180
May Day, 138–39, 150, 218–19
media. *See* radio broadcasts
Mei-Ami, 120
Me'ir, Me'ir, 168–69
Mekorot (Israel's water company), 119
Meretz Party, 125n
Meron, 88
Metannes, Metannes, 164n
methodology, xi–xii
Mghar, 119, 207, 221–22
Mi'ar, 101–3
Mi'ari, Muhammad, 218
Michael, Michael, 62, 178
Mikve Yisrael (highschool), 12
military government and Arab responses,
    xi, 2, 3, 4, 5, 6, 7, 9, 11, 20, 21, 27, 30, 33, 36,
    40, 41, 42–44, 51–52, 56, 59, 60, 62, 64,
    65, 68, 72–73, 96, 101, 110, 114, 119, 123,
    128, 134–35, 136, 137, 140, 141, 143, 145,
    148, 150, 157 (fig.), 158n, 159, 162, 177, 178,
    181, 183–85, 204–5, 206, 207, 208, 210–11,
    212, 214, 216, 217, 219–20, 222, 223, 225,
    226, 227, 235, 236, 237; accusations of cor-
    ruption, 19, 35, 183; Arab support of, 61,
    72–73, 172, 173n, 199; collaboration with,
    13, 23, 26, 28n, 35, 51, 79, 83–4, 85–86, 98,
    115, 128, 131–32, 133, 182–83, 188, 192, 193,
    200, 218, 225, 231, 233; end of, 227; estab-
    lishment of, 13–17. *See also* Regional Com-
    mittees on Arab Affairs
M'ilya, 77, 177, 205, 210, 228
Ministry of Agriculture, 27, 103–4, 106
Ministry of Defense, 161–2, 180, 181, 216
Ministry of Education, 124 (fig.), 140, 144,
    149, 169–70, 199, 221, 222, 224, 235
Ministry of Foreign Affairs, 11, 22, 33, 47,
    70n, 174, 179, 193
Ministry of Health, 134
Ministry of Housing, 201n
Ministry of Interior, 60, 99, 101, 204, 205–
    9, 214, 217, 221, 226

Ministry of Minorities, 20, 46, 109, 112
Ministry of Police, 40, 44, 79
Ministry of Religions, 77, 156, 166–67, 170,
    223, 234
Ministry of Transportation, 221
Ministry of Welfare, 222–23
minorities, among the Arabs in Israel, 159–
    194. *See also* Bedouins; Christians; Cira-
    cassians; Druze
Minorities Battalion, 159, 162–63, 166, 168,
    175, 180, 185, 202, 224
Al-Mirsad, 170
Mishmar, 54, 116
Mishmar Ayalon, 34
mitzpim (Jewish settlements in the Gali-
    lee), 97
"moderates." *See* loyalty
Mokdi, Amos, 114
Motza, 34
Mt. Carmel, 154, 161, 166n, 173n
Mt. Meron, 171
Mt. Tabor, 23, 47, 49, 127
Mu'adi, Jaber, 61, 63, 79, 160, 161, 165 (fig.),
    167, 173n, 211, 225
Mu'adi, Marzuq Sa'id, 159
Mu'allim, Salim, 226
Mughar al-Kheit (al-Druze), 171–72
mukhtars, 2–3, 6, 14, 15, 18, 25, 27, 35, 36, 40,
    46, 77, 79, 85–86, 98, 99, 100, 197 (fig.),
    113, 128, 134, 159, 202–6, 224
municipalities. *See* local councils and
    municipalities
Muqeible, 80
Murqus, Hanna Mu'allim, 156
Musa, Jamal, 147
Musa, Nadim, 43, 56
Muslims and Islam, 3, 10, 48, 56, 67, 72, 75,
    76, 77, 91, 97, 130, 134–35, 137–38, 139,
    150, 156, 160, 179, 180, 181, 208, 214, 216,
    223, 228, 231, 257n55; Ciracassians, 177–8;
    Druze and, 163, 164n, 167n, 168, 170–72,
    227; *See also* religious identities
Musmus, 152

Nablus, 84, 88
Nahal Corps, 120
Nahal Oz, 67n
Nahariya, 104–5

Nahf, 111, 218
Nahmani, Yosef, 112–13, 226
Najjada (Palestinian organization), 53–55, 57
Nakba, and commemoration of, 4, 132n, 139, 142, 144, 149, 151, 218–19, 234, 237
Nakhle, Elias, 61, 63 (fig.)
Napoleon, 125
Naqura (Nablus), 83
narratives. *See* discourses and historical narratives
Nassar, Fu'ad, 57–58
Nasser, Gamal, and Nasserism, 9, 38, 63–64, 112, 128, 129, 130–31, 132, 141, 142, 143, 144, 151, 152, 154, 155, 164n, 178, 219, 227, 237–38
National Guard (Jordanian), 28
National Liberation League (communist), 42, 55
National Water Carrier, 118, 119–20, 225
nationalism, 179. *See* Arab nationalism
Nation's Fund (Palestinian), 47
Na'ura, 23, 77
Nazareth, 6, 16–17, 18, 23, 24 (fig.), 39, 40, 42, 44, 49–50, 53, 56, 57, 58, 62, 80, 81, 113, 114, 124 (fig.), 128, 129, 131, 138, 142, 149, 151, 156, 157 (fig.), 208, 211, 220, 223, 224, 227, 228; Upper Nazareth, 97, 111
Nazism, 11–12, 28, 111, 132
Nebi saleh, 216n
Nebi Shu'eib, 164–65, 167–68
Negev, 6, 8, 16, 17–18, 22, 36, 73, 87, 97, 123, 154, 158, 181–94, 202, 206–7, 221, 226
Netanya, 196
Nimrodi, Ya'akov, 189
Nin (village), 22, 23
1921 riots/uprising, 195, 201
1929 riots/uprising, 45–46
1948 War/Independence War, 1, 3, 4, 9, 13, 14, 15, 16, 18, 22, 25, 26, 29, 31, 40, 41–42, 46, 47, 55, 66, 69, 70, 71, 73, 75, 84, 98, 104–5, 107 (fig.), 124–25, 129, 139, 150, 157, 177, 182–83, 187, 188, 196, 104, 205, 214–15, 221, 231, 234, 237; Arab and Jewish atrocities during, 46–7, 92, 92n, 105–106, 124–25n, 215; Bedouin in, 185; Druze in, 165–66; responsibility for, 54. *See also* Nakba

1956 War. *See* Sinai Campaign
1967 War, 58, 87, 128, 227–29, 236, 238
Novoselski, Ovadiah, 30

Oman, 133
Oslo Agreements, 224

Palestine (usage of the term), 119–120n, 152
Palestine Rescue Organization, 119
Palestinian Authority, 224
Palestinian identity, 3, 9, 38, 119, 119n, 140–41, 155, 174, 179; and Druze, 173, 231, 233, 237–8. *See also* discourses and historical narratives
Palestinian national movement, 4, 5, 9, 13, 100, 149, 179, 182, 224, 229
Palestinian nationalist ideology, 20, 37, 47, 54, 58, 65–66, 97, 133, 138. *See also* resistance
Palmon, Yehoshua, 11–13, 54, 60, 72, 96n, 167, 170, 203n
pan-Arabism, 3, 9–10, 81, 129–30, 237. *See also* Arab nationalism; Nasser
Paradise Lost, 124–25
Parliament. *See* Knesset and MKs
partition borders, 21, 41, 50, 56, 66, 178
partition plan (1947), 23, 42, 58, 232, 247n38
passivity, 6, 21, 38, 46, 109, 115, 151
Peres, Yohanan, 7
permits (arms, residency, travel), 26, 28–30, 33, 36, 44, 53, 56, 60, 62–63, 79, 95–96, 116, 163, 178, 205, 206, 212–15, 217, 223
personality assessments (by the security agencies), xi, 25, 30, 83, 114, 203–4, 219
Petah Tikva, 83, 198
petitions (public), 51, 114, 162, 171, 198, 219–20, 228
planning and building, Jewish towns, 110–11, 234; control of, 6, 36, 208, 214; for internal refugees, 198. *See also* Karmiel; Nazareth
PLO, 125
police, xi, 5, 11, 13, 14, 17, 19, 20, 25, 30, 33, 49, 52, 55, 56, 59, 60, 65, 79, 88n, 91, 92, 93, 94, 99, 101, 104–5, 106, 107, 108–10, 113–5, 116, 120–21, 126, 127, 133, 134, 138, 140n, 142–43, 144, 145, 146–47, 149–50, 154, 158, 159, 164n, 177, 180, 190, 196,

police *(continued)*
198, 199, 204–5, 211, 213–15, 218, 220, 226–28, 235, 238; Acre police, 78, 103; arrests, 49, 56, 59, 61, 66, 70, 77, 78, 83, 88n, 106, 114–15, 116, 125, 138–39, 146, 158, 160–62, 171–2, 177, 186, 190, 198, 199–200, 204, 207n, 218–19, 227; and Bedouins, 183, 186, 187, 191; Bolshevik police, 127; Border Police, 91, 135; British, 12, 14, 92; Central District, 217n; and Druze, 160–62, 171–72, 173; Hadera, 25, 79, 154; Haifa District, 18; and infiltration, 65–82; informers of, 6, 15–16, 21, 26, 30, 33, 77, 78, 81–82, 85, 115–16, 128, 212; Jordanian, 28n, 60, 82, 84; Karkur station, 18, 30; Lebanese, 90; letters to, 39–40, 77, 81, 102, 131; minister of, 22, 44, 79; Nazareth, 18, 39, 44–45, 62, 80, 131; Northern District, 52, 104, 113, 121, 145n, 200n; political reports by, 67, 59, 62, 68, 75, 156n, 202, 216n; Ra'anana, 83; Ramla, 145, 216–17n; in RCAA, 8, 36, 107, 202, 213–15, 225; relations with security agencies *(see also* RCAA), 33–35, 62, 206; Safed, 45; Southern District, 198; special branch, xi, 45, 78, 79, 88n, 116n, 139–40, 156n, 198, 200n, 215n; Structure of, 240; Tiberias, 50; Yizrael (Jezreel) Subdistrict, 62, 156n, 215n
Popular Front, 112, 135, 137–38, 223, 224, 229
Popular Front for the Liberation of Palestine, 229

Qabalan family, 171–72
Qalansawa, 78
Qalqilya, 82, 84, 86
Qardush, Mansour, 128, 219
Qasem, Ibrahim Khalil, 196
Qasem, Samih, 131, 224
Qasis Mas'ad, 211–12
Qassam, Izz al-Din, 121
Qastina, 189
Qa'war, Salman Qasem, 222
Qawuqji, Fawzi, 13, 16, 43, 46, 66, 81, 98
Qays, Hajj Muhammad 'Omar, 28, 88, 177
Qrinat, sheikh 'Ali, 158n

Queen Esther tomb, 109
Quran, 78, 91
Quteina, Yusef, 189
Qutub, Jamil, 221

Rabinowitz, Dani, 4, 151
Al-Rabita, 47
radio broadcasts, 81, 139, 152, 153 (fig.), 155, 156, 177, 224, 234
Rakah, 4. *See also* Communist Party
Ramadan, 170
Ramallah, 35, 179, 224
Ramat HaKovesh, 196
Rambam hospital, 103
Rameh (also: Rami) (village), 27, 98, 162, 205
Ramla, 75–77, 143, 157, 216n
Ras Atiah, 86
Red Army, 12
refugees, 1, 4, 5, 6, 9, 14, 17, 29, 46–47, 52–53, 54–55, 65–67, 67n, 69, 70, 72, 77, 78, 79, 80, 85, 87, 88–89, 90, 92–93, 95, 96, 130, 152, 168, 177, 178, 188n, 224, 232, 237; internal refugees, 26, 27, 41, 50, 73n, 76, 96–97n, 99, 100–10, 129–30, 134, 157; Jewish refugees, 47; refugees property, 31, 98, 110; return, 29, 32, 46–47, 50, 52–53, 54, 65, 70, 95, 96, 98, 99–101, 104, 109–10, 133, 152, 224, 232. *See also* absentee property; infiltrators
Refugee Rehabilitation Authority, 101
Regional Committees on Arab Affairs, xi, 8, 10, 36, 140n, 201, 202, 205–6, 207, 211, 213–14, 218, 220, 224, 233; Galilee (Northern), 107, 114, 173, 202–3, 205, 209–10, 211–12, 217, 218, 219–26; Negev, 194, 206–7, 226; Triangle (Central), 203–4, 211, 215–16
Reihaniyya, 28, 88, 177–78
Reine, 17
Rekhess, Elie, 7
religious identities, 3, 10, 163, 173–74, 178–79, 179–80, 208
retaliation operation, 85–88, 92n
Riklin (police officer), 83
Rishpon, 84, 196
Robinson Shira, 7
Rohan, Michael, 58

Roosvelt, Eleanor, 184 (fig.)
Rosh HaNikra, 12

Saʿdi, Ahmad, 7, 119, 155
Safed, 109, 110, 171
Saffuri, 16, 107
Sajara, battle of, 98
Sakhnin, 5, 17, 94, 100, 106, 112n, 118, 119,
   147–48, 218, 225
Sakhnini, Raja, 148
Sakran, Khaled, 89–91
Salim, Naʾif, 40
Salman, Nur, 119
Salman, ʿUrsan, 209–10
Samʿan, Amin, 212
Samʿan, Fawzi, 134
Samaria, 12, 195. See also West Bank
Samwili, Mustafa, 34–35
Sarayʿa (Bedouin tribe), 187–88
Saʿsa, 26, 89, 108
schools. See education
Sbeih, Arab al-, 175
Scouts, Arab, 53; Catholic, 49–51; Druze,
   168; Israeli, 216n
Sea of Galilee, 118
Segev, Shmuel, 111–13
Segev, Yitzhak, 62
Shaʿab, 100–6
Shabak. See General Security Service
Shadmi, Yiska, 135
Shaghur lands, 117, 119
Shai (the Hagana intelligence service), 11,
   13, 14–15. See also Haganah
Shalhut, Shafiq, 222
Shamir, Yitzhak, 182 (fig.)
Shani, Yitzhak, 96n, 183, 205
Sharett, Moshe, 22, 70n, 167, 174, 177, 179
Sharon, Ariel, 34
Sharon (region), 75, 82, 195
Shatta prison, 190–91
Shefaʿamr, 17, 29, 49, 71–72, 89, 161–62,
   168, 208, 227
Shemaʿayya and Avtalyon, 109
Shibli (tribe, village), 107
shin Bet. See General Security Service
Shitrit, Bechor shalom, 22, 44, 46, 79
Shlomi, 110

Shlush, Aharon, 35, 139–40, 145, 173
Shomera, 91
Shufaniyya, Salah, 168
Shvili, Yitzhak, 65–66
Sidon, 89
Sinai Campaign, 128, 135, 137, 156–157, 158n,
   164n, 193, 227
Sindianah, 85
Singer (police officer), 183
Six Day War. See 1967 War
Smooha, Sami, 7
smuggling, 2, 34, 36, 67–71, 75, 77–81, 85,
   94, 187–92, 226; arms in 1948, 31; "legal
   smuggling," 27–28, 33, 137, 164, 236
Social Security Institute, 221
Sofia, 12
Soltz, Elisha, 17
spies and spying, 51, 67, 81, 88n, 93, 94, 146–
   47, 152, 187–89
Sprinzak, Yosef, 162
Srour, Freij, 46
Stalin, 49
Steinberg, Zeʿev, 33–34, 86
sulha, 51–2, 144 (fig.), 204
Supreme Committee on Arab Affairs, 36
Supreme Court, 31, 50–51, 58, 71, 79, 101–2,
   108, 111, 142n, 177, 201n, 249n12; Sharʿi
   Supreme Court, 156
Supreme Muslim Council, 179n
Syria, 12, 28, 53, 68, 81, 82, 88, 91–93, 101,
   128–29, 131, 132, 139, 159, 160–61, 173, 177,
   189, 219

Tabari, Musa, 138, 156
Tabari, Taher, 156, 257n55
Tamra, 17, 63–64, 72, 78, 106, 129, 132–33,
   149, 205, 212, 213 (fig.), 225
Tamra Zuʿbiyya, 23
Tanenbaum, Elhanan, 61
Tantura, 124
Tarafa, Rashid, 91
Tarif, Amin, 136 (fig.), 164–72
Tarif, Kamel Salman, 159
Tarif, Salman, 166
Tarif, Suleiman Sirhan, 159
Tarif family, 160
Tarshiha, 48, 110, 177, 205, 228

Taybe (Ramallah), 179
Taybe (Triangle), 11–14, 59–61, 83, 94, 128, 173n
Taybe-Zuʻbiyya, 23
teachers, 108, 123, 129, 139–150, 154, 156, 164n, 169–70, 194, 199, 210, 221–22, 223, 224, 228, 233, 235, 237; dismissal of, 221; employment for loyalists, 221. *See also* education
Tel Aviv, 54, 75, 136 (fig.), 206
Tel Mond (prison), 93
Tel al-Safi, 188n
Tepner (Major), 62
terminology, xii
Tiberias, 51, 110
Tira, 14, 26, 83–84, 128, 151, 153 (fig.), 195–200, 211
Tiyaha (tribes), 181
Tokatli, Nissim, 169, 228
Toledano, Shmuel, 96n, 179, 208
Toubi, Tawfiq, 5, 44, 58, 59
Touma, Emil, 57
Triangle (region), 6, 8, 11, 13–16, 18, 19 (fig.), 19–20, 25, 26, 27, 28, 30, 35, 36, 59, 60, 61, 73, 75, 78, 80, 84, 85, 89, 97, 120, 150, 152, 155, 186, 193, 194, 196, 199, 200, 202, 203, 207n, 212, 215–16, 218, 219
Tuhtuh, Nimer, 91
Tulkarem, 13, 28, 36, 60, 78, 82, 85
Tumarkin, Yigal, 114
Turʻan, 80, 92, 131, 152–53, 212, 214n
Turkey, 12, 13, 175
Tyre (Lebanon), 77
Tzvia Yaʻakov, 163n

ʻUbeid, Diab, 60–1
ʻUbeid, Hasan, 59–61
ʻUbeid, Kamel, 60
ʻUbeid, Qays, 61
Umm al-Fahm, 13, 15–6, 80, 120–2, 125, 138, 147, 204, 211, 228
Umm al-Zeinat, 106
Unit 101, 34–5, 226
Unit 154 (military intelligence, later 504), 30, 93, 186–7, 189–91, 202, 226
United Arab Republic, 129, 132, 139, 199, 219, 227, 234
United Nations, 21, 54, 193, 232

United States, 6, 156
Upper Nazareth, 97, 111

Vardi, Rehavia, 26
Vatican, 47, 49
Vilner, Meir, 43
voting patterns. *See* elections

Wadi ʻAra, 15, 18, 80, 152, 205. *See also* Triangle
Wadi Hamam, 221
Wagmeister, Oded, 226
Walaja, 87
waqf, 216
weapons, 189; collection of, 14–15, 17, 30, 79, 83, 105–6; illegal, 40, 80; in 1948 War, 31, 41–2, 55, 104, 105, 187, 220, 245n4; licenses, 5, 18, 29–30, 60, 62–3, 73, 100, 160, 178, 192, 212, 220, 222, 225–7, 236; smuggling to Jews, 22, 31; as a symbol, 29
wedding songs, 9, 118, 129–31, 139, 151, 152, 212, 224, 233
Weitz, Yosef, 96n, 181
Weizmann, Haim, 48 (fig.)
West Bank, 5, 13, 29, 61, 87, 88, 98, 99, 119n, 120, 185, 187, 189, 190, 226, 238; after the Israeli occupation, 229–30, 238
World War II, 53

Al-Yawm, 57, 121, 156, 170, 224
Yadin, Yigal, 181
Yanai, Amnon, 166–67
Yanni, Yanni, 133, 210–11
Yanuh, 166, 167n
Yarka, 159
Yediʻot Aharonot, 111, 181
Yefet, Moshe, 159
Yehushua, Yaʻakov, 166
Young Communist League, 115
Yunis, Mahmoud, 15
Yunis family, 203–4

Zayyad, Tawfiq, 119, 211n
Zevulun Valley, 99, 106, 209
Zilberman, Rabbi, 109
Ziv (police officer), 140
Zohar, Uri, 114
Zuʻbi, Mahmoud, 156

Zu'bi, Muhammad Sa'id, 22
Zu'bi, Sayf al-Din, 22, 23, 24 (fig.), 31, 59,
63, 211, 212
Zu'biyya family and villages, 17–18, 23,
77–78

Zureiq, Lutf, 50
Zureiq, Mu'in, 39–40, 52
Zureiq, Suheil, 50–52
Zureiq clan, 46, 50–52

Text:	11.25/13.5 Adobe Garamond
Display:	Perpetua
Compositor:	BookMatters, Berkeley
Printer and binder:	Maple-Vail Book Manufacturing Group